# Texas State Parks

Other Books by George Bristol

*Glacier National Park: A Culmination of Giants*

*On Politics and Parks*

*Visual Voices*

# Texas State Parks

## The First 100 Years

### 1923-2023

**GEORGE BRISTOL**

with contributions by
Jennifer L. Bristol and Cynthia A. Brandimarte

A Joint Project of the
Center for Texas Studies at TCU
and TCU Press

Fort Worth, Texas

TCU Box 298300
Fort Worth, Texas 76129

Design by Bill Brammer

Cover art is the property of the Texas Parks and Wildlife Department
and is used with permission. Creative and Interactive Services, Texas Parks
and Wildlife Department, Austin, Texas.

## Dedication

This book is dedicated to all those—named and unnamed—
who trod the trails of our parks with me,
especially those I hold most close:

my mother and brother, Lottie Bristol and David Bristol

my children, Jim Bristol, Mark Bristol, and Jennifer L. Bristol
Andrea Denny and Samuel Alexander Denny

my grandchildren, Evelyn and Walter Bristol and Sam and Henry Rosenzweig

and my beloved wife, Gretchen Denny

# Foreword

It has been a long time coming. One hundred years long, in fact. Perched atop the geodetic dome at Enchanted Rock and on the sun-drenched sands of Galveston, under the sprawling pictographs at Fate Ball Shelter, and beneath the towering canopy of the "Big Tree" at Goose Island, few would argue whether or not it was worth the wait.

I surely wouldn't.

In 2023, the State of Texas will proudly celebrate the centennial of its state parks system, an anniversary of note for all Texans—then, now, and to come. The state parks system's genesis was anchored in notions as relevant then as they are today—sentiments that were borne as much out of a deep pride of place as they were a recognition of the wisdom, if not criticality, of providing places of respite and recreation in the great outdoors for the state's citizenry.

The urgency of the idea was not a universally embraced one. Thankfully, the original architects and advocates for the parks—an eclectic lot of politicians, philanthropists, landowners, garden and women's club members, businessmen, sportsmen, and outdoor enthusiasts—weren't easily dissuaded by a sometimes-indifferent, and occasionally recalcitrant, state government. Neither were subsequent generations of parks champions, including this book's author, Texas Parks and Wildlife commissioners, a procession of state parks directors—from Colp and Neff to Dabney, Leisure, and Franklin—and many, many friends of the parks along the way.

Over time, their fortitude, persistence, and sanctity of purpose carried the day. Generous supporters, communities, and landowners donated tracts of land and money. The National Park Service lent much-needed expertise and startup capital. The men of the Civilian Conservation Corps crafted many of the parks' original buildings, camps, and structures. Political leaders and citizen advocates navigated the machinations of state politics to help keep the parks afloat through the rough years. Department staff very capably developed and ably managed the parks and their programs through floods and fires, hurricanes and droughts, wars and pandemics. Meanwhile, a coterie of dedicated supporters never abandoned the notion that state parks—treasures of all Texas and for all Texans—should be funded sustainably and predictably as points of pride, not parsimony.

One of those unabashed and unrelenting warriors is George Bristol, a native son imbued at an early age with a deep reverence for the outdoors. Bristol's life is a case study in giving back, particularly to parks. As a young man, he spent summers working at Glacier National Park in Montana. Later, he went on to serve as a board member of the National Park Foundation. When he turned his considerable energy and immutable focus to remedying the Achilles' heel of funding for Texas state parks, it didn't hurt that the award-winning conservationist, poet, author, raconteur, hotelier, lobbyist, and consigliere to senators and presidents alike brought to the fight a bird-dog-like nose for the state's political winds, along with a lifetime of friendships with business and political leaders from both sides of the aisle.

Suffice it to say, if there was such thing as a patron saint for Texas state parks in the twenty-first century, it most assuredly would be Bristol. Not quite single-handedly, but pretty close to it, he cheerfully carried the proverbial water for nearly two decades in coordinating, corralling, and cajoling the state and its political leaders to invest more in the future of the parks. And, with the overwhelming support of the Texas state legislature and through citizen passage of Proposition 5 in 2019—the statewide constitutional amendment ensuring dedicated parks funding from the Sporting Goods Sales Tax—his work was roundly validated across Texas.

So when George Bristol talks about parks, he knows of what he speaks. Within these pages, he shares for all to digest and enjoy an eloquent and meticulously well-researched narrative about the people who gave life and vitality to the Texas state parks system in its first hundred years of existence. From Texas history buffs to outdoor enthusiasts, from political junkies to conservationists, anyone with the slightest bit of interest in our state parks will find this book well worth the read.

As Texans, our home ground is uniquely ours—ours to enjoy, ours to steward, and ours to pass along to those who come after us. Nowhere is that more manifest than in the ecologically, recreationally, and culturally rich Texas state parks system, where the life, histories, and stories of our great state are captured like nowhere else.

Encompassed within the parks are extraordinary places, from the birthplace of Texas to the homeplace of presidents; fields of battles won and lost; ancient pictographs and frontier presidios; desert oases and lost pines; sky islands and spring-fed streams; bison herds and bat caves; and shimmering lakes and barrier islands. These are the places where people from all areas and of all ages come to camp, kayak, hike, bike, climb, bird-watch, hunt, fish, learn, explore, and simply make lasting memories in the outdoors.

I hope you will join us in celebrating this centennial year, not only by savoring this exceptional historical account of our state parks and their inception, but also by getting out and visiting our parks. The Texas Parks and Wildlife Department team will be thrilled to welcome you at the front gate. Thanks for caring about our wild things and wild places. They need you now more than ever.

Carter P. Smith, *Former Executive Director*
Texas Parks and Wildlife Department

# Preface

Why parks? I don't know how often I've been asked that question.

It could be a query of why I, after most of my career, was drawn to spending the last third of my life devoting my time and treasure to the well-being of parks: national, state, and local.

Or it could be an exploration of why parks should receive public support (funding) over other equally important responsibilities of our government.

Or it could be an inquiry of (usually with a bit of curled lip) why parks at all?

Because all, in varying degrees, are legitimate questions, they deserve legitimate answers.

I hope to use the coming pages to answer these questions by exploring those American and Texas leaders who embraced and then championed the concept of public lands for all our citizens.

To begin, I can't imagine a time when I wasn't exposed to parks or park-like settings: swimming holes, public pools (a number built by the Civilian Conservation Corps), roadside picnic tables, Texas beaches, and state parks and historic sites.

Sometime in 1947, following the death of my father, when my mother, brother David, and I lived in Beeville, Texas, a genuinely nice woman who knew my mother through her organ and piano music at church offered to take us to her ranch for the weekend. I can't remember the exact location of her property, but I have to think it was near the small South Texas town of Goliad. Either coming or going, we stopped to explore Goliad State Park and Historic Site, which recently had been restored by the Civilian Conservation Corps. While David and I (ages five and seven, respectively) probably had only a passing interest in that beautiful setting and Mission Espíritu Santo, which dominates the site, we were old enough to know that Mother loved Texas history, so we obediently went along with the tour.

As we were leaving and walking to the parking lot, we spotted a man coming toward us dressed in a cowboy outfit from head to toe. Even at that age, we immediately assumed he was one of our Saturday movie matinee heroes—Gene Autry. Running up to him, we yelled, "It's Gene! It's Gene Autry!" He kindly bent down to us and said, "Boys, I'm not Gene Autry, but he's a good friend of mine. I'm Monte Hale."

So, we started chanting, "It's Monte Hale!" Turned out, it was true.

That incident left a positive, yet undefined, feeling for parks and historic sites, which would only grow over a lifetime.

The author (right) and his cousin Judd Holt, natural from the beginning, ca. 1945. Author's collection.

Years later, in 1986, I had the opportunity to meet Gene Autry. He came to Texas to help celebrate the state's sesquicentennial. He flew into Austin on his private plane with his wife and another couple—the Monte Hales. That evening at a reception, I had the pleasure of introducing Autry and his guests. I led with the Goliad State Park story. Before I could finish, Hale broke in and laughingly recalled, "I remember that day and those two towheads yelling, 'It's Gene!'"

Fortunately, several other individuals also functioned as boosters and signposts for me along the way.

Former Congressman (later Speaker of the House) Jim Wright played the pivotal role in my careers in politics and parks, although there were plenty of boosters and signposts before May 1961, when I found myself without a summer job. Fortunately, I had worked for Jim on his US Senate race in the spring of 1961—a race to fill the vacancy when Senator Lyndon Johnson was elevated to the vice presidency. Jim lost but carried the counties surrounding Austin that I had been charged with organizing. Don't ask how. I never could figure it out. But Jim took notice.

I thought I'd like to go to Washington and help with President Kennedy's New Frontier. So, I went to see State Representative Don Kennard, a staunch Wright supporter and friend. Don called Jim, and Jim called his friend former Congressman Stewart Udall, whom President Kennedy had recently appointed as secretary of the Interior. It would not be a job with an office next to President Kennedy—but one in Glacier National Park: two wonderful summers (1961 and 1962) in that natural paradise, and the conservation hook was set.

On my return from the park to Austin in August 1962, Jim called. He stated he'd recommended me to Congressman Homer Thornberry, the occupant of the Tenth Congressional District of Texas—the district that I'd worked. Thornberry was thought to be in political trouble and needed help with students and other constituents in the district. He asked for my help.

I accepted. Thornberry won (big) and asked me to go to DC with him—and the political hook was set.

Thirty years later, politics and parks would flow together and make it possible for me to be appointed to the National Park Foundation Board of Directors in 1994 by President Clinton and Secretary of the Interior Bruce Babbitt, with behind-the-scenes support from Secretary of the Treasury Lloyd Bentsen. It was the best nonpaying job I've ever had and, most likely, the best job, period. Imagine going out to our national parks for board meetings with the Tetons, Mesa Verde, or, yes, Glacier in the background.

From that moment forward, I became devoted not only to the awesome landscapes and historic sites of our country but also their national purpose, articulated by the men and women who led the way through the nineteenth and twentieth centuries and carry forward into the twenty-first.

In a little more than a hundred years, they nurtured a hopeful thought into an idea so strong and universally acceptable that it was proclaimed "America's Best Idea" by Wallace Stegner in 1983.

One carryover was the rise of the state parks movement. This centennial book is written for all those who breathed life into Texas's state parks over the first hundred years—and a prayer that others will follow to leave footprints into and over the next hundred years.

# Special Acknowledgments

For me, this is the most difficult part of a book to write: I am always afraid there's someone who will be left out. To any and all I might have overlooked, I regret the oversight. If we never meet, know it was not intentional. If we should meet, I will personally and promptly apologize—and do so as well in my next book, should I write one.

Without funding over a three-year period (in the middle of a pandemic), I could not have started nor finished this undertaking. Adelaide Leavens, the Amon G. Carter Foundation, Rod Sanders and the Heritage Foundation, the Sid W. Richardson Foundation, and the Jacob & Terese Hershey Foundation—all contributed generously.

Carter Smith, former executive director of the Texas Parks and Wildlife Department, encouraged me to write a history of Texas state parks for the 2023 state parks centennial and suggested that I operate under the auspices of the Texas Parks and Wildlife Foundation. Both Carter and the foundation's staff have been supportive partners every step of the way. So have staff members of the Texas Parks and Wildlife Department, especially Texas State Parks Director of Interpretation Ky Harkey, Chief Curator Sally Baulch, and Chief Photographer Chase Fountain, who helped with material on segregation in the parks, historic and photographic research, matters pertaining to the book, and the department's centennial plans.

Among the staff, a special acknowledgment and thanks must be given to Allison Winney, intergovernmental affairs specialist with the Texas Parks and Wildlife Department. With patience, good humor, and grasp of numbers, she guided me through the ever-shifting sands of legislative budgets. Also, Kevin Good, recently retired as special assistant to the director of the State Parks Division, was always available for a phone call and proved to be invaluable in providing answers to my many questions about all things pertaining to parks.

In addition, a special word or two must be reserved for three past Texas Parks and Wildlife Department employees who epitomize the dedicated public servant. Walt Dabney and Brent Leisure served back-to-back as Texas State Parks directors and managed to modernize the agency's system, staff, and operations, even in those years of limited budgets. They were supported every step of the way by David Riskind, who led the modernization efforts as director of the Natural Resources Program. Because they believed, they inspired others in and out of the agency to follow suit. They (and all the other employees of the Texas Parks and Wildlife Department) deserve recognition for their many good works—year after year. Because of their leadership, they readied the agency for the time when appropriations began to flow at their maximum.

I also would like to thank Dr. John Crompton of Texas A&M University, whose help and support have been vital through the years. He and Dr. Ji Youn Jeong worked tirelessly to provide the supporting data we needed to make our case for parks and historic sites to the legislature, state agencies, and private organizations and corporations. A special thanks to Vicki Betts for sharing her article "For the Citizens of East Texas: The Desegregation of Tyler State Park." It was most helpful in focusing my thoughts on a most difficult subject—prejudice in the parks.

I also must mention Dr. David Hill, who has been a steady provider of public opinion surveys in Texas for several decades, first for the Trust for Public Land (1999) and then for the Texas Coalition for Conservation (2005 to 2019). Dr. Hill's reputation as one of America's leading pollsters on matters concerning conservation and the environment initially drew me to him. His consistent professionalism made him a continuing partner up to and through the monumental constitutional amendment election on November 5, 2019.

No history of Texas parks can be written without first reading James Wright Steely's *Parks for Texas: Enduring Landscapes of the New Deal.* It is marvelous background material. And if you can get him on the phone, he's a conversationalist par excellence.

While most of this book was written by the author, I felt two chapters should be addressed by others dedicated to our parks. In chapter two, my daughter, Jennifer L. Bristol, a former employee of the Texas Parks and Wildlife Department, has penned a fine piece on the role of women in the parks' history, particularly those who led the charge in the formative days before, during, and after ratification of the Nineteenth Amendment in 1920. Jennifer's contribution highlights the connection between the Texas Garden Clubs, Federation of Women's Clubs, and Daughters of the Republic of Texas, who pushed for a state parks system and influenced its formation. The chapter also celebrates more recent contributions by conservationists such as Lady Bird Johnson, Jane Sibley, and Madge Lindsay.

The other piece was written by one of America's leading authorities on the Civilian Conservation Corps, Cindy Brandimarte, former director of the Historic Sites and Structures Program at the Texas Parks and Wildlife Department. Cindy is the finest historian on the role the Civilian Conservation Corps played in Texas in the 1930s. No book on the centennial of state parks would be complete without sharing her insight and wisdom on this Depression-era program that literally became the foundation of our state parks system. Her astute contribution can be found in chapter four. Cindy would like to acknowledge Jennifer Carpenter, Elizabeth O'Brien, John Higley, John Anderson, Anne L. Cook, James Steely, Dan Utley, Tom Shelton, and Martha Norkunas, who helpfully provided photography research, historical context, and other information and materials.

Finally, while all mentioned here played significant roles throughout the writing of this book, there is one who was—and is—indispensable. She is an editor without peer, a designer without equal, and a soothing influence when the going became overly frustrating. Sharon McKone has been essential to my ability to put words and images on page after page in an orderly manner.

# Chapter 1

# Genesis:
# The National Parks

*Everybody needs beauty as well as bread, places to play in and pray in, where nature may heal and give strength to body and soul.*[1]

**JOHN MUIR**

No treatment of the first hundred years (1923 to 2023) of Texas's state parks history can be complete without some understanding of the rise of the conservation and public park ethic that began early in America's journey across the uncharted majesties of waters, mountains, valleys, and endless, beckoning horizons.

At first, it was the tales of fur trappers and mountain men that conveyed the wonder of discoveries of landscapes and wildlife, but there was never a call to conserve what they found. In fact, both the lands and the animals that lived on them existed mainly for the taking. But there is no question that those explorers' praising observations struck a chord in the hearts of many intrigued with the call of the West. Among them were those who saw benefit in conserving parts of nature for the common good.

While it is impossible to know those who first put thought to voice, what can be found are early observers who expressed the need to set aside, in some fashion, landscapes of "supreme" treasure.

# The National Park Concept in America

Thomas Jefferson, ca. 1805. Courtesy of Gilbert Stewart, Bowdoin College Museum of Art via Adobe Stock.

There's no question that some citizens of the new republic—the United States—voiced their eloquent influence about the growing need for public and shared ownership of natural resources for mutual recreation, renewal, and preservation. None actually coined the phrase "national park," but some came close. From 1800 to 1860, seeds were sown; some took root.

Two were authors and leaders of the American Romantic and Transcendental movements who lent their strong voices concerning man's relationship between God and nature to the cause, arguing that some parts of those natural domains must be set aside for all citizens, not just the wealthy and landed.

Three were presidents, all of whom by their pocketbook (personal or public) and/or power caused certain private and public lands to be preserved with an eye to the future, but certainly without a central, formal plan in mind.

Two were artists, one of Western scenery and Native Americans (both of which he believed were in danger of ruination and extinction), and the other, a new breed of artist—a landscape architect who had recently designed the first urban landscape park in the United States: Central Park in New York City.

Such advocacy and actions, though noble and ultimately lasting, were hit-and-miss at best, without form or governance. But that advocacy was brought to life and sustained by this relatively small group of men (and, later, women) scattered across the new country who were influential, even after death in some cases, in keeping those ideas and sites before the public until other contemporaries or future advocates could assume the cause.

Bless all these and others who had the vision and voice to convey the significance of the concept and the importance of the places, even if their callings received no immediate national acceptance.

But like the ripple on a lake, a small puddle's rings lift one leaf, then another, until a mosaic of leaves are perceived as a grand design, which, in the case of national parks, became a source of national pride and acceptance from post-Civil War years into the twentieth century, then to the present.

Before taking a look at these leaders, it is necessary to examine a trend that began to take root before the Civil War and took wings afterward.

Because the terrible drain of war stifled a great deal of original thought concerning land use and, certainly, action to acquire land—with one monumental exception that took place in 1864—nothing transpired on this front until after the signing of the surrender at Appomattox. Then, after the bitter residue of Reconstruction that created as many new grievances between citizens of the North and South as before the war, the country began to turn and move toward the beckoning West again.[2]

Even with the disruption of battle, people from the North and South had continued to trickle west. That trickle turned into a national tidal wave after the war, continuing for twenty-five years or so until 1890, when the US census would proclaim that there was no more frontier.[3] We as a nation had spread from "sea to shining sea," but in doing so, we had not left a shining example. In our rush to push west, forests were obliterated, mountains were scarred, rivers were dammed, and all manner of animals were killed to near extinction—as were many Native Americans.

Fortunately, some of the settlers, including recent trespassers, turned their gazes backward and were horrified by the waste and blight laid upon our natural resources. They began to think individually, then collectively, that amends needed to be made—and soon. One occurred from 1864 to 1865 with the transfer of Yosemite to California as a state park. Another occurred in 1872, when President Ulysses S. Grant created one of our first sacred natural treasures—Yellowstone National Park. From that point forward, the name "national park" took on permanency.

By virtue of the Yellowstone National Park Protection Act, future parks fulfilled the public park concept and assumed the role of national healer through citizen pride and common citizenship—shared ownership by all, North and South.

BELOW
One of America's natural wonders, Natural Bridge, Virginia, ca. 1903. Courtesy of Carleton H. Graves, Library of Congress Prints and Photographs Division, Washington, DC, LC-DIG-Stereo-1s16288.

Natural Bridge, Virginia, now a state park,
date unknown. Adobe Stock.

## Rise of the Public Park Concept

One of the earliest observers of the public park concept was one who would soon become a primary advocate for revolution and discovery—President Thomas Jefferson.

On a profound and personal level, Jefferson would, by chance of ownership of land, begin to set the stage for America's fascination with wilderness and a growing sense that at least some of the more spectacular parts of the purchased discoveries should be set aside for the pleasure of all.

In 1774, Jefferson would come upon what is now Natural Bridge State Park in Virginia. Awestruck by its beauty, he paid twenty shillings to King George III for the bridge and surrounding 157 acres. On a personal level, Jefferson was one of those who was enthralled by such scenery and did something about it. Though the land would remain in Jefferson's hands throughout his life and under private ownership until 2014, it was one of the first recognitions by a public figure "of the bounty of the Creator's handiwork in America and [deserving of] its preservation relevant to the individual and the nation as a whole." In fact, Jefferson swore in the conveyance that he "viewed it as a public trust."[4] Not quite there—but moving toward the possibility and recognition of a place for the public in nature. Years later, in 1806, once the Louisiana Purchase was complete, Jefferson sent Lewis and Clark on their journey not only to survey the boundaries of the newly obtained holdings but also to catalog plants, animals, mountain passes, and roaring rivers. Their findings were the spark that detonated the explosion of "westward ho." But even as wave after wave moved across the plains toward the unknown, some began to contemplate the future and possibility of conservation.

Ralph Waldo Emerson and Henry David Thoreau came into their own fifty years after Jefferson's purchase, which began to define places to set aside for preservation. Both, in their own ways, became Romantic-era authors who had a reverence for nature as well as for individual freedoms. Among everything was the thought that nature should be accessible to all. Thoreau wrote:

Ralph Waldo Emerson, ca. 1906. Courtesy of the Library of Congress Prints and Photographs Division, Washington, DC, LC-USZ62-73430.

> Why should not we, who have renounced the king's authority, have our own preserves, where no village need be destroyed, in which the bear and panther, and some even of the human race, may still exist, and not be civilized off the face of the earth, our forests, not to hold the king's game mainly, but hold and preserve the king himself also, the lord of creation, not for idle sport or food, but for inspirations and our own true re-creation?[5]

In 1832, noted Western and Native American artist George Catlin gave the name to those lands that would later capture the country's consciousness: "nation's parks." While his ideas were not immediately entertained, Catlin had a solid reputation, and his observations of the growing plight of the Plains Indians and bison and the need to conserve lands for their preservation in a "magnificent" park setting for future generations planted seeds:

> . . . for ages to come, the native Indian in his classic attire, galloping his wild horse, with sinewy bow, and shield and lance, amid the fleeting herds of elks and buffaloes. What a beautiful and thrilling specimen for America to preserve and hold up to view of her refined citizens and the world, in future ages! *A Nation's Park* [emphasis author's], containing man and beast, in all the wild and freshness of their nature's beauty![6]

Henry David Thoreau, date unknown. Courtesy of the Library of Congress Prints and Photographs Division, Washington, DC, LC-USZ62-19291.

Thoreau's Cove, Lake Walden, Concord, Massachusetts, ca. 1900–1910. Courtesy of the Detroit Publishing Company Photograph Collection, Library of Congress Prints and Photographs Division, Washington, DC, LC-DIG-det-4a18296.

Portrait of George Catlin, 1849. Courtesy of William Fisk, National Portrait Gallery, Smithsonian Institution via Wikimedia Commons.

*A Small Crow Village*, ca. 1855–1869. Courtesy of George Catlin, Paul Mellon Collection via Wikimedia Commons, NGA_50334.

Lest the reader conclude that this would be a natural Disneyland, Catlin suggested that such a "park" be preserved "by some great protecting policy of government." Somewhere, at some time, someone picked up on the idea and passed it on, culminating in the creation of Yellowstone National Park in 1872.

In the same year as Catlin's proclamation—1832—President Andrew Jackson and Congress nominated Hot Springs, Arkansas, as the first federal reservation. By a whisker, it missed national park status. That would come in 1921.

Some still hold to its designation as the first national park. It was—and is—the first federal land set aside for public recreation. It is storied that President (and citizen) Andrew Jackson partook of its hot baths to treat his rheumatism and other ailments.

By all rights, the first national park should have been Yosemite. Yes, even amidst the carnage of civil war, voices for nature's well-being and purpose arose out of the wreckage (a practice that would continue throughout the nation's great conflicts). These voices were projecting past the war with an eye toward a united and peaceful union. One voice would set the precedent for public ownership of nature's wonders. The other would articulate the national purpose for such "parks." Still others in greater numbers and rapid order would follow suit.

The Honorable John Conness, United States Senator, ca. 1855–1865. Senator Conness was the author of the bill transferring land in Yosemite Valley and the nearby Mariposa Big Tree Grove to the State of California in 1864. Courtesy of the Brady-Handy Photograph Collection, Library of Congress Prints and Photographs Division, Washington, DC, LC-BH82- 4567 C [P&P].

In 1864, Senator John Conness of California rose on the Senate floor and introduced an unprecedented bill: the setting aside for public purpose and further enjoyment for all a state-owned tract of land. It passed, President Abraham Lincoln signed it into law, and, by that action, the landscape known as Yosemite was transferred from the federal government to California as a state park. Why was it transferred? Because the state could better protect and preserve it. And why was that important? Because Conness, Lincoln, and others, even in a time of civil war, had come to realize that there was more to possession of acreage than mere ownership. That moved Lincoln, the second advocate in this original act of national public ownership, to exclaim that Yosemite was "the greatest glory of nature . . . the union of the deepest sublimity with the deepest beauty."[7]

Frederick Law Olmsted left New York City, having completed his initial design and construction of Central Park, to work in California and visit the site called Yosemite. His reasoning for doing so was simple: no work was available for landscape architects during the Civil War years, not even for America's most renowned landscape architect.

His arrival could not have been timelier. The measure transferring the lands from the federal government to the state was now the law of the land. It is interesting to note that

Abraham Lincoln, February 9, 1864. Courtesy of Anthony Berger, Library of Congress Prints and Photographs Division, Washington, DC, LC-DIG-ppmsca-19305.

in order to gain approval, Conness had to assure his congressional colleagues that while the land and adjoining Mariposa Big Tree Grove were wonders of the world and should by preservation flow to the benefit of all, they would require no expenditure of federal funds. That argument would be used time and time again in the establishment of future national parks. Some at both the national and state levels eventually came to believe this and used it to deny adequate funding (or to provide none at all). This will be a common theme throughout this book.

Fortunately, Olmsted was appointed chair of the commission that would give guidance to Yosemite, and he was tasked to write the report. Wisely, he set forth the economic benefits of tourism first. Better the dollar before the ethereal. He compared the financial opportunities of Yosemite to those communities and resorts in the Swiss Alps where many wealthy tourists, including Americans, traveled.[8]

To the economic argument, he added a prophetic note. "That when it shall become more accessible, the Yosemite will prove an attraction of a similar character, of wealth to the whole community, not only of California but of the United States, there can be no doubt."[9] Because there were—and always are—doubters, let me point out that Yosemite presently hosts millions of visitors and generates more than $300 million annually!

Next, Olmsted pointed out that parks were good not only for the pocketbook but also for the mental, physical, and spiritual health of those who experienced the wonders of the outdoors.

> It is a scientific fact that the occasional contemplation of natural scenes of an impressive character, particularly if this occurs in connection with relief from ordinary cares, change of air, and change of habits, is favorable to the health and vigor of men, especially to the health and vigor of their intellect beyond any other conditions that can be offered them, and not only gives pleasure for the time being but increases the subsequent capacity for happiness and the means for securing that happiness. Thus, the establishment by the government of great public grounds for the free enjoyment of the people under certain circumstances is . . . justified and enforced as a political duty.[10]

Most important here was Olmsted's adamant call for protection of the natural scenery that would draw visitors to Yosemite and future parks, giving those visitors benefit to both mind and body. His argument applied to the preservation of flora and fauna in the present as well as the future, when the number of visitors to national parks would be measured not in the hundreds but the millions—331 million nationwide by 2017![11] Yosemite alone surpassed five million visitors in 2016.[12]

However, it is here that Olmsted's dual call for necessary accommodations for visitors and preservation of natural scenery would almost immediately fall into conflict, a vexation that exists to this day, growing more complicated with each new million tourists who pass through the entrance stations of our national and state parks.

The conflict was incorporated in the language of the legislation establishing the National Park Service in 1916, known as the "Organic Act": "which purpose is to conserve the scenery and the natural and historic objects and the wildlife therein and to provide for the enjoyment of the same in such a manner and by such means as will leave them unimpaired for the enjoyment of future generations."[13]

To Olmsted's credit—and that of the National Park Service—that dual management task has been honored for the most part to the greatest degree possible. Most of the acreage of our great parks remain in a wilderness state by law or in practice.

Sadly, Olmsted was neither honored nor given due credit for his formulation of what amounted to a coherent and passionate guide for the continued well-being of Yosemite and park governance in the decades to come. Because that denial of honor and credit is so tied to the current dilemma that faces most of our parks systems—national, state, and local—it warrants an expansion of the Olmsted-Yosemite situation.

Even though his Yosemite report was initially met with enthusiasm and a seemingly unanimous vote of approval by his fellow commissioners, Olmsted left California and Yosemite Valley too soon—and forever. In doing so, he left the future of the report in conflicted hands, and, in his absence, the opposition carried the day.

Frederick Law Olmsted Sr., 1893. Courtesy of James Notman, The World's Work via Wikimedia Commons.

For all the wisdom with which Olmsted foretold how this national magnificence would become an attraction of the first order, bringing tourists from near and far who would spend countless dollars viewing a God-wonder kept pristine and regulated by a responsible government for the enjoyment of all, then and now, he made an honest, but fatal, recommendation.

Olmsted was not only an artist with an eye for the possibilities, he was also a practical businessman and, thus, ended his report with a practical initial budget: $37,000.[14] No matter the amount, others on the commission had their eye on the funds for other uses and convinced the governor to bury the report, which he did.

The full report was not discovered until 1962.

Fortunately, Olmsted had discussed and shared his thoughts and theories with other national opinionmakers. Fifty-one years later, in 1916, many of the report's suggestions were incorporated into the Organic Act establishing the National Park Service. Little wonder. Most of the act was written by his son, Frederick Law Olmsted Jr.

More fortunately, a prophet of biblical stature was waiting in the wings to pick up where Olmsted left off, expand on the concept, and, as a result, receive the recognition and accolades his predecessor never enjoyed. At the same time, he would also fortify the spiritual legitimacy of man's relationship to nature.

John Muir, born in Scotland and raised in Wisconsin, was an inventor with a flair for business who knew most of the Bible by heart. But neither profit nor prophet was in his blood—or at least not a prophet of religion. His would be the religion of nature, and Yosemite would be his principal temple.

His arrival in the wilds of Yosemite in 1868 proved transformative. As he would later describe it,

> We are now in the mountains and they are in us, kindling enthusiasm, making every nerve quiver, filling every pore and cell of us. Our flesh-and-bone tabernacle seems transparent as glass to the beauty about us, neither old nor young, sick nor well, but immortal. I am a captive. I am bound. Love of pure unblemished nature seems to overmaster and blur out of sight all other objects and considerations.[15]

At last, preservation and parks had an advocate of rare combination. Muir embodied the talents of preacher, organizer, and publicist. He would convert disciples who would become not simply followers but generals of various ranks in Muir's army: George Bird Grinnell, Robert Underwood Johnson, Louis Hill, Stephen Mather, and Franklin Delano Roosevelt, among others. But in the immediacy, there was Teddy!

If John Muir was the quiet voice of shadows and sunlight playing across the face of nature and the need to protect that scenery, Theodore Roosevelt would become the bugler, sounding the charge for conservation and the "essential democracy" of parks.

When joined in harmony, Muir and Roosevelt would add their voices, pens, and power to a growing chorus for preservation and conservation. They would become an irreversible force of nature.

Both men found greatness in the other (a relationship cemented at Yosemite in 1903 over a period of three days, when the two of them alone devised a plan not only for Yosemite but for national parks in general) and set forth on a course for conservation that would not only see the transfer of the Yosemite Valley and Mariposa Grove back to the federal government and the existing Yosemite National Park but an explosion of parks, forests, and national monuments, many under the broad umbrella of the Antiquities Act of 1906. That law would be one of the most significant acts, along with the establishment of the National Park Service in 1916, in America's march toward conservation and

*Forest and Stream* magazine cover, November 1921. Courtesy of *Forest and Stream*, Charles Hallock, publisher.

**RIGHT**
"A Summer Hunt with the Pawnees" by George Bird Grinnell in *Forest and Stream* magazine, October 10, 1889. Courtesy of *Forest and Stream*, Charles Hallock, publisher.

222 FOREST AND STREAM. [Oct. 10, 1889.

## The Sportsman Tourist.

### A SUMMER HUNT WITH THE PAWNEES.

From a forthcoming volume of "Pawnee Hero Stories and Folk-Tales."

BY GEO. BIRD GRINNELL ("YO").

I.

IT was in the month of July, 1872. The Pawnees were preparing to start on their semi-annual buffalo hunt, and only the last religious rites remained to be performed before the nation should leave the village for the buffalo range.

"*Eh, idadi, whoop,*" came from without the lodge; and as I replied, "*Ehya, whoop,*" the sturdy figure of *Le-ta-kats-ta'-ka* appeared in the doorway.

"*Lau, idad, tŭt-tŭ-ta-rik ti-rah-rĕk*—Come, brother, they are going to dance," he said, and then he turned and went out.

I rose from the pile of robes on which I had been dozing, and, after rolling them up, strolled out after him. The village seemed deserted, but off toward the medicine lodge, which stood upon its outskirts, I could see a throng of Indians; and a low murmur of voices and of footsteps, the hum which always accompanies any large assemblage, was borne to my ears on the evening breeze. The ceremonies, which comprised the consecration of the buffalo staves and the buffalo dance, were about to begin. The great dirt lodge was crowded. I pushed my way through the throng of women and boys, who made up the outer circle of spectators, and soon found myself among the men, who made way for me, until I reached a position from which I could see all that was going on within the circle about which they stood.

For several days the priests and the doctors had been preparing for this solemn religious ceremonial. They had fasted long; earnest prayers had been made to *Ti-ra'-wa*, and sacrifices had been offered. Now the twelve buffalo skulls had been arranged on the ground in a half-circle, and near them stood the chiefs and doctors, reverently holding in their hands the buffalo staves and sacred bows and arrows, and other implements of the chase. For a little while they stood silent, with bowed heads, but presently one and then another began to murmur their petitions to *A-ti-us Ti-ra'-wa*, the Spirit Father. At first their voices were low and mumbling, but gradually they became more earnest and lifted their eyes toward heaven. It was impossible to distinguish what each one said, but now and then disjointed sentences reached me. "Father, you are the Ruler—We are poor—Take pity on us—Send us plenty of buffalo, plenty of fat cows—Father, we are your children—help the people—send us plenty of meat, so that we may be strong, and our bodies may increase and our flesh grow hard—Father, you see us, listen." As they prayed they moved their hands backward and forward over the implements which they held, and at length reverently deposited them on the ground within the line of buffalo skulls, and then stepped back, still continuing their prayers.

It was a touching sight to witness these men calling upon their God for help. All of them had passed middle life, and some were gray-haired, blind and tottering; but they prayed with a fervor and earnestness that compelled respect. They threw their souls into their prayers, and as a son might entreat his earthly father for some great gift, so they pleaded with *Ti-ra'-wa*. Their bodies quivered with emotion, and great drops of perspiration stood upon their brows. They were thoroughly sincere.

After the last of the articles had been placed upon the ground, their voices grew lower and at length died away. A moment later a drum sounded, and a dozen or twenty young warriors sprang into the circle and began the buffalo dance. This was kept up without intermission for three days, and as soon as it was over, the tribe moved out of the village on the hunt.

From the village on the Loup, we traveled southward; for in those days the region between the Platte and the Smoky rivers swarmed with buffalo. With the Pawnees were a few Poncas, Omahas and Otoes, so that there were about four thousand Indians in the camp. It was the summer hunt of the tribe. Twice each year the agent permitted them to visit the buffalo range. The meat which they killed and dried on these hunts, the corn and squashes which they grew on their farms, and the small annuities received from the Government, were all they had to subsist on from season to season. Thus the occasion was one of importance to the Indians. Perhaps only the older heads among them fully appreciated its economic interest; but for all it was a holiday time; a temporary escape from confinement. Life on the reservation was monotonous. There was nothing to do except to sit in the sun and smoke, and tell stories of the former glories of the nation; of successful fights with the Sioux and Cheyennes, and of horse stealing expeditions, from which the heroes had returned with great herds of ponies and much glory. Now, for a little while, they returned to the old free life of earlier years, when the land had been all their own, and they had wandered at will over the broad expanse of the rolling prairie. Now, for a time, it was as it had been before the cornfields of the white man had begun to dot the river bottoms, before the sound of his rifle had made wild their game, before the locomotive's whistle had shrieked through the still, hot summer air. Half a year's provision was now to be secured. The comfort—almost the existence—of the tribe for the next six months depended on the accumulation of an abundant supply of dried buffalo meat, and no precaution was omitted to make the hunt successful. It would not do to permit each individual to hunt independently. Indiscriminate buffalo running by six or eight hundred men scattered over the prairie, each one working for himself alone, would result in the killing of some few buffalo, but would terrify and drive away all the others in the neighborhood. This matter was too important to be trusted to chance. The hunting was systematized.

The government of the hunt was intrusted to the Pawnee soldiers. These were twenty-four warriors of mature age, not so old as to be unfitted for active work, yet with the fires of early youth somewhat tempered by years of experience; men whose judgment and discretion could at all times be relied on. These soldiers acted under the chiefs, but the practical guidance of the hunt was wholly in their hands. They determined the direction and length of each day's march, and the spot for camping. They selected the young men who should act as scouts, and arranged all the details of approach and the charge when a herd of buffalo was discovered large enough to call for a general surround. All the men were under their control, and amenable to their discipline. They did not hesitate to exercise their authority, nor to severely punish any one who committed an act by which the success of the hunt might be imperilled.

The scouts sent out by the soldiers were chosen from among the younger men. They acted merely as spies, their office was to find the buffalo. They moved rapidly along, far in advance of the marching column, and from the tops of the highest hills carefully scanned the country before them in search of buffalo. If a herd was discerned they were not to show themselves, nor in any way to alarm it. Having found the game, their duty was to observe its movement, learn where it was likely to be for the next few hours, and then to report as quickly as possible to the camp. The soldiers then determined what action should be taken. If the news was received late in the day, and the buffalo were at some distance, the camp would probably be moved as near as practicable to where the herd was feeding, and the chase would take place in the early morning. If, on the other hand, the scouts found the herd in the morning, the men would start off at once for the surround, leaving the women to follow and make camp as near as possible to where the dead buffalo lay.

Day after day we traveled southward, crossing the Platte River, and then the Republican about due south of the present flourishing town of Kearney. South of the Platte a few scattering buffalo were found, but no large herds had been met with—nothing that called for a surround. At length we camped one night on the Beaver, a small affluent of the Republican, emptying into it from the south.

II.

With the gray dawn of morning, the camp, as usual, is astir. By the time our little party have turned out of our blankets some of the Indians have already finished eating, and are catching up their horses and preparing to ride off over the bluffs, leaving the squaws to take down the lodges, pack the ponies, and pursue the designated line of march. Before we are ready to "pull out," most of the ponies have been packed, and a long, irregular line of Indians is creeping across the level valley, and beginning to wind up the face of the bluffs. The procession moves slowly, proceeding at a walk. Most of those who remain with the column are on foot, the squaws leading the ponies, and many of the men, wrapped in their blankets, and with only their bows and arrows on their backs, walking briskly over the prairie, a little to one side. These last are the poorer Indians—those who have but few horses. They travel on foot, letting their horses run without burdens, so that they may be fresh and strong, whenever they shall be needed for running the buffalo.

Side by side, at the head of the column, walk eight men who carry the buffalo staves. These are slender spruce poles, like a short lodge-pole, wrapped with blue and red cloth, and elaborately ornamented with bead work, and with the feathers of hawks and of the war eagle. These sticks are carried by men selected by the chiefs and doctors in private council, and are religiously guarded. Upon the care of these emblems, and the respect paid to them, depends, in a great measure, the success of the hunt. While borne before the moving column, no one is permitted to cross the line of march in front of them.

Close behind the staff bearers follow a number of the principal men of the tribe; the head chief, old *Pĭ'ta Le-shar*, and a dozen or fifteen sub-chiefs or head men, all mounted on superb horses. Behind them comes the camp at large, a fantastically mingled multitude, marching without any appearance of order. Here most of the individuals are women, young girls and children, for the men who accompany the camp usually march singly, or by twos and threes, a little apart from the mob. Most of those rich enough in horses to be able to ride at all times, are scattered over the prairie for miles in every direction, picking up the small bands of buffalo, which have been passed by the scouts as not large enough to call for a general surround. The hunters are careful, however, not to follow too close upon the advance line, whose movements they can readily observe upon the bare bluffs far ahead of them.

At the time of which I am writing the Pawnees had no wagons, all their possessions being transported on pack horses. The Indian pack pony is apt to be old and sedate, requiring no special guidance nor control. A strip of rawhide, knotted about the lower jaw, serves as a bridle, and is either tied up to the saddle or held in the rider's hand. In packing the animals a bundle of lodge-poles is tied on either side of the saddle, one end projecting forward toward the horse's head, the other dragging on the ground behind. This is the *travois*. Cross poles are often tied between these two dragging bundles, and on these are carried packages of meat and robes. Often, too, on a robe stretched between them, a sick or wounded Indian, unable to ride, is transported. The lodge-poles having been fastened to the saddle, the lodge is folded up and placed on it between them, and blankets, robes, and other articles are piled on top of this until the old horse has on its back what appears to be about as much as it can carry. The pack is then lashed firmly in position, and pots, buckets and other utensils are tied about wherever there is room.

On top of the load so arranged one or two women, or three or four children, clamber and settle themselves comfortably there, and the old horse is turned loose. Each rider carries in her hand a whip, with which she strikes the horse at every step, not cruelly at all, but just from force of habit. If the pack is low, so that her feet reach down to the animal's sides, she keeps up also a constant drumming on his ribs with her heels. The old horse pays not the slightest attention to any of these demonstrations of impatience, but plods steadily along at a quiet walk, his eyes half closed and his ears nodding at each step. If the riders are women, each one holds a child or two in her arms, or on her back, or perhaps the baby board is hung over the end of a lodge-pole, and swings free. If the living load consists of children, they have in their arms a lot of puppies; for puppies occupy with relation to the small Indian girls the place which dolls hold among the white children. Many of the pack animals are mares with young colts, and these last, instead of following quietly at their mothers' heels, range here and there, sometimes before and sometimes behind their dams. They are thus constantly getting lost in the crowd, and then they charge backward and forward in wild affright, neighing shrilly, until they have again found their place in the line of march. Many of the yearling colts have very small and light packs tied on their backs, while the two-year-olds are often ridden by the tiniest of the Indian boys, who are now giving them their first lesson in weight-carrying. Loose horses of all ages roam about at will, and their continual cries mingle with the barking of dogs, the calling of women and the yells of boys, and make an unceasing noise.

The boys are boiling over with animal spirits, and like their civilized brothers of the same age, are continually running about, chasing each other, wrestling, shooting arrows and playing games, of which the familiar stick game seems the favorite.

Whenever the column draws near any cover, which may shelter game, such as a few bushes in a ravine, or the fringe of low willows along some little watercourse, the younger men and boys scatter out and surround it. They beat it in the most thorough manner, and any game which it contains is driven out on the prairie, surrounded and killed. The appearance even of a jackass rabbit throws the boys into a fever of excitement, and causes them to shriek and yell as if in a frenzy.

All the morning I rode with the Indians, either at the head of the column, chatting as best I could with *Pĭ'ta Le-shar* and other chiefs, or falling back and riding among the women and children, whom I never tired of watching. Frequently during the day I saw at a distance, on the prairie, small bunches of buffalo in full flight, hotly pursued by dark-skinned riders, and occasionally two or three men would ride up to the marching columns with heavy loads of freshly-killed meat. The quick-heaving, wet flanks of the ponies told a story of sharp, rapid chases, and their tossing heads and eager, excited looks showed how much interest they took in the hunt.

The report of firearms was seldom heard. Most of the Indians hunted with the primitive weapon of their forefathers—the bow and arrow. For buffalo running an arrow is nearly as effective as lead. The power of the bow in expert hands is tremendous. Riding within half a dozen yards of the victim's side, the practiced bowman will drive the dart so far through the body of the buffalo that its shaft may project a foot or more from the opposite side—sometimes, indeed, may pass quite through. Besides, the bow can be used very rapidly and accurately. I have seen an Indian take a sheaf of six arrows in his hand, and discharge them at a mark more rapidly and with more certainty of hitting his target than I could fire the six barrels of a revolver.

III.

It was nearly noon, and I was riding along at the head of the column. I had but one horse, and did not care to wear him out by chasing around over the prairie, preferring to save him for some great effort. We were traveling along a smooth divide between two sets of ravines, which ran off, one to the east and the other to the west. *Pĭ'ta Le-shar* had just informed me by signs that we should make camp about two miles further on, by a stream whose course we could trace from where we then were. Suddenly, without the slightest warning, the huge dark bodies of half a dozen buffalo sprang into view, rising out of a ravine on our left not a hundred yards distant. When they saw the multitude before them, they stopped and stared at us.

They were too close for me to resist the temptation to pursue. As I lifted the reins from my pony's neck and bent forward, the little animal sprang into a sharp gallop toward the game, and as he did so I saw half a dozen Indians shoot out from the column and follow me. The buffalo wheeled, and in an instant were out of sight, but when I reached the edge of the bank down which they had plunged, I could see through the cloud of dust, which they left behind them, their uncouth forms dashing down the ravine. My nimble pony, as eager for the race as his rider, hurled himself down the deep pitch, and sped along the narrow broken bed of the gully. I could feel that sometimes he would lengthen his stride to leap wide ditches, where the water from some side ravine had cut away the ground, but I never knew of these until they were passed. My eyes were fixed on the fleeing herd; my ears were intent on the pursuing horsemen. Close behind me I could hear the quick pounding of many hoofs, and could feel that one of the horses, nearer than the rest, was steadily drawing up to me—but I was gaining on the buffalo. Already the confused rumble of their hoof-beats almost drowned those of the horses behind me, and the air was full of the dust and small pebbles thrown up by their hurrying feet. But they were still ahead of me, and the gulch was so narrow that I could not shoot. The leading horseman drew nearer and nearer, and was now almost at my side. I could see the lean head and long, slim neck of his pony under my right arm, and could hear the rider speak to his horse and urge him forward in the race. My horse did his best, but the other had the most speed. He shot by me, and a moment later was alongside the last buffalo.

As he passed me the young Indian made a laughing gesture of triumph, slipped an arrow on his bowstring, and drew it to its head; but just as he was about to let it fly, his horse, which was but a colt, took fright at the huge animal which it had overtaken, and shied violently to the right, almost unseating its rider. At the same moment the buffalo swerved a little to the left, and thus lost a few feet. Truly, the race is not always to the swift. As I passed the Indian, I could not restrain a little whoop of satisfaction, and then swinging my rifle around, I fired. The buffalo fell in its stride, tossing up a mighty cloud of the soft yellow earth, and my pony ran by him fifty yards before he could be checked. Then I turned and rode back to look at the game. The other Indians had passed me like a whirlwind, and, close at the heels of the herd, had swept around a point of bluff and out of sight. Only my rival remained, and he was excitedly arguing with his horse. The logic of a whip-handle, applied with vigor about the creature's ears, convinced it that it must approach the dead buffalo; and then the rider dismounting, and passing his lariat about the animal's horns, drew the pony's head to within a few feet of the terrifying mass, and fastened the rope. When he had accomplished this, he grinned pleasantly at me, and I responded in kind, and in dumb show transferred to him all my right and title in the dead buffalo. At this he

Dr. and Mrs. George Bird Grinnell on Grinnell Glacier, date unknown.
Courtesy of the Glacier National Park Archives, National Park Service.

"Crown of the Continent" by George Bird Grinnell in *The Century Magazine*, September 1901. Courtesy of *The Century Magazine*, Scribner & Company: The Century Company, publisher, via the University of California.

preservation sanity. Within its loosely worded parameters was permitting language that allowed a president of the United States to act unilaterally to protect "historic landmarks and historic and prehistoric structures," adding "and other objects of historic interest." It was tailor-made for a president of action, and Theodore Roosevelt fit the bill. Since then, seventeen presidents have designated at least one landscape or monument, totaling 158 as of 2021.[16]

Roosevelt would eventually proclaim eighteen national monuments, fifty-one federal bird sanctuaries, four national game refuges, and a hundred million acres of national

James J. Hill and Louis W. Hill, 1912. Courtesy of the James J. Hill Papers, Minnesota Historical Society, St. Paul, Minnesota, James J. Hill 387.

forest reserves. To top it off, he added five national parks: Crater Lake National Park in Oregon, Wind Cave National Park in South Dakota, Sullys Hill National Game Preserve in North Dakota (now White Horse Hill National Game Preserve), Mesa Verde National Park in Colorado, and Platt National Park in Oklahoma (now Chickasaw National Recreation Area). But his most defining contribution to conservation was to empower and legitimize the cause. He made it not only the popular thing to do but also the right and patriotic thing to do.

If John Muir and Teddy Roosevelt were the soul-sharing twins of preservation and conservation of parklands who gave national purpose to the cause, George Bird Grinnell and Louis Hill were two who, inspired by both, used their God-given talents to create a national park in the far west corner of Montana: Glacier in 1910.

Before Grinnell completed his life's work, he initiated campaigns to end predatory market hunting and game poaching in Yellowstone that led to the Yellowstone Park Protection Act. He also founded the Audubon Society of New York that was the precursor to the National Audubon Society. And, with Teddy Roosevelt, he founded the Boone and Crockett Club. His power was derived by the pen and the purse, principally through his ownership of *Forest and Stream* magazine—now *Field & Stream*. That pen and influence of the club saved the bison from extinction. He wrote nearly thirty books on Native American life, conservation, and sport hunting. And he took up the fight for national park status for Grand Canyon and Olympic National Parks.

Grinnell first came to the Glacier area in 1885. By 1891, he was thinking about national park status for those wild and haunting places of mountains, valleys, rushing waters, glimmering lakes, and glaciers. Grinnell became so enthralled with the area that he gave it a name, "Crown of the Continent," in 1901 and began to actively champion its inclusion as a national park. He drew many supporters to the cause, including Louis Hill of the Great Northern Railroad.

Born in 1872, Hill was the third of nine children of James J. and Mary T. Hill. He would rise to lead the Great Northern Railroad founded by his father, first as its president in 1907 and then as board chairman in 1912.

Ironically, it would be a boyhood trip to Yellowstone on his father's chief competitor's line, the Northern Pacific, that planted the seed for Louis Hill's love of nature and Western scenery, which eventually blossomed into support for the national park concept. Specifically, as he matured and began to take charge of more aspects of the Great Northern's business, he would come to recognize an opportunity for his railroad to have its own national park: Glacier. In doing so, he would also bring American tourists west on his passenger cars to "See America First."

It would take all the effectiveness of Grinnell's pen and Hill's power to persuade a reluctant Congress to act.

But together, Grinnell, Hill, and their allies would hammer Congress into submission through their genius of the pen, public relations, and sheer political muscle. On May 11, 1910, President William Howard Taft signed into law the act creating Glacier National Park.

Interestingly enough, the two founding partners in the drive to create Glacier National Park apparently did not personally meet until 1912—or thereafter.

> Two days later, as he and [Luther] North rode toward East Flattop, they met three horsemen, Grinnell recorded. The leader spoke and at length asked if this was Mr. Grinnell's party and if I was Mr. G. Just before we turned off to McDermott (now Swiftcurrent Lake), they stopped again and the leader introduced himself as Mr. Louis Hill (president of the Great Northern Railroad). We had a long talk . . . Hill seemed a very bright, energetic, and determined fellow. He will do much for the park and I told Jack (Monroe) he is a good man to tie up to.[17]

## Stephen Tyng Mather: The Essential Genius

Among park champions past and future, none played a more significant role than Stephen Mather, the National Park Service's first superintendent. I rank him with the two Roosevelts, Muir, and President Lyndon and Lady Bird Johnson. His influence stretched far beyond most others in the landscape of citizen perception and acceptance.

On his first inspection trip as assistant to the secretary of the Interior, he became convinced that the roads (or lack of roads) in Glacier and other parks were terrible and needed to be addressed to meet the rising American love affair with the automobile. He also saw that Glacier required a new headquarters, bought the necessary land out of his own pocket, and gave it to the park.

When necessary (which in the formative years of the park service was often), he would take on the high and mighty to establish firm jurisdiction of the agency so that policy would not be whipsawed by politics, power, or profit. He most often won. His sense and flare for public relations, his passion for parks, and his personal wealth all contributed to his success.

Mather's business was Borax, a common commodity that he took to new commercial heights by advertising it as the "20 Mule Team Borax." His endeavors were successful and made Mather a millionaire several times over. By 1914, at the age of forty-seven, he was rich for a lifetime and sought other ways to fulfill his restless drive. He also needed another outlet to tame his periodic bouts with serious depression. Already a devoted outdoorsman and hiker, he turned to the Western mountains to calm that depression. During that period (1904 to 1914), he would meet John Muir, join the Sierra Club, and become a lifetime devotee of Muir and his philosophy for national parks.

He also became a staunch advocate for cleaning up the disarray and disrepair that had befallen the parks and was recruited to do just that by the secretary of the Interior. If the original national parks movement was loaded with first-team talent, its second-generation bench was equally impressive. None was more important than Mather in establishing a coherent system for supervising the growing number of parks whose governance had been wholly lacking, spread over several agencies, and desperately underfunded.

First and foremost was the need to establish a national park service, then get it functioning and funded. But to get the credibility and funding necessary, a national public relations campaign would have to be devised. To accomplish this, Mather would use his own public relations genius, fortified by his former newspaper colleague Robert Sterling Yard, an editor at the *New York Herald*. Mather got Yard by personally paying his $6,000-a-year salary. He would also pay part of Horace Albright's salary out of his own pocket. Together, they directed the charge for the national park service cause.

As the parks became more popular, the second leg of the movement kicked in: recreation. Preserved for now and the future, owned by its citizens, then made accessible to all, lands of the natural environment would serve the spiritual, physical, and mental well-being and recreation needs of the nation.

But if increased park visitation were to be realized, better and more accommodations and roads to service the tourists would have to be built. The publicity and increased visitation were essential to persuade a reluctant Congress to appropriate funds.

All had to be packaged and fit between 1914 to 1915, not only to meet Mather's personal deadline (he originally promised

Yellowstone National Park Superintendent and National Park Service Deputy Director Horace M. Albright (left) and National Park Service Director Stephen T. Mather (right) standing next to a Packard with license plate U. S. N. P. S. 1, 1924. Courtesy of the National Park Service, Harpers Ferry Center, West Virginia.

a year's commitment), but to create a critical mass of public support among growing numbers of park visitors in order to foster legislative action. While support was growing in the hinterlands for more parks and a national park service (Rocky Mountain National Park was established in 1916), Congress was another matter. Mather's first budget for more staff and roads was cut. Limitations on per-park spending were adopted. Mather then found he could not personally pay for a road in Yosemite without congressional approval. He got the law changed, convinced his wealthy friends and the Sierra Club to buy the road, then gifted it to Yosemite.

The policy of road development became one of Mather's most lasting legacies. How to accommodate the rising number of automobile visitors required roads—good, new roads. But good roads bumped up against the preservation clause of the "Organic Act." Only a genius with a sense of the practical, coupled with an eye for nature's majesty, could connect the two with minimal damage to either.

In the development of Glacier National Park, Mather found the answer: adopting a single route for the "Going-to-the-Sun" highway that would be adequate for the growing number of visitors while causing the least environmental disruption.

Stephen Mather's one-road policy seemed to answer both sides of the conflicting charges of the Organic Act: conservation (proper use of nature) and preservation (protection of nature from any use). In large part, that policy has held and served the intent of the dual purposes well.

Stephen Tyng Mather plaque at Zion National Park, Utah, 2009. Courtesy of the National Park Service via Wikimedia Commons.

Undeterred by the challenges he faced, Mather headed out of Washington for a series of conferences to generate support among elected officials, business leaders, and organizations such as the General Federation of Women's Clubs, whose two million members were already working for the establishment of more national parks and a national park service. They also had at the ready a 250,000-strong mailing list. (That potential powerhouse of organizers and voters did not go unnoticed by Pat Neff a few years later when he ran for Texas governor in 1920.) On August 25, 1916, after unrelenting pressure on Congress, the National Park Service was established and signed into law by President Woodrow Wilson.

At that moment, there were thirty-five national parks and monuments, with several others under consideration.[18] As of 2020, there were 423 parks in the national parks system, with sixty-three designated as "national parks."[19] Thanks to Stephen Mather's vision and perseverance, our national parks fit into his primary requirement of "supreme" excellence.

Rather than a year's commitment, Mather, with Albright and Yard by his side most of the way, would remain with the National Park Service for fourteen years. His accomplishments touched every region of the country and all areas of governance. The proof of his success lies in the fact that all his park additions remain intact and popular. And his contributions to good governance and practical regulation placed the men and women of the National Park Service near the top of the most admired government employees.

> He laid the foundation of the National Park Service, defining and establishing the policies under which its areas shall be developed and conserved unimpaired for future generations. There will never come an end to the good he has done.
>
> *Inscription on Mather plaques*
> *placed in national parks across the US*

# Chapter 2

# Texas Women in the State Parks Movement

Contributed by **Jennifer L. Bristol**

The Second Industrial Revolution was in full swing by the 1880s. Steel plants churned out the necessary materials to fuel new skyscrapers in the cities and provide the railroads with tracks to extend west to fertile farmlands and onward to timber country in the Northwest. While factories and cities grew, so, too, grew pollution and the trappings of urban life. Out of the urban cores, a new class emerged, stronger than ever. The middle class consisted of small business owners, lawyers, doctors, accountants, and other professionals who could earn enough money to no longer be counted as poor—but who were not yet rich enough to be part of the wealthy elite.

While the number of middle-class citizens was increasing in the United States and Europe, the strict rules of social conduct of the Victorian era were tightening. Under these rules, there was little room for error for middle-class women. There was also little room for achieving political influence, higher education, or financial independence. These restrictive norms left many women longing for more than just being a reliable mother or dutiful daughter. Slowly, women began to gather at luncheon groups to share ideas, listen to intellectual speakers, share gardening tips, and focus on social issues.

Jane Croly, 1904. Courtesy of *Memories of Jane Cunningham Croly*, G.P. Putnam's Sons, publisher, via the Library Company of Philadelphia.

After the Civil War ended, women's clubs began to spring up across the country, and, by 1890, the General Federation of Women's Clubs had been organized. Earlier, Jane Croly, a professional journalist, had formed the Sorosis Club after being denied entry—based on her gender—to listen to a lecture by novelist Charles Dickens. The Sorosis Club's original intent was to bring intellectual enrichment to women through guest speakers, book recommendations, and informal classes. To celebrate the club's twenty years of existence, Jane Croly and others organized a convention in New York City. They brought together leaders from other women's clubs from around the country and organized the federation.[1]

Throughout the 1880s and 1890s, women's clubs were popping up across Texas in towns both large and small. During that same time, the city of Galveston had become a boom town and the main port from which vast Texas farms and ranches exported cotton, cattle, and other goods. Two Galveston women, Betty Eve Ballinger and her cousin, Hally Ballinger Bryan Perry, met in the library of the Ballinger family home in Galveston, known as The Oaks, to discuss their concerns about the diminishing memory—and fading fighters—of the Texas Revolution. Betty Ballinger's maternal grandfather, William Houston Jack, had fought in the Battle of San Jacinto and later became a prominent lawyer. Hally Ballinger had the distinction of being the grandniece of Stephen F. Austin, one of the first Anglo colonizers in Texas.[2]

The two dutiful daughters wanted to honor the memory of those who had fought in the Texas Revolution. They also wanted to honor their families. In 1891, they traveled to Houston to meet fourteen other distinguished women in the home of Mary Jane Harris

**RIGHT**
Betty Eve Ballinger, cofounder of the Daughters of the Republic of Texas, 1891. Courtesy of the Daughters of the Republic of Texas Museum, Austin, Texas.

**FAR RIGHT**
Hally Ballinger Bryan Perry, cofounder of the Daughters of the Republic of Texas, date unknown. Courtesy of the Daughters of the Republic of Texas Museum, Austin, Texas.

Briscoe. Mary Jane Briscoe was the wealthy widow of a Texas patriot and businessman, Andrew J. Briscoe. Also in attendance was the widow of Anson Jones, the last president of the Republic of Texas. Mary Smith Jones was acquainted with Hally Ballinger's father, Guy Bryan, through the Texas Veterans Association, and was instrumental in bringing the two groups together.[3]

The women collectively agreed to take action and form an association first called the Daughters of Female Descendants of the Heroes of '36, which later became the Daughters of the Republic of Texas. The charter for the club was not ratified until 1895, when the Texas Veterans Association formally requested that the Daughters of the Republic of Texas carry forward their memory and honor the past. Mary Smith Jones was the first president of the new organization.[4]

Daughters of the Republic of Texas with members of the Texas Veterans Association arriving at the San Jacinto Battlefield, ca. 1894–1897. Courtesy of Cecil Thomson, San Jacinto Museum and Battlefield Association, LaPorte, Texas, 14885c0352.

The first actions of the Daughters of the Republic of Texas focused on preserving documents, collecting stories from the aging veterans and their families, and establishing celebrations that honored specific dates relevant to the establishment of Texas. Deeply committed to the power of education, they also influenced the teaching of Texas history in public schools.

Knowing time was of the essence to capture the fading memory of the Battle of San Jacinto, they worked with veterans to map the battlefield on the grounds where the final battle between the mighty Mexican Army and the rebellious Texans took place. The preservation of Civil War battle sites such as Shiloh and Vicksburg were occurring in other states, which further fanned the flames of the Daughters of the Republic of Texas to focus their efforts on purchasing the land as a memorial park and erecting markers to designate the conflict and honor the fallen Texans. After several failed attempts, they finally found a willing legislative sponsor in Senator Waller Thomas Burns of Houston, who agreed to sponsor a bill to establish the battlefield as a memorial park. In 1897, with political support from Senator Burns and the constant persuasion and perseverance of the Daughters of the Republic of Texas, the Texas legislature appropriated $10,000 for the purchase of the battlefield, thus making San Jacinto the first state-owned park in Texas.[5]

By 1907, the park consisted of 336 acres, with land being added over time to encompass the twelve hundred acres of the current historic site. The San Jacinto Park Commission was established to manage the property, with support from the Daughters of the Republic of Texas to help raise additional funds and host events. In 1919, the state

Visitors gathering at the Brigham
Monument at the San Jacinto Battlefield,
December 19, 1893. Courtesy of Henry
Stanton, San Jacinto Museum and Battle-
field Association, LaPorte, Texas, 3585c3.

Front of the Alamo through the compound gate, ca. 1922. After their victory with the San Jacinto Battlefield, the Daughters of the Republic of Texas set their sights on preserving the Alamo and, in 1905, convinced the state legislature to purchase the remaining buildings and name the Daughters of the Republic of Texas as the permanent custodian of the site. That agreement remained until 2015, when custodianship was transferred to the Texas General Land Office. Courtesy of Underwood & Underwood, Library of Congress Prints and Photographs Division, Washington, DC, cph 3b34239.

established the Board of Control, an oversight board tasked with overseeing state historical parks and local commissions. In 1965, the San Jacinto Commission was dissolved, and management of the land was transferred to the Texas Parks and Wildlife Department. In 2019, after approval of House Bill 1422, the Eighty-Sixth Texas Legislature shifted management of the battlefield and monuments when they transferred the properties to the Texas Historical Commission.[6]

After the success of the establishment of the San Jacinto Battlefield park, the Daughters of the Republic of Texas set their sights on additional locations associated with the Revolution, including the Alamo, Fannin and Gonzales battlefields, Refugio public square, and Washington-on-the-Brazos. These additional properties sparked the notion to follow the national park model to create a state parks system.

The idea and desire for parks came late to Texas. The first urban parks consisted of cemeteries such as Glenwood Cemetery in Houston (established in 1871) and Oakland Cemetery in Dallas (established in 1891). The logical progression was to establish memorial parks to honor the Texas Revolution, Civil War battlefields, and other culturally significant places that were relevant at the time. While the establishment of those types of memorial parks was underway, Texans also acknowledged their deep love of nature and desire to have parks for living people as well as parks to honor the dead.

Additional women's clubs were emerging across the state, and, in 1897, twenty-one
clubs gathered in Waco to form the Texas Federation of Literary Clubs. The name
changed in 1898 to the Texas Federation of Women's Clubs, when members agreed to
expand their focus beyond education and enrichment to include community service,
arts, welfare of the poor, support of Native Americans, and parks and playgrounds.[7]
Women of color were initially included—and then later excluded—from the Texas Federation of Women's Clubs, so in 1905, they formed their own powerful network known
as the Texas Federation of Colored Women's Clubs.[8]

A group of women marching in a suffrage parade under the Texas banner in Washington, DC, April 7, 1913. Courtesy of W. R. Ross, Library of Congress Prints and Services Division, Washington, DC, cph 3a10923.

The devotion to education and literacy by the women of the Texas Federation of Women's Clubs cannot be overlooked. Today, more than 85 percent of Texas public libraries are a result of the work of the Texas Federation of Women's Clubs or the Texas Federation of Colored Women's Clubs and their volunteers. An equally important component to consider is the aspiration of the women in the Texas Federation of Women's Clubs and the Texas Federation of Colored Women's Clubs to have the power of the vote and become an essential part of the political process. Alongside their sisters in other states, they organized, wrote letters, marched, and held luncheons for elected officials. Had the founding fathers of the Republic of Texas followed Sam Houston's sage advice to grant women the right to vote, Texas would have again turned the tide of history. Instead, women—and a handful of men—struggled to obtain that right for eighty-three more years. Texas granted the right for women to vote in the state primaries in 1918 and, in June 1919, became the ninth state—and the first southern state—to ratify the Nineteenth Amendment, which enfranchised women.[9]

Poll taxes and local voting intimidation laws and practices obstructed men and women of color from voting for decades. Many White women were forbidden by their parents or husbands to vote, work outside the home, or run for office, which slowed the social transformation the suffragettes had envisioned. There also remained a contingency of women who believed it was not the place of women to enter into decision-making roles outside the confines of raising and educating children and/or tending to their families.

In Texas, male elected officials and lobbyists took notice of the powerful women-run networks that emerged during the struggle to win the vote and called on them to help sway the legislature and local governing bodies on a number of issues.

With the end of World War I and passing of the Spanish flu epidemic, industrialized countries roared into the 1920s. New innovations infiltrated all facets of life, including transportation, women's fashions, farming methods, and social constructs. Not everyone embraced the age of innovation and shedding of strict Victorian and Edwardian values, however. Prohibition was in full swing by 1920 with passage of the Eighteenth Amendment. The Ku Klux Klan, otherwise known as the invisible empire, was also in full swing, especially in Texas, where the rapid expansion of agriculture and construction infused the workforce with Hispanic and African American labor. The revolution in Mexico (1910 to 1920) also displaced large numbers of Mexican families, who were trying to escape the chaos by fleeing to the United States. With the expansion of newspapers and radio, conflicts that would generally have been swept under the proverbial rug were brought into the households of average Americans. By the 1920s, the hard-fought wins of the Progressive Era were being tested.

Transportation was also changing, and the post-World War I automobile age pulled onto fertile ground in Texas. Farmers and ranchers embraced trucks to haul their goods to smaller markets, rail yards, or shipping hubs. Merchants and salesmen discovered a faster, more efficient and independent mode of transportation to sell their wares. The increasing middle class recognized the automobile as a means to transport them out of the hot, dusty, and often smoky cities to the countryside to spend their newly found leisure time. All these new autos required gasoline and motor oil, a resource that ran deep in Texas.

The new auto age, however, lacked two things: good roads and public points of interest beyond cemeteries and historic sites. Inspired by the national parks movement, modern travelers wanted places to escape into the wilderness, marvel at nature, canoe down a river, swim or fish in a lake, hunt game, or reunite with their family and friends. The Texas Federation of Women's Clubs advocated for improved roads, recognizing the need to transport rural school children safely to community schools and provide them with better access to local medical services. They also recognized that good roads strengthened business communities in their towns, which made it possible to achieve projects such as local libraries, parks, and cultural centers, to name a few. As early as 1915, the Texas Federation of Women's Clubs formed a committee under the Rural Life Division to advocate at the local and state levels for improved transportation.[10]

One of the many men who recognized the potential and understood the necessity to improve auto transportation was Governor Pat Morris Neff. Neff was born in 1871 in McLennan County outside Waco to Isabella and Noah Neff. The young couple built a home in Coryell County along a clear, cool spring they called Neff Spring. Life was not easy on the Texas frontier, where Comanches were always on the lookout for homes to raid and horses to liberate from the pioneers who penetrated deeper into their homelands. Despite the hardships, Isabella loved the freedom of country life, and she deeply loved the land.[11]

A young Pat Neff, ca. 1890s. Courtesy of the Pat Neff Archive, Texas Collection, Baylor University, Waco, Texas.

Isabella and Noah welcomed nine children into the world; Pat was the youngest of the brood. For many years, the family flourished at the farm and in the community. However, typhoid hit the Neff family, and, in the span of a few years, Isabella lost a daughter, a son, and her beloved Noah in 1884. Isabella was left to manage the farm with five children. Two of her older sons turned to a life of crime; one was convicted of murder and the other was imprisoned for robbing a train. Devoted to the salvation offered through a good education, she pushed her remaining children even harder to pursue their studies. She also instilled in them a deep love of nature and often gathered with friends and family on their farm at a special place called the Grove near the Leon River.

Pat earned an undergraduate degree from Baylor University and a law degree from the University of Texas. In 1899, he entered the Texas House of Representatives and, in 1903, became the youngest speaker of the House. He took a break from politics in 1905 to practice law and attend to his family in and around Waco. In 1920, Neff saw an opportunity to run for governor as a strong advocate of Prohibition and reform. In his campaign, he covered more than six thousand miles of Texas, visiting counties that had never received a visit from a candidate for governor. Many of the roads he traveled were little more than unimproved wagon routes. Neff enjoyed camping and, frugal to the core, often camped while on the campaign trail instead of staying in hotels or boarding houses.[12]

After his victory, Neff met staunch opposition to his progressive ideas regarding water conservation, efficiency in government, and prison reform. His idea to follow the national park model to create a state parks system also fell on uninspired—if not deaf—

ears at the State Capitol. Despite opposition, Neff was able to establish the State Parks Board to gather information and make recommendations on where to establish parks. He appointed David Colp as board chair. Colp had been secretary of the Texas Highway Commission and was the point man for promoting "good roads." Neff and Colp saw the connection for promoting a state parks system in conjunction with a state highway system.[13]

When Pat Neff was elected governor, his mother strongly supported many of his campaign ideas, and the concept of parks where people could gather and relax in nature especially intrigued her. In 1916, she donated six acres of land along the Leon River to be enjoyed by the public as a place to picnic, gather with family, or rest in the shade of a majestic pecan grove. Sadly, she died in 1921 during Neff's first year as governor. In her will, she requested that the six-acre grove be donated to the state for the purpose of a park. Governor Neff proclaimed the donated land to be the first state park in Texas that was established solely for the purpose of outdoor recreation and not a memorial park such as the San Jacinto Battlefield. Neff later included an additional two hundred fifty acres of his own property to increase the size of the park. Mother Neff State Park officially opened in 1937.[14]

Influenced by the Texas Garden Clubs, the Texas Federation of Women's Clubs expanded its scope of work to include a Parks and Playgrounds Division under the club's Department of Conservation and Natural Resources. The other divisions under that department included: Forestry and Wildlife Refuges; Natural Scenery; Billboard Restriction; Birds, Flowers, and Gardens; Highways and Memorial Tree Planting; Waterways; Historic Spots and Buildings; and Soils and Minerals. Each of the divisions was chaired by women who spanned the far reaches of the state, from Alpine to Port Arthur and Amarillo to Brownsville. Despite not having modern conveniences such as cell phones, computers, highways, or Fun Fares on Southwest Airlines, the women communicated frequently via letter, in person, and, occasionally, by telephone, which was becoming more prevalent even in rural communities. They waited patiently to hear from

Original Texas State Parks Board members, 1924. From left, David E. Colp, chairman; Phebe K. Warner, secretary and statistician; Pat M. Neff, governor; Mrs. W. C. (Florence) Martin, vice chairman; Robert M. Hubbard, State Highway Commission chairman; Mrs. James (Katie) Welder, historian; and Hobart Key, attorney and sergeant at arms. Courtesy of Curatorial Services, Texas Parks and Wildlife Department, Austin, Texas, 2017.3.2.

Phebe Kerrick Warner, date unknown. Courtesy of the Texas Parks and Wildlife Department, Austin, Texas.

each other before taking action that required or warranted the approval of the collective. When necessary, they put their trust in a single individual to represent the federation in her subject matter of expertise.

Heeding the call of Governor Neff and the call for "good roads," the federation called on its members to support national and state highway systems. In a 1923 article in the McKinney, Texas, *Courier-Gazette*, Decca Lamar West, chair of the Good Roads Division of the Department of Conservation of the Texas Federation of Women's Clubs, made an appeal to rally support for a state highway amendment. That article was published in newspapers around the state. The constitutional amendment was to go before voters to establish a state highway system that would construct and maintain roads and allow the state to levy a tax for that purpose. The Texas Federation of Women's Clubs noted the value in the amendment as twofold: first, it would allow for reliable transportation of rural school children, and second, it would lay the foundation for the creation of a state parks system that was already being discussed at the national level by Stephen Tyng Mather, director of the National Park Service, and the General Federation of Women's Clubs.[15]

Even though Governor Neff was met with fierce resistance to his idea of a state parks system from the legislature, he was able to get Senate Bill 73 passed to establish the first State Parks Board in 1923 and appointed five members: David E. Colp from San Antonio, Phebe Kerrick Warner, Florence Martin, Katie Owens Welder, and Hobart Key Sr., a businessman from Marshall. All three women held leadership roles in the Texas Federation of Women's Clubs.

Prior to serving two terms on the State Parks Board, Phebe Kerrick Warner of Claude, Texas, was a journalist for twenty-two years, writing a regular column in the *Fort Worth Star-Telegram* and periodic articles for other newspapers and journals across the state. She had a distinct journalistic style that captured the Panhandle and West Texas lifestyle and addressed many of the issues that communities faced, including the enfranchisement of women, hazards of industrial farming, county-based government, "good roads," and, above all, improvement of the quality of rural life. She championed the effort to set aside Palo Duro Canyon State Park. In 1929, President Herbert Hoover appointed her to the national Home Builders Committee, and she later ran unsuccessfully for the United States Congress.[16]

Florence Martin, more often referred to as Mrs. W. C. Martin, served as vice chair of the State Parks Board until the 1930s. She is best known for her efforts to improve the lives of tenant farmers and for introducing a revolutionary farming system model in Darco, Texas.[17] She was chair of the Texas Federation of Women's Clubs Country Rural Life Division, became the first woman chair of the National Farm Bureau, and spent a great deal of time writing and speaking on the topic of rural life. Governor Pat Neff thought highly of Florence Martin and appointed her to be the only woman on the Penitentiary Relocation Board as it wrestled with the issues of prison farms and prison labor. Above all, she loved Texas and believed that each person should "know their state first." In an article she wrote for the *Fort Worth Star-Telegram* on July 13, 1924, she articulated her feelings on the topic:

> It should be our first duty, to know our own state, and our first trips should be made there. When, after that ground has been covered and the family has been educated it is time to take a post graduate course, and go on into the neighboring states. The great transcontinental highways and our state and national parks have also made traveling by motor a real recreation.[18]

Like Phebe Warner, Florence Martin was a strong advocate for good roads to improve rural life and increase recreational travel. In the same article, she wrote about the "Glacier to Gulf Highway," which was a concept to create a major highway system that ran from Glacier National Park to the Gulf of Mexico, with state and national parks located on or near the highway every hundred miles or so.

Mrs. W. C. (Florence) Martin posing in a Cadillac Model E automobile, 1906. Courtesy of F. Ed. Spooner, Lazamick Collection, National Automotive History Collection, Detroit Public Library, na004066.

Katie Owens Welder was born in Victoria County, Texas, during the Civil War and married James Francis Welder, a prominent rancher and banker, in 1889. In 1912, she formed the Mother's Club to support St. Joseph's School in Victoria and continued to serve that club for more than thirty years. She was honored several times by the pope for her charitable work with the church. In addition to serving on the State Parks Board and Texas State Parks Association, she held various leadership roles in the Texas Federation of Women's Clubs, including serving as chair of the Permanent Headquarters Committee to secure funding and oversee construction of the federation's clubhouse in Austin.[19]

Governor Neff had chosen his board members well and set them to work immediately. Part of their charge was to inventory the state to look for places of interest that willing landowners would donate to be developed into roadside parks. Governor Neff and David Colp envisioned securing smaller parks of fifty acres or less. Board member Phebe Kerrick Warner and several of the club's leaders in West Texas had their eyes on bigger prizes and continually made the case for larger parks. Despite having a strong team assembled for the State Parks Board, they needed an ally to lobby on their behalf.

Marian Rather Powell in front of a painting of her grandchildren, circa 1950s. Courtesy of Nancy Powell Moore and family.

In 1925, the Parks and Playgrounds Division of the Texas Federation of Women's Clubs was chaired by one of the most capable and well-connected women in Texas: Marian "Mamie" Rather Powell of Austin. Born in Huntsville, Mamie Powell followed in her parents' footsteps to pursue a college education. She graduated from the University of Texas in 1902 and promptly returned to Huntsville to start her teaching career at the high school. She was a skilled teacher who was appointed by the governor to the staff at Sam Houston Normal Institute in 1909. Per state law regarding teaching and marriage in Texas in 1913, she stepped down from her prized teaching duties at the college after she married a local up-and-coming attorney, Benjamin "Ben" Harrison Powell III.[20]

Mamie Powell did not go quietly into married life, never to be heard from again. With the support of her husband, she fought vigorously for women's rights, education, and improvement of the lives of economically disadvantaged families. She chaired the Walker County Suffrage Association, served on the board of the Red Cross, and was the first woman to serve on the Huntsville School Board.

Mamie and Ben Powell welcomed their first son, Benjamin H. Powell, in 1915 and their second son, Rawley R. Powell, in 1918. Texas Governor William P. Hobby appointed Ben Powell III to the Twelfth District Court in 1919, and, from 1920 to 1927, he served on the Commission of Appeals to the Texas Supreme Court. The dynamic couple moved to Austin in 1920 and immersed themselves in the energy of the city. Tragedy struck in 1923, when their youngest son, Rawley, died at the age of five while undergoing a tonsillectomy that went horribly wrong. Their child bled to death on the operating table. Bereft, the Powells created the Wildwood Sanctuary, a four-acre wooded area at the Oakwood Cemetery in Huntsville in his honor.

Mamie Powell channeled her grief into one of the things she did best—public service. After all, service was in her blood. Her mother had been president of the Daughters of the American Revolution, and her father had served as mayor of Huntsville. Mamie was well respected in her own right as a brilliant mind who was fiercely organized; however, she also knew how to leverage the connections from her parents and husband. The bridge clubs and garden parties held at the Powell home were filled with a who's-who list of Texas movers and shakers and their savvy spouses. These connections would serve her well as she stepped forward to embark on the journey to become the State Parks Board's secret weapon.

The letters retained by the Powell family offer a priceless account of exactly how integral Mamie Powell and the Texas Federation of Women's Clubs were in inventorying existing local parks across the state, securing additional lands to be donated to the state, and, most importantly, helping secure passage of the legislation that allowed the state to accept the donated lands for the purpose of parks.

As chair of the Parks and Playgrounds Division of the Texas Federation of Women's Clubs, Mamie Powell established a strong relationship with David Colp and the other

State Parks Board members. With the help of the vast membership of the Texas Federation of Women's Clubs, which numbered more than fifty thousand, the State Parks Board had been able to inventory and identify twenty-seven potential parks with willing landowners who would deed the lands to the State of Texas. However, with Pat Neff out of office by this time, the Thirty-Ninth Texas Legislature had cooled its interest in accepting the lands or creating a state parks system. The State Parks Board needed a change agent to contextualize the relevancy of parks, mobilize a grassroots movement, influence the inner circle of power, and do it all for free. Mamie Powell was just the person to do so.

At the annual Texas Federation of Women's Clubs convention in Dallas in November 1926, a resolution was adopted to "petition the 40th Legislature of Texas to accept titles to certain park sites offered the State by patriotic citizens refused by the 39th Legislature." At the convention, the president of the Texas Federation of Women's Clubs, Florence B. Fields of Haskell, and the other leaders expressed their confidence in Mamie Powell to champion the cause and represent the federation in all things regarding parks, even though Mrs. L. A. Wells of Amarillo was chair of the Department of Conservation of Natural Resources. Mrs. Wells was devoted but too far removed from the hub of political activity in Austin. In a letter dated January 26, 1927, from David Colp to Mamie Powell, Colp states, "I am also in receipt of a letter from Mrs. Wells, of Amarillo, advising that she is asking you to represent her as a member of the Board of Directors of the Parks Association during her absence."[21]

Another ally arrived at the State Capitol in 1926, when Margie E. Neal of Carthage clicked her heeled shoes up the granite steps and through the sturdy wooden doors of the State Capitol to be sworn in as the first woman senator in Texas. Margie Neal had already proven herself to be a savvy business owner and journalist when she owned the *East Texas Register* newspaper. She had been an astute teacher and well-respected member of the Texas Federation of Women's Clubs. In fact, she served on many club committees alongside Florence Martin and Phebe Warner. Margie Neal had advocated for political equality in the suffrage movement and started her public service with an appointment to the State Teachers College Board of Regents. While in Austin during the legislative session, she often played bridge and visited the home of her longtime friend, Mamie Powell.[22]

With the Texas Federation of Women's Clubs on board and Senator Neal in the state House, David Colp and the State Parks Board now had the right team to encourage the legislature to accept the donated lands as parks and create a state parks system. In February 1926, Colp wrote to Mamie Powell to request that she and Mrs. E. A. Bellis of Fort Worth engage the Texas Federation of Women's Clubs in a letter-writing campaign to support Senate Concurrent Resolution 13 accepting the donations of lands that was introduced by Senator Neal. Colp suggested that a hundred letters would be a good number to sway the State Affairs Committee. Within weeks, more than four hundred letters poured in from influential women across the state.[23]

Senator Margie E. Neal, ca. 1929. Courtesy of the State Preservation Board, Austin, Texas, 1989.605.

The first meeting before the State Affairs Committee did not go well, and all was almost lost. No shrinking violet, Mamie Powell did not hold back in her letter to David Colp to express her displeasure in how the matter was handled.

> *Yesterday afternoon Miss Neal and I appeared before the State Affairs Committee in the interest of the resolution sent by you and introduced by her. Had you been here to give them actual information of the individual advantages of each site, I think the result would have been more favorable. As it was, neither Miss Neal nor I had visited each tract and could not assure them of particular merits. I was prepared to argue for acceptance alone unhampered by a program of maintenance, but when Senator Wirtz said he favored a State Park program but could not agree to accept the entire string of tracts, since he understood many were better fitted for county or town projects, I was silent except to say a very splendid group of citizens composing of Parks Board members having visited them were recommending them. I cannot understand why some members of the Parks Board did not consider the resolution of sufficient importance to come here to help meet the objections.*

Colp later wrote and apologized that he was detained on other business in the Rio Grande Valley.[24]

In January 1927, Colp wrote Mamie Powell asking her and her committee members to concentrate on Senator Edgar E. Witt of Waco and Senator John H. Bailey of Cuero to win them over, as both had been against the idea of the state owning lands for the purpose of recreation. At the end of February, Mamie Powell wrote to Colp to share that she had personally spoken with Senator Witt, "whom I've known for many years and who appeared ready to be convinced." She reiterated her disappointment that she was the only person showing up at meetings to advocate for the parks.

> *The suggested low level implied in tourist parks ruined our proposition. Had an informed person been present to take each tract up and show why it should be set apart from State maintenance, I believe it would have gone out favorably and carried through the Senate. This resolution is dead unless you or someone, who can give the information, comes before this sub-committee.*[25]

Colp heeded her message and did not miss another hearing. By mid-March, the tide had turned, thanks to Mamie Powell's constant presence at the Capitol, phone calls and letters to Texas Federation of Women's Clubs members, and communication with the media. Senator Neal had a reputation for getting her bills passed and leaned on the senators who needed a final push.

Even in the flurry of activity, Mamie Powell maintained her busy family life with great care and affection. In a letter from Mamie to her mother, we have a window into the pleasures and demands of her personal life. She beautifully describes her son and his friends gathered upstairs playing ping-pong, while one of the younger visitors quietly reads a book in her favorite corner of the house. The additional children were staying with the Powells because her friend's youngest child had come down with chicken pox, and her friend needed a safe place for her older children to stay.[26]

Mamie also includes that she played bridge the previous day with her friends: Mrs. Bobbit (wife of the Speaker of the House), Mrs. Matson, Miss Margie Neal (senator), Mrs. Barry Miller (wife of the lieutenant governor), and Mrs. Moody (wife of the governor). She also writes that during and after the game, they discussed the park resolution, which she describes in detail. In the following paragraph, she asks her mother to help her repair the lacework on her dress the next time she is in town. She concludes with how much she is enjoying her work on the park resolution and with the federation and admits it is much more rewarding than cleaning the house or cooking.

On March 17, 1927, Colp wrote Mrs. Bellis, "I suppose you had the pleasure of reading in the press this morning the final acceptance of twenty-three of our parks by the legislature, the John H. Kirby State Park at Fort Worth being among the number. We certainly owe you and Mrs. Powell a vote of thanks for your loyal cooperation."

In the same letter, Colp adds that while the parks had been accepted, advocates still needed to secure the appropriation of $50,000 and convict labor to get the parks ready for use. He requests that Mrs. Bellis be ready to organize another letter-writing campaign.[27] While twenty-three parks were listed in the resolution, there were actually twenty-four lands donated to the state when the earlier gift from Isabella and Pat Neff was included.

Every major newspaper and many of the smaller ones picked up the story to celebrate the passage of Senator Margie Neal's resolution to accept twenty-four parks totaling 1,858 acres across Texas. The *Austin American-Statesman* reported, "State Accepts 24 New Parks, Mrs. Ben Powell, Austin, Presses Resolution in Legislature." The article credited Senator Neal, Mamie Powell, and the Texas Federation of Women's Clubs for their skillful efforts in achieving passage of the resolution, which the governor approved on March 28, 1927.[28]

Securing the appropriations took a second burst of energy, and, in a letter to Julia Owens of Navasota, Colp explained that the House was willing to support the expense; however, the Senate again was repelling the idea. He added, "I am going to Austin today for a conference with Mrs. Powell and shall be governed largely by Mrs. Powell's recommendations, believing that if she is given a free hand that she may be successful with this as she was in securing the acceptance of the parks." Establishing a reliable method for funding state parks would take decades.[29]

David Colp and the State Parks Board searched for funding to staff and improve

Beatrice Pickens (right) with husband T. Boone Pickens (center) and Sidney Tassin, assistant vice president of finances at Mesa Petroleum Company, May 13, 1985. Courtesy of Lennox McLendon, Associated Press via Shutterstock.

Terry Hershey, August 30, 2011. Courtesy of Brian Swett, Jacob & Terese Hershey Foundation.

the parks for years until a windfall occurred during the Great Depression of the 1930s. The Civilian Conservation Corps was established under the New Deal. Men were offered jobs and housing to make public improvements around the country, including building needed roads, dams, trails, lodging, and administrative facilities at Texas's new state parks.

Each of the aforementioned women focused her particular abilities and interests to significantly contribute to forming and sustaining the Texas state parks system. These women did not just lay the foundation, they also gathered their friends and families to clear the grounds, mix and pour the cement, and host a luncheon to celebrate their collective achievements. They juggled the demands of family life, the challenges of expanding social norms, and the doubts of the established power structure to serve the greater good of their fellow citizens and leave a legacy that their children and all future generations could enjoy.

After these courageous women assisted in establishing the state parks system in Texas, it would take sixty-four years before a woman would again serve in a leadership role on the governing body for the Texas Parks and Wildlife Department. Beatrice "Bea" Pickens, wife of oilman T. Boone Pickens, was appointed to the Texas Parks and Wildlife Commission in 1987 by Governor Bill Clements. At the time, she was the director of the National Fish and Wildlife Foundation and an avid hunter who understood the need for good habitat to support fish and game. Her appointment opened the door for a succession of women to serve on the commission. In 1991, Governor Ann Richards appointed Terry Hershey to the commission, quickly followed by Mickey Burleson in 1993. Both women advocated for more and improved parks for people, conservation of species and habitat, and less focus on hunting and fishing.

Beyond service on the State Parks Board, which later became the Texas Parks and Wildlife Commission, an entire cast of women has contributed to the addition of state parks, advocating for conservation easements on private lands or championing policies that protect endangered species and their habitats. Three such women stand out with significant contributions to the history of state parks: Lady Bird Johnson, Jane Dunn Sibley, and Madge Lindsay.

Lady Bird Johnson is well known for her contributions to the environmental movement. According to the First Lady's official website, ladybirdjohnson.org,

> More than two hundred laws related to the environment were passed during the Johnson Administration, many of which were influenced by Mrs. Johnson's work. Among the major legislative initiatives were the Wilderness Act of 1964,

Lady Bird Johnson in a field of wildflowers in the Texas Hill Country, May 10, 1990. Courtesy of Frank Wolfe, White House Photo Office Collection, Lyndon Baines Johnson Presidential Library, Austin, Texas, D9081-6.

the Land and Water Conservation Fund, the Wild and Scenic Rivers Program, the 1965 Highway Beautification Act, and many additions to the National Park system. . . .

The President thanked his wife for her dedication on July 26, 1968, after signing the Department of the Interior Appropriations Bill. He presented her with fifty pens used to sign some fifty laws relating to conservation and beautification and a plaque that read: "To Lady Bird, who has inspired me and millions of Americans to try to preserve our land and beautify our nation. With love from Lyndon."

Lady Bird Johnson's work did not stop once President Johnson's term ended. She returned to Texas and continued her conservation work.[30]

In 1976, Charles H. Moss and his wife, Ruth, had too many health issues to continue managing their ranch and private park operations surrounding the granite domes known as Enchanted Rock. The couple hoped to sell the lands to a conservation buyer to be

Enchanted Rock State Natural Area, 2015. Courtesy of Jonathan Vail, Jonathan Vail Photography.

managed as a park; after all, outdoor enthusiasts had enjoyed the property since 1927. A conservation buyer did not appear quickly, so in 1977, Moss indicated they would sell to any buyer, especially after receiving word that the state was not interested in purchasing it as a park. The Nature Conservancy was contacted but initially passed on the project, remarking that they were not interested in running a park or managing a concessionaire. Two problem solvers stepped up to the plate: James Bryce, a local Austin attorney connected with the Nature Conservancy, and Lady Bird Johnson.[31]

The Moss family had contacted the Texas Parks and Wildlife Department as early as 1962 to indicate they would be interested in selling the significant geological domes and surrounding property to them. As the department inventoried the state and considered the lands they wished to set aside as parks or state natural areas, Enchanted Rock ranked a mere fifty-third on the list.

Lady Bird Johnson was familiar with the property, as it was not far from the family ranch outside of Johnson City. She also understood the historical and natural value of the granite domes. After learning the property was up for sale, Lady Bird quickly went

Enchanted Rock State Natural Area, 2013. Courtesy of Jonathan Vail, Jonathan Vail Photography.

to work. She knew how to leverage her connections and, most importantly, understood the funding mechanisms of the Land and Water Conservation Fund that she had helped enact. The first lever she pulled was a phone call to Pat Noonan, president of the Nature Conservancy. When Lady Bird Johnson calls and says, "I need you to come to Texas," you get on a plane and go, which is exactly what Noonan did. She explained the urgency of the situation: the failing health of the landowners, the lack of interest from the Texas Parks and Wildlife Department, and the potential of a mining and quarry company purchasing the property. Noonan saw the natural and cultural significance of Enchanted Rock and vowed to take action.

Lady Bird Johnson worked in the background with her influential friends to garner the interest of the Texas Parks and Wildlife Department to get the project moved up the list. The primary focus of Texas Parks and Wildlife during this time was on hunting and fishing, not as much on conservation or nature exploration. In 1977, President Jimmy Carter created the National Heritage Program and asked states to inventory their lands to identify and preserve natural and cultural areas that were significant to the region. The

Jane Sibley, date unknown.
Courtesy of the Sibley family.

University of Texas stepped in to assist with the inventory. The program helped create a sense of urgency to purchase the Enchanted Rock property. At the urging of Lady Bird Johnson and Pat Noonan, the Department of the Interior requested that matching funds from the Land and Water Conservation Fund be reserved if the Nature Conservancy could secure the purchase, with the understanding that Texas Parks and Wildlife would take ownership of the property. With all the pieces in place, the land was acquired on March 1, 1978, with James Bryce managing the transaction. On March 6, 1978, the Texas Parks and Wildlife Department purchased the property from the Nature Conservancy, positioning it to become one of the first state natural areas in Texas.

Lady Bird Johnson's legacy reaches far beyond the boundaries of the 1,640-acre park. Without her, no Texan today would have the privilege of climbing to the top of the granite dome to gaze out over the rugged Texas Hill Country and see for a moment what the Tonkawa, Apache, and Comanche saw in their day.

In 1965, the Johnsons donated their ranch outside Johnson City to the Texas Parks and Wildlife Department for the purpose of a park and history center. Lady Bird continued to reside and entertain in a portion of the ranch until she passed away in 2007.

In 1968, on the other side of the state, the US Army Corps of Engineers was supervising the construction of Amistad Dam along the Rio Grande just north of Del Rio. The National Park Service was working feverishly to remove more than a million artifacts and document the rock art of the soon-to-be flooded zone. That same year, Texas Governor John Connally was gearing up for the World's Fair at the HemisFair in San Antonio, with the idea of celebrating the rich diversity of Texas's people, ingenuity, and natural wonders. One of the ideas floated was to remove the rock art located along the Pecos River. Engineers from Brown & Root researched the idea and informed the governor that removing the paintings would destroy them and that it would be more sensible to enjoy them at the location.

The state's archeologist, Curtis Tunnel, invited two of his friends, Dr. D.J. and Jane Sibley, to tour the future lake to share the wonders of the rock art. The Sibleys were longtime advocates for historic preservation, and Jane Sibley, in particular, had a special love of the arts and regional culture. She is often referred to as the "Savior of the Austin Symphony."

Jane Sibley was from a prominent ranching family in Alpine and later moved to Austin with her husband after oil was discovered on their West Texas land. She was instantly enchanted with the rock art; however, she was not able to take action as her husband suffered a relapse of tuberculosis, which required her attention until 1970.

In 1970, Jane had a conversation about the remaining rock art along the Pecos River with her archeologist friend, Solveig Turpin, who informed her, "Oh, Jane, the vandalism is just awful." Jane decided to take action and quickly recruited her longtime friend Rose Mary Jones, who was also from a successful West Texas ranching family. The three

Seminole Canyon State Park, 2008. Courtesy of Chase Fountain, Texas Parks and Wildlife Department, Austin, Texas.

women went to work to protect the historic site. The Sibleys were well connected and respected, an asset Jane Sibley leveraged when she invited Texas Governor Preston Smith to tour Panther Canyon. Admittedly, the governor neither knew nor cared about the rock art, but he appreciated the cultural value—and Jane Sibley's tenacity—so he appointed her to the Texas Historical Commission that year.

Unlike the rapidly paced acquisition of Enchanted Rock, it would take more than twelve years to convince the state to preserve, purchase, and open Seminole Canyon State Park and Historic Site. In her autobiography, *Jane's Window: My Spirited Life in West Texas and Austin*, Jane reflects on that time.

> We soon discovered that it can take years of patient persuasion to get the legislature to create a new park, even one containing works of art found nowhere else in the world. To speed up that laborious prospect, Rosie [Rose Mary Jones] worked on the ranchers, and I worked on the politicians. Solveig

provided us with the scientific and archeological backup. Somehow, it all came together. Between 1973 and 1977, the State of Texas bought 2,172.5 acres along Seminole Canyon.[32]

When the park was finally completed and ready to open in February 1980, Rose Mary Jones called the Texas Parks and Wildlife Department to inquire about its plans for a dedication ceremony. Upon finding out that the state did not have the money for such an event, Rose Mary and Jane Sibley footed the bill and organized a grand event that included Wendell Chino, chief of the Mescalero Apaches; Lieutenant Governor Bill Hobby; and an army of journalists. Jane cites in her book that in 2006, more than forty-one thousand visitors toured the remote Seminole Canyon State Park and Historic Site. In 1991, she and her friends formed the Rock Art Foundation to purchase and protect a property adjacent to the park called the White Shaman Preserve.

In the early 1990s, the Texas Parks and Wildlife Department and a number of other state agencies began tracking outdoor recreation and tourism trends. The data demonstrated that the economic powerhouses of hunting and fishing were declining, while activities such as camping, bird watching, and nature exploration were on the rise. By 1990, the majority of Texans were living in urban settings with less connection to private lands where a hunting ethic could be fostered. The interest in fishing remained stable; however, decreasing spaces were available for urban-based citizens to participate in the sport. While sales for hunting and fishing licenses dropped 10 percent from 1983 to 1993, visitation to Texas state parks increased by 40 percent.[33]

This trend was not isolated to Texas but was consistent across North America. Urban centers and suburban communities did not offer the same connection with nature that previous generations had enjoyed. What people lacked was access and confidence to pitch a tent, bait a fishing hook, hike a trail without getting lost, or face an encounter with wildlife. They were certainly less likely to take up hunting without having a connection to the sport in an earlier stage of their lives. Young parents were particularly less likely to try a new outdoor skill that required either specialized equipment or the knowledge to explain that skill to their children.

In 1992, Clemson University conducted a survey to capture the attitudes of Americans toward outdoor recreation and tourism in general. The survey found that people who traveled specifically to explore nature or historic sites wanted to be involved in the experience, not just be a passive tourist. They wanted targeted, meaningful activities where they could learn about—and be enveloped in—nature while also being physically active. The study also found that nature tourists would go out of their way to see an important or interesting bird, flower, or phenomena.

A separate 1994 report from the Eco-Society included data from the World Travel and Tourism Council, which stated that wildlife viewing was the most popular nature

Great Texas Coastal Birding Trail, 2013. Courtesy of the Texas Parks and Wildlife Department, Austin, Texas.

sport in the country, with 76.5 million people participating in the activity. By comparison, hunting had only 14.1 million participants. The statistics all pointed to the same conclusion: it was time to embrace nature tourism as an economic driver and popular pursuit.

At approximately the same time, the American Birding Association surveyed its member list and found that Texas ranked number one five years in a row as the place its members traveled to see birds. Both the American Birding Association and National Audubon Society reported that birders were affluent, savvy travelers who stayed longer in an area if there was a wide variety of birds and access to multiple birding locations.

According to Texas Department of Commerce 1993 data, tourism was the third-largest industry in Texas and generated $23 billion in business. Governor Ann Richards requested that a state task force be formed to consider what the state could do to enhance nature tourism. The task force was cochaired by Andrew Sansom, then executive director of the Texas Parks and Wildlife Department, and Deborah Kastrin, executive director of the Texas Department of Commerce. Sansom tasked Madge Lindsay from the Wildlife Diversity Program to coordinate the project. She skillfully shepherded the twenty-member task force through the visioning process to create a plan that could be adapted to urban or rural communities wanting to grow their economy through nature tourism.

Armed with the data and surrounded with innovative minds, Sansom saw birding as the nexus for meeting the shifting public demand and intentionally influencing econom-

**ABOVE**
Map of the Lower Texas Coast segment of the Great Texas Coastal Birding Trail, date unknown. Courtesy of the Texas Parks and Wildlife Department, Austin, Texas.

**LEFT**
Bird-watching at Estero Llano Grande State Park during the Great Texas Birding Classic, 2016. From left, Jennifer L. Bristol, unknown Texas Parks and Wildlife Department staff member (standing), Superintendent Javier DeLeon, Valarie Bristol, Thomas Nilles, and volunteer Huck Hutchens. Courtesy of Jennifer L. Bristol.

ic growth through creating access to nature. One of the ideas brought forward by Madge Lindsay and Ted Eubanks (an indispensable consultant with the task force) was to create the Great Texas Coastal Birding Trail, the first in the country. The concept was to develop a map that included the best birding sites along the coast. Signs would be erected at each of the locations. The innovative project was awarded a $1.5 million grant from the Texas Parks and Wildlife Department through a federal program for highway enhancements. In 1995, the first sign along the five-hundred-mile Great Texas Coastal Birding Trail was unveiled at the Connie Hagar Cottage Sanctuary in Rockport.[34] In 2020, the program (later renamed the Great Texas Wildlife Trails) celebrated its twenty-fifth anniversary and now includes nine distinct ecoregions of the state.

While developing the birding trails, Madge Lindsay used a brilliant idea—hatched by a birding think tank that included Victor Emanuel and Greg Lasley—to start a birding competition modeled after a golfing classic. She and the think tank wanted the competition to have a cup or trophy inscribed with the winning team's name each year. Entrance fees and donations would collectively pay for conservation projects. The Great Texas Birding Classic was hatched.[35] According to Shelly Plante, nature tourism manager at the Texas Parks and Wildlife Department, in its first twenty-six years, the classic funded $1,116,000 in projects that support nature tourism, avian habitat restoration, and land conservation. She has been a team player and the keeper of the birding classic and Wildlife Viewing Trails since Madge Lindsay hired her as an intern in 2001.

With the success of the Great Texas Coastal Birding Trail, the Texas Parks and Wildlife Department was ready to try an even bolder approach to enhancing nature tourism. In 1996, the concept of the World Birding Center in the Rio Grande Valley was born. Sansom again assigned Madge Lindsay to coordinate the effort. As the project gained momentum, she moved from Austin to the Rio Grande Valley in 1998 to manage the local task force.

The task force, in partnership with the Texas Parks and Wildlife Department, set the parameters for what each birding center site should offer in order to be awarded funds and carry the brand of the World Birding Center. The task force also had the duty of sharing nature tourism economic impact data with the communities in the valley. It didn't take long for the cities to see the value.

Gillian Swanson reported in her article "Mid-Valley City Shows Interest in Birding Center" in the September 1997 McAllen, Texas, *Monitor*, Weslaco –

> The battle for the birds has begun. Weslaco this week publicly announced its hopes of landing the multimillion-dollar World Birding Center. Harlingen and McAllen already have revealed their wishes to win the facility, which will house exhibits, maps, guides, and up-to-date bird sighting information for expert birders, tourists, and community members alike.[36]

Madge Lindsay, date unknown. Courtesy of Madge Lindsay.

Ranger Hannah Buschert teaching children about bird migration and food webs, Bentsen-Rio Grande Valley State Park, 2014. Courtesy of Jennifer L. Bristol.

Indeed, the competition became heated. Cities pulled together packages that included land, matching funds, private partnerships, and community input. The project grew in scope to include a central education center and nine satellite centers. The most popular idea was to have a centrally located main center, which put Weslaco at the top of the list since land was already being purchased there for the purpose of creating a new state park.

Then the Texas legislature got involved. Cheryl Smith of the McAllen, Texas, *Monitor* reports in an April 1999 article, "World Birding Center will nest in Mission":

Surprise decision comes after legislature intervenes. The Texas legislature's appropriations committee took the bird by the beak Thursday when members voted to award the coveted World Birding Center's headquarters to Mission, stripping the Texas Parks and Wildlife Department of any decision-making authority on the site. In a surprise move, the House of Representatives Appropriations Committee's Conference Committee agreed to provide the Texas Parks and Wildlife Department with $35 million in additional funds on the condition that Mission be selected as the headquarters for the World Birding Center. "About $5 million of the approved Parks and Wildlife funds are earmarked for the center," said state Representative Ismael "Kino" Flores, D-Palmview, who serves on the House Appropriations Committee. Flores pushed for Mission to be awarded the WBC headquarters.

The article goes on to mention that the mayor of Mission was Representative Flores's second cousin.[37]

The decision by the legislature was a surprise and a blow to the Texas Parks and Wildlife Department and task force. It undid much of the goodwill and trust that had taken years to build. Instead of crumbling, Madge Lindsay and the task force members pressed on. Cities saw the economic value, while conservationists saw the need to set aside as much land as possible in the rapidly growing Rio Grande Valley. The Texas Parks and Wildlife Department was already well down the path of transforming two of its parks into birding centers and adding an additional park.

The original 587 acres of Bentsen-Rio Grande Valley State Park in Mission were donated to the state in 1944 by the Bentsen family for the purpose of a park. The ebony-forested park opened to the public in 1962. Additional purchased and donated lands

World Birding Center groundbreaking at Bentsen-Rio Grande State Park, date unknown. Madge Lindsay is far left in the white shirt. Courtesy of the Communications Division, Texas Parks and Wildlife Department, Austin, Texas.

were added to the park for the new World Birding Center headquarters complex and additional parking.

Weslaco continued its plans of creating a new state park and World Birding Center site on the edge of town. The Weslaco Economic Development Corporation, City of Weslaco, and a number of other entities were tasked with piecing together the additional land. The City of Weslaco and the Texas Parks and Wildlife Department requested that the Nature Conservancy assist them with brokering the deal to purchase the Lakeview RV Park that abutted the agricultural land already purchased. Former Texas Parks and Wildlife Department Executive Director Carter Smith was the Nature Conservancy's South Texas regional manager at the time and in charge of brokering the agreement.

In an interview, Smith shared that the negotiation was incredibly difficult and sensitive because it involved closing an RV park where dozens of residents lived. The issue was exacerbated by the fact that the property owner lived in California and required the sale be kept "top secret" until the last minute so as not to lose revenue.[38]

Smith also shared that Madge Lindsay was an "artisanal wellspring of energy" who knew how to keep the big personalities focused and moving toward the goal. Smith also credits self-taught naturalist and volunteer Richard Lehmann as being relentless in finding solutions.

When it came time for the Nature Conservancy to close the sale of the property and transfer it to either the Texas Parks and Wildlife Department or the City of Weslaco, neither wanted to take ownership because of the vocal renters who lived in the RV park. The Nature Conservancy was stunned. Carter Smith and Madge Lindsay summoned

Dragonfly overlook at Resaca de la Palma State Park, 2008. Courtesy of Earl Nottingham, Texas Parks and Wildlife Department, Austin, Texas.

all of the involved parties and negotiated an arrangement that everyone could support. Eventually, the City of Weslaco decided to allow the residents to leave on their own terms. The Estero Llano Grande State Park and World Birding Center Site opened in 2006 and, by 2021, all but one renter had moved on.

In 1977, the state acquired twelve hundred acres of land outside Brownsville for the purpose of a park. However, resources were lacking to create the infrastructure needed to open the park until Madge Lindsay and her team helped secure the funds for a World Birding Center site. The resulting Resaca de la Palma State Park and World Birding Center Site opened to the public in 2008.

In addition to opening two new state parks and enhancing a third, six local parks or nature centers were added or upgraded to complete the network of World Birding Center sites in the Rio Grande Valley. By 2010, an estimated $125 million had been infused into the valley's economy by nature tourists, with a primary focus on bird-watching.

According to the Texas Parks and Wildlife Department, visitation at the three state parks that are identified as World Birding Center sites increased by 68 percent—from 660,000 visitors to 1,106,000—between 2019 and 2021. This rise during the COVID-19 pandemic demonstrates the public's need and desire for more outdoor opportunities for local residents and travelers alike. With the Rio Grande Valley having the eighth-largest population in the United States, each of the World Birding Center sites is an important piece of the conservation matrix.

Madge Lindsay's legacy reaches beyond the borders of Texas as the birding trails inspired other states to implement their own versions. The World Birding Center inspired the addition of more than fifteen additional nature centers throughout the Rio Grande Valley for birders to enjoy. The focus on nature tourism and birding has also inspired many Texas state and local parks to add bird blinds, hawk watch towers, and boardwalks from which to enjoy viewing the birds. In addition, more than forty states now have wildlife viewing trails based on the Texas model.

Hawk watchtower at Bentsen-Rio Grande Valley State Park, 2004. Courtesy of the Texas Parks and Wildlife Department, Austin, Texas.

While the first women on the State Parks Board were able to influence the creation of a state parks system from within the political structure, it took decades to reestablish that level of influence. Lady Bird Johnson and Jane Sibley are examples of women who used their power and influence to establish new state parks from outside the inner workings of the Texas Parks and Wildlife Department and Texas Parks and Wildlife Commission. Madge Lindsay is an example of a woman working within the agency to champion a vision and connect outside partners to achieve a complicated goal. While all these women are pioneers, there are certainly additional unsung women heroes who assisted in establishing and sustaining state parks in Texas.

# Chapter 3

# Genesis:
# The State Parks

*After all, nature has to give some help in establishing a state park. It requires more than a cow pasture and an excited Chamber of Commerce to make a park go.*

TEXAS STATE REPRESENTATIVE **W. R. CHAMBERS**
*Dallas Morning News* August 28, 1945

S tephen Mather did not invent state parks, but he was wise enough to see that they could play a major role in supplementing national parks, primarily by redirecting the growing phenomenon of family outings in the automobile and by encouraging state programs to take the pressure off the many requests for Mather and Congress to create new national parks. Furthermore, Mather already had in mind a set of high standards for national park qualification, and he wanted the states (without so stating) to take on landscapes that did not meet Mather's "supreme" natural criteria. No Texas sites were even considered for federal protection as national parks. The reason was simple. Unlike other Western states, Texas had retained control of its public lands when it was annexed to the United States. The federal government had no say in what Texas did with its land. But by the new century, interest was growing among people of influence across the Lone Star State to begin to discuss and advocate for national parks in Texas.

First national conference on state parks in Des Moines, Iowa, 1921. Via Rebecca Conard, "The National Conference on State Parks: Reflections on Organizational Genealogy," The George Wright Forum 14, no. 4 (1997): 28–43.

David Colp, first chairman of the newly created Texas State Parks Board, date unknown. Courtesy of the Texas Parks and Wildlife Department, Austin, Texas.

According to an account of the first nationwide conference on state parks in 1921 (instigated by Mather), Edgar R. Harlan, curator of the Iowa State Historical Department and secretary of the Iowa Board of Conservation, offered the following observation: "On the morning of Monday, January 10, in the capacious rooms of the splendid Fort Des Moines Hotel, at 11 o'clock, [a] far-fetched assembly, representing twenty-five states … got down to business and made history with definite and precisioned step."[1]

Even though this pronouncement was overstated by several degrees, the conference, which was attended by some two hundred or more interested parties, set in motion a number of organizations over the decades whose purpose was the advancement of state parks ideology, purpose, and programs. The original organization formed at the Des Moines assembly—which would later become the National Conference on State Parks— would spark debate (or, rather, further debate) on the proper role of parks: conservation (recreation) versus preservation of natural blessings. That debate continues today at the national and state levels. Though maddening at times, that delicate balance keeps both goals in view, even when one seems to outweigh the other.

Nonetheless, there was much to discuss and absorb at that first meeting. Even though the governor-elect of Texas, Pat Morris Neff, did not attend the Des Moines conference, there is no question that he was interested and was informed about its deliberations and recommendations. In fact, Neff was fired up by the possibilities of multiple state parks throughout his beloved Texas. Furthermore, he took to using in his later speeches two slogans: "See Texas First" and "A State Park Every Hundred Miles!"[2] Not only was Neff inspired by the recommendations of the conference, he would also soon be in a position to do something about it. One week later, on January 18, 1921, he was sworn in as the twenty-eighth governor of the State of Texas. At the time, only twenty states or so had some state parks and/or a semblance of an official parks system. Texas had none. Neff meant to change that.

It would take time. Journeying to Austin from Waco that week before his inauguration, it is fair to assume that the ramrod-straight, six-foot-tall man dressed in black had more on his mind than just state parks.

As Neff prepared for his new role in Austin, there was much to ponder about a Texas that had grown in population from 3.9 million in 1910 to more than 4.6 million in 1920. The state was still rural (two-thirds of Texans lived in the country), but more people were coming off the farm and from other

Governor Pat Neff signing a bill at his desk, 1923. Courtesy of the Pat Neff Archive, Texas Collection, Baylor University, Waco, Texas.

states and foreign countries into expanding towns and cities. For the most part, that growth was initially welcomed but was beginning to rub. All too soon, the Ku Klux Klan would rear its ugly head again. For a short time in the 1920s, the Ku Klux Klan would become a major political force across Texas. It is thought by some that the Ku Klux Klan controlled the legislature and that Neff secretly supported them—untrue. But he did little to thwart their activities.

If Teddy Roosevelt and Stephen Mather, who expanded and enhanced the concept and system, first by Roosevelt's "bully pulpit" oration and pen and then by Mather's passionate genius for publicity and organization, were the leading all-stars on the national park team in the last decade of the nineteenth century and early decades of the twentieth, then Texas, likewise, was blessed by the rise of Governor Pat Neff and David Edward Colp, a San Antonio car dealer and "good roads" promoter whom Neff would appoint as chairman of the newly created State Parks Board in 1923.

As recounted in the previous chapter, both Mather's national park efforts and those of the Texas State Parks Board were backed by powerful women and their organizations. It can be said, with little fear of contradiction, that the women helped hold things together throughout the first ten lean years (1923 to 1933) of Texas's emerging parks system.

Like Mather, Neff and Colp would encounter opposition from beginning to end of the first decade. Also, like Mather, they had flaws, but, between the two of them—with the help of Phebe Kerrick Warner, Texas State Senator Margie Elizabeth Neal, Marian "Mamie" Rather Powell, and their organizations—they muddled through that first decade.

## A Decade of Darkness—Then Light

Following his election as governor in 1920, Neff was met with barriers erected by hostile legislators, some of whom became so by way of the moralistic and uncompromising new governor himself.

Pat Neff was a product of this transitory time. Born and reared in Central Texas's Coryell County in the rural village of Eagle Springs, his life on the farm—with its native wildflowers, animals, and rivers—and, most certainly, his parents, particularly his mother, formed his thoughts about nature. Baylor University in Waco (undergraduate degree) and the University of Texas in Austin (law degree) molded his career as a lawyer and politician.

As he made his way to Austin for his inauguration by automobile or private railroad car (in those days, elected officials were given free passage on the rail lines), I am sure the governor-elect watched Central Texas unfold with kind thoughts of his father, who had died when Neff was twelve, and his eight siblings, pausing longer to savor the fond images of his mother, Isabella Neff, who hailed from Virginia before migrating with Noah Neff to Central Texas. Mother Neff (as she was called) imparted to her ninth child a lifelong love of nature, literature, and God. When asked why she had nine children, she

**ABOVE**

A young Pat Neff and his mother, Isabella, date unknown. Courtesy of the Pat Neff Archive, Texas Collection, Baylor University, Waco, Texas.

**ABOVE LEFT**

Neff family pavilion, ca. 1920s. Occasionally, community groups would ask to use the riverbank area on the Neffs' property, so the Neffs built this pavilion for community gatherings. Courtesy of the Texas Parks and Wildlife Department, Austin, Texas.

**LEFT**

Pat Neff at the Mother Neff State Park dedication ceremony, May 14, 1938. Courtesy of the Pat Neff Archive, Texas Collection, Baylor University, Waco, Texas.

Pat Neff breaking up illegal drinking and gambling in Mexia, Texas, 1922. Courtesy of the Pat Neff Archive, Texas Collection, Baylor University, Waco, Texas.

exclaimed, "If I hadn't had nine, I wouldn't have had Pat!"[3] As noted in the previous chapter, she would set aside land for public use—at first, six acres of the family farm on the Leon River in her will, then 250 more when her son, then governor of Texas, deeded the acreage to the state. She would pass away less than four months later on May 18, 1921. Her death and gift were the emotional spark for the creation of a state parks system.

Although Neff's family and parks were of tantamount importance, it is a given that, with the legislature set to convene less than a week after the conference, Neff had to turn his attention to a broader agenda. For a moment, we need to turn our attention to how he got to this moment and the primary focus behind his run for governor in 1920: Protestantism, Progressivism, Prohibition, and the women's right to vote (PPP&W). He supported all with equal fervor, and he ran openly for them, while his opponent, a long-time power in the Democratic party, former US Senator Joe Weldon Bailey, opposed. With the PPP&W behind him, Neff, who had become enamored with automobile travel, struck out across the state in his car, often camping out, covering six thousand miles, and meeting potential voters in places where no candidate or official had ever darkened a door. He often stated he was the first candidate to campaign by automobile and fly to a destination. He did it all without polls, media buys, managers, or headquarters. But he caught the tidal wave of issues coming in as the old ways flowed out.

He also had the gift of oration, a first-class mind, and the foundation of a moralist, which stood him well on the campaign trail but became a hindrance when he began to deal with the legislature, since he would not compromise on most of the issues he championed as governor: education, prison reform, health, and taxation. These issues were often met with no action or failure on the floor of the Texas House or Senate. Neff did not take defeat kindly and had little use for compromise.

But all that lay ahead as he rode toward Austin and his destiny.

To understand Pat Neff's destiny, it would help to understand Texas, its economy, and its politics.

As mentioned previously, Texans in 1920 still lived on the farm (more than three million men—women and children were uncounted).[4] Many who lived in larger towns and the "big" cities were tied to agriculture through trade and strong family connections. Cotton was still king, with cattle, timber, railroads, and a newly emerging oil industry following close behind. By 1920, Texas was producing 515 million barrels of oil per year—and that was only the beginning. Mass production of goods and the beginning of mass consumption were also on the horizon. A bull market back East was beginning to snort and charge and would help sustain the country on an upward trajectory until it imploded in 1929.

But one item coming down the road was set to touch every aspect of life: the automobile. Gasoline stations, repair shops, refineries, motels, and good highways were enthusiastically accepted in many areas of the state. By 1929, there was one car for every 4.3 Texas citizens—and not only for commerce but to take the family to Grandma's for Sunday dinner after church and out into the country to stay connected with nature.

Like the economy, politics and governance of the state were in transition. Here again, the rise of the automobile played a significant role. Goods and people were moving about the state in greater amounts and numbers. To improve on that, a better, more coordinated system needed to take the place of the loose and inefficient highway and county road systems.

In 1917, the Texas Highway Department was created by the state legislature. At the time, twenty-six highways spanned nine thousand miles. By 1927, there were eighteen thousand miles of "good roads" that connected farms and ranches to growing cities and oil-boom towns. But it was not until 1924 that the department took over the financing of highways and management of construction. In the 1930s, the department would take over the roadside park program that numbered several hundred sites.

## Rise of the Texas State Parks Concept

As embodied in the national park concept by the creation of the first national park in 1872—Yellowstone—and formalized as a federal system in 1916 with passage of the Organic Act establishing the National Park Service, public lands for public pleasure and preservation was a foreign idea to most Texans. Texas's annexation into the Union in 1845 held a unique proviso: all lands in the public domain were retained by the state rather than passing to the United States.[5] Thus, from that time forward, most Texans ignored federal land policy. They had enough of their own to manage, sell, or give away—225 million acres.

That is not to say nothing happened conservation- or public lands-wise before the 1920s, when Governor Pat Neff proposed a state parks bill. But he addressed a mixed bag of trial-and-error laws and rules that often faded away due to lack of funding or retained interest.

As early as the 1860s, Texas joined a number of Western states to enact laws to protect fish and wildlife against commercial catch. In 1907, the Texas Game, Fish and Oyster Commission was created for "the protection of wildlife."[6] But in a developing pattern of lack of support, Texas legislatures would enact the enabling measures, appropriate little or no funding, scurry back home to take credit for saving wildlife, then slip back to Austin to starve the agency or commission. Without true and sustainable leadership, the people and their elected officials soon moved on to other pressing issues of the day.

But there were those who were probably aroused by the same waves of "nature excitement" that began to prick the conscience of other Americans, as the names Yosemite, Yellowstone, and Rocky Mountains began to lure citizens into the sphere of national shared parks for the people and family vacations by car. As Neff noted in *The Battles for Peace,*

The early RV: family camping, ca. 1920. Circa Images via Alamy Stock Photo.

Texas should have led all other states in the Union in ownership and maintenance of state parks, especially in view of the fact that, of all the forty-eight states, Texas was the only state that once owned title to all its lands. By the 1880s and 1890s, however, Texas had sold (at rock-bottom prices) or given away practically all of its public lands, aggregating 172 million acres. Texas did not reserve one beauty spot or set aside any places to be used and enjoyed by the public in the name of the State.[7]

**ABOVE**
Texas Governor John Ireland, 1875. Courtesy of
the Texas Jurists Collection by Jack Pope, Jamail
Center for Legal Research, Tarlton Law Library,
University of Texas at Austin, Austin, Texas, TJ4.

**ABOVE RIGHT**
Alamo street scene, ca. 1915. Courtesy of
N. M. Wilcox, Places Collection, Prints and
Photographs Collection, Archives and Information Services Division, Texas State Library
and Archives Commission, Austin, Texas,
1/103-648.

**RIGHT**
San Jacinto Monument, ca. 1936–1939.
Courtesy of the San Jacinto Museum and
Battlefield Association, LaPorte, Texas,
L3910-592.

Houston community leader and Texas Centennial Celebrations
Chairman Jesse H. Jones at the dedication of the San Jacinto
Monument, April 21, 1939. Courtesy of the San Jacinto Museum
and Battlefield Association, LaPorte, Texas.

Congressman John Hall Stephens of Wichita Falls, early champion of public lands, 1912. Courtesy of G. V. Buck, Library of Congress Prints and Photographs Division, Washington, DC, LC-DIG-ppmsca-12904.

Although it wasn't for public lands for conservation/preservation/recreation, in 1883, Texas Governor John Ireland stepped in and created the land grant program and saved twenty-seven million acres in West Texas to establish a long-lasting (up to and including today) income stream—oil!—for the permanent school fund. In the same session of the Texas legislature, he, with visionary, progressive skill, convinced the legislators to purchase the fast-deteriorating Alamo as well as ten acres on the site of the Battle of San Jacinto. None would qualify as a park, but there was a dawning recognition that the state was, from time to time, required to step in and secure sites that needed protection for the appreciation of the past and benefit of future generations.

Throughout the 1890s and into the early years of the twentieth century, other venues (mainly historic) were secured by various groups (principally women) centered around the organizing and advocacy skills of the Daughters of the Republic of Texas. Through their efforts, the Alamo and San Jacinto areas were financed and expanded to the point where, in 1907, the San Jacinto site was "hereafter [to] be known and styled 'San Jacinto State Park,'" the first that was officially so named.[8]

However, the competition for what venue would become the first official state park played out over several years, from the turn of the century until Governor Neff put an end to the dispute, more or less, by naming Mother Neff State Park the winner without debate. Along the way, Neff managed to anger constituents who had worked hard and raised funds to pay for the earlier sites and restore some of Texas's most hallowed grounds.

In 1908 (and again in 1911 and 1915), US Congressman John Hall Stephens of Vernon introduced bills to establish a "national forest reserve and park" in Palo Duro Canyon.[9] It had the full support of the Canyon City Commercial Club as well as state senators and representatives. The wings of public conservation and parklands were spreading, but they were not strong enough to break the chains of the ongoing and growing dispute between the federal Agriculture and Interior departments as well as questions over land ownership at the state level. The bills failed to pass.

The Interior/Agriculture dispute bears some explanation because no dispute better tells the conservation/preservation conflict tale than the Hetch-Hetchy battle for the heart of the environmental movement and the controversy over the proposed building of a major dam in a pristine valley of Yosemite National Park.

The issue centered around the need to create a permanent water supply for the citizens of San Francisco after the massive earthquake of 1906. On one side were the conservationists, led by Gifford Pinchot, head of the US Forest Service and a personal friend of Teddy Roosevelt. His quote concerning conservation has become its permanent definition: "The purpose of conservation: The greatest good for the greatest number of people for the longest time."[10]

Palo Duro Canyon, one of the first large-park prospects, date unknown. Courtesy of the Texas Parks and Wildlife Department, Austin, Texas, 2005.1.2.

Hetch-Hetchy Valley, California, before and after construction of the O'Shaughnessy Dam, ca. 1919 and 1923. The building of the dam was an early conflict between conservationists and preservationists. Courtesy of the San Francisco Public Utilities Commission via the *San Francisco Chronicle* Photo Archives, San Francisco, California.

John Muir, on behalf of preservation, countered: "God has cared for these trees, saved them from drought, disease, and a thousand tempests and floods. But he cannot save them from fools. The clearest way into the Universe is through a forest wilderness. The mountains are calling, and I must go."[11]

Muir and his followers mounted a huge nationwide campaign to thwart the dam project, arguing that the Hetch-Hetchy Valley was truly God-created and God-given and should be left in its wild state of being.

Eventually, Pinchot would win that particular battle, but in doing so, he stirred up a hornets' nest of interest in pure preservation, so much so that when the language of the Organic Act establishing the National Park Service was written from 1915 to 1916, both the conservation and preservation positions were incorporated.

By incorporating both, Frederick Law Olmsted Jr. (with the agreement of others) inscribed a permanent tension that has served as a perpetual counterbalance. It is by no means perfect, but it is enough that the park pendulum has swung back and forth in timed arches over the National Park Service's first hundred years, allowing both to exist to the benefit of all and to one another.

Nothing demonstrates the constructive role of the conservation ethic in Texas better than the life work of William Goodrich Jones, a banker and businessman from Temple. In boyhood, his father took him on a walking tour of the Black Forest of Germany. Somewhere in there, the beauty and commercial possibilities of a well-managed forest took root that would hold for the remainder of his life.

Clearly, Jones's philosophy was influenced by the work ethic of the local foresters and villagers: they planted, cultivated, and rotated cutting using methods that would guarantee a continuous living decade after decade.

This was in real life practice the epitome of Pinchot's definition. Jones began his life's work by urging his fellow citizens to follow a similar pattern of planting—and re-planting—trees. Soon, Jones caught the eye of other forestry managers to the point that, in 1914, he was invited to a White House conference on conservation. Soon after, he formed a Texas forestry association, which led the Texas legislature to create the Texas Department of Forestry. It even led to funding, which led to a system of state forests in the 1920s.[12]

I have spent this time on the constructive work of William Goodrich Jones for two reasons: first, to point out that by the 1920s, the Texas legislature was willing to appropriate funds for forestry and forestlands; and, second, to demonstrate that the conservation ethic of Jones was the proper one to gain the support of Texas leadership, including lumber and timber businessmen. According to Robert S. Maxwell in his article on Jones, "Jones was not a wilderness advocate but rather a supporter of conservation for prudent use of Texas."[13]

Preservation projects would come in their own good time. These included wildlife management areas. Unlike most state parks (although many parks have areas of preservation within them), wildlife management areas encourage little human impact and are set aside for the pure joy and protection of nature in and for itself.

Yet pure joy of nature requires a key element missing before the 1920s—parks for the people and people in the parks.

## Colp Tries to Secure Neff's Parks

It appears that Governor Neff knew before passage of his parks bill in a special session in 1923 how he wanted the commission to be governed, whom he wanted to represent the five regions he had devised, and whom he wanted as chairman of the newly created State Parks Board. David Colp of San Antonio was his man. Others on the board gave balance to the state's five regions. As noted in chapter two, a majority of the board's members were women, many in leadership positions, in recognition of their growing political power. They had been helpful in Neff's election for governor and had shown a willingness to support and raise money for parklands and park issues.

David E. Colp was born in 1867 near Bowie, Texas, later moving to a family ranch near Hondo, where he cowboyed and followed with a number of other low-level jobs. By 1920, he was established in San Antonio as an automobile dealer and recognized statewide as an astute and honest highway manager and expert. From the turn of the century forward, he was actively involved in various aspects of "good roads," including as secretary of the Texas Good Roads Association and co-manager of three major interstate highways: the Old Spanish Trail, Meridian Highway, and Glacier to Gulf Highway. Perhaps because of his rural upbringing, he had an appreciative eye for nature's bounty that surely could be connected to those new highways, giving motor tourists rest areas along their journey or, perhaps, a place for a quiet picnic with the family. With each passing year, more automobiles were rolling off the assembly lines. Ford produced a new car every minute in 1914 and one every ten seconds by 1925, and Colp wanted as many of those cars as possible on his highways.[14]

Among his other attributes, Colp was a keen observer. He recognized early on that roadside parks and good roads went hand in hand and that both were good for business. Good (and more) roads and more tourists meant more dollars for local merchants, cities, counties, and the state, and Texas parks would bring more tourists to Texas who might otherwise visit Yellowstone, Yosemite, or other out-of-state national or state parks. "See Texas First" and "A Park Every 100 Miles" became the bumper sticker logos before there were bumpers or logo was a word.

At some point, other park advocates such as Phebe Kerrick Warner, a journalist from Claude, Texas, and one of Pat Neff's appointees to the parks board in 1923, began to tout other benefits of good parks: clean air and water, wildflowers and wild game, forest trails and waterfalls—all could contribute to the betterment of Texas's touring citizens and out-of-state visitors.

It is here I want to explain a difference that might be overlooked by the casual reader. At the outset, both Neff and Colp were advocating a series of small-acreage parks, much like the roadside parks (or picnic areas) that we know today. The big, expansive vistas of the Western states were the furthest thing from all but a few minds in the public and legislative scheme of things. That position was where "good roads" chairman Colp started. It is not where he ended.

The indifference in the legislature turned to open hostility due to Neff's "patronizing superiority" when it came to legislative issues early in his first term in 1921. To understand how such a break could have occurred during the first weeks of his maiden session, one has to know more about Pat Neff's character.

Charismatic, deeply religious, handsome, and physically imposing, he was a hands-on leader, fiercely patriotic, and a defender of individual liberty. He was an accomplished orator, capable, some said, "of talking a hungry dog off a meat wagon."[15]

But Neff, even though he had served as Speaker of the Texas House from 1903 to 1905, never learned or accepted the art of compromise; thus, he rarely took legislative defeat with grace. When it came to right or wrong, there was no middle ground for Neff. Many would say that "after he came along, they broke the mold." His critics often declared that was a good thing.[16]

It is here that the mystery of Governor Pat Neff's lack of action during his first term begins. He had campaigned on the issue of state parks and had received the support of cheering crowds and newspaper accolades across the state. While he almost immediately ran into legislative hostility on many fronts, it did not seem to carry over to parks. But no bill or suggested outline of the governor's wishes were forthcoming. It must be noted here that then (and now), the legislature rarely goes looking for additional workload, regardless of the issue, particularly to accommodate the unspoken wishes of an already unpopular governor. Again, because he had been Speaker of the Texas House, Neff should

From left, Phebe Warner, Pat Neff, and David Colp at Palo Duro Canyon, date unknown. Courtesy of the Panhandle-Plains Historical Museum, Canyon, Texas, 1988-45/1-61.

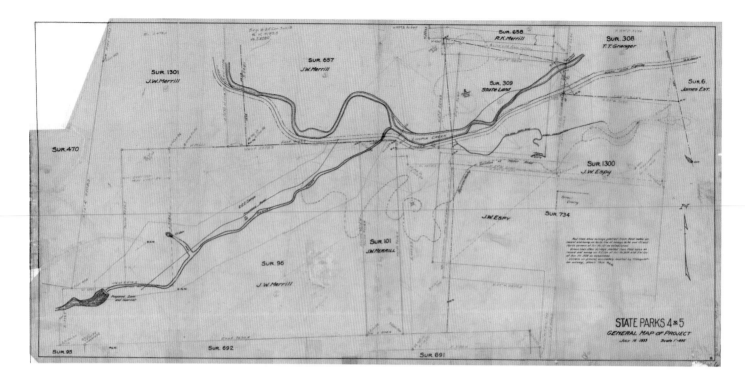

Original general map of Davis Mountains State Park, July 16, 1933. The Texas State Parks Board Civilian Conservation Corps map (black ink and red, green, and gray pencil on wax tracing paper) shows Limpia Creek and Keesey Creek, with numerous block boundaries demarcated. Courtesy of the Prints and Photographs Collection, Archives and Information Services Division, Texas State Library and Archives Commission, Austin, Texas, SP.47.6.

have realized this and reached out to key supporters in the House and Senate. Maybe the answer lies in his failure to reach out to colleagues on the appropriate committees or powerful members to swing those committee chairs and other members. Maybe he had no such friends or supporters. I have found no mention of trusted lieutenants who could carry the ball and deliver votes. Certainly, this appears to be the case in 1921. Failure to create or pass a bill created a vacuum that allowed Texas Representative W.W. Stewart of Reeves County to author his own bill and move it through both houses, ready to send to the governor for his signature.

It was a simple bill and, under most circumstances, non-controversial, but it was also a monumental break with Neff's (and Colp's) vision of a multitude of small parks. The bill would create a joint committee of the House and Senate to study the possibilities of converting scenic mountain landscapes in the Davis Mountains into a state park. Stewart suggested three ways (two on which Neff campaigned) such parks would benefit local and state residents. The parks would keep those tourist dollars within the state, and they would act as wildlife preserves. Finally, through the judicious construction of dams, attractive lakes would be created in the parks for recreational purposes as well as a reclamation irrigation system for farming, which would add to the commonwealth.[17] Conservation best-use practice at its best—or worst.

The bill, as well as a companion bill, passed both houses in the waning days of the special session and was promptly sent to the governor. Apparently without consideration or fanfare, Neff, the "father of Texas state parks," vetoed the bill. The chasm between governor and legislature widened—never to narrow again. An angry legislature overrode his veto in the second-called special session, appointed House and Senate members as part of the special inspection committee, and went home.[18]

There were other reasons that played a role in the immediate split and thereafter.

A sizable number of House and Senate members were past supporters of Joe Weldon Bailey, whom Neff had defeated in 1920. The bitterness still lingered. There were others who fit in the Bailey column but also were in the anti-Prohibition column—some were both. Neff also had no chief of staff or secretary to whom he could delegate matters, unlike today when, perhaps, we have allowed that office and others to become overstaffed. Neff was no delegator. He had no campaign manager in 1920 and saw no need as governor to have a competent staff member.

Someone has to mind the store, particularly when the boss is away, and nothing points out that situation more vividly than the prolonged illness of Neff's beloved mother, ending with her death on May 18, 1921. Neff cancelled most engagements and stayed by her side at the governor's mansion for several weeks—at a crucial time of the legislative process. With no Neff, no floor managers among the House and Senate members, and no "go-to" trusted staffer, I can imagine how Representative Stewart's parks bill passed in the coming special-session period.

After receiving a unanimous report from the joint committee that the legislature should pass a bill to create state parks and game preserves—and a governing system of sorts—the 1923 session of the Texas legislature did just that. It called for the creation of a non-salaried state parks board (the Texas State Parks Board) that would be authorized to investigate sites across the state that could be donated to the state for parks. Sometime during this period, Governor Neff began to listen to the growing number of "big park" advocates. Upon the creation of the State Parks Board, he declared, "By such action, the government of Texas would 'establish, before it is too late, a system of state parks where the rank and file of the people of Texas and elsewhere may go and forget the anxieties, the strife, and vexations of life's daily grind.'"[19]

While the majority of his speech speaks to the benefits of nature for all citizens and the imperative of the state to protect and preserve, Neff also pointed out the real possibility that by doing so, Texas would become "the Mecca of auto tourists."[20] For all the reasons of health, welfare, happiness, and the pocketbook, Governor Pat Neff brushed aside the naysayers who saw parks as a frivolous and needless expenditure and deemed these necessities shades of Teddy Roosevelt's "essential democracy." Even though lingering animosities remained between the governor and the legislature, the recommendations of the special committee were so positive that they smoothed things over on park issues long enough to gain passage with little opposition.

In mid-October 1923, Governor Neff made his selections to the parks board and spelled out their charges, most importantly "to approach landowners in such a manner

GOV. PAT M. NEFF AND DAUGHTER MISS HALLIE MAUD; MISS GIBSON WHO INTRODUCED GOVERNOR NEFF AT A LUNCHEON WITH THE CITIZENS ON MONAHAN AND VICINITY WHILE ON AN INSPECTION WITH STATE PARKS BOARD - JULY 1924.

Pat Neff (middle) with daughter Hallie Maud Neff (right) and Miss Gibson (left, first name unknown) during a series of trips around the state to visit proposed park sites, July 1924. The establishment of a state parks system ranks as one of the greatest achievements of Neff's political career. Courtesy of the Pat Neff Archive, Texas Collection, Baylor University, Waco, Texas.

as to induce [them] to donate land to the state, or with a view of purchasing it at the lowest terms possible."[21]

It was the governor's fondest hope that by demonstrating a commitment to obtaining *potential parklands by donation* [emphasis author's], future legislatures would see the wisdom of appropriating adequate sums for purchases and maintenance.

In David Colp and his fellow board members, Neff found five citizens with the ability and personal reputation to sell landowners and community leaders on the benefits of parks for present and future generations of Texans.

In addition to the appointment of members to the State Parks Board and spelling out of the standards for membership, Neff and the members knew they had to generate support from the public as well as motivate the donation of lands to meet the specifications of the Texas legislature. While Pat Neff was unpopular with a large number of legislative members, he was still immensely popular with the people. If he could sell the citizenry, he could create pressure on the legislature and, at the same time, stir the landowners to generously support their communities (shades of Mather's strategy). The first trip was planned for November 1923 to the Panhandle. It was rescheduled to March 1924.

In the meantime, Colp and the other board members, particularly Phebe Warner, went about the task of building a statewide organization county by county. Again, they turned to women's organizations such as the Texas Federation of Women's Clubs and Texas Women's Garden Clubs. In turn, county leaders were tasked with the responsibility of finding suitable land and willing landowners. To qualify, each piece of landscape had to meet certain criteria: be near a state highway, have water and shade, and possess historical significance or exceptionally meritorious scenery.[22] To keep it all together and running, David Colp wrote upwards of five hundred letters of explanation, encouragement, and ego flattering.

The first trip got off in March 1924. It would be headlined by Governor Neff, his daughter, and State Highway Commissioner George Armistead. It was scheduled for ten days and would cover fifteen hundred miles. If anyone doubted the tie-in of parks and highways, they only had to look at the makeup of the delegation and the itinerary.

From the start, the trip appeared to be a success. The first donation for a state park

**ABOVE**

A crowd of ten thousand (including two thousand automobiles) rallying for a state park and highway for Meridian, Texas, May 1924. Courtesy of Preservation Services, Texas Parks and Wildlife Department, Austin, Texas.

**ABOVE**

*Waco News-Tribune* newspaper article touting the new state parks system, May 10, 1924. The size of the crowd in Meridian (ten thousand strong) demonstrated the popularity of parks and their champion, Governor Pat Neff. Courtesy of the *Waco News-Tribune* via Newspapers.com.

**ABOVE**

Governor Pat Neff drumming up support for parks in Meridian, Texas, May 1924. Courtesy of Robert Runyon, Robert Runyon Photograph Collection, Dolph Briscoe Center for American History, University of Texas at Austin, Austin, Texas, RUN02897.

Main Street in Alpine, Texas, ca. 1920.
Courtesy of the Archives of the Big Bend,
Bryan Wildenthal Memorial Library,
Sul Ross State University, MSSC338
A2f2014b_9.

was secured. The media coverage was statewide and enthusiastic, and the message continually reminded Texans of the mission: to develop a system of state parks for the benefit of all citizens of Texas, with the added goal of establishing three national parks. By journey's end, the *San Antonio Express* proclaimed that fifteen sites had been secured and another eight had been assessed.[23]

The follow-on trip in May 1924 would be even more exciting. At one of the first stops in Meridian, a section of the highway was named in honor of Governor Neff, and a "Big Jubilee" was held on the proposed site, which was filled with buggies, wagons, and—new to the scene—two thousand cars—all producing a crowd of ten thousand![24] As the principal speaker, Neff talked the "hungry dog off the meat (barbeque) wagon."[25] "See Texas First" was his theme. "The more the people of Texas comingle in travel, the more they will know about the history and appreciate the beauty of this beautiful state," he stated.[26]

Successful though the trip was, there was much left to accomplish. Neff had promised the legislature fifty state parks by the time they met in January 1925—the end of his term. Colp and the other board members worked around the clock to ensure that goal was

Pat Neff visiting Monahans Sand Domes (now Monahans Sandhills State Park), July 1924. Courtesy of the Pat Neff Archive, Texas Collection, Baylor University, Waco, Texas.

reached, hopefully by the beginning of an upcoming trip to West Texas. In a sense, the West Texas trip would be the "do-or-die" effort.

In preparation, Colp sent out five or six hundred additional letters. Phebe Warner and Mrs. W. C. (Florence) Martin cranked out articles for publication in local West Texas papers. Colp worked several national magazines for favorable stories. On July 14, 1924, several cars carrying the governor, the entire board, members of the highway commission, highway engineers, representatives of the National Park Service, and representatives of six of the largest newspapers headed out again.

It should be noted that because of the tireless work of Colp, Phebe Warner, and Florence Martin, there would have been ample coverage, but now, the possibility of one or two national parks increased the interest of the press as well as elevated excitement and support from local and state leaders—elected and business—particularly since there was such a large contingency of federal and state highway personnel on board. In a two-thousand-mile barnstorming journey, mass meetings were held in Boerne, Alpine, Marfa, Van Horn, Pecos, Kerrville, Monahans, and a dozen smaller cities along the way.

But the highlight of the trip in terms of awe-inspiring landscape and national park possibility fell to the Big Bend/Davis Mountains region. Again, the crowds were large and cheering at every stop on the route. Yes, they wanted a state or national park. Yes, they wanted good roads, but they also wanted to hear from their much-admired governor, who, by the way, was the first governor to visit this area in the history of Texas. The results: fifteen more parks of between fifteen and a thousand acres were added, with others promised. By the time the tired troop returned to San Antonio on July 26, the State Parks Board had twenty-nine park prospects in hand. They were halfway home on the

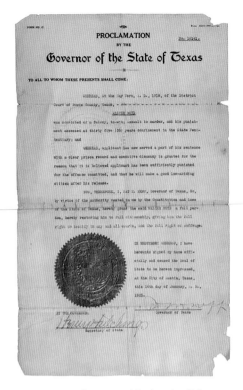

Document pardoning Huddie (Lead Belly) Ledbetter, 1925. Courtesy of the Lead Belly Estate via Smithsonian Folkways Recordings.

mission of fifty parks by 1925.

But, to the best of my research, not a single House or Senate member was part of the traveling entourage or was an invited guest! That oversight, purposeful or not, would come back to haunt the efforts of Neff, Colp, and the others who had given life not only to a state parks system but had spurred a growing call for at least one national park. The depth of the lingering animosity—a result, in part, of ignoring legislative representation on the park fact-finding trips—showed in the 1925 legislative session. Neff, Colp, and company offered up fifty-two potential sites, with a request for an appropriation of $50,000 for repair and maintenance expenses. By February 1925, with Neff gone from the governor's office, the legislature voted to fund not a dime and even prevented the state from accepting the hard-won tracts unless the donors themselves guaranteed the maintenance and upkeep of the parks. This was a personal slap in Neff's face and a blow to David Colp and the board. Lesser men and women would have resigned, tucked tail, and run.

But Governor Pat Neff had known his man. David Colp stayed hitched. In 1927, Colp secured twenty-three parks from a legislature composed of many of the same members who had rejected Neff in 1925. The only catch again was that Colp had to guarantee that each park would be self-sustaining. Nonetheless, Colp hung on, regardless of the fact that little of positive note happened to or for parks for several years—until 1933, to be exact!

On a side note not pertaining to parks but, perhaps, shining a small light on what influenced Neff's thinking (in this instance, on prison reform), two of Neff's brothers had committed crimes and served time. One of Neff's last acts as governor in January 1925 was pardoning a Black prisoner by the name of Huddie Ledbetter, better known by his stage name, "Lead Belly." Ledbetter was an American folk and blues singer, songwriter, and musician who had been convicted of the murder of one of his relatives during a fight. After serving the minimum time of his sentence and exhibiting good behavior while in prison, he caught the attention of Neff, a strong advocate for prison reform, while Neff was on a prison visit. He heard Ledbetter sing a song asking for a pardon.

If I had you, Governor Neff,
Like you got me/
I'd wake up
In the morning, and I'd set you free.

Huddie Ledbetter
"Please Pardon Me"

Unfortunately, Ledbetter would later commit attempted murder, be sentenced, and serve time again. He was released in 1934 and went on to musical fame at the behest of folklorists John and Alan Lomax. He would perform with greats such as Woodie Guthrie, but it was his songwriting talent that gave him immortality. "Goodnight Irene," "The Midnight Special," and "Rock Island Line" became—and are—standards of the genre. Unfortunately, his fame—and royalties—came after his death in 1949. His repertoire included five hundred songs.[27]

Whether by inspiration or motive, Pat Neff did the world a favor. According to Roger Catlin in *Smithsonian Magazine*, George Harrison of the Beatles once said, "If there was no Lead Belly, there would have been no Lonnie Donegan; no Lonnie Donegan, no Beatles. Therefore, no Lead Belly, no Beatles."[28]

After leaving office, Neff would return to Waco and the practice of law. In 1926, Calvin Coolidge appointed him to the newly created United States Board of Mediation for a term ending in 1928. Neff also served as president of the Baptist General Convention of Texas from 1926 until 1928, was president of Baylor University from 1932 until 1947, and, even with that full load, was president of the Southern Baptist Convention from 1944 to 1946. Through tireless work and strict discipline, Neff is credited with saving Baylor from financial ruin.

During that same period (1925 to 1933), the much-maligned, often-disappointed, and sometimes-disappointing Chairman David Colp kept the faith and fires for state parks burning, even when the glow from the coals was faint. By this time, Colp had grown from simply a good roads booster to an advocate for a state parks system that would better the lives of all Texans while preserving the landscapes and wildlife. Furthermore, he came to see the need for parks grander than roadside rest stops for those highway tourists. So trudge on he did, seemingly often alone, not knowing that with each passing year, he and parks were drawing closer to brighter days of hope. It was ironic that those bright rays shone from the darkness of the Great Depression.

Though uncompensated with either salary or most expenses, Colp stuck to the task, even when legislators failed to appropriate any funds. Colp was a successful car dealer, but he had more than a desire to sell cars. He genuinely believed in parks for the public. For ten years, he traveled the state, sometimes with Neff, but always in touch with the leaders of the cause, particularly the leaders of the major women's organizations.

Huddie (Lead Belly) Ledbetter, 1948. Courtesy of Austin Wilder, *New York World-Telegram* and Sun Newspaper Photograph Collection, Library of Congress Prints and Photographs Division, Washington, DC, LC-USZ62-120591.

## The Lean Years: 1923–1933

According to Jeffrey Fritz Crunk in his comprehensive thesis on Neff, Colp, and the early Texas state parks system,

> Colp was drawn to the state parks movement in part because he was convinced that parks would benefit Texas highway travelers and the cities and businesses that these highways connected. He remained chairman of the Texas State Parks Board because he wanted a system that would enhance Texans' lives, in addition to their pocketbooks.[29]

That commitment had to remain strong. From the time he became chairman in 1923 until 1933, he met disappointments (some would say failures) and frustrations, but he seemingly weathered every Texas legislative snub and denial as well as that of other state officials and local leaders. By the early 1930s, the State Parks Board was nearly forgotten and almost irrelevant.

In fact, during the first ten years of the State Parks Board's existence, there were only two successes:

1) Legislative action (in 1927) allowed for twenty-three new state parks (see Appendix B) to be accepted by the State Parks Board, a first for the land donation package. It must be pointed out here that most of these "parks" were small roadside venues of limited acreage.

2) Colp obtained legislative authority to acquire land and then, in 1932, cobbled together a deal for 426 acres near Burnet, Texas, which came to be known as Longhorn Cavern State Park.

There were no legislative appropriations attached for operations or maintenance, but, over time, concession income paid off the note.

Coupled closely with this latter success was the re-emergence of Pat Neff, then president of Baylor University, onto the state parks scene. Early in Miriam "Ma" Ferguson's second term as Texas governor (1933, six years after her first), she appointed Neff to the State Parks Board, which he had championed and passed by legislation in 1923. He accepted but did not ask to be its next chairman. I think it showed the high regard Neff had for Colp. He recognized in Colp the loyalty and perseverance of his friend, who had unsuccessfully planned for a vibrant state parks system over the lean years of 1923 to 1933. Though seemingly hopeless, the cause was right, and that was all-important to Neff. He was also impressed by the dogged determination he saw in Colp.

To demonstrate his regard for Colp, on Thanksgiving Day 1932, Neff gave the dedication address at the newly renamed Longhorn Cavern State Park—Colp's only tangible state park deal, composed of a land donation and concession agreement to operate the park. The property, known as Sherrard's Cave, was compared to Carlsbad Caverns National Park and had a popular dance hall in its interior.[30]

Together—a team again—they and their fellow board members, with support from Governor Ferguson (finally) and President Roosevelt's New Deal Civilian Conservation Corps, were about to make lasting state parks history.

Dancers at the Sherrard's Cave (soon to become Longhorn Cavern State Park) dance hall, date unknown. Courtesy of the Texas Parks and Wildlife Department, Austin, Texas, 2015.41.35.

Migrant mother with her daughter in the door of their trailer home near Weslaco, Texas, February 1939. Courtesy of Russell Lee, Office of War Information Photo Collection, Farm Security Administration, Library of Congress Prints and Photographs Division, Washington, DC, LC-DIG-fsa-8a24988.

But first, there had to be a bit of turf fighting to establish jurisdiction over park planning, placement of Civilian Conservation Corps encampments, and federal funding. Several histories need to be played out to set the stage for this struggle throughout 1933.

Beginning in 1929, the economic catastrophe that became known as the Great Depression suppressed everything—not least of which were state governments and their programs, including those to enhance and expand state parks systems.

If the fate of the newly enacted state parks system was dim and growing darker, the economies of the nation and Texas were glowing and growing throughout the 1920s, fueled by booming growth in population. The population in Texas increased to nearly six million over the decade, representing an increase of more than one million people—an almost 25 percent gain.[31]

While cotton was still king, lumber, South Texas crops of fruit and vegetables, livestock, and oil and gas added greatly to the bottom line of the state and its citizens. Most of these cash crops were little dependent on the ebb and flow of the "back-East" stock and bond booms that rarely made the news in Texas.

Then on "Black Tuesday," October 29, 1929, there came a bust—the Crash! Those booming, never-declining Wall Street dream makers lost 40 percent of their value over the next several months. Yet even as the crisis deepened on the East Coast among speculators and stock gamblers, Texas seemed to weather the storm and did so for the first year of the economic debacle, propped up by continuing good prices for its primary industries: cotton, cattle, oil, construction, and railroads.[32]

By 1931, however, the shallow waves of bad news from the East became a tidal wave of overwhelming dimensions in Texas. To compound the growing effects from without, cracks were appearing from within. Agriculture, oil and gas, and timber prices fell. Farm foreclosures grew, and thousands of farmers and sharecroppers began to leave the land. Many never returned to the rural life that had been their core existence for generations.

With no serious thought of aid from federal or state governments, leaders from the private sector tried to help. Fort Worth publisher Amon Carter, for instance, backed a fundraising tour by Will Rogers. It may have raised spirits for an evening, but it didn't feed hungry mouths or pay off loans.

Throughout 1932, damage from the Great Depression deepened throughout Texas. Banks failed, unemployment rose, cotton prices dropped to five or six cents a pound, "Hooverville" tent cities and camps sprang up in a number of towns, and soup and breadlines circled the blocks of many major cities. And this was just the plight of White men and boys.

If times were tough for White men, the economic plight of people of color was tougher. The average annual wage for a Black family fell from $978 in 1928 to a low of $874 in 1933. By 1935, an estimated 90 percent of Black farm laborers could not find work.[33]

**ABOVE**
Hispanic women pecan shellers at work in a union plant in San Antonio, Texas, March 1939. Courtesy of Russell Lee, Office of War Information Photo Collection, Farm Security Administration, Library of Congress Prints and Photographs Division, Washington, DC, LC-DIG-fsa-8b21319.

**LEFT**
Depression-era billboard, date unknown. Courtesy of Wikimedia Commons.

Menacing black clouds of dust rising over the Texas Panhandle, March 1936. Courtesy of Arthur Rothstein, Office of War Information Photo Collection, Farm Security Administration, Library of Congress Prints and Photographs Division, Washington, DC, LC-DIG-fsa-8b27276.

The same conditions applied to Mexican Americans, but there was the added degradation of deportation. Because they would work for lower wages, Mexican Americans became the target of the anger of poor White workers and were summarily rounded up for deportation by the United States Immigration Service. Between 1929 and 1939, 250,000 were returned to Mexico.

Even Texas women—of all colors—were criticized for working at jobs to the detriment of out-of-work men. Nonetheless, more than half a million women worked for wages.

At the depth of the Depression in 1933, the gross national product sank by 29 percent, consumption by 18 percent, and investment by 98 percent, while unemployment shot up to 25 percent—higher among young men nationwide—with similar numbers in Texas.

To add insult to injury, drought set in during the last half of the 1930s, accompanied by winds (some tornadic "black blizzards") and erosion. The Dust Bowl had arrived and, by 1935, covered a hundred million acres. Throughout the 1930s and well into the 1940s, these conditions destroyed the once-rich soils of Texas, New Mexico, Oklahoma, Kansas, and Colorado.

But more than soil was lost. Farm equipment was ruined. Lives were lost; many were permanently blinded, and others suffered debilitating lung disease. The elderly and very young were the most affected. Between 1935 and 1937, more than 34 percent of farmers left the land.

For all the scenes of Depression tragedy that moved across the destroyed landscape and economy of Texas and other states, help was emerging. Some of it would be directed at parks—national and state.

Voices at the national and state levels spoke to the benefits of parks as public works projects. The Reconstruction Finance Corporation, established in 1932 by President Herbert Hoover, was formed to aid banks, railroads, and corporations, but it was soon amended to include agriculture and state and local public works—including parks. Though timid in action and short of vision, it was the beginning of federal support for financing work relief in parks. More importantly, the old walls of go-it-alone state pride were beginning to crumble.

Building the Rim-to-Floor Road, Palo Duro Canyon State Park, 1933. The first and most extensive Civilian Conservation Corps project at Palo Duro Canyon was building a two-lane automobile road from the rim headquarters area to the floor of the canyon. Although Civilian Conservation Corps enrollees used dynamite and had dump trucks at their disposal, they also accomplished a good portion of the work by hand. Courtesy of the National Archives and Records Administration, College Park, Maryland.

Phebe Warner, the Texas State Parks Board member and Panhandle columnist from Claude, Texas, wrote in 1933, "Tragic as the Depression has been, state parks projects have thrived under it as the parks furnished an opportunity for public works . . . we may just as well be at work building this road [for Palo Duro Canyon] across our county as sitting around idle and cussing the Depression."[34] Other prominent park planners and advocates would, in varying degrees, champion Phebe Warner's West Texas practical logic: Robert Moses, New York State Council of Parks chairman; Horace Albright, who followed Stephen Mather as national parks director; Jesse Jones of the Reconstruction Finance Corporation; but none more so than newly elected President Franklin Delano Roosevelt.

Roosevelt did not come late to the parks/public works frame of mind.

He "felt the scars and exhaustion of the earth almost as a personal injury" and meant to use his presidency to right those wrongs—for the land and for the youth of America.[35]

Even without a formal body to administer them, funds began to be committed to Texas—some $2.5 million in January and February of 1933—but without accountability from the state.

In early February, A. W. McMillan, field representative of the Reconstruction Finance Corporation, wrote to Governor Ferguson a questioning letter. "These funds," he asked, "are not in lieu of, but are merely supplementary to, state and local efforts."[36] In other words, the Reconstruction Finance Corporation wanted to know what the Texas government had contributed to match the federal funds.

Franklin D. Roosevelt (seated in car) shaking hands with a farmer while on a stop en route to Warm Springs, Georgia, October 23, 1932. Courtesy of the Franklin D. Roosevelt Presidential Library and Museum, Hyde Park, New York, 48-22:3704(419)c.

It is rare to see the governor and Texas legislature move in concert and with all due speed. But with future funding from Washington as the carrot, and loss of it the stick, move they did.

On March 1, the governor, by executive order, created the Texas Relief Commission, placed all responsibility for distributing federal relief funds with the new commission, and appointed Lawrence Westbrook as executive director. The governor also ended the questionable practice of distributing the funds through favored private chamber of commerce offices. Simultaneously, the legislature began considering transforming the Texas Relief Commission into a full-fledged state agency and proposed a bond package to be taken to the voters as soon as possible. That ballot measure would take place on August 26, 1933, and by a two-to-one margin, allowed for the sale of up to $20 million in relief bonds. While Ferguson and the legislators were cleaning up their houses to comply with Washington's demands and threats, Roosevelt, his cabinet, and Congress were moving quickly to stem the tide of economic wreckage from the Great Depression.

First on the agenda was swift congressional action to stabilize the banking system, which was in freefall. But even as that essential bill moved through the US House and Senate, Roosevelt laid out a plan to put five hundred thousand men to work on various conservation programs. The working group consisted of the departments of Interior, Agriculture, War, and Labor. On March 14, 1933, the Civilian Conservation Corps was proposed. In the first round of the proposal, the program was limited to forestry and erosion projects and included 250,000 enrollees. Within two weeks (March 31), a bill known as the Emergency Conservation Work Act passed, and, on April 5, Roosevelt signed an executive order creating the Civilian Conservation Corps.

It would be assumed that with such rapid action and solid backing from the president and $300 million from the Reconstruction Finance Corporation, 1933 would generate balances that would guarantee all would be happy and hitched to the same wagon of positive results.

But within weeks of passage, the decade-long feud between the National Park Service and the US Forest Service broke out anew—if, indeed, it had ever ceased. After much back-and-forth, backstabbing, and positioning, the army, with the blessing of the president, stepped in to organize the growing mess. It was done in rapid order, and, in the process, the National Park Service broke away from the Forest Service and established its

Franklin D. Roosevelt signing into law the Emergency Railroad Transportation Act with US Senator Clarence Dill (left) and US Representative Sam Rayburn (right) looking on, June 16, 1933. Courtesy of the Sam Rayburn Papers, Dolph Briscoe Center for American History, University of Texas at Austin, Austin, Texas, di_03285.

own districts. Soon, with the backing of Texas's powerful delegation (and its ever-present Vice President John Nance Garner), ten Texas state parks were on the approved list for Civilian Conservation Corps camps and funding.

Even with that clarion call to action, political maneuvering was at play. It seems that every park on the list fit nicely into a supporting senator's or representative's congressional district. But without that support, it is doubtful that state parks development would have reached the independence and prominence it would soon obtain for the immediate present and future.

Colp, for his part, was only involved in the possible development of Palo Duro Canyon, going so far as to apply for a $141,000 loan from the Reconstruction Finance Corporation to acquire and develop the proposed park.

To fill the void, Westbrook and his newly legislated and renamed Texas Rehabilitation and Relief Commission went to work to control all park projects throughout the state—without any consultation with Colp. Some would attribute this slight to the fact that the State Parks Board had fallen to a disgraceful level of irrelevance, so why bother contacting him? Others would see that Westbrook and the Fergusons wanted all the projects and funding under their control. To solidify their position, Ferguson wrote to the National Park Service director that the State Parks Board had no staff, offices, or

Postcard of Palo Duro Canyon, which was considered for national park status but became a state park in 1934, date unknown. Courtesy of the Texas Parks and Wildlife Department, Austin, Texas, 2007.144.66.

Postcard of Palo Duro Canyon from a different location, date unknown. Courtesy of the Texas Parks and Wildlife Department, Austin, Texas, 2007.144.68.

fiscal setup, and to remedy this situation, she recommended that all administration and funds be directed to the Texas Rehabilitation and Relief Commission. She wrote that Colp approved of this arrangement. If it came to pass, the Fergusons and Westbrook would stand to control all funding, site selection, and ability to dole out lucrative jobs and accounts to favored banks. From the outset, they proceeded to do just that.

Once again, it would appear that Colp and the State Parks Board were left out in the cold.

Fortunately, both Colp and Neff had friends in high places, both in Texas and Washington. And state parks projects continued apace, including Colp's pet Palo Duro, though not without delay and roadblocks—most of which were probably thrown up by Westbrook.

From June through the fall of 1933, fifteen Civilian Conservation Corps camps were established and activated. By the first of July, Roosevelt had met his revised goal: the placement of 274,374 men in life-saving work.[37]

During the formative months of 1933, Interior Secretary Harold Ickes assigned National Park Service Director Horace Albright as his representative to Roosevelt's cabinet. Conrad Wirth, Albright's assistant, filled his position when Albright resigned later in 1933. In turn, Wirth hired Herbert Evison from the National Conference on State Parks to coordinate "state park emergency conservation work." Evison knew the parks people from that first meeting of the National Conference on State Parks and had an ongoing relationship with Colp and, surely, Neff.

By July 1933, the alarm bells of slipping authority went off in Colp's head. On July 7, 1933, he called a formal meeting of the State Parks Board, the first in several years.

Among its actions was a resolution establishing (or re-establishing) full authority over all matters pertaining to state parks under the directives of the National Park Service. The board went on to complain that no one in Westbrook's Texas Rehabilitation and Relief Commission had bothered to consult with the State Parks Board on any matters or projects pertaining to state parks.

Over the next several months, the legislature, bowing to Ferguson and the people's vote approving the $20 million bond issue, approved $5.5 million to match federal assistance. The stakes for control just got higher.

Westbrook raised hell and alarms. "Ma" called a joint meeting of the State Parks Board and the Texas Rehabilitation and Relief Commission. Though much was left unresolved, the State Parks Board agreed to ask the legislature for $25,000 to fund a two-year parks maintenance program to match federal dollars. The appropriation failed. Some saw the hand of Westbrook again at play.

The failure to appropriate matching funds and the actions behind that failure caused Colp and the other members to put their collective feet down. They sent a telegram to

Gretchen Denny and the author at Palo Duro Canyon State Park, July 19, 2012. Author's collection.

National Park Service Assistant Director Wirth. They argued that the 1923 establishment laws, fortified by laws passed in 1923 and 1933, placed firm control with the State Parks Board.[38]

Wirth telegraphed Governor Ferguson asking what was going on: "Please advise by wire whom we are to deal with in connection with state park emergency conservation work."

Apparently, the governor suggested a legal opinion from the attorney general of Texas was in order. James Allred was the attorney general whose early legal career was enhanced when he was appointed district attorney by Pat Neff. The opinion was forthcoming in early November.

Allred ruled that the Texas State Parks Board was responsible for the administration and construction of Texas state parks, not the Texas Rehabilitation and Relief Commission.[39]

Westbrook threw in the towel.

Later in 1933, Westbrook admitted before a Texas State Senate investigating committee, "I know that in some instances outright fraud has been committed, forgeries, misapplication of funds."[40]

Westbrook went to Washington with no apparent punishment. By 1934, the situation had been rectified and the Ferguson money machine smashed.

Major work on parks continued. The Civilian Conservation Corps grew in stature. The State Parks Board was finally and firmly in control of all Depression park relief work in Texas.

Remnants of a Civilian Conservation Corps
structure, Fort Worth Nature Center & Refuge,
May 3, 2016. Photo by George Bristol,
author's collection.

Due to politics, however, Colp was soon out of a job. He died in 1936.

The Civilian Conservation Corps was created with the goal of putting 275,000 to work by July 1933. From 1933 to 1942, more than three million young men between the ages of seventeen and twenty-eight passed through the program. They were given a job and $30 a month, of which $25 was sent home to Depression-stricken families. The men were provided shelter, clothing, and food. Equally important, they were given a lifetime of experience in the great American outdoors, coupled with the opportunity to learn a trade. And they were given hope.

Roosevelt would go on to become a new champion among presidents for creating and restoring parks and historic sites.

Nearly $220 million was spent within the national parks. But Roosevelt's conservation policies for national parks did not end with the Civilian Conservation Corps. Seven national parks were added to the system, including the Great Smoky Mountains and Shenandoah in the East. Furthermore, Roosevelt created by executive order numerous national monuments, many of which caused immediate transformation and enlargement of the park service in 1933. Military parks, historic battlefields and monuments, the Statue of Liberty, Mount Rushmore, the Washington Monument, and Lincoln Memorial

Tour of the Fort Worth Nature Center & Refuge, May 3, 2016. Photo by George Bristol, author's collection.

were transferred to the National Park Service. Now the service not only encompassed the great vistas of natural America but also its history and shared ideas.

The Civilian Conservation Corps, to my mind, was one of the most noble and effective programs of the New Deal. In Texas, Civilian Conservation Corps–operated camps, with populations ranging up to nineteen thousand men (enrolling nearly fifty thousand Texans over the course of the camps' existence from 1933 to 1942), developed forty-one parks, of which thirty-one are still operating, including Bastrop, Davis Mountains, Garner, Goliad, and Palo Duro Canyon. In Tarrant County, Lake Worth was a beneficiary of the Civilian Conservation Corps effort at Mosque Point and what is now the Fort Worth Nature Center & Refuge. Serving the Lake Worth area from 1934 to 1938, Civilian Conservation Corps Company 1816, Lake Worth Camp Sp-31-T, planned and supervised the completion of foot and auto bridges, shelters, picnic and campground facilities, roads, foot trails, landscaping, tree planting, drinking fountains, toilets, water lines, fire protection amenities, and more, some of which are still standing at the Nature Center. What is not known is why this project was not completed to state park status—speculation, but nothing concrete.

By July, the "CCC boys" in Texas were at work on twenty-six park projects. Many were on Colp's wish list. For all his woes and missteps, David Colp saw his dream of a state parks system through to his end. This quote summarizes him perfectly:

Success consists of going from failure to failure without loss of enthusiasm.[41]

SIR WINSTON CHURCHILL

# Chapter 4

# A New Deal for Texas State Parks

Contributed by **Cynthia A. Brandimarte**

W ith Attorney General James Allred's November 1933 decision, the State Parks Board had finally secured its role as the official agency in Texas in charge of all matters related to state parks. Granted, its activity had sometimes been listless, but as its title bespoke, it was already largely functioning in that capacity. After all, Texas landowners who had already donated small parcels for parks did so to the State Parks Board during the 1920s. And it was the State Parks Board that Texans thought to contact about adding large scenic areas. Consequently, in important ways, Allred's decision changed little, simply reinforcing what had been a tacit understanding, despite Lawrence Westbrook and others' efforts to muddy the waters. Yet in one important way, it changed a great deal. As the recognized state parks agency, the State Parks Board could identify the camp locations to receive federal funding and hire multidisciplinary expertise to build a Texas state parks system. The designation was a game changer.

Before New Deal programs came to Texas, the State Parks Board was little more than a loosely functioning committee that was spread across the state at a time when letters, telegrams, and phone calls were the methods of communication. In fact, before the arrival of federal support, board members met infrequently, recorded no minutes, and exercised modest oversight of David Colp. The State Parks Board was without a state budget other than travel reimbursements and without a stable location for its office.

From left, David Colp, Conrad Wirth, Herbert Maier, Olin Boese, Herbert Evison, and George Nason (representatives of the Texas State Parks Board and the National Park Service) at a Gunter Hotel luncheon in San Antonio given by Reagan Houston to consider a national park site north of the city, 1935. Courtesy of *The San Antonio Light* Collection, University of Texas at San Antonio Institute for Texan Cultures, San Antonio, Texas, Friday, August 2, 1935.

None of these early shortcomings, however, had stopped board members from launching into and becoming embroiled in large and complicated endeavors. Admittedly, they were sometimes nudged by boosters. By the time the federal government intervened, the State Parks Board had managed to become mired in a time-consuming Palo Duro land deal and land deals involving the Chisos Mountains and Caddo Lake, which were, nonetheless, singular Texas landscapes and important projects. Further complicating the board's agenda were the dozens of donors of small tracts of land spread around the state who turned to the State Parks Board expecting it would transform their parcels into parks.

Early on, conflict between the Texas Rehabilitation and Relief Commission and the State Parks Board's authority over parks had delayed any meaningful collaboration between federal agencies and the board. And when National Park Service power figures such as Herbert Maier and Herb Evison did confirm the Texas State Parks Board as its state partner, they soon learned how dramatically they, with their paid positions and federal budgets, exceeded the resources of the fledgling board and its lack of legislative funding.[1] This asymmetry weighed on the federal/state alliance throughout their interactions. But since both parties were yoked by a common focus on creating and developing parks, they strove to forge and sustain a working partnership.

## The Great Depression

The partnership between the National Park Service and the State Parks Board began in 1933, the worst year of the Great Depression and the culmination of years of extravagance during the 1920s. As president after 1928, Herbert Hoover had for four years relied mainly on reduced government spending to restore business confidence and on voluntary local and private sources of relief to lessen the ordinary American's plight. His measures were in step with economic doctrine at the time, but accepted *laissez-faire* ideas and largely voluntary aid efforts proved to be ineffective in the face of the unprecedented economic collapse that unfolded between 1929 and 1932: factories shuttered, banks and companies bankrupt, and a quarter of all workers unemployed. As noted in the previous chapter, agricultural income had plummeted, and debts, exacerbated by dire drought in the Southwest, had driven many farmers from their lands.[2]

The brunt of economic disasters came slowly to Texas, however. Holding steadfast to optimism and frontier resourcefulness, Texans took solace in their somewhat diversified economy—agriculture, lumber, oil, and gas.[3] They also paid little attention to troubles in distant places like New York and stock market matters they considered not germane to their lives; instead, they pointed to thriving Texas cities such as Houston and Corpus Christi that initially seemed immune to the Depression. But when economic consequences reached Texas, Texans could not ignore the faces captured by the Farm Security Administration's photographers, the misery of neighbors, or the hunger in their own stomachs.

A change was needed, and this was what Democratic candidate Franklin Delano Roosevelt offered in the runup to the presidential election of 1932. His promise of a New Deal for America appealed to many voters, and his selection of Texan John Nance

Unemployed workers gathered outside the US Labor Bureau office on Dolorosa Street in San Antonio, 1933. US Department of Labor Employment Service enrollees were eligible for food, checks, and seasonal public works jobs under the Federal Emergency Relief Administration established under Franklin D. Roosevelt. Courtesy of *The San Antonio Light* Collection, University of Texas at San Antonio Institute for Texan Cultures, San Antonio, Texas, L-0049-A.

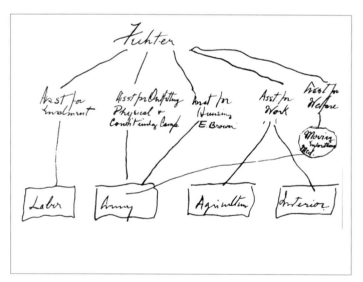

Three of a seven-member Oklahoma family camping by the roadside near Blythe, California, hoping to find work in the cotton fields, August 17, 1936. Courtesy of Dorothea Lange, Office of War Information Photo Collection, Farm Security Administration, Library of Congress, Washington, DC.

Dust storm approaching Spearman, Texas, April 14, 1935. Courtesy of the Franklin D. Roosevelt Presidential Library and Museum, Hyde Park, New York.

Franklin D. Roosevelt's sketches on a napkin showing a rough organizational chart of the Civilian Conservation Corps, 1933. The chart, created a few days before Roosevelt signed the executive order establishing the Civilian Conservation Corps, demonstrates how the Corps' director, Robert Fechner (whose name he misspelled), would draw on the resources of the departments of War, Labor, Agriculture, and Interior. Courtesy of the Franklin D. Roosevelt Presidential Library and Museum, Hyde Park, New York.

Garner as his running mate secured the votes of Texans and Southerners more widely. The ticket won the November 8, 1932, election by a landslide, and when Roosevelt took office on March 4, 1933, he launched into solving the nation's crises.[4]

Two of the problems facing the country were its demoralized populace and degraded physical landscape. Despondence was manifest in "a cheerless time of pay cuts, part-time labor, distracted social volunteers, apple vendors, bank closures, panhandlers, men on park benches."[5] Many of the fourteen million jobless were young men whose adult lives had been upended before they had really begun. Hopelessness threatened to consume an entire generation. The degraded physical landscape resulted from lands west of the Appalachians having been cleared, plowed, and grazed with abandon for a century or more. Consequently, topsoil that was no longer grounded by root systems of native grasses became blowing dust as winds swept over land made dry by a terrible drought. Six out of every ten inhabitants of the Southwestern states fled to the country's West Coast to escape the Dust Bowl, a migration dramatized by John Steinbeck in *The Grapes of Wrath*. Moreover, unchecked lumbering in the country's Western regions had left lands vulnerable to floods. Where once there had been eight hundred million acres of forest, by 1933, only one hundred million remained.

Roosevelt had a long-held and deep belief that physical vigor and spiritual health were intertwined. In what was perhaps his first written expression of this, Roosevelt outlined a federal program that would prove to be a centerpiece of his New Deal, a program to provide employment and vocational training for unemployed youth who would, in return, assist in protecting natural resources by carrying out a nationwide conservation program in forests, parks, and farmlands. Roosevelt introduced this Civilian Conservation Corps to Congress on March 21, 1933, just days after swearing his oath of office. Nicknamed sardonically "Roosevelt's Tree Army," CCC enrollees were soon rehabilitating land damaged by fires, lumbering, and erosion with millions of newly planted trees; digging untold numbers of ditches and canals; stocking lakes and rivers with upwards of a billion fish; restoring historic battlefields as memorials; and building hundreds of campgrounds and structures in previously empty locations. A crucial aim of this undertaking was to renew the spirits of dispirited young men. As Roosevelt said when he introduced the CCC in an address to Congress,

> More important . . . than the material gains will be the moral and spiritual value of such work. The overwhelming majority of unemployed Americans, who are now walking the streets and receiving private or public relief, would infinitely prefer to work. We can take a vast army of these unemployed out into healthful surroundings. We can eliminate to some extent at least the threat that enforced idleness brings to spiritual and moral stability.[6]

## New Deal Politics

To accomplish these twin goals—lift the spirits of America's unemployed youth and restore and conserve the nation's natural resources—Roosevelt wanted to hit the ground running when he entered the White House. Instead of creating and funding an entirely new agency, he used structures that were already in place. Initially, the Department of Labor in Washington was put in charge of selecting Civilian Conservation Corps enrollees; to do this, it cooperated with county welfare agencies to find and certify enrollees.[7] The departments of Agriculture and Interior selected projects from among those proposed for the CCC to carry out. The War Department (today's Department of Defense) had multiple responsibilities: assess and approve CCC campsites for water supply and sanitation; supervise camp construction, maintenance, and administration; ensure the health, welfare, and discipline of workers in camps; and oversee payrolls. The War Department was also charged with selecting and supervising camp administrative per-

Vice President John Nance Garner (left) with US House Majority Leader Sam Rayburn (right) and US House Speaker William B. Bankhead (son of John H. Bankhead, for whom the Bankhead Highway was named), July 18, 1939. Courtesy of the Dolph Briscoe Center for American History, Austin, Texas.

sonnel, including camp teachers and advisers selected by the Office of Education. The Department of the Interior was responsible for planning, executing, and administering projects, including hiring and supervising project directors and officers to liaise between directors. Overall, the War and Interior departments had the most important roles, the former being responsible for camp operations, the latter for delivering all sorts of completed projects.

Roosevelt had full power to authorize projects no matter if the land on which they were to occur was owned by a local or state governmental entity or private citizen. The president appointed a Civilian Conservation Corps director, and Congress approved the appointment in line with its sole authority as the legislative branch. The director was given discretionary power over the functioning of the CCC, including allotments made to other federal departments and agencies. If the director had no jurisdiction in a particular case, then it fell to the president to exercise it. Thus, the power of the executive branch in the work of the CCC was absolute.[8] The initial executive order and subsequent legislation in 1937 pertaining to the CCC gave Roosevelt *carte blanche* in distributing a large amount of federal funds, though the overall CCC budget was not as large as that of other federal agencies. As involved as Roosevelt wanted to be with the CCC's workings after its creation, other responsibilities demanded his attention. He chose labor leader Robert Fechner to serve as director of Emergency Conservation Work, the official name of the program under which the CCC first operated.[9]

The allotment of projects to Texas was enhanced by the political web between Texas and Washington. The state's connections with Washington were strong, and they yielded much influence. Before serving as Roosevelt's vice president, John Nance Garner from Uvalde, and for whom Garner State Park was later named, held the position as speaker of the US House of Representatives and had strong political allies in Washington. In addition, there was US Congressman Richard M. Kleberg, for whom the CCC's "Camp Kleberg" at Lake Corpus Christi State Park was later named. There was US Congressman Sam Rayburn, Speaker of the House from East Texas, an advocate of soil conservation, farming, and lakes in his region. US Senators Morris Shepard and Tom Connally were early supporters of New Deal programs and were instrumental in securing the bounty that Texas received in the form of state parks. Also notable was Lyndon Baines Johnson, who eventually became director of the National Youth Association, another of Roosevelt's work projects. Behind the Texas politicians, and sometimes leading them, were boosters and promoters who often were members of local chambers of commerce and who worked hard to benefit their local economies by touting in grandiose terms the virtues and promise of their communities.[10]

There was no lack of proposed park sites in Texas from which to choose. Wish lists abounded.[11] Governor Miriam Ferguson had one list she passed to Lawrence Westbrook of the Texas Rehabilitation and Relief Commission.[12] State Parks Board Chairman Pat Neff had a long list, too. Some counties and municipalities had, or soon devised, their own lists.

## The Master Plan

In order to obtain federal funds for building state parks, a state had only to promise two things: to work with National Park Service professionals in designing parks and to operate and maintain parks once they were built. The former was easier than the latter, although both were difficult in Texas.

If the process of planning, designing, and building state parks had gone smoothly, it would have unfolded along these general lines: the State Parks Board would provide an office where personnel of both the National Park Service and the board would work; equipped with drafting tables, the office would be the hub of park planning. The board would have secured both the deed to the intended park property and a map with its boundaries. In concert with each district, the State Parks Board would have hired "technical men" for its central design office, who would further identify areas within the boundaries that were to be altered or left untouched and who would indicate how

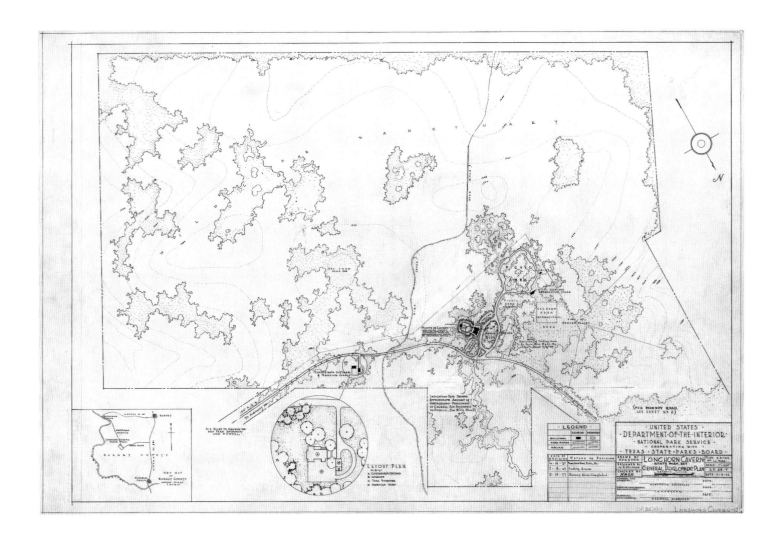

people and automobiles were expected to circulate in each park. The experts would then continue to refine plans for each state park's development and design the early primitive facilities to be built by the CCC. In Texas, the Austin design professionals would work with veteran park planners in the district office, in this case, District III in Oklahoma City, and with the National Park Service field staff assigned to Texas to develop a master plan with permanent buildings, structures, and features that could be built by workers unfamiliar with building trades but under the guidance of skilled locals and technical men in the field. National Park Service inspectors would provide quality control. The Army finance officer would pay the bills, and the State Parks Board would act as the procurement agency. The state parks authorities would handle the camps, and, although paid out of federal funds, camp superintendents and technical men who supervised the work would report directly to the state parks authorities.[13]

Longhorn Cavern State Park General Development Plan, November 16, 1936. Courtesy of M. E. Delonge, architect and artist, and Paul R. Roesle, artist, Prints and Photographs Collection, Archives and Information Services Division, Texas State Library and Archives Commission, Austin, Texas, SP.35.10.1A.

THE MASTER PLAN
BALMORHEA STATE PARK
TEXAS

UNITED STATES
DEPARTMENT OF THE INTERIOR
NATIONAL PARK SERVICE

COOPERATING WITH

TEXAS STATE PARKS BOARD

Cover sheet for Balmorhea State Park plans and drawings, ca. 1935–1938. Possibly by Olin Boese, architect (Boese designed the shelter featured on the cover), Prints and Photographs Collection, Archives and Information Services Division, Texas State Library and Archives Commission, Austin, Texas.

Completed by Austin-based designers and approved by the district, the resulting master plans would generate specific projects. The project or park superintendent would initiate a Job Application and Completion Record, which would include the project name and cost estimate based on materials and estimated number of workdays. An example of a job might be landscape planting or construction of a concession building. Based on approval by the National Park Service inspector for each Texas region, the job application would be funded and the job would proceed, with a tabulation of any remaining funds or overages at the project's completion. Most jobs were to be completed within a certain time period, typically six months, and usually from October through March and April through September. There were to be nineteen six-month periods that ran from June 1933 through July 1942. Signing off on the project was a park authority, notably William J. Lawson, David Colp's successor, the first board secretary and its first paid employee. Ultimately, each Job Application and Completion Record form for Texas parks projects was to be thoroughly reviewed by the District III office and identified by its designated park number. For example, as the first CCC park in Texas, Caddo Lake was designated SP-1.[14]

Meanwhile, the State Parks Board would continue to be responsible for liaising with chambers of commerce and park user groups, interacting with members of the public, and answering to elected members of the Texas legislature. Seeking state funds was constant and particularly intense when lawmakers gathered for each biennial session. Workloads varied, depending on the number of camps operating in any given period. Fluctuations were also the result of varying federal fund allotments, which had to be divided between both national and state parks; the relative strength of Texas's political influence; and the quality of the project applications. But there was never a shortage of work to go around.

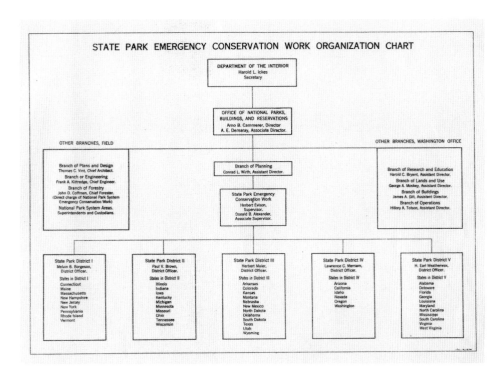

Formal organizational chart of the Civilian Conservation Corps, 1934. A year after Roosevelt sketched his idea for organization of the Civilian Conservation Corps, this formal chart was firmly in place for the Department of the Interior. The National Park Service had overarching duties in developing state parks. At this time, Texas fell into District III. Courtesy of the Prints and Photographs Collection, Archives and Information Services Division, Texas State Library and Archives Commission, Austin, Texas.

Yellowstone National Park, Madison Museum, 1929, Herbert Maier, architect. The museum was considered one of the best examples of rustic architecture in the National Park System and served as a model for Texas park buildings during the 1930s. Courtesy of the Library of Congress Prints and Photographs Division, Washington, DC.

# Design Inspiration and the National Park Service

Each state was assigned to a district led by a district leader. Assigned to District III, Texas was fortunate to have the expertise of Herbert Maier, who set the National Park Service design standard.[15] The National Park Service acting director in charge of state park projects in Texas, Maier was an accomplished architect who had designed park buildings for Yellowstone, Glacier, and Yosemite during the 1920s. Like others of his generation, he was influenced by prevailing notions of nature's beauty that had evolved over several decades and become a credo for park architects and planners. The naturalistic parks of Frederick Law Olmsted Jr., the designer of Central Park in New York City, and the Romanesque buildings of Henry Hobson Richardson in Central Park strove for a seamless blending of modern buildings and natural settings.

The parks and buildings of Olmsted, Richardson, and their contemporaries greatly influenced the Arts and Crafts Movement, which, during the twentieth century's early years, pursued alternatives to revivalist historical styles and factory-like buildings stemming from the Industrial Revolution. Publications such as *The Craftsman* spread the new architectural ideas to a wide audience, making rustic stone bungalows and hand-made furnishings popular. Frank Lloyd Wright disdained formal architectural styles and developed an "organic architecture" in which buildings "grew" naturally from their environments and took on forms that reflected qualities of the materials used to construct them. National Park Service architects gave life to these newly fashionable ideas in parks they designed during the 1920s and 1930s.

Oriented primarily toward the design of suburban houses and other types of buildings, the ideas of Olmsted, Richardson, Wright, and others were well suited to parks in natural settings. Earlier resort hotels in natural settings were of ornate Victorian-style architecture, with elaborate wood exteriors painted and trimmed in bright colors. Finding these artifacts of the Victorian era jarring to the eye when located in a dense forest, near a hot spring, on a canyon rim, or nestled at the base of a majestic mountain, designers during the 1920s and 1930s strove for styles more in tune with such landscapes. The plans they provided for CCC parks were for structures that would be unobtrusive in natural settings. These structures were to consist of local stone, timber, and other materials easily obtainable in or near where each park was to be created. Construction of buildings would involve straightforward masonry and carpentry techniques, and buildings would have simple horizontal lines and low silhouettes that would not distract from the natural setting each park celebrated.

Bastrop State Park cabin, ca. 1930s. Hugging the hillside at Bastrop State Park, this cabin displays the horizontal line favored by architect Herbert Maier. Courtesy of the Texas Parks and Wildlife Department, Austin, Texas.

The strong emphasis on low and horizontal rather than sharply vertical structures and buildings stemmed from what Herbert Maier termed "the Horizontal Key." As architectural historian James Wright Steely describes this, "You see a consistent horizontal orientation of the fabric—no matter what the fabric is. And that puts it in line with the ground, close to the ground."[16] Employing arches as a central design element helped implement Maier's Horizontal Key. In Texas and elsewhere, National Park Service architects routinely insisted on arches that would break up the facades of park buildings and blend them with the landscape. Visually, arches provide an orderly rhythm in large structures, and they figure prominently in many imposing buildings the CCC built in Texas.

National Park Service Assistant Director Conrad Wirth and Herb Evison, who was in charge of National Park Service cooperation with state parks, together with George Nason, the senior National Park Service inspector for Texas, did much to translate Maier's designs into reality, as did others who worked under Maier. Maier sought to hire camp inspectors who were experienced in landscape architecture, engineering, and forestry, although few of them had worked in park and recreation planning and development. With private construction having dried up during the Depression and with unemployed professionals seeking work where they could find it, those fortunate to be hired readily adapted to park recreation principles and requirements.[17] Those who found their way to the State Parks Board would learn park design from Maier via a scrapbook he made of designs that the new planners could model.

## Planning Texas Parks

The start was slow, however. The first period, which was from June 1933 to the fall, was spent in work that was light on design: latrines and picnic tables based on drawings generated by the National Park Service in Washington.[18] Twelve Texas state parks were on the list for that first period, along with fifteen companies, and among the parks were Caddo Lake, Davis Mountains, and Palo Duro. The latter two were so large that they each required two CCC companies, yet neither was developed in any major way during this early stage.

Slowly during 1933, fledgling park planners from the disciplines of architecture and landscape architecture were added to the Austin office, and soon, design professionals were situated near important projects: Bonham, Lake Corpus Christi, and Bastrop, for example. Coordinating with the District III office, the Austin planners drew master plans that generally led automobile visitors through formal portals made of local stone,

Stone bridge with symmetrical culverts at Lake Corpus Christi State Park, 1935. Courtesy of the Texas Parks and Wildlife Department, Austin, Texas.

Unpaved road leading automobiles through the portals of Goose Island State Park, ca. 1930s. Courtesy of the Texas Parks and Wildlife Department, Austin, Texas.

**OPPOSITE (TOP)**
Road leading to the Goose Island State Park concession building, which was constructed of shellcrete blocks formed onsite at both Goose Island and Lake Corpus Christi state parks, ca. 1934–1935. Courtesy of the National Archives and Records Administration, College Park, Maryland.

**OPPOSITE (BOTTOM)**
Boathouse and pier at Bonham State Park, October 17, 1936. Courtesy of the Texas Parks and Wildlife Department, Austin, Texas.

followed by drives on winding roads crossing crafted stone bridges and culverts before arriving at a main building, variously called a refectory, combination, or concession building, also made of local stone and wood. There, they would be able to obtain park information, use areas for groups to gather, purchase food and supplies for camping, take advantage of well-constructed restrooms, and have access to patios. Master plans for parks containing lakes specified boathouses, beach shelters, and bathhouses. Play areas were built for parks with only swimming pools. Plans for larger parks, such as those to be built at Bastrop, Lake Brownwood, Daingerfield, Garner, and Palo Duro Canyon, included simple cabins to be used for overnight and longer stays. National parks served as models for these.

Judging from their designs, planners in Texas studied Maier's album that he called "The Library of Original Sources" and learned lessons from national parks, aspiring to execute the overall design philosophy of naturalism.[19] Regarding every building, picnic shelter, and signpost as a potentially intrusive element, the aim was to harmonize each feature to the maximum extent possible with the environment surrounding it. Among the notable figures in the planning group was the University of Texas-educated Arthur Fehr, an energetic and gifted architect to whom we are grateful for his overall work as "architect-foreman" at Bastrop State Park.[20] Working with Fehr was the chief landscape architect for the State Parks Board, Norfleet Bone, a graduate of Texas A&M University's horticulture program who left his mark on many a Texas state park landscape as designer, inspector, and administrator during his long tenure with the Texas parks system. Accompanying these two professionals were many whose careers had been temporarily upended by the Depression: Samuel Charles Phelps Vosper, who was principal designer at Goliad State Park and Longhorn Cavern State Park; architect Guy Carlander at Palo Duro State Park; architect Olin Smith and landscape architects Mason Coney and C.C. Pat Fleming at Palmetto State Park; architect Guy Newhall, landscape architect Stewart King, and engineer W. K. Adams at Mother Neff State Park; and Olin Boese, who designed the refectories at Lake Corpus Christi, Bastrop, and Abilene State Parks.[21]

Adequate staffing and federal funding quickened the pace of Texas park development. Between the third period, April through September 1934, and the ninth period, April through September 1937, activity reached its high point. New Deal support and federal funding remained steady, and the National Park Service and State Parks Board

partners kept their respective doubts at bay in order to realize their common purpose. As planners forged ahead with designs, their plans addressed a score of new or upgraded state parks and set the stage for construction work by some of the fifty thousand Civilian Conservation Corps enrollees in Texas during the ensuing decade.

## The Enrollees

Desperation drove the young men who traveled to county welfare offices in order to enroll in the Civilian Conservation Corps. Russell Cashion was one of them. He lived with his sharecropper parents and five siblings in Johnson County, Texas. Faced with poverty and few prospects beyond low-paying farm work, he later recalled, "As I grew older, I became depressed and wanted to run away, and that's why my dad got me in there, in the three Cs."[22] Another Texas youth, W. R. Patrick, described the circumstances that propelled him this way:

> My dad had always . . . made a little bit of money—it wasn't [m]any dollars and cents; it was just good at the time. Everything was cheap. He was a carpenter and contractor. When he died, we just lost that. I had just [gotten] out of school. Three months after he died, I got in the three C camp, sent twenty-five dollars home. My mother and three sisters were still there. That helped them. There ain't no doubt about that . . . there's no doubt in my life that it didn't save my life.[23]

Like those two enrollees, young men who enrolled in the Civilian Conservation Corps were probably unaware of the national or state politicians and promoters behind the work relief effort. Few would have heard much about the Texas State Parks Board, the National Park Service, or some of the other state and federal players who played a role in creating their new opportunity. But the men who were fortunate enough to be selected or "certified" as eligible for the CCC soon came face-to-face with personnel from the War Department, who arranged transportation from their home to their camp assignments.

Most of the successful applicants were US citizens between eighteen and twenty-three years old, unmarried, unemployed or needing employment, not in legal trouble, willing to support dependents, in good physical and mental health, and with good character and motivation. Most applicants met these criteria, but some took liberties in stating their actual circumstances or age. Julian Cavazos of Karnes City enrolled at age fifteen.[24]

The eligible age range was expanded to include war veterans when awareness of their economic plight became widespread. The Veterans Administration, rather than the

Civilian Conservation Corps Company 3822(V) enrollees (consisting of World War I veterans) constructing the massive stone masonry walls for the Mission *Nuestra Señora de Espíritu Santo de Zúñiga* at Goliad State Park, ca. 1930s. Courtesy of the Texas Parks and Wildlife Department, Austin, Texas.

Department of Labor, selected men who had served in the Spanish American War and World War I and were in their thirties and forties. These enrollees served in companies designated with a "V" affixed to their company number, thus leading to a distinction between junior and veteran companies.[25]

Most enrollees were White because the Civilian Conservation Corps was designed to mirror the racial percentages of the American population. Although economic hardships hit some groups more severely, as when Blacks lost jobs to Whites during the Depression, enrollee numbers did not reflect relative need, only proportions of the total population. Thus, approximately 10 percent of enrollees were Black, and 10 percent were Latino; the number was capped at ten thousand at any one time for Native Americans. Blacks tended to work in segregated companies, especially projects located in the South; Latinos worked predominantly on projects located in the Southwest; and Native Americans worked on reservations.

Once certified as eligible to enroll, a man was transported to an assigned camp, where he received a vaccination, a uniform—often ill-fitting—and a locker. Meeting fellow enrollees and getting used to camp rules and routines preoccupied him during his first days. Like others new to the camp, he may have been on the receiving end of a joke or other rite

Junior Civilian Conservation Corps company enrollees traveling to their work assignments at Bastrop State Park, ca. 1930s. The seats and railing added a layer of safety for the men during truck transport. Courtesy of the Texas Parks and Wildlife Department, Austin, Texas.

Civilian Conservation Corps workers well along in the construction process of the refectory at Bastrop State Park, ca. 1936. Much of the masonry was in place, but enrollees continued to frame the roof and work the stone to add dimension. Courtesy of the Texas Parks and Wildlife Department, Austin, Texas.

of passage as men formed friendships. Short-sheeting beds or hiding a sawed-off broom at the foot of one's bed with the bristles poking a sleeper's feet were popular pranks. Gardner Hill, who worked at Lake Brownwood, confided, "It wasn't so good when they was [sic] doing it to me, but when it got to be my turn—oh, it was enjoyable then."[26]

An enrollee's day began when reveille sounded at 6:00 a.m. He arose, made his bed, helped clean the barracks, participated in a morning exercise routine led by one of his company's officers, then ate a breakfast of eggs, bacon, cereal, and milk before drawing tools and reporting to a job site. After a morning of hard work, he ate lunch back at camp or munched sandwiches at the job site before working until late in the afternoon. Returning to camp, he enjoyed evenings involving supper, courtesy of an enrollee cook, as well as some combination of a study program, library time, and recreation that often involved a competitive team sport before it was time for lights out. This routine surely tried one's patience, but for most men, it was bearable and, most of the time, worth what they received in exchange: a monthly cash stipend of $30 for the five-day workweek, keeping $5 and sending $25 home to their families; three full meals a day; lodging; clothes; footwear; and medical and dental care.

While US Army personnel controlled the living arrangements in Civilian Conservation Corps camps and enrollees followed a military regimen when in camp, work sites were supervised by representatives of one or another federal agency, usually the National Park Service, Forest Service, or Soil Conservation Service. Enrollees tasked with building state parks in Texas learned to clear brush, make adobe bricks, haul rocks, and pour concrete. Most of this work required limited training and involved hard manual labor, usually under a blazing sun. "Locally Experienced Men" (abbreviated as LEMs) were hired to supervise the manual labor. LEMs were mature artisans with carpentry, stone masonry, electrical, plumbing, or blacksmithing skills that enabled them to guide teams of unskilled workers. Some workers observed and learned from LEMs' expertise and that of the National Park Service and Texas State Parks Board professionals. Enrollee Thomas Earl Jordan recalled,

Physical training, a requirement before breakfast and the beginning of the workday, at a Civilian Conservation Corps camp, ca. 1930s. Courtesy of the National Archives and Records Administration, College Park, Maryland.

> . . . we had adult, older instructors. There was a guy named Floyd and myself—
> we called him Pretty Boy Floyd . . . He and I were on a surveying crew with an
> albino named Dozier, a little short fellow. Really enjoyed working with him
> because he'd explain things to you and you could understand—how to shoot
> to make contour maps, how to enter in the book, how to figure the math on it,
> all that kind of stuff. I turn in all that to him, he'd draw a contour map for the
> park service.[27]

Most Civilian Conservation Corps enrollees had been unable to find jobs in depressed economic conditions at home. Some hailed from nearby Texas farming communities, but many came from distant cities in the Northeast who were rounded up to get them off the streets. Few had job experience or training beyond simple farm duties or other rudimentary skills, and few had more than a primary education.

Civilian Conservation Corps Company 845 enrollees in Beaumont (at the city's Tyrrell Park), 1935. Educational courses provided key elements of a public school curriculum, enabling enrollees to complete basic requirements for high school graduation. Courtesy of the National Archives and Records Administration, College Park, Maryland.

## Education and Recreation in the Camps

"We had classes we could enroll in—carpentry, metalwork, mathematics, and car repair—whatever they had a teacher for," remarked one enrollee. "I took carpentry and typing. I still type. Your fingers don't forget."[28] Often conducted in partnership with local schools or businesses and often utilizing moonlighting or unemployed local teachers who were paid by the Works Progress Administration for their time, evening classes ranged from academic training to social skills. The formal educational programs complemented on-the-job vocational training and, in the case of some subjects like mechanical drawing, radio servicing, and auto mechanics, expanded enrollees' vocational knowledge.

Several of the Civilian Conservation Corps camps in Texas took special pride in these programs, likely prompted by a particularly dedicated educational adviser provided by the Office of Education. The camp at Cleburne published illustrated teaching outlines of their own for original courses in addition to those prepared for all CCC enrollees. At Mother Neff State Park, men were able to select from twenty-nine classes, ranging from elementary school to college-level courses.[29] Classes in art, music, dancing, and typing helped the men enjoy and master what they pursued during their spare time, whether it was playing in bands, reading books and magazines in camp libraries, publishing camp newspapers, or just socializing.

While the daily CCC routine provided discipline, training, and structure for enrollees, there was still time for recreation and relaxation. Canteens sold candy and tobacco. Some camps had halls where enrollees played cards, board games, table tennis, and billiards. Enrollees sang along as some played their guitars or the camp's piano. They wrote letters home, got a haircut, read *Life Magazine* or *National Geographic* in the camp library, or listened to news and music on the radio. Others escaped such evening activities by hiding out in cars in nearby woods or sneaking out to buy alcohol from local bootleggers.

On weekends when they did not need to finish a work project, the companies held barbeques and sporting contests. Enrollees competed at softball, boxing, baseball, track, and tennis. Camp teams played one another in the region and in district-wide tournaments. Coached by a company officer who had played with the Chicago Bears, Civilian Conservation Corps Company 854 working at Blanco State Park in 1933 had an excellent football team that traveled around Texas for matches with other CCC camps.[30]

Members of Civilian Conservation Corps Company 3804 spending their leisure time shooting pool and playing cards, table tennis, and the piano in the recreation hall at Cleburne State Park, ca. 1930s. Courtesy of the National Archives and Records Administration, College Park, Maryland.

Civilian Conservation Corps Company 849 posing for a photograph of an archetypal construction feat at Lake Brownwood State Park, ca. 1937. Above them is the lookout shelter atop the stairway; below, the pier to the lake. Courtesy of the National Archives and Records Administration, College Park, Maryland.

Enrollees also competed at less physically strenuous games like spelling bees and arithmetic contests and matched skills with one another in extemporaneous speeches, typewriting, and first-aid ability.

Enrollees could read *Happy Days*, the national journal of the Civilian Conservation Corps, or *Chips*, the official information bulletin of the district headquartered at Fort Sam Houston, or *The Roundup* newsletter, which served parks in West Texas. Many camps also chose to produce their own company newspaper and read about workmates and friends. Stories focused on camp antics and achievements, highlighting athletic victories of enrollees and teams. Almost a hundred camp newsletters were produced across Texas, ranging from *The Windy Rim* published in Canyon to *The Mosquito* published in Karnack. The newsletters provided interesting and entertaining glimpses of life in the camps and promoted feelings of community. There were articles about work, healthcare, education, athletics, social events, religion, and the local community.

One enrollee summarized the whole of his time in the Civilian Conservation Corps, including not only his job experience but also "soft skills" he acquired by virtue of living among fellow "CCCers": "It's been invaluable to me throughout my life. I learned to work. I grew up into manhood in there. I learned how to associate with people, work with them, plan with them, play with them. Not all was hard work. It has been invaluable to me, like I said. We were not as regimented there as we were in the military later. It was a more pleasurable time."[31]

## Civilian Conservation Corps Camps and Local Communities

As zealous as members of some Texas communities were to obtain a Civilian Conservation Corps camp, community members were often suspicious of outsiders coming into their locales. But where positive relationships were developed between a camp and a local community, a camp's success was assured. By buying supplies from merchants and

Dance at a Civilian Conservation Corps camp, 1933. Residents from the adjacent town were invited, and local bands provided entertainment. Courtesy of the National Archives and Records Administration, College Park, Maryland.

spending their discretionary $5 per month on goods and recreation in town, camps and enrollees became part of local economies.

Many Texans welcomed enrollees into their homes, hosted events for camps, and donated books to camp libraries. Local church members embraced enrollees who attended worship services, and churches were places where enrollees met and mingled with community residents. Enrollees' church attendance lessened the concerns of local citizens, who were wary about the strangers in their midst. Churchgoing enrollees were well aware this was one way to gain acceptance by the local community.

Enrollees no doubt had other sorts of mingling in mind, too, when it came to going to town or church. "They had a café," one camp worker explained. "They had a service station. They had a general merchandise store with a fountain in it, where you could get fountain cokes, ice cream sodas, things like that. The main thing they had was a bumper crop of girls." The churches in town held special appeal:

All these girls went to church. So us boys who courted these girls went to church. They didn't have church every Sunday at each church. We'd go to the First Christian church one Sunday. We'd go to the Baptist church the next Sunday. We'd go to the Methodist church next Sunday. Every once in a while, the holy rollers would come around, pitch a tent, and have a tent revival. We'd go to that.[32]

CCC CO. 888 WECHES TEXAS OCT. 1934
1st. Lt. J. R. Secker Jr. ← CAPT. HERMAN H. SPOEDE COM'D'G. → 1st. Lt. M. M. Dornaudt Med.
MR. HARRY LONG SUPT.

Enrollees attended community dances and patronized local theaters. At Daingerfield and elsewhere, CCC trucks transported local women to the camps for dances that sometimes lasted until well after midnight before the trucks returned the women to town. Town residents were often invited to attend entertainments, watch events like boxing and wrestling matches, or see movies at the camp. Not surprisingly, some enrollees eventually married women living in the local communities, as did some officers.

## Discrimination

The experiences of African Americans and Mexican Americans in the camps also involved long workdays and three daily meals, but sometimes their work assignments and recreational activities differed from those of White enrollees. The differences are captured in anecdotal evidence of racial discrimination within Civilian Conservation Corps companies and camps.[33] Stories survive of racist remarks made by Army officers and Forest Service personnel, for example, and if the victims complained about discriminatory incidents, they risked being ignored, disciplined, or transferred. In some instances where African American enrollees found their situations intolerable, they responded by refusing to work and deserting the camps. Photographs showing Black enrollees posing separately from White enrollees, wearing different uniforms, and huddled far from where officers and mascots were located testify to tense race relations.

Approximately 250,000 African Americans served in the Civilian Conservation Corps nationwide, and an estimated five thousand did so in Texas, where there were twenty-three CCC companies consisting solely of African Americans. Two of those companies were composed of World War I veterans. When it was conceived, the CCC was intended to be a fully integrated organization, and it had the goal of enlisting African Americans as 10 percent of all enrollees, a proportion that matched that of African Americans in the general population at the time. This ignored the fact that unemployment and impoverishment among Black men were twice the levels of White Americans.

For all its progressive accomplishments, the CCC could not escape its cultural milieu, and in 1935, it was forced to bow to social pressures and segregate its companies of enrollees. Even in integrated companies, African American enrollees were often assigned humble tasks preparing meals in kitchens or serving them to others in dining rooms, similar to the assignments of African Americans in the US military. It was also a practice to exclude African Americans from educational and other special programs.

Even before the CCC instituted a policy of segregating Black and White companies, some sought subversive ways to make that happen. One state's relief administrator proposed that by assigning African Americans to kitchen duty, they would necessarily eat apart from those whom they served and thus remain segregated from White enrollees.

The men of Civilian Conservation Corps Company 3807(C) preparing the dam site on the Navasota River to create a lake for Fort Parker State Park, 1935. Considered particularly suited for intense labor requiring little training, Black workers were supervised by White bosses. Courtesy of the Texas Parks and Wildlife Department, Austin, Texas.

After 1935, African Americans in the Civilian Conservation Corps nationwide were usually placed in segregated companies, where they performed work identical to those in White companies—planting trees, fighting fires, constructing parks, and alleviating soil erosion—not relegated strictly to cooking meals and kitchen cleanup. To the extent that African Americans participated in all aspects of building parks, in Texas and elsewhere, they did so prevailingly in Black companies. Yet even in those companies, they were not allowed to serve in most supervisory positions.

In Texas, some Black companies encountered vociferous local community opposition to their arrival, and this forced companies to relocate to areas of the state less opposed to their presence. For example, Company 1823 (CV), a unit for "colored veterans," was forced to move from its initial assignment at Sweetwater's municipal park because of local protest about a group of mature Black men being in town. Originally an integrated company of two hundred Whites and twelve Blacks, all of them WWI veterans, Company 1823 (V) became Company 1823 (CV) when CCC Director Fechner mandated segregated units as national policy, bowing to the Southern states. Abilene was the first to embrace Company 1823 (CV) by recognizing the enrollees' construction skills and welcoming the company's musical talent at local events. The men likewise enjoyed Abilene's movie theaters, concerts, and other entertainments. Later, other towns like Kerrville, Ottine near Gonzales, and Huntsville greeted a Black company as the means to gain a park, and, ultimately, exclusively Black CCC companies contributed importantly to building Palo Duro, Abilene, Daingerfield, Palmetto, Goose Island, and Fort Parker, as well as other parks.

For Mexican American enrollees, situations varied. Some classes were taught in Spanish, as was a 1934 first aid class for Company 879 at Fort Davis (Davis Mountains State Park) because Spanish-speaking members comprised more than half of the company. In February 1940, three quarters of Civilian Conservation Corps enrollees building a park at Garner were Mexican Americans. But while Whites and Mexican Americans worked side by side at Garner, they lived in segregated barracks and socialized in separate circles. One former White enrollee at Garner recalled, "If they had a dance, the Whites stayed away. If the Whites had a dance, the Mexicans stayed away." Another White enrollee recollected Mexican American company leaders keeping "their" enrollees "in line," citing an occasion when some "stuck their heads" into a White dance and a Mexican American leader came to get "hold of them." In a time when interracial marriage was scorned and illegal in many states, racial distinctions clearly existed in the CCC.

Thanks to John Collier, whom Roosevelt appointed as commissioner of the Bureau of Indian Affairs, the US Congress created the Indian Emergency Conservation Program, a CCC program for reservations. Initially, fourteen thousand enrollees lived and worked at reservations, primarily in New Mexico and Arizona, and between 1933 and 1942, some eighty-five thousand Native Americans were in the CCC. The Public Works Administration, Works Progress Administration, and National Youth Administration also hired Native Americans due to Collier and other reformers' efforts.

Discouraged historically from joining the paid workforce, women during the Depression struggled to support themselves and their families. They were excluded from joining the Civilian Conservation Corps as it was originally conceived by President Roosevelt. But concerned by the program's gender inequality, women's rights activist and First Lady Eleanor Roosevelt proposed the creation of camps focused on education and the environment for unemployed young women. She brushed aside the phrase "She-She-She Camps" and worked with Secretary of Labor Frances Perkins, the nation's first female cabinet member, to establish Camp Tera in New York in 1934. Around the country, existing facilities were used to house some 8,500 women at ninety residential camps, where young women generally took education courses and did public service for six to eight weeks, but its curriculum and goals were vague. The small-scale effort was also short-lived.[34]

It may be tempting to conclude that because the Civilian Conservation Corps enrolled only men, women played no role in or were absent from the building of Texas state parks during the 1920s, 1930s, and early 1940s. Yet appointments to the first State Parks Board included Florence George Martin from Dallas, who served as the first vice chair of the board; Phebe Kerrick Warner from Claude as its secretary and statistician; and Katie Owens Welder from Victoria as its historian. The appointments extended into the 1930s. Hired as "stenographers," women worked as clerical and administrative employees for the State Parks Board. In the field, women accompanied husbands who

Louise Sellers posing in front of the Balmorhea State Park bathhouse and facing the pool during a rare February snowstorm, 1937. Courtesy of the John Dunbar Sellers Collection, Texas Parks and Wildlife Department, Austin, Texas.

worked for the Army or who were National Park Service and board inspectors. Ruby Lee Bone lived with her husband, Norfleet, and their two children at unfinished Buescher State Park while he collaborated on its landscape design and development. Louise Sellers, a bride from big-city Dallas, married and soon ended up in Balmorhea, population five hundred (which some said included cattle), when her Army Reserve groom was assigned to operate the camp. Proud of her trousseau, Sellers recalled nighttime trips to the outhouse in her negligee and days when dust storms blew over the flat plain. A neighbor gave the newlywed some perspective and admonished her not to fear, "They're gonna bury you in that dust one of these days."[35] At least one woman served as superintendent when the male superintendent was relieved of his position at Caddo Lake State Park. Other intrepid women joined superintendent husbands at parks and lived in buildings still under construction. Later, some also stepped up to operate parks during their spouses' military service during World War II.

## Dissatisfactions

Not all of those who could enroll in or worked with the Civilian Conservation Corps were unequivocally happy to be involved. State Parks Board architects, landscape architects, and engineers in the camps were grateful for the paid work, but it was a relatively small sum compared to previous salaries in private practices. The work relief experience was generally not something about which they later boasted. Some Army cavalry soldiers, pulled away from what they loved and for which they had trained, did not enjoy their roles as caretakers of CCC enrollees.

In the camps, there was some danger, especially for enrollees working outside, sometimes in wilderness settings and at new tasks using unfamiliar equipment. Injuries happened as men moved rocks, felled trees, cut wood, drove vehicles, and operated machines. They received safety training, and Locally Experienced Men (LEMs) supervised their work, yet the CCC safety office reported injuries and even deaths.[36]

There were garden-variety complaints from those living in new surroundings—the food was not satisfactory; some of the men did not get along; the regimen was insufferable; and the like. More than a few enrollees were just plain homesick in spite of camp facilities and activities. They resented Civilian Conservation Corps work practices and camp discipline as harsh and unjust.[37] Homesickness and resentment contributed to desertions. For some, the CCC was not a worthwhile experience, and they fled it as soon as they could. But available evidence clearly indicates that for the great majority of enrollees, the CCC was a home away from home and a solution to grave financial hardship.

Outside the camps, there was dissatisfaction when local community members expressed disappointment that "they didn't finish our park." Shortages of gasoline, tires, and other commodities in the year or so before 1942 dogged park development. Building supplies were scarce or at a premium, and the war swept many supervisors and artisans into the military. As Americans, Texans understood the call of national defense, but residents of some communities still felt that promises to construct nearby parks had been broken. They clamored for completing a dam, lake, cabins, picnic tables, trails, or park roads that had been promised before war erupted.

Some South Texas and Hill Country residents wanted all twenty-six of the cabins planned for Garner State Park to be finished because when the war began, only fourteen had been completed. Elsewhere, some local residents thought progress building nearby parks was insufficient and demanded that land donated for them be returned to the donors. A proviso attached to the donation of land at Possum Kingdom called for returning the land to the Brazos River Conservation and Reclamation District if the National Park Service and State Parks Board failed to initiate park construction. A Civilian Conservation Corps camp had been established there in May 1941, and it remained active until July 1942, although that was too little time to realize the full-blown master plan and satisfy all park enthusiasts. As at Fort Griffin and Inks Lake, other parks with approved camps and companies got too late a start or had to stop before implementing the original park plans fully. Communities across Texas regarded plans for nearby parks as assets that had been promised but not delivered, and they sometimes did not fully appreciate the wartime exigencies responsible for their disappointments.

## Abrasions

Between the two major entities collaborating on state parks in Texas—the State Parks Board and the National Park Service—there were continuing abrasions that had plagued their partnership from the beginning. The board manifested its relatively weak status in the state government by its lack of an office, which reflected its lack of state funding. It had initially situated itself in San Antonio's Bedell Building at 116 Broadway before moving to Burnet in 1932 to be near the major work taking place at Longhorn Cavern. By the time the National Park Service arrived the following year, the board had set up a small shop in Committee Room 7 in the Capitol's House of Representatives. Later, it shifted to a senate room until it ended up in the rotunda of the Capitol on the third floor.

Not until 1936 were the State Parks Board, National Park Service procurement staff, and National Park Service inspector's office together in a space inside the Texas Game, Fish and Oyster Commission in the Walton Building in downtown Austin. Finally in 1937, the State Parks Board and National Park Service office staff found a home at 106 East Thirteenth Street overlooking the northeast Capitol grounds.[38] The irony that the board, responsible for determining park locations around the entire state of Texas and securing state ownership of park sites, could not even secure a long-term office space until 1937 was not lost on those involved.

The disparate locations of staff and workers made the coordination process bumpy. Communications about disputed deeds, differences of opinion about the merits of park sites, conflicting ideas about design, inevitable modifications, and lack of clarity about roles heightened tensions. The State Parks Board frequently complained about the National Park Service's tendency to plan parks without board input, instancing both the design of state parks and the National Park Service's collaborations with entities like counties and municipalities to construct parks that lay beyond the board's purview.

From the beginning, the National Park Service had been frustrated by the lack of state resources to justify federal investment in Texas state parks, a frustration first expressed by Herbert Maier in 1933, when he learned that the State Parks Board had no office, no employees, and essentially no budget. The mismatch of federal and state resources continued until it reached a tipping point in June 1934 at a late-night meeting in Waco of the board and the newly promoted chief inspector for Texas, George Nason. When the board complained to ECW District III Director Herbert Maier about Nason, the inspector requested a meeting. At issue were Nason's habits of transferring or removing superintendents at parks, telling park personnel that he was the one to whom they should listen rather than the board, chastising park superintendents for failing to properly credit the National Park Service in park publicity, and making decisions without consulting the board. Although diplomatic, Nason addressed each complaint and added his disappointments about a range of issues concerning the board: superintendents whom he thought ill-suited for the job, all-too-rare opportunities to meet with the board, and the paucity of "technical men" hired, which required district office designers to work beyond plan reviews.

Nason saved his last criticism as the most important: "I have hoped of solving the one thing that I believe is causing more trouble in Texas than any thing [sic] else, and that is the lack of a central office."[39] Nason had figured that a small amount of the Texas legislature's special allotment of $25,000 could be spent for that purpose, unaware that it was all the serious money the State Parks Board had ever received and that it was being spent on board expenses such as equipment and travel. Several times during the Waco meeting, Nason repeated that the federal government was spending $200,000 per month on parks in Texas, and he clearly hoped that he could convince board members to

offer more resources so that the National Park Service would not cut the number of park projects in Texas as it had threatened to do. The need for a central office, both Nason and Colp agreed, would allow decision-making in a streamlined manner, with consensus among the parties. Without a central office, progress was splintered and too much decision-making was taking place on the spot and in the field.

Log veneer cabins at Caddo Lake State Park, which used the natural materials abundant in the Texas Pineywoods and mirrored the region's vernacular architecture, 2001. Courtesy of the Texas Parks and Wildlife Department, Austin, Texas.

## The Works Progress Administration and the National Youth Administration

The preponderance of park construction in Texas was accomplished by Civilian Conservation Corps enrollees under the direction of the National Park Service, but other New Deal agencies contributed significantly to the parks story in Texas. In 1936, these agencies were on view together at the Centennial of Texas Independence, which was celebrated at the Art Deco buildings in Dallas's Fair Park. On the grounds of the exposition was one rustic cabin that was given over to these New Deal agencies and their complementary goals. The CCC, Works Progress Administration, and National Youth Administration created exhibits highlighting their work and accomplishments, and representatives from each agency took turns staffing the exhibit.[40]

The agencies crossed paths in a number of ways besides on the centennial grounds. Created in spring 1935 during what has been referred to as the Second New Deal, the Works Progress Administration and National Youth Administration (which was under

Franklin D. Roosevelt shaking hands with a young Lyndon B. Johnson in Galveston, Texas, May 12, 1937. Texas Governor James Allred stands with the president and the newly elected Texas congressman. Courtesy of Wikimedia Commons.

Early mill building at Bastrop State Park, ca. 1930s. The building served as a carpentry shop where Civilian Conservation Corps enrollees fashioned furniture, architectural decoration, and even boats. Courtesy of the Texas Parks and Wildlife Department, Austin, Texas.

the WPA at first) were part of Roosevelt's escalating determination to expand assistance to those who continued to suffer unemployment, an unstable economy, and effects of the Dust Bowl. The agencies helped him achieve this by prioritizing work relief programs over direct relief. The WPA undertook much-needed public works construction projects such as bridge and school building. Frequently, counties applied for its funds to complete projects in their areas. Under the guidance of engineers and other professionals, local unemployed men were hired to do such work and thus did not live in distant camps like Civilian Conservation Corps enrollees did. Some of these men were skilled, some not, but all had been certified by the local welfare office as needing work.[41] When National Park Service park planners disallowed swimming pools and frowned on golf courses being built by the CCC, WPA labor constructed pools and built fairways within state parks.[42] The WPA gave Bastrop State Park its swimming pool and worked on its golf course. At Caddo Lake State Park, landscape architect Norfleet Bone required CCC enrollees to build their barracks by using half-cut logs, calculating that the logs could be used later for cabin veneers, and it was the WPA that finished the cabin work.

Like the Civilian Conservation Corps, the National Youth Administration promoted work projects and jobs for youth ages eighteen to twenty-five who were attending (or had dropped out of) high school or college. It was somewhat more accepting of diverse groups, including women and men, whether Black, White, or Brown. The NYA worked through local school programs and emphasized vocational education while providing pay for after-school jobs. Some youth worked on NYA construction and maintenance projects, but they also had jobs in schools and libraries. Lyndon Johnson led the NYA in Texas from 1935 to 1937 and worked with local committees around the state to make it as robust as possible. The agency also had resident training camps, where students stayed and worked for short periods of time, usually during summers.

A number of state parks hosted National Youth Administration students after the Civilian Conservation Corps vacated the facilities. At Bastrop State Park, for example, the NYA staffed the mill where workers made furniture, and they occupied the old CCC barracks. When suspected spontaneous combustion burned the building down, the NYA rebuilt the warehouse and mill and fitted it out with machinery needed to resume work. Occupying CCC-built facilities at Mother Neff State Park, a group of NYA girls from Temple cleared campsites, buildings, and grounds and constructed several simple cottages for the park to rent.[43] Near Longhorn Cavern and Inks Lake state parks, the NYA constructed a federal fish hatchery to provide fish for lakes created by the Public Works Administration's damming of the Colorado River. After completion of that project in 1940, the NYA camp was converted into the Inks Dam War Work Center, where young men and women could choose the type of skill they wanted to acquire and apply in their work: machine shop, radio, electrical, or sheet metal work, which were applicable to jobs in defense industries.

## World War II and the New Deal's End

Civilian Conservation Corps enrollees of Company 3803, 1940. Enrollees working at Fort Griffin State Park learned the basics of metalworking at nearby Albany Public High School. Courtesy of the National Archives and Records Administration, College Park, Maryland.

By the late 1930s, successes of the Civilian Conservation Corps were widely recognized, and there were attempts to turn it into a permanent federal agency. Nevertheless, the CCC faced tough questioning by some lawmakers, including some Texans who had supported Roosevelt's early New Deal programs. There was suspicion that some of the highly touted infrastructure projects could have been completed more efficiently with already trained local labor forces. Some lawmakers questioned why schools were not a better place to educate youth, despite the CCC's excellent educational programs. The recession of May 1937 to June 1938 exacerbated reluctance to make the CCC permanent, and it forced reductions of National Park Service personnel and camps. The indefinite future of the CCC as an organization plus budgetary and personnel reductions led to low morale in National Park Service and CCC camps and to desertions that shrank the numbers of persons working on national and state parks.

As the 1930s ended, the US turned its eyes to Europe, especially after Germany invaded western European countries in the spring of 1940. Although the US was largely isolationist following World War I and during the Depression, the deteriorating military situation in Europe was impossible to ignore. It became clear by the late 1930s that the US would need to mobilize industrial production to assist allies and protect itself.

As overall camp numbers slowly declined, Civilian Conservation Corps education programs began to emphasize subjects considered necessary to national defense, including basic engineering. Some CCC companies moved to military bases, where they constructed buildings, airfields, and artillery ranges. Defense industries and their need for workers grew steadily. Some reserve Army officers in charge of CCC camps were gradually withdrawn and put on active military duty; some experienced mechanics were lured away to work at high-paying defense jobs; and some enrollees had other job opportunities. These changes made CCC recruiting more difficult. Then in September 1940, Roosevelt signed the Selective Service Act, which required all males ages twenty-one to forty-five to register for military service.

Despite those developments, CCC camps in Texas remained intact at Lake Brownwood, Garner, Goliad, Fort Parker, Tyler, Huntsville, Fort Griffin, and Inks Lake State Parks during late 1940 and early 1941. In late 1941, with the exception of Goliad, Tyler, and Garner, CCC camps continued at these parks, while a camp at Possum Kingdom State Park was added, albeit with less than the full complement of a two-hundred-man company.[44] Perhaps to acknowledge continued federal support and to try to be accommodating, the State Parks Board assured the War Department in Washington that park buildings and facilities in Texas would be made available for military use. Governor W. Lee O'Daniel welcomed the board's offer and turned several parks over to the military to use as training camps.[45] The military soon requested permission to use still other parks for temporary troop staging areas and for rest and recreation.

When the Japanese bombed Pearl Harbor on December 7, 1941, the Texas State Parks Board was holding its quarterly meeting in Fort Worth. Its agenda was filled with reports about the Special Park Fund, updates on remaining projects at CCC parks, and news of the Big Bend Land Purchase Program. It had recently recognized the likelihood

Postcard of Bastrop State Park swimming pool, 1941. Soldier Bill Walters enjoyed relaxing at the pool during maneuvers and later mailed this postcard to his mother in Ruston, Louisiana. By the time he posted it on November 5, 1941, from Camp Hulen near Palacios, the weather had chilled. He wrote, "We're out in the field on more war games. Brrrr! It is cold!" Courtesy of the Texas Parks and Wildlife Department, Austin, Texas.

Lockhart State Park refectory, 1935. Having already completed the waney edge cladding of the refectory, enrollees prepare the roof for wooden shingles. Courtesy of the Texas Parks and Wildlife Department, Austin, Texas.

of losing CCC camps, but it was still hopeful that the Works Progress Administration could be enlisted for continued state parks support. By the end of December, the National Park Service had terminated all CCC projects not relating to the war effort, so only eighty-nine camps were operating nationwide by the start of 1942. Of these, just nine were in state park areas, and two of those remained in Texas—Huntsville and Possum Kingdom. The CCC itself was terminated before the dam at Huntsville State Park could be stabilized and before Possum Kingdom State Park could be completed. With Congress debating appropriations, Roosevelt argued for funding an extension of the CCC, but Congress defied him and funded only $8 million to cover costs of closing the CCC and ending it on July 2, 1942.[46]

**ABOVE**

Longhorn Cavern State Park administration building, ca. 1934–1938, Charles S. P. Vosper and George Walling, designers. Built with limestone dug from the cavern, the structure's interior features quartz details. Courtesy of the Texas Parks and Wildlife Department, Austin, Texas.

**LEFT**

Red sandstone arches at the Abilene State Park refectory, 2008. Courtesy of John B. Chandler, Texas Parks and Wildlife Department, Austin, Texas.

## A State Parks
## System to Admire

Picnic table at Blanco State Park, ca. 1933–1934. The table stretches seventy feet in length, and its concrete top rests on waist-high masonry pedestals. The bench seats that completely surround the table were constructed of stone, as was the nearby fireplace. Courtesy of the Texas Parks and Wildlife Department, Austin, Texas.

Before the Civilian Conservation Corps left Texas, it had fundamentally changed the landscape of Texas by emphasizing some of the state's natural resources in inspiring buildings and features at scenic destinations. For example, vibrant red sandstone formed the Romanesque arches of Abilene State Park's signature concession building. Locally harvested timber provided the material for Lockhart and Bastrop State Parks. Thatches of palmetto leaves comprised the roof of the remarkable refectory at Palmetto State Park. Locally quarried limestone, plentiful in some areas of Texas, shaped building walls and

**ABOVE**
Masterful use of materials for a retaining
wall and culvert at Bastrop State Park, 1933.
Courtesy of the National Archives and Records
Administration, College Park, Maryland.

**LEFT**
Stone façade of the interpretive center at Palo
Duro Canyon State Park, ca. 1930s. Originally
known as the Coronado Lodge, the center was
designed to mimic the canyon wall. Courtesy of
the National Archives and Records Administration, College Park, Maryland.

Indian Lodge just after completion of construction and before painting, 1935. Built of native clay formed into adobe bricks, the lodge blended almost seamlessly into the landscape of Big Bend. Courtesy of the Archives of the Big Bend, Alpine, Texas.

other features at Blanco and Longhorn Cavern State Parks. To avoid buildings being humdrum, designers produced imaginative combinations of locally available materials such as stone and wood at Bastrop State Park—but stone and adobe at Indian Lodge at Davis Mountains State Park.

Sometimes, park visitors must look twice to discern what is natural and what is built, so unobtrusive are the constructions. Designers and planners worked hard to select locations where buildings and structures would appear to be a simple extension of the ground on which they sat. Thus, cabins and shelters at Bastrop State Park seem to be part of a natural depression in the ground. Palo Duro Canyon State Park's interpretive center, originally designed as a lodge, perches on the canyon's rim and seems to be simply an extension of the cliff wall below it. Whether located at high or low elevations, park structures were systematically subordinated to the landscape and made it more interesting.

Ingenious visual and tactile blending extended to screening some park infrastructures. Designers kept complex mechanical and maintenance systems generally out of public view and, where possible, designed them according to the National Park Service aesthetic. To minimize intrusiveness, roadway designs limited speed and noise and allowed automobiles to glide through natural settings. Below and to the sides of park roads, stone-lined drainages and culverts were in harmony with the stone constructions of bridges. Walking trails meandered to scenic overlooks, with stone benches for viewing. At well-situated picnic areas, stone ovens and tables catered to hungry visitors.

When designing the parks, maintaining continuity with the past was as important as achieving continuity with landscapes. The National Park Service philosophy of architecture taught that park buildings should reflect the history and material culture of the local region. In heavily forested Northeast Texas, where log structures had dotted the

landscape during the nineteenth and early twentieth centuries, architects prescribed log buildings for Caddo Lake State Park. The design for Indian Lodge in Davis Mountains State Park drew inspiration from Native American pueblos in nearby New Mexico. At Goliad, National Park Service preservation architects and archaeologists, inspired by Southwestern mission architecture, guided CCC workers in the reconstruction of several buildings from the extensive ruins of the eighteenth-century Spanish Mission *Nuestra Señora del Espíritu Santo de Zúñiga*.

Given such achievements, it is remarkable that not all states welcomed the CCC in the manner that Texas did. In Idaho, for example, the CCC concentrated on fire suppression because of a spate of fires that had devastated the state's woodlands and forests.[47] California, having a surfeit of talented landscape architects and other design professionals, had less need for additional expertise than Texas had. In Oregon, park leaders preferred their nature untouched and park development kept light; the state's parks engineer, Samuel Boardman, agreed with critics who accused the CCC of prettifying nature when it needed to be preserved. He complained about National Park Service planners, whom he accused of liking "to hang the garland on the crag" and wanting to "festoon the stars and moon."[48] Texas was a different story. Spared widespread threats to forests and lacking both an abundance of landscape architects and animosity toward the design profession, elected state officials were eager, some downright greedy, for federal dollars

Custodian's cottage at Goliad State Park, ca. 1936–1937. Designed by Charles S. P. Vosper with Raiford Stripling, the building and grounds were used as an architectural studio and laboratory where designers experimented with restoration techniques. Thanks to a grant from the Texas Department of Transportation, the building is now part of El Camino de Los Tejas National Historic Trail and serves as a visitor center for area historic sites surrounding Goliad State Park and Historic Site operated by the Texas Parks and Wildlife Department. Courtesy of the Raiford Stripling Collection, Cushing Memorial Library and Archives, Texas A&M University, College Station, Texas.

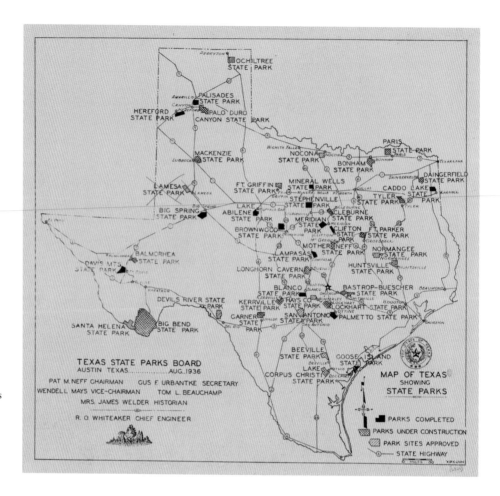

Map of completed and in-progress parks, approved park sites, and highways, August 1936. The drawing lists members of the Texas State Parks Board along with Chief Engineer R. O. Whiteaker. Courtesy of the Prints and Photographs Collection, Archives and Information Services Division, Texas State Library and Archives Commission, Austin, Texas.

to hire professionals that they could not.

Like many states in 1933, Texas was not geared to accept the number of workers and volume of resources that federal agencies brought to the state. During each of the nine-plus years of its life and the nineteen periods of work, Civilian Conservation Corps funding in Texas fluctuated, as did the number of camps, companies, and projects. But even in the leanest years, there was more development than could ever have been mustered by just the members of the State Parks Board working with the Texas legislature. When the CCC ended in 1942, the board could be proud of the distance it had traveled over many rocky roads.

Before the New Deal, the State Parks Board had followed a course plotted during 1920 road trips in which its members accumulated small acreages. With the influx of federal funds, the board could now boast of Big Bend State Park in the Davis Mountains, Palo Duro Canyon State Park in the Panhandle, Caddo Lake State Park in the Piney

Roadside park in Williamson County on US Highway 81, March 3, 1939. Roadside parks ranged from sites with a few amenities, such as this park that offered a chance to cook out, picnic, and camp, to those with only a small parcel of land. Courtesy of the Texas Department of Transportation, Austin, Texas.

Woods, Palmetto State Park as a tropical oasis near Austin, historic Goliad State Park along the San Antonio River, Bastrop State Park in the Lost Pines, Longhorn Cavern State Park carved from Hill Country limestone, and Lake Corpus Christi State Park in Texas's Coastal Bend. These and thirty-three other distinctive parks constructed during the New Deal transformed the nascent Texas parks system into a series of statewide destinations.

When Roosevelt created the nationwide Civilian Conservation Corps, he set in motion a string of events that resulted in some three billion trees being planted, more than three hundred thousand dams being built for erosion control, and 125,000 miles of roads completed. His multi-agency force had built more than 560 non-federal park areas, a whopping 10 percent of them in Texas.[49] In the process, the CCC, along with other New Deal agencies buttressed by the state's political heavyweights, gave the fledgling state parks system in Texas an undeniable solidity. This was an accomplishment to applaud at any time but especially during the Great Depression's rampant despair.

# Chapter 5

# War, Peace, Drought, and a War Within

A s with most major conflicts, World War II inspired national, state, and individual acts of generosity. In Texas, more visitors wanted to enjoy parks and natural areas. Servicemen and servicewomen led the way because they were given full and free access to their parks. In fact, Bastrop State Park hosted a picnic/barbeque for two thousand soldiers and their families. But close behind were all those Texans who did not go off to war but turned to state parks because, while they had good wages in their war-economy pockets, they were limited by rationing of gasoline and tires in what they could do with those dollars and where they could spend them. Vacationers turned to close-to-home state parks in increasing numbers. To ease the situation, many who owned cabins and houses in or near parks opened them freely to members of the armed forces. Another subgroup of visitors was the "CCC boys." During and after the war, many hastened to take their families and friends to see the forty-one parks they had helped build.[1] They were welcomed back with open arms—to a point. The influx of visitors aside, there were other problems with the parks, not least of which was the almost overnight disappearance in 1942 of the Civilian Conservation Corps/National Youth Administration and their infusion of federal dollars. All funds were reallocated to the war effort. So were the young men who were working in the parks. Many of the "CCC boys" went off to war. Many never returned.

The Gap, Big Bend National Park, 1943. This early photograph was taken not long before Big Bend became a national park. Courtesy of Curatorial Services, Texas Parks and Wildlife Department, Austin, Texas, 1997. 35.814.

Some parks were damaged by wartime usage, including cattle grazing and oil and gas leasing. Others, such as Longhorn Cavern State Park and Inks Lake, were caught in an ongoing feud with the powerful chairman of the State Board of Control, who had the idea of converting the abandoned Civilian Conservation Corps facilities into mental health treatment hospitals. Fortunately, saner minds and generosity prevailed.

For instance, Mr. and Mrs. Lloyd Bentsen Sr. of McAllen, parents of Lloyd Bentsen Jr.—future congressman, business leader, US senator, vice presidential candidate, and secretary of the Treasury—deeded over 764 acres in 1944 for a state park: the Bentsen-Rio Grande Valley State Park. The creation of parks moved forward.

In fact, the most significant occurrence in state parks history was the establishment of Big Bend National Park, Texas's first national park. In a reversal of the Yosemite transaction—a federal transfer of land to a state (California)—Texas, after years of advocating for a national park, was, at last, ready to transfer state land to the federal government for the purpose of creating Big Bend National Park.

**ABOVE**
Native American mortar at Chisos Basin, Big Bend area, 1936. Courtesy of Curatorial Services, Texas Parks and Wildlife Department, Austin, Texas, 1997.35.821.

**LEFT**
Visitors enjoying Easter Sunday in Bentsen-Rio Grande Valley State Park, 1962. The Bentsen family donated the land for the park around 1945. Courtesy of the Texas Parks and Wildlife Department, Austin, Texas.

Chisos Mountains, Big Bend area, 1935. Courtesy
of Curatorial Services, Texas Parks and Wildlife
Department, Austin, Texas, 1997.35.830.

Amon Carter delivering the deed of cession to
Big Bend to President Franklin Delano Roosevelt,
June 6, 1944 (D-day). Courtesy of the *Fort Worth
Star-Telegram* Collection, University of Texas
at Arlington Libraries, University of Texas at
Arlington, Arlington, Texas, AR406-6 Carter
Files 07/01/1964.

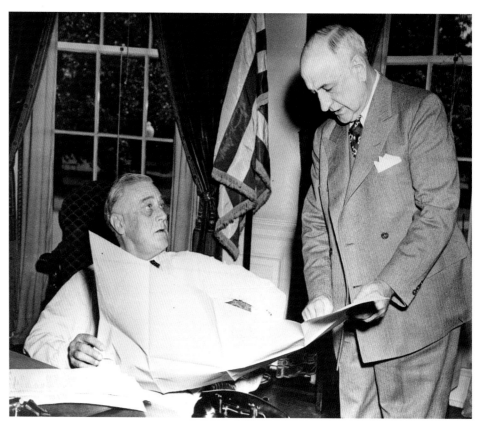

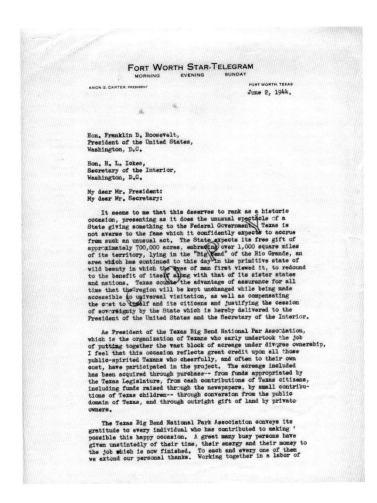

FORT WORTH STAR-TELEGRAM
MORNING    EVENING    SUNDAY

AMON G. CARTER, PRESIDENT                          FORT WORTH, TEXAS

June 2, 1944.

Hon. Franklin D. Roosevelt,
President of the United States,
Washington, D.C.

Hon. H. L. Ickes,
Secretary of the Interior,
Washington, D.C.

My dear Mr. President:
My dear Mr. Secretary:

It seems to me that this deserves to rank as a historic occasion, presenting as it does the unusual spectacle of a State giving something to the Federal Government. Texas is not averse to the fame which it confidently expects to accrue from such an unusual act. The State expects its free gift of approximately 700,000 acres, embracing over 1,000 square miles of its territory, lying in the "Big Bend" of the Rio Grande, an area which has continued to this day in the primitive state of wild beauty in which the eyes of man first viewed it, to redound to the benefit of itself along with that of its sister states and nations. Texas counts the advantage of assurance for all time that the region will be kept unchanged while being made accessible to universal visitation, as well as compensating the cost to itself and its citizens and justifying the cession of sovereignty by the State which is hereby delivered to the President of the United States and the Secretary of the Interior.

As President of the Texas Big Bend National Par Association, which is the organization of Texans who early undertook the job of putting together the vast block of acreage under divorse ownership, I feel that this occasion reflects great credit upon all those public-spirited Texans who cheerfully, and often to their own cost, have participated in the project. The acreage included has been acquired through purchase-- from funds appropriated by the Texas Legislature, from cash contributions of Texas citizens, including funds raised through the newspapers, by small contributions of Texas children-- through conversion from the public domain of Texas, and through outright gift of land by private owners.

The Texas Big Bend National Park Association conveys its gratitude to every individual who has contributed to making possible this happy occasion. A great many busy persons have given unstintedly of their time, their energy and their money to the job which is now finished. To each and every one of them we extend our personal thanks. Working together in a labor of

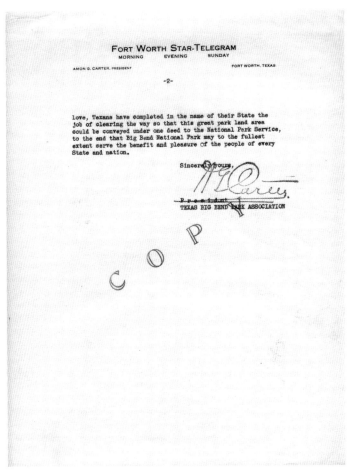

FORT WORTH STAR-TELEGRAM
MORNING    EVENING    SUNDAY

AMON G. CARTER, PRESIDENT                          FORT WORTH, TEXAS

-2-

love, Texans have completed in the name of their State the job of clearing the way so that this great park land area could be conveyed under one deed to the National Park Service, to the end that Big Bend National Park may to the fullest extent serve the benefit and pleasure of the people of every State and nation.

Sincerely yours,

W G Carter.

President,
TEXAS BIG BEND PARK ASSOCIATION

COPY

What further distinguishes this transfer is that it occurred on the day of the greatest battle for democracy in World War II: June 6, 1944, D-day.

Because that massive invasion raged all day and into the next several weeks, few noticed that Amon G. Carter Sr. of Fort Worth, Texas, a leader in the Big Bend movement for national park status, delivered the deed of cession during a personal meeting with President Franklin Delano Roosevelt (a dear friend) in Washington, DC.

A deed of cession (or cession deed) is used by a government agency to transfer property rights to another government authority. In this case, the State of Texas conveyed Big Bend State Park property rights to the federal government so that, on official acceptance, it could reopen as Big Bend National Park.

It should be noted that Carter and his newspaper, the *Fort Worth Star-Telegram*, were staunch supporters of parks before, during, and after the championing of the Big Bend effort and have remained so up to and including the Texas constitutional amendment that secured permanent funding for Texas parks in 2019.

**ABOVE**
Letter to President Franklin D. Roosevelt and Secretary of the Interior Harold Ickes, June 2, 1944. Signed by Amon G. Carter, president of the Texas Big Bend Park Association, the letter conveyed the deed of cession to transfer Big Bend State Park to the National Park Service and was delivered in person to Roosevelt on June 6, 1944. Courtesy of the Amon G. Carter Sr. Collection, Mary Couts Burnett Library Special Collections, Texas Christian University, Fort Worth, Texas.

*Fort Worth Star-Telegram* article about the Big Bend transfer, June 7, 1944. Courtesy of the *Fort Worth Star-Telegram*, McClatchy.

Again, as was the case with Abraham Lincoln's transfer of what would become Yosemite National Park in the midst of the Civil War in 1864 and Woodrow Wilson's signature establishing the National Park Service in 1916 in the looming shadow of World War I, the conservation of America's supreme landscapes would continue to be an ongoing part of America's "essential democracy" legacy, even in the worst of times.

What was not recognized on that day (there was no possible way to know) was that in the darkness before the dawn of D-day lay one of the last dreadnought ships—the Battleship *Texas*—whose thunderous guns would pound the enemy as it had during World War I, thus affording it the honor of serving in both world wars. In doing so, a future centerpiece of the Texas state parks system would survive World War II and arrive in 1948 to be dedicated in a berth near Houston at the Battleship *Texas* Historic Site.

Unfortunately, the saltwater elements at the Texas Parks and Wildlife Department berth in LaPorte, Texas, along with sporadic and inadequate legislative funding, has done what no enemy guns could do—cause irreparable damage of rust and rot that has put the great ship in danger of sinking in the not-too-distant future.

Damage to the Battleship *Texas*, 2022. Courtesy of Leroy Williamson, Texas Parks and Wildlife Department, Austin, Texas.

The Battleship *Texas* in a repair dock for damage inspection, 2022. Courtesy of Leroy Williamson, Texas Parks and Wildlife Department, Austin, Texas.

St. Helena Canyon, Big Bend area, 1935. Courtesy of Curatorial Services, Texas Parks and Wildlife Department, Austin, Texas, 1997.35.836.

Timaja Reed Plateau, Terlingua, Big Bend area, 1936. Courtesy of Curatorial Services, Texas Parks and Wildlife Department, Austin, Texas, 1997.35.820.

In 2020, in a last-ditch effort to save the Battleship *Texas*, the legislature authorized a memorandum of understanding between the Texas Parks and Wildlife Department and the nonprofit Battleship *Texas* Foundation transferring operational control of the ship to the foundation. The foundation then contracted with Valkor LLC to manage the task of transporting and repairing the Battleship *Texas* and returning it to a location (to be determined) as its final designated docking location.

On October 27, 2021, the Battleship *Texas* Foundation announced it had signed a contract with Gulf Copper Corporation to float the battleship to a drydock in Galveston and make repairs.

**ABOVE AND RIGHT**
Big Bend National Park, 2018. Photos by
George Bristol, author's collection.

# Big Bend: Texas's First National Park

As recounted in John Jameson's well-regarded history of Big Bend National Park, *The Story of Big Bend National Park*, according to local folklore, an old forgotten cowboy at the turn of the century gave directions to Big Bend by telling travelers to "go south from Fort Davis until you come to the place where rainbows wait for rain, and the big river is kept in a stone box, and water runs uphill. And the mountains float in the air, except at night when they go away to play with other mountains."[2] Decades later, Secretary of the Interior Stewart Udall described the "awesome, silent splendor of Big Bend," with its "spectacular mountain and desert scenery, the myriad of wildly improbable geological structures, all enclosed in the great bend of the Rio Grande," all of which "combine

Lady Bird Johnson and Stewart Udall arriving at Big Bend National Park, April 2, 1966. Courtesy of Robert L. Knudsen, White House Photo Office Collection, Lyndon Baines Johnson Presidential Library, Austin, Texas, C1628-2.

Davis Mountains State Park, 2010. Photo by George Bristol, author's collection.

to provide an unearthly sense of visiting another world."[3] Udall visited Big Bend National Park in April 1966 with Lady Bird Johnson to promote the "See America First" campaign and call attention to the fiftieth anniversary of the National Park Service.[4]

Big Bend is an appropriate inclusion in the Depression/Civilian Conservation Corps/World War II Texas story because it is all-encompassing: from the beginnings of the national and state parks movements; through Teddy Roosevelt's Bully Pulpit conservation charge; to Governor Pat Neff's call to create a state parks system; to David Colp (who should be measured by his strides, not his stumbles) for holding all the reins until the State Parks Board was awarded jurisdiction and funding for Texas during the Depression.

As the decade of the 1920s drew to a close and the black clouds of what was to become the Great Depression loomed just beyond the horizon, Texas was still without a national park or forest. It was not for lack of interest or influence.

Beginning in 1872, men like Frank Collinson, former Texas Ranger Everett E. Townsend, and Robert Hill began to write about and illustrate the unusual and ghostly beauty of the landscapes they encountered. Townsend went so far as to exclaim to have seen "God as [I] had never seen Him before" and vowed that "upon the arrival of my ship, I would buy the whole Chisos Mountains as a hunting and playground for myself and friends and that when no longer wanted I would give it to the State." Townsend's devotion to and love for this desert wilderness would grow into a lifetime commitment to seeing it become a national park. So great was his influence that somewhere along his historic journey, he was deemed "the father of Big Bend National Park."[5]

This drumbeat for a large park began to gather strength after the turn of the twentieth century, culminating in 1935 with congressional authorization on June 20 and concluding with the official establishment of Big Bend as the twenty-seventh national park on June 12, 1944.[6]

The years in between witnessed periods of stops and starts—but for the first twenty years, mainly stops—with one exception: the establishment of the State Parks Board in 1923, when the Texas legislature enacted Governor Pat Neff's parks proposal.

It must be noted again that the same legislature that created the State Parks Board failed to appropriate funds for land purchases or monies for development or repairs. This led to the lean years of denial and disappointment for Chairman Colp and the board

throughout the 1920s and early 1930s, with the exceptions of the 1927 legislation enabling the State Parks Board to accept twenty-three "small-park" donations and the 1931 concession deal for Longhorn Cavern State Park. Yet the same legislature passed, without consulting Colp, a bill authorizing the highway department to develop the Davis Mountains State Park Highway.[7] This was the legislative acceptance of the large-park advocates' position, in contradiction to the Neff/Colp small-park roadside concept (although both Neff and Colp would eventually come to support the "big park" concept).

It can't be stressed enough how great the suspicion was when it came to any relationship with the federal government pertaining to land ownership. However, the prospect of big tourist dollars flowing into the state, down its highways, and stopping off to trade with local merchants was enough to turn most skeptical heads.

As noted in chapter three, throughout the remainder of the 1920s, several large-park projects moved forward in some form or fashion without influence by or advocacy from the State Parks Board. These potential large parks included the Davis Mountains, Big Bend, Frio River, Palo Duro Canyon, and Caddo Lake.

Lighthouse Rock, Palo Duro Canyon State Park, 2010. Courtesy of Bryan Frazier, Texas Parks and Wildlife Department, Austin, Texas.

At some point in the largely failed years, David Colp perceived that large parks had a role to play and got behind the Palo Duro Canyon State Park project. It was about this time that men and women in leadership positions also began to advocate for a national park.

But it would be several years before Colp's and others' support would bear fruit.

In the interim (1927 to 1933), other events such as the 1928 Democratic National Convention in Houston and the impending centennial celebration of Texas's independence in 1936 drew widespread support and funding for historic sites, including San Jacinto Battleground State Historic Site and the Alamo. Through other-than-State Parks Board sponsorship, several historic sites moved to state park or potential state park status: Goliad State Park, Goose Island State Park, Caddo Lake, and a contract between the local landowners of Palo Duro Canyon and chamber of commerce to allow public access.[8] Even though these accomplishments by local committees shut out Colp and the State Parks Board, there was clearly a growing excitement across the state for more parks—big parks for a big state. Statewide pride had kicked in and overridden suspicion surrounding the concept of public lands for public recreation and renewal.

As discussed more in depth in chapter three, though disappointment after disappointment befell Colp, he appears not to have thrown up his hands in despair but continued to look for opportunities. Thanks to State Senator Margie Neal, a bill was passed in 1931 allowing for more concessions on donated state parklands.[9] This led to the creation of Longhorn Cavern State Park in 1933—Colp's single park success during the first decade of the State Parks Board's founding.

Though a small accomplishment in the scheme of things, the securing of the Longhorn Cavern deal in late 1932 and Pat Neff's dedication speech on Thanksgiving Day surely gave Colp and the other board members a boost—so much so that "little-park" David Colp threw most of his attention behind his new favorite project, Palo Duro Canyon. He did so with the hope of financing it with a loan from the newly created federal Reconstruction Finance Corporation.

But that prospect as well as others would take time, and more importantly, the inauguration of Franklin Delano Roosevelt in March 1933 would need to occur for the full force of his New Deal conservation programs to take place.

Nonetheless, the dawn of a new beginning for the State Parks Board and a state parks system was at hand for Texas, and it included action on projects such as Palo Duro Canyon and Big Bend.

But questions abounded, not least of which was whether one or more might gain national park status.

# Full Acceptance of the National and State Parks Concept

I have before me information based on actual experience of the National Park Service . . . It is estimated that the federal government would spend $225,000 annually for maintenance and protection of the park. Then projecting 120,000 out-of-state visitors spending an average of $4 per person per day over seven days, it would bring to the state $3,360,000 in expenditures every year. Not only would the park prove valuable from this standpoint, but it would add much enjoyment of citizens throughout the state.[10]

> TEXAS GOVERNOR W. LEE O'DANIEL
> *To the Texas legislature as lawmakers considered the economic impact of a bill appropriating funds for land purchase and conveyance of Big Bend to the federal government*
> 1939

From left, Ross A. Maxwell, superintendent of Big Bend National Park; Thomas Morse, president of the National Conference on State Parks; and Frank David Quinn, director of the Texas State Parks Board, October 11, 1950. Courtesy of the Texas State Parks Board Big Bend National Park Files, Prints and Photographs Collection, Archives and Information Services Division, Texas State Library and Archives Commission, Austin, Texas, 2005/147-2.

With this positive economic impact analysis coming from the governor and Texas House and Senate sponsors cleverly side-stepping any mention of state appropriations, the bill transferring Big Bend State Park to the federal government appeared to simply name the area "Big Bend National Park." This would also help continue to break down resistance to any public use/ownership of state lands.

Funding would come later.

In 1941, the traditionally miserly Texas legislature would appropriate $1.5 million for land purchases to meet the commitment Texas made to the National Park Service to secure national park status for Big Bend. They would need a person to make it all come together.

Perhaps not as well-known as Neff, Colp, or other park players, Frank David Quinn was, nonetheless, a significant factor in the well-being and expansion of the Texas parks system from 1939 until his death in 1971. His tenure would include a depression, a world war, the finalization of land purchases to seal the deal to create Big Bend National Park, and a financial recovery marred by segregation in the parks with a subsequent struggle to make things right. He was further confronted by a ruinous drought that stifled Texas throughout the 1950s. Quinn was appointed executive director of the State Parks Board in 1939, serving until 1945, at which time he resigned to enter private business. Even then, he remained a constant influence on the State Parks Board as a board member until 1961. He would also chair the National Conference on State Parks and bring its annual meeting to Bastrop State Park in the 1950s. In his final decade of life, with no official title, he worked tirelessly on state and local parks projects, specifically Bastrop and Buescher State Parks, and on the Parks and Recreation Board of the City of Austin.[11]

Like all other leaders of the parks movement, there were aspects of his youth and early career that shaped his life and prepared him to take on the growing parks system with all its attendant opportunities and headaches.

Frank Quinn was born in Mississippi in 1894. It seems his formal schooling ended in Tennessee in 1913, when he completed courses in shorthand and bookkeeping. He immediately took his training to work for L. K. Salsbury of the Delta Pine and Land Company, known as the "world's largest cotton planation." He would become manager, get married, and move to Tyler, Texas. Like many at that time, he would join the oil business—first in East Texas and then in the Seguin area of Central Texas. He would add to his sphere of influence by becoming president of the local chamber of commerce.[12] Standing in support of Quinn, apparently since early in his East Texas days, was Tom Beauchamp, who had Governor O'Daniel's ear on all manner of state affairs, including parks.

Of immediate concern upon taking office was the need to renegotiate new contracts with park concessionaires. With his business background and accounting training, Quinn knew exactly how to fashion contracts more favorable to the State Parks Board—85 percent to the board and 15 percent to the concessionaires—and he pushed them through in short order.[13] On a number of other fronts, Quinn brought a sense of reality and better system management practices to the fore.

Quinn was not averse to making deals with any and all agencies that had excess funding to help the State Parks Board bridge the financial gap created by the reduction in federal Civilian Conservation Corps allocations. Between 1939 and 1943, the agencies, with the support of Texas's powerful congressional delegation as well as growing support at the state level, would step outside Depression-dictated reliance on federal Civilian Conservation Corps appropriations.

From late 1939 into the war years of 1942 to 1945, there was less money to go around, even as the members of Civilian Conservation Corps camps remained in the camps. But there was money in the National Youth Administration account (thanks to former Texas Director Lyndon B. Johnson) for a number of projects involving parks. When the furniture shop at Bastrop State Park was abandoned by the National Park Service and the Civilian Conservation Corps, Quinn moved quickly to award furniture contracts from wood shops in Bowie, Vernon, and Wichita Falls for twenty sets of furniture to be delivered to Balmorhea State Park in deep West Texas. Recently elected Congressman Lyndon Johnson would then move to create a fifteen-hundred-student craft center at Inks Lake. Since Bastrop State Park's furniture shops were silent, they were put back to work as a residence center for the National Youth Administration.

This scheme of diversification first put into play by the Neff/Colp team was enhanced by Quinn and the State Parks Board, when they signed a major contract with the Texas Highway Department to complete maintenance work within the parks. That diversification process remains today. All park roads are designated as State of Texas roads and are funded by a separate parks road fund set aside as part of the Texas Department of Transportation's budget.

In August 1941, Quinn was given the largest—and probably most complex—task of his career: consolidating for purchase more than six hundred thousand acres of land necessary to fulfill the requirements and specifications of the National Park Service to create Big Bend National Park.[14]

In a wholly unexpected move, the Texas legislature appropriated $1.5 million to the State Parks Board for the creation of Big Bend National Park. By all accounts, Quinn seems to have carried out his mission with a fair but firm hand. Interestingly, he appeared to have spent little time in the Big Bend area and ran most of the land dealings from Austin.

The purchase project spanned from 1941 to 1942 and involved several sources before it was completed: first was a 158,960-acre purchase from state school land, then came purchases of foreclosed ranches and purchases made with federal drought funds, culminating with the 1941 state contribution of $1.5 million. There was finally enough land assembled to transfer 691,338 acres to the federal government, thereby formalizing the transformation from Big Bend State Park to Big Bend National Park.

By 1944, upon final completion of all the moving parts of the Big Bend National Park effort and the handing off of the mountainous landscape to the National Park Service, Quinn resigned to return to business, but he continued to keep his hand on the parks' pulse. He would remain active in parks matters until his death in 1971.

# Post-World War II and Drought

The war, for all its deaths and horrors, changed the face of Texas forever. Seemingly overnight, the state transformed from an agricultural powerhouse into an urban-industrial economic giant.

Population shift alone proves the point: in 1945, some five hundred thousand Texans left two hundred rural counties to join the wartime industrial workforce in the fifty-four urban counties. The 1950 census reported for the first time that more Texans lived in the city than in the country.[15]

Post-closure of a bridge on the Canadian River near Pampa that had become too dangerous to use, 1951. Drivers who took their chances crossing the dry river bed sometimes had to be hauled out by tow trucks. Courtesy of the Texas Highway Department Records, Prints and Photographs Collection, Archives and Information Services Division, Texas State Library and Archives Commission, Austin, Texas, 2002/101-70.

Farm population fell from 1.5 million in 1945 to 215,000 in 1980. By 2020, only 3 percent of Texans worked in agriculture and other industries tied to rural areas.

If the wartime and postwar lure of the cities didn't attract people, the drought years of the 1950s did.

Cities not only sprang upward but outward. Immigration not only came from the farms and rural Texas but from other states and across borders, principally from Mexico. By 1980, Mexican Americans became the largest minority group in Texas. Altogether, 82 percent of Texans lived in major cities. Three—Houston, Dallas, and San Antonio, with Austin closing fast—surpassed one million each.[16]

For all the growth in urban areas, there was always a sense of belonging in the outdoors. Even in a time of war, drought, and rural abandonment, millions of Texans felt the need to get out of the crowd and into the "out there"—into our state parks, which were among the most popular destinations. Just how popular—and necessary—they were was borne out in 2019, when 88 percent of Texans voiced positive approval for the Proposition 5 constitutional amendment that provided permanent funding for our state parks, and again from 2020 to 2021, when, in the jaws of the first wave of the pandemic, Texans rushed back to nature, buying all manner of sporting goods as they went.

Even though prosperity swept the nation after World War II, the 1950s were not kind to Texas or its parks. Texas has always been known for its repeated dry spells, but the drought of the 1950s was historic—and horrific. From 1950 (some say 1947) to 1957, Texas experienced the most severe drought ever recorded. Total rainfall was less than 40 percent of normal levels, and excessively high summer temperatures made the situation worse.

I don't remember the exact year—probably 1950 to 1951—but the sky in and around Weatherford, Texas, was so filled with blowing dust that midnight began at noon. The air was so thick and biting that my mother, brother David, and I had to lay out water-soaked towels and rags along the window seals and other cracks to ward off the chattering, pebbled assault.

We had no way of knowing that those dry winds, accompanied by the lack of rain and searing rise in temperature, would eventually produce a drought that spanned nearly a decade until torrential rains caused flooding along every river and stream in the state. By the time the rains (in partnership with hailstorms and tornadoes) came in early 1957, the drought was "the costliest and one of the most devastating droughts in six hundred years."[17]

Two hundred forty-four of 254 counties were under federal disaster relief. Seventy-five percent of Texas measured below-normal rainfall, and half the farming in Texas was gone—forever.[18] To add to the drought-caused damage, floods, hail, and a hurricane added $126 million to nature's devastating tab.

Towns and cities shared in the disaster. In 1952, Lubbock received not a drop of recorded rain. Lake Dallas fell to 11 percent of capacity. Most of the state's municipalities were under strict water rationing, and many had to truck in drinking water from Oklahoma.

The drought devastated lakes and reservoirs and, coupled with destruction from Hurricane Carla in 1961, caused serious damage to Texas state parks. At the same time, the parks were facing increasing numbers of visitors, fueled by the introduction of the interstate highway system and a higher standard of living that brought vacations within reach of the middle class.

Suddenly, facilities that were adequate in the 1930s were looking tired and unkempt. Yet in spite of the clear popularity of Texas's parks with the public, the legislature again failed to meet the demands of their constituencies. Their appropriations, coupled with

One of Lubbock's many water supply projects, 1956. In 1952, Lubbock did not record even a trace of rain. Courtesy of the Texas Highway Department Records, Prints and Photographs Collection, Archives and Information Services Division, Texas State Library and Archives Commission, Austin, Texas, 2002/101-83.

**ABOVE**
Monahans Sandhills State Park, 2010. Photo by
George Bristol, author's collection.

**RIGHT**
The author's grandsons at Monahans Sandhills
State Park, December 26, 2014. Photo by
George Bristol, author's collection.

revenue from various concessions, failed to meet expenses for operations and main-tenance, let alone for repairs and upgrades—certainly nothing for acquisition of new properties.

Ironically, in the middle of the drought (1953) and despite the lack of funding, a new state park was added—Monahans sandhills! Some cynics might question the appropri-ateness of adding a park composed of sand dunes in a state choked on dry, blowing dust, but its magnificent, mysterious beauty would far outweigh such considerations. Today, it is one of the jewel-box venues among the eighty-nine existing parks.

Several other new parks also came into existence during this time, including Hunts-ville State Park.

Not all was negative in the postwar/drought years of the late 1940s and 1950s.

In 1950, the Dingell-Johnson Act created a federal fund from a dedicated tax on fishing equipment, which financed construction and restoration of more than twelve hundred fishing venues and boat-launching facilities. This new money supplemented funds from the 1937 Pittman-Robertson Act, which financed a variety of programs cen-tered around wildlife conservation, operation of wildlife management areas in Texas, and hunting regulations.

To meet the challenge of future droughts, Texas created the Water Development Board in 1957. Its creation was coupled with an amendment to the Texas constitution that allowed issuance of $200 million in loans for conservation and development of wa-ter resources.[19]

By 1980, more than 126 major reservoirs had been created. Today, Texas has more surface area of lakes than any state except Minnesota. Fortunately, many of these reser-voirs would lend themselves to state park sites. If, and when, other reservoirs are built, adjacent parklands should be required to be set aside, with acreage and location compa-rable to the reservoir's size and shoreline.

## The War Within—
## The Stain of Segregation

Among the millions who had traveled the journey from the Great Depression through the hell of World War II to the postwar years, when Americans went about settling into more productive and tranquil lives—some were written out of the book of possibilities.

Minorities, in general—but African Americans, in particular—were stopped at the gates of the very landscapes that appeared to be dedicated to a mutual sharing among *all* citizens. The reality of deep-seated prejudice, partially ignored during the Depression and war, seemed to reappear at every entrance to Texas's state parks. To worsen the slight,

Bicycling at Brazos Bend State Park, November 7, 2020. Courtesy of Earl Nottingham, Texas Parks and Wildlife Department, Austin, Texas.

that denial also applied to returning Black veterans, some of whom had worked on Civilian Conservation Corps projects during the 1930s and early 1940s.

Natural settings of a public nature are the Creator's temples. No one should be turned away, especially for the color of one's skin, which is also the result of the Creator's handiwork.

It is not surprising—but sad, nonetheless—that as late as 2016, very few Black citizens of Cedar Hill, Texas, which is 65 percent Black, visited adjacent Cedar Hill State Park. That situation holds true in varying degrees in many of our national and state parks—in contrast to local city parks, which are filled to capacity on weekends and most holidays with patrons of all colors.

Why? That answer is multifaceted and complicated.

National and state parks avoidance, at its core, is best defined by Dr. KangJae "Jerry" Lee, assistant professor in the Department of Parks, Recreation and Tourism Management at North Carolina State University:

> How do you expect today's African Americans to appreciate [parks] if their parents couldn't appreciate them, their grandparents were not able to appreciate them. It's a socialization process. African Americans have had limited opportunity to develop a recreational culture. It is sort of a legacy of racial discrimination.[20]

Or to paraphrase Charles Jordan: "Why should an African American go out into the unfamiliar and set up a tent for the night next to someone who has a case of beer and might be looking to reignite the Civil War when he and his family could stay close to home and gather in a city park?"[21] Jordan would have known. He has been recognized nationally as the country's premier public parks visionary and has gained fame for his work as park director in Portland, Oregon, and Austin, Texas. He is also known worldwide for his leadership in engaging African Americans in the conservation movement. In Portland, he promoted forty-four new recreational facilities and natural areas, heavily involving Americans who happen to be Black.

But until President Lyndon Johnson's monumental passage of the Civil Rights Act of 1964 and the Voting Rights Act of 1965, Texas state parks were as segregated as the rest of Southern society.

Clearly, not all White people were (or are) segregationists. Some spoke out and tried to help change policy. But by the time of President Johnson's action, the hook had been set. Regardless of what the law of the land was (or is), Blacks did not trust their acceptance in the framework of something that should be more than just shared ownership—it should be a shared experience. That is too bad. Prejudice is so wasteful and belittling. Sunrises and waterfalls should be meant for all.

In the year of the establishment of the State Parks Board (1923), the Ku Klux Klan reared its ugly head again in Texas.[22] In 1922, Earl Bradford Mayfield, the Klan-endorsed candidate for the US Senate, was elected. In 1923, Klan-backed candidates took control of city governments in Dallas, Fort Worth, and Wichita Falls—and probably a majority of the Texas legislature in the thirty-eighth (1923) session.

All this is to say that any thoughts of public parks for *all* were shared by few and spoken by fewer from the outset of the Texas parks movement to the late 1960s.

But by then, the damage of history was done and lingers to this day. It is sad because many polls point to the fact that, even though use of state parks is not great among Blacks, they generally support the concept. This points to an opportunity: they would like to come if the comfort level could be raised.

To my mind, what primarily congealed Blacks' negative attitudes toward state parks were incidents involving the treatment of World War II veterans, some of whom not only fought for America but also worked with the Civilian Conservation Corps on Texas state parks, where they were denied entry upon returning home.

Such was the case of Millard Fillmore Rutherford, who labored on a Civilian Conservation Corps crew that restored Fort Parker and built the dam that created Lake Springfield. After his stint in the corps, Rutherford went off to war, returned, married, and took his bride to see the park he had so proudly helped restore and build. They were not allowed to enter.[23]

Denial of entry was not limited to East Texas or to African American citizens. Balmorhea State Park is located in deep West Texas in the foothills of the Davis Mountains off US Highway 10. Its main attraction is the San Solomon Springs (originally Mescalero Springs) that flow into a swimming pool area built by the Civilian Conservation Corps between 1936 and 1941. It is reported that on several occasions, Mexican Americans (perhaps some who had also served their country) were turned away from the cooling waters of the springs. This occurred in an area that is predominantly populated by Mexican Americans whose ancestors had lived in and farmed the area for centuries.

All aspects of segregation in our state parks system can be summarized in the progression of events that took place at Tyler State Park during the period of roughly 1930 to 1960.

Tyler State Park was a product of the Depression, created in 1934 in a partnership between all levels of government—city, county, state, and federal (as well as, I am certain, the chamber of commerce and other civic-minded groups). Its stated purpose was for "the pleasure, the benefit, and the recreation for the citizens of East Texas."[24] The

Young birder with a spotting scope, Resaca de la Palma State Park & World Birding Center, 2008. Courtesy of Earl Nottingham, Texas Parks and Wildlife Department, Austin, Texas.

Depiction of the segregation found at Tyler State Park, 2018. Until 1964, all state parks in Texas were segregated. Courtesy of the Texas Parks and Wildlife Department, Austin, Texas.

soon-apparent flaw was that the word "citizens" was not fully defined. It should have read, "except African Americans."

From the late 1930s forward, this essential right was requested by all manner of non-threatening organizations and individuals: Black 4-H clubs to Texas College in Tyler, a successful barber school owner, a White car dealer—even citizens who just wanted a place to fish. Such requests (and subsequent denials) continued throughout World War II. The war not only gave Blacks an opportunity to fight for their country, it also instilled in many the courage to stand and fight for those rights supposedly afforded to *all* citizens, including the right to share in the beauty and recreation derived from those taxpayer-built and -maintained facilities. By 1949, the denials had grown so ridiculous that state officials hoisted themselves on their own petards.

If the state insists on the luxury of segregation, it must also assume the burden of providing, *at any cost*, equal accommodations for the persons or groups "segregated." To fail to do so would surely lead to a lawsuit. On December 29, 1949, such a suit was filed to end segregation in Tyler State Park and all other Texas state parks. That suit was titled *T.R. Register, et al v. J.D. Sandefer, Jr., et al.* The federal judge hearing the case gave the state time to demonstrate "real effort to equalize park facilities for Whites and Negroes" during the upcoming special session in January 1950.[25]

The legislature promptly reaffirmed the segregation of state parks but declared that "separate facilities shall be furnished, and impartial provision shall be made for both races."[26] However (in a continuing tradition), no funds were appropriated for additional

Two friends fly fishing on a Texas river, May 13, 2021. Courtesy of Sonja Sommerfeld, Texas Parks and Wildlife Department, Austin, Texas.

facilities. Even when the State Parks Board developed a budget to upgrade parks to accommodate Blacks, the legislature again failed to appropriate the necessary funds.

However, the legal heat was on, and the state was running out of excuses. To blunt the critics, a state senate committee approved a separate area at Tyler State Park for Blacks, which had been recommended by the National Association for the Advancement of Colored People, along with two new Black state parks and parts of four others.

After a few adjustments, including a new road for Blacks to use, Tyler State Park was reopened with a separate (but hardly equal) facility on July 4, 1951. In their haste to comply, state officials failed to include any of the amenities—such as a bathhouse, beach, boathouse with equipment, dance hall, playground, wading pool, or miniature golf course—that the main area of the park enjoyed.[27] The new, paved road to the Black

From left, Jennifer L. Bristol, Rodney Franklin, and the author, 2018. Courtesy of Jennifer L. Bristol.

area was designed in such a way that Blacks wouldn't mix with Whites while passing through to their totally inadequate side of the lake.

Despite several state and federal lawsuits, none fell on the side of justice for African Americans. Even when the US Supreme Court ruled that places of public recreation must be opened to all, the State of Texas's answer was to raid the state offices of the National Association for the Advancement of Colored People. Intimidated, the National Association for the Advancement of Colored People was stripped of its dignity and much of its standing in the community.

Tyler State Park and others would remain segregated and unequal. Nothing constructive occurred until 1964, when a Texan, President Lyndon Johnson, pushed through the Civil Rights Act. At some point after its passage, the segregation signs were quietly removed, and the Black and White roads were connected. No ceremonies were held, and no notices were published in the local newspapers.

Tyler State Park was finally open to all citizens.

That would be the case for all public parks in Texas and the nation. From first-hand knowledge, I know the present administration at the Texas Parks and Wildlife Department is trying all sorts of programs and park incentives to make the park/nature experience a meaningful one, regardless of color. Texas Parks and Wildlife system leadership, under the caring guidance of its former executive director, Carter Smith, has set the best example: in 2018, Rodney Franklin, an able American who happens to be Black, was selected as the Texas State Parks Division director. Only good can come of that decision.

# Chapter 6
# President and Mrs. Lyndon B. Johnson: Forces for Nature

The grounding foundation of both President Lyndon B. Johnson and Claudia Alta "Lady Bird" Johnson took root in the rural settings of the Hill Country and East Texas. Both grew from childhood to adulthood cherishing the waters, wildlife, flowers, and landscapes that surrounded them in the early years of the twentieth century.

Both had other meaningful experiences that molded them. Lady Bird's passion for all things wild grew before, during, and after the White House years, and she embraced national parks, urban planning, and highway beautification. Early on, President Johnson would witness the ravishing waste of neglected youth. It would remain with him throughout his political career, leading him to speak often and forcefully of its evils, even on his election eve in 1964.

> I learned . . . when I was the NYA [National Youth Administration] director
> that poverty and ignorance are the only basic weaknesses of a free society, and
> that both are only bad habits and can be stopped.[1]

Later, Johnson would explain that his work with the National Youth Administration had opened his eyes further to "real poverty . . . to the problems of Black economic opportunity, and to an interest in parks and conservation."[2]

**ABOVE**

Lady Bird and Senator Lyndon B. Johnson in a 1934 Ford Phaeton parked on a dam in the Pedernales River at the LBJ Ranch near Stonewall, Texas, December 1959. Courtesy of Frank Muto, Lyndon Baines Johnson Presidential Library, Austin, Texas, 59-12-91.

**RIGHT**

Lyndon B. Johnson at the Welhausen School in Cotulla, Texas, with his first students (fifth, sixth, and seventh grades), 1928. Courtesy of the Lyndon Baines Johnson Presidential Library, Austin, Texas, 28-13-4.

When linked with his teaching experiences in Cotulla in deep South Texas, where he taught for a year, the Lyndon Johnson who would become president of the United States thirty-five years later began to be permanently shaped. His twenty-nine students in the fifth, sixth, and seventh grades lacked for everything: no books, no pencils, no lunchrooms or lunches, and no playground facilities.

Johnson took money from his own account and "invested" in his students. His caring commitment, coupled with his organizational abilities, earned him the position of principal during his second semester.

The National Youth Administration was established on June 26, 1935, and operated for eight years.[3] Lyndon Johnson was Texas's first director, serving for two years (1935 to 1937). The NYA's purpose was to provide part-time work for students in high school and college. Unlike the Civilian Conservation Corps, it was open to young men and women between the ages of sixteen and twenty-five at pay scales ranging from $6 to $20 per month. Its students lived at home rather than in camps like the "CCC boys." The students worked on a variety of projects: clerking as well as maintenance on highways, roadside parks, playgrounds, schools, and recreational parks across the state.

Lyndon B. Johnson visiting a National Youth Administration project at a highway park in Seguin, Texas, ca. January–February 1936. From left, R. W. Jacobs, Lyndon B. Johnson, and unknown (probably a highway foreman). Courtesy of the Lyndon Baines Johnson Presidential Library, Austin, Texas, 36-1/2-1.

To make it all work, Johnson and his staff established state and local advisory committees in most counties. From each of these bodies, Johnson was constantly on the lookout for those who demonstrated organizational talent. Many of these young men and women would become the base for Johnson's political machine, which dominated Texas politics from his first congressional race in 1937 until well after his presidency ended in 1969. But for the moment, the committees' responsibility was to keep Texas youth in school and working. Johnson would make that crystal clear in an interview with the *Daily Texan*. "Let it be understood once and for all that the NYA [National Youth Administration] is not a movement. It is a program . . . based strictly on American traditions."[4]

# The National Youth Administration: A New Beginning for the Nation's Youth

"The young are rotting without jobs, and there are no jobs to be had."[5]

The United States Employment Service stated in 1933 that youth between sixteen and twenty-five years old accounted for one-third of the nation's unemployed workers.[6] Unfortunately, most of Franklin Delano Roosevelt's early recovery programs were targeted at young men over twenty-five and older men who were out of work.

The Civilian Conservation Corps program was providing a great service among the men it targeted, but it completely missed those young men (and women) who wanted part-time work and a chance to complete their education.

After two years of lobbying by Eleanor Roosevelt and her allies, Roosevelt launched the National Youth Administration in June 1935 by Executive Order No. 7086. Its mission was twofold, as stated by the president: to provide financial assistance to high school and college students and to provide employment for young people between sixteen and twenty-five years old who were no longer in school.

During the next four years, the National Youth Administration would provide funds to more than 600,000 college students and 1.5 million high school children through its student aid program. Additionally, more than 2.6 million were employed in the NYA work program. All in all, the national program would directly touch four million young people and indirectly affect countless other lives.

The National Youth Administration would, at the outset, have a $50 million budget with which to work. Lyndon Johnson's Texas program was allocated $90,000 per year, a number that would cause a lesser person to throw up his hands in despair before the first bell sounded.

But like Governor Pat Neff, Lyndon Johnson could talk a dog off a meat wagon. And talk and persuade he did. To Texas Governor James Allred, he requested $50,000 from the state and got it. He sought cosponsorships from the Texas Highway Department, Texas Relief Commission, other county and city agencies, and private individuals. So persuasive was his pitch to Gil Gilchrist, head of the Texas Highway Department, that by March 1936, the Highway Department was a cosponsor with Johnson's National Youth Administration on 142 work projects, many of them roadside parks.

Starting in 1935 with the $90,000 federal budget allocation, Lyndon Johnson had compiled a statewide program that would cover $450,000 worth of programs for Texas youth by March 1936!

His organizational and fundraising abilities would be noticed by Franklin and Eleanor Roosevelt. Both made trips to Texas to inspect his successes firsthand. Being touted and blessed by the Roosevelts caught the attention not only of other highly placed officials in Washington but also of the leaders and citizens of the Texas Tenth Congressional District.

When the congressman from the tenth district died in 1937, Lyndon Johnson entered the race and won by three thousand votes. Again, his effective organization and persuasiveness would rule the day.

From his first days in Congress to his last days on Earth, Johnson would recall the deep pride he had for his National Youth Administration accomplishments.

He also never forgot his deep roots in the Hill Country and the need to conserve and protect its beauty and natural resources. Both the National Youth Administration programs for youth and the conservation of natural landscapes would become two of the three mainstays of his dreams for a "Great Society"—the third being civil rights.

These early experiences would mold both the Johnsons into caring public servants. Both would have a profound effect on the environment for the public good, be it a magnificent national park or a small local one.

During his days in the National Youth Administration, Johnson was on the lookout for top talent from the University of Texas and his alma mater, Southwest Texas Teachers College (now Texas State University). Among those chosen were a future governor, John Connally; two future congressmen, Ray Roberts and Jake Pickle; Willard Deason; Sherman Birdwell; and Jesse Kellam, who would follow Johnson as director of Texas's NYA

Letter from Lyndon B. Johnson to John Connally congratulating him on his University of Texas at Austin Students' Association president win, April 13, 1938. Courtesy of the John B. Connally Records Collection, Lyndon Baines Johnson Presidential Library, Austin, Texas.

President Lyndon B. Johnson signing the 1964 Civil Rights Act as Martin Luther King Jr. and others look on, July 2, 1964. Courtesy of Cecil Stoughton, White House Photo Office Collection, Lyndon Baines Johnson Presidential Library, Austin, Texas, 276-10-WH64.

programs when Johnson resigned in 1937 to run for Congress. All would work for and with him throughout his long political career.

Even though Johnson tried (with limited success) to carve out programs for Black and Mexican American communities, most of Texas's National Youth Administration programs worked for the betterment of its White participants: some 175,000 received enough work aid to finish their educations, and 75,000 were employed in out-of-school programs. In fact, his organizational and planning skills were often cited as role models. His attempts to help minority communities did not go unnoticed, however, and were appreciated in the political years that followed.

Today, National Youth Administration work can be viewed by visitors to Bastrop State Park, Inks Lake State Park, the Little Chapel in the Woods at Texas Woman's University in Denton (a site Eleanor Roosevelt would visit in the 1940s for a dedication ceremony), Prairie View A&M University, and other monuments to the NYA's work in Texas.[7]

Johnson would go on to pass some three hundred bills during his presidency (1963 to 1969) that were aimed at all aspects of conservation and preservation. Unfortunately, his accomplishments (until recently) were overshadowed by the crippling horrors of the Vietnam War. Interestingly enough, like Lincoln's action transferring Yosemite during the height of the Civil War and Roosevelt's multiple actions during the Great Depression and World War II, Johnson began to right the wrongs of years of abuse to America's waters, air, and lands throughout these bloody conflicts. I enumerate many of his

environmental victories and contributions, but for the purposes of examination, I will concentrate on the Land and Water Conservation Act of 1964 and Johnson's efforts to create more national parks—fifty in number, and certainly more than his heroes in conservation, Teddy and Franklin Roosevelt.

> The water we drink, the food we eat, the very air that we breathe, are threatened with pollution. Our parks are overcrowded, our seashores overburdened, green fields and dense forest disappearing. For once the battle is lost, once our natural splendor is destroyed, it can never be recaptured. And once man can no longer walk with beauty or wonder at nature, his spirit will wither, and his sustenance be wasted.
>
> LYNDON B. JOHNSON
> *Commencement (Great Society) Speech*
> *The University of Michigan*
> May 22, 1964

Even before President Johnson uttered these words, he had his cabinet and Congress working on every aspect of the country's environmental challenges. By the end of his first full year in office, he would sign into law the Clean Air Act (1963), the Wilderness Act (1964), and the Pesticide Control Act (1964).

The following year, with an overwhelming election mandate by the American people at the polls in November 1964, a blizzard of environmental laws would follow and keep coming through the remainder of his presidency. The laws would address every issue set forth in his 1964 speech. They would drastically reduce the levels of pollution in our air, water, and food while heightening Americans' consciousness of these problems.

Johnson would also ensure that there were more parks, wildlife, and recreational areas accessible to more people, especially among the exploding populations in urban centers.

Before his full term was finished, Lyndon Johnson's three hundred bills addressed every aspect of conservation, preservation, and the environment. Although watered down and attacked in Congress and the courts, most are still on the books, continuing to provide protection against despoilers while at the same time providing greater opportunity for outdoor experiences with nature and historic sites and better access for all American citizens.

No act during that time has touched more lives and communities than the Land and Water Conservation Fund (1964)—the "Mystery Act"—signed on the same day as the more ballyhooed Wilderness Act (the long-awaited and heavily lobbied cause advocated by nearly the entire spectrum of environmental organizations).

Why the Mystery Act? Because it was barely recognized at the signing on September 3, 1964, and has been left off most compilations of Johnson's triumphs. And a triumph it has been and will continue to be, having been fully secured and permanently funded as part of the Great American Outdoors Act, a bipartisan masterpiece signed into law on August 4, 2020.

Unfortunately, over the fifty-six years between 1964 and 2020, the engine driving the original act was often thwarted by Congress, which, more often than not, failed to supply the engine with fuel.

The Land and Water Conservation Fund authorized $900 million annually to acquire park inholdings that would open access to more outdoor activities.[8] It also provided matching grants to state and local communities. Even with congressional cuts and denials (the $900 million was fully funded only twice between 1964 and 2020), enough slipped through to finance landscape protection in all fifty states and more than forty-two thousand state and local projects in every county in the US. Many such projects became part of the Texas landscape and local park grants programs. But with $22 billion diverted over the same period, many projects across the nation and in Texas were left on the drawing board or in the incomplete column, even as population and park visitation were increasing by the millions.

Mission San José, San Antonio Missions National Historical Park, date unknown. Courtesy of the National Park Service, Harpers Ferry Center, West Virginia.

Fortunately, millions across the nation and in Texas demonstrate strong support—public opinion polls show upwards of 70 percent or more—for parks and for their sustainable and substantial funding.

In spite of the setbacks at the national level, Texas, over the ensuing five decades (1965 to 2019), received approximately $589 million in national, state park, and local grants as well as for other worthy conservation projects.

At the national park level, many Texas additions were funded by the Land and Water Conservation Fund, including the Big Thicket Preserve, Padre Island National Seashore, San Antonio Missions National Historical Park, and Guadalupe Mountains National Park, among others. Of these, Guadalupe Mountains National Park's founding and funding deserve special recognition and explanation.

Although the Guadalupe Mountains found its way onto several state parks "wish lists" in the first half of the twentieth century, the movement for park status gained little traction until supporters with influence stepped up to the national park plate. A combination of powerful ranchers, congressmen, US Senator Ralph Yarborough, Secretary of Interior Stewart Udall, and, to cap it off, President and Mrs. Lyndon B. Johnson would weigh in at the right moments to push the project along. President Johnson signed off

Guadalupe Mountains National Park, date unknown. Courtesy of Derrick Neill via Adobe Stock.

on its creation in 1966—again, like some of his predecessors, in the midst of a national crisis—Vietnam.

But what made the support of President Johnson unique was not just the creation of the park but the method of financing. Johnson proposed to use revenue from the recently enacted Land and Water Conservation Fund to purchase the lands offered by the ranchers who had held onto their holdings in hopes of selling them for national park use. It would be the first federal purchase of private lands for public park purposes. It would not be the last.

Texas state parks and local programs were granted some $188.3 million over the same period from the Land and Water Conservation Fund, most in matching fund partnerships with the Texas Parks and Wildlife Department.

Among the state parks benefiting from Land and Water Conservation Fund funding were Palo Duro Canyon State Park, Bastrop State Park, Big Bend Ranch State Park, and McKinney Falls State Park, to name a few.

Add to this the many hundreds of local parks and recreation grants (all of which must be matched at the local level in order to qualify for federal/state funding), and much has been accomplished over the past decades in spite of congressional and Texas state legislative appropriation cuts and diversion of funds.

Thus, it can be said that President Lyndon Johnson, by means of his growing commitment to a better America through a more robust enhancement of its natural and historic gifts, left a legacy unsurpassed by all presidential predecessors while at the same time creating a major source of funding for his beloved Texas and, yes, the other forty-nine states as well.

Lady Bird Johnson, Stewart Udall, and group rafting down the Rio Grande in Big Bend National Park, April 3, 1966. Courtesy of Robert L. Knudsen, White House Photo Office Collection, Lyndon Baines Johnson Presidential Library, Austin, Texas, C1626-18a.

Lady Bird Johnson, Secretary of the Interior Stewart Udall, NPS Director George Hartzog, and party hiking the Lost Mine Trail at Big Bend National Park, April 1966. Courtesy of the National Park Service, Harpers Ferry Center, West Virginia.

Official White House diary entry detailing Lady Bird Johnson's arrival at Big Bend National Park, April 2, 1966. Courtesy of the Lady Bird Johnson White House Diary Collection, Lyndon Baines Johnson Presidential Library, Austin, Texas, ctjd-ctjdd-19660402.

THE WHITE HOUSE
WASHINGTON

MRS. LYNDON B. JOHNSON, *Daily Diary*

Mrs. Johnson began her day at (Place) *Tropicana Motel, San Antonio*     Date *Saturday, April 2, 1966*

*Dictated: Infos*

| Entry No. | Time | Activity |
|---|---|---|
| ① | 7:55 | with Udalls departed motel via official car. |
| | 8:00 | Arrived Alamo and took short tour. |
| | 8:15 | Departed |
| | 8:35 | Arrived San Antonio Airport and boarded chartered plane |
| | 9:00 | with staff and press departed San Antonio |
| ② | 10:09 | Arrived Presidio County Airport. Short receiving line and ceremony |
| | 11:15 | With Udalls left via motorcade. |
| ③ | 12:40 | Arrived Big Bend National Park   for luncheon |
| | 2:15 | With Udalls departed |
| | 2:33 | Arrived Park Basin and went to cabins:110 |
| ④ | 3:40 | With Udalls departed Basin and motored to beginning of Lost Mine Trail~Red umbrella |
| | 3:48 | Arrived Lost Mine Trail and hiked to top and back. |
| | 5:22 | With Udalls and party returned to Basin again. |
| | 5:30 | To Cabin 110 |
| ⑤ | 6:40 | Joined VIPs and accompanying press: campfire and dinner on grounds immediately in back of cabin 110. |
| | 10:50 | Returned to 110 and retired |

Official White House diary entry depicting Lady Bird Johnson's rafting trip down the Rio Grande River at Big Bend National Park, April 3, 1966. Courtesy of the Lady Bird Johnson White House Diary Collection, Lyndon Baines Johnson Presidential Library, Austin, Texas, ctjd-ctjdd-19660403.

THE WHITE HOUSE
WASHINGTON

MRS. LYNDON B. JOHNSON, *Daily Diary*

Mrs. Johnson began her day at (Place) *Big Bend*     Date *Sunday, April 3, 1966*

| Entry No. | Time | Activity |
|---|---|---|
| ① | 7:05 | with Se. and Mrs. Udall to Basin Center for outdoor breakfast, short church services and planting tree. |
| | 8:15 | returned to Cabin 110 |
| ② | 8:37 | With Mrs. Udall departed Basin via car. Picked up Se. Udall walking down road |
| | 10:28 | Arrived Raft Debarkation site on Rio Grande |
| | 10:37 | With Sec and Mrs. Udall and staff and press debarked in rubber rafts. Paddled down Rio Grande and Mariscal Canyon.   Canyon wrens singing |
| | 12:18 | Arrived Rattlesnake Sand Bar for lunch. Sat around & talked with reporters |
| | 12:47 | Back on Rafts for more paddling down river. |
| ③ | 4:10 | Arrived landing site |
| | 4:18 | with Sec and Mrs. Udall left for Camp Ground. Saw road runner |
| ④ | 5:17 | Arrived Rio Grand Village Camp Ground and had Odessa Chuck Wagon steak fry dinner with Udalls, Geroge Hartzog, local VIP's and press |
| | 8:20 | Left with Udalls |
| | 9:35 | Arrived Basin and to cabin 110 and retired |

Enchanted Rock State Natural Area, 2012. Courtesy of Chase Fountain, Texas Parks and Wildlife Foundation, Austin, Texas.

To aid him in this monumental undertaking, Johnson had the good fortune to have a great lifetime partner with an equally strong devotion to nature—Lady Bird Johnson.

To my mind, her greatest contribution was that she kept the president and the nation's eyes focused on the need for and benefits of national parks, state parks, and wild things throughout Johnson's presidential years—and then on her own in the years following his death in 1973.

During the height of the Vietnam War, Lady Bird set out to keep that focus on the creation and conservation of America's parks and wildernesses. With Secretary of the Interior Stewart Udall, National Park Service top brass, key leaders, and the press in tow, she hiked trails, floated rivers, called attention to flora and fauna, and constantly pointed out how nature is beneficial for all. Like Lincoln, Wilson, and Teddy Roosevelt, she knew in her nature-uplifted heart that our soldiers, their families, and America's citizens would need these places for renewal and recreation during and after the war. Certainly, her devotion to these natural treasures would only grow stronger during and after Johnson's presidency.

Buildings and wildflowers at the Lady Bird Johnson Wildflower Center, ca. mid-1990s. This photo is from Mrs. Johnson's personal collection. Courtesy of Greg Hursley, Through the Lens Management, Inc., Lyndon Baines Johnson Presidential Library, Austin, Texas, D11243.

In 1967, Mrs. Johnson personally called Texas State Senator Joe Christie, author of the necessary Guadalupe Mountains National Park legislative conveyance of mineral rights to the federal government, to see how plans were going with the legislation and to ask if there was anything she could do to help.[9]

I am sure there was, and I am sure she did!

In 1977, as described in chapter two, she also sprang into action to save Enchanted Rock, a unique granite-domed outcropping near the LBJ Ranch. Time was of the essence. She called Patrick Noonan of the Nature Conservancy in Arlington, Virginia, and urged him to come quickly. Two days later, he and Mrs. Johnson were climbing the rock and enjoying dinner. Shortly thereafter in 1978, the Nature Conservancy bought Enchanted Rock land for $1.3 million, then deeded it to the State of Texas.[10] In 1984, the Enchanted Rock State Natural Area opened to the public.

And in 1982, as a gift to herself on her seventieth birthday, she deeded land she owned near Austin to create the National Wildflower Research Center (now known as the Lady Bird Johnson Wildflower Center). It is a major tourist attraction, as is Lady Bird Johnson Lake in Austin. Both are daily reminders of her devotion to all things wild and free.

At the end of his presidency, the Johnsons returned to the LBJ Ranch fifty miles west of Austin for solace and renewal. They lived there before, during, and after the presidency, and are buried in the natural, peaceful landscapes that gave meaning to their lives. To honor and memorialize their commitment to Texas and the nation, the Johnsons deeded the LBJ Ranch, Johnson's boyhood home, and their ranch residence to the National Park Service and the Texas Parks and Wildlife Department in 1969. It is appropriate that the free-flowing Pedernales River connects the Lyndon B. Johnson National Historic Site with the LBJ State Park and Historic Area.

Although I have written of the Johnsons' accomplishments on behalf of conservation and preservation of the American environment as two separate efforts working toward the same goal, the truth is they acted as one. Whispering in the president's ear on behalf of some national park or wilderness area was Mrs. Johnson's stock-in-trade to persuade and keep the president focused on the task at hand. Johnson, in time, more than likely used that whispered conversation to convince a member of the House or Senate that the bill at hand was of particular interest to their friend Lady Bird.

MRS. LYNDON B. JOHNSON, *Daily Diary*

Mrs. Johnson began her day at (Place) *The White House* _____ Date *Friday, 26 July 1968*

| Entry No. | Time | Activity ND |
|---|---|---|
| | 10:15 | Breakfast |
| | 10:25 | Departed W.H. for funeral of Mrs. Price at St. John's Episcopal Church<br> Sat in car because late - and went to cemetery |
| | 11:25 | Mrs. Krim left |
| | 11:45 | Returned to White House and went to President's office<br>President gave me a display of pens used to sign all the beautification bills. |
| | 11:50 | Liz, Simone, Tom Wolf, Howard K. Smith, M/M Jensen and John Lynch in to see me. |
| | 12:10 | Left President's office but returned for purse |
| | 12:25 | Returned to second floor |
| | | To Yellow Oval Room to meet with Liz, Simone, Tom Wolf, Howard K. Smith,<br> M/M Jensen and John Lynch<br> Served ice tea and sandwiches |
| | 2:00 | Departed W.H. for Navy Photo Center with Liz and others |

**ABOVE**

President Lyndon B. Johnson presenting Lady Bird Johnson and Secretary of the Interior Stewart Udall with shadow boxes containing the fifty pens he had used to sign fifty laws pertaining to conservation, preservation, and beautification, July 26, 1968. From left, Secretary Udall, President Johnson, Lady Bird Johnson, and Udall Chief of Staff Henry Kimelman. Courtesy of Yoichi Okamoto, White House Photo Office Collection, Lyndon Baines Johnson Presidential Library, Austin, Texas, A6605-3.

**LEFT**

Official White House diary entry listing President Johnson's gift of fifty pens used to sign conservation acts during the Johnson years, July 26, 1968. Courtesy of the Lady Bird Johnson White House Diary Collection, Lyndon Baines Johnson Presidential Library, Austin, Texas, ctjd-ctjdd-19680726.

President Lyndon B. Johnson and Lady Bird Johnson walking through a field of flowers at the LBJ Ranch near Stonewall, Texas, July 5, 1968. Courtesy of Frank Wolfe, White House Photo Office Collection, Lyndon Baines Johnson Presidential Library, Austin, Texas, D915-16.

Though they worked as one, even the president of the United States knew who the driving force in these efforts was and recognized that devotion to nature in a special way.

On July 26, 1968, Johnson presented Lady Bird with fifty pens he had used to sign fifty laws pertaining to conservation, preservation, and beautification, accompanied with an inscription that read, "To Lady Bird, who has inspired me and millions of Americans to preserve our land and beautify our nation. With love from Lyndon."[11]

The smiles on their faces signaled their sense of accomplishment and the depth of admiration each held for the other. I believe the lands and waters also smiled at that moment.

# Chapter 7

# The Golden Years: 1963-1980

H ow could a man who looked as urbane and sophisticated as Governor John Bowden Connally Jr. of Texas have had such an abundant and lasting interest in state parks, so much so that he placed the merger of the two state agencies tasked with nurturing Texas's natural resources, the money to pay for their upkeep, and a major park expansion through acquisitions high on his first legislative agenda in 1963?

Why was he so devoted? First, Connally was a product of rural Texas, growing up on a farm near Floresville south of San Antonio. He never lost his love of the land and landscape. Later in life, he bought ranchland in the area (including the acreage that contained his boyhood home), built a suitable house, and retreated there whenever possible. Like his friend and mentor, Lyndon B. Johnson, he drew renewal and peace from the sunrises, sunsets, and wildlife he found on his ranch.

Second, University of Texas student leader Connally held a position under Johnson in Texas's National Youth Administration in the 1930s. Although it was only a minor position, Connally surely observed how working on those Depression-era projects benefited the young men (and later women) in the National Youth Administration. I strongly suspect that an ambitious and alert Connally filed away those observations with a promise to continue the work should the opportunity arise.

John Connally served in the Navy from 1941 until the end of combat in the Pacific in 1945. He returned home as a lieutenant commander and hero and immediately jumped into business, law, and politics. He was a founder and investor, with other veterans, of radio station KVET (1946 to 1949); became a new member of an Austin law firm; and was

John Connally as the University of Texas at Austin Students' Association president-elect, 1938. Courtesy of the Cactus Yearbook Collection, Texas ScholarWorks, University of Texas Libraries, University of Texas at Austin, Austin, Texas.

campaign manager for Lyndon Johnson's 1946 US congressional re-election and hotly contested 1948 US Senate race. That political partnership would endure through both the failed 1960 and wildly successful 1964 presidential races.

Again, two men and a woman (Lady Bird Johnson), all products of the Texas landscape, would not only carry their love of the outdoors through their lifetimes, but would all devote large parts of their lives to ensuring that nature's treasures could be shared with all who wished to find comfort and renewal there.

Following his stints in radio ownership and management of Lyndon Johnson's political races, John Connally was hired by Fort Worth oilman Sid Richardson and his nephew Perry Bass to handle legal affairs and lobbying in Washington and Austin. In 1962, Connally was elected governor and, in August 1963, signed into law the act consolidating the State Parks Board—which was, according to Connally, "sick to the point of dying"—with the older, more-established Game & Fish Commission to create the Texas Parks and Wildlife Department. It caused criticism upfront—"a Connally power grab," with attendant grumbling and finger-pointing—but it soon became very popular and raised more revenue than expected. By 1967, the department was held in such high esteem and parks were in such high demand that Connally passed a $75 million bond package for park acquisition. The bond package was matched by millions in federal dollars (originally, the match was 60 percent state and 40 percent federal).[1] In the twenty-five years after the merger of the agencies, Texas purchased sixty-three parks.[2] During that period and onward, several of Fort Worth's leading citizens played significant roles in the governance and future of both the Texas Parks and Wildlife Department and parks themselves. Three served as chairman of the Texas Parks and Wildlife Commission at some point: Perry Bass, Lee Bass, and Ralph Duggins. Amon Carter Sr. and his *Fort Worth Star-Telegram* provided early and ongoing support, which continues to the present day. State senators Don Kennard and John Montford (both from Fort Worth) sponsored and passed major park financing bills.

But John Connally would lead the way in the early 1960s.

Our present state parks system is sick to the point of dying. Our parks are many, scattered, and without tourist-attracting features needed for effective use. I propose the consolidation of the State Parks Board and the Game & Fish Commission under a three-member commission . . . We must make giant strides because time has run out. We must decide what we want in the way of parks and what it will cost, then provide this service to our people or not attempt to engage in the activity at all.

JOHN B. CONNALLY JR., GOVERNOR OF TEXAS
*Address to a Joint Session of the*
*Fifty-Eighth Texas Legislature*
*Inaugural State of the State*
January 16, 1963

Even though there was opposition—some strong and vocal—the Texas legislature responded quickly and favorably, passing House Bill 21 on April 17, 1963. Connally signed it into law. Henceforth, the new agency would be known as the Texas Parks and Wildlife Department.

Pat Neff's and David Colp's State Parks Board, created forty years previously in 1923, ceased to exist.

To make his case, Governor Connally used his significant attributes—charm, knowledge, and political adroitness—to sell the merger and the renewal of the parks system. He also had the recent findings of a State Parks Board-commissioned study (1958) on the needs of the parks and lack of sustainable funding. The study was conducted by Texas Tech College (now University). With park attendance reaching more than five million visitors annually and with many of the parks reaching twenty-five to thirty years of constant use (with a lack of repair and maintenance), the study called for the acquisition of

**ABOVE**

Texas Governor John B. Connally, a major influence on Texas state parks, ca. 1967–1968. Courtesy of the Texas Parks and Wildlife Department, Austin, Texas.

Amon Carter Sr., 1955. Carter was the owner of the *Fort Worth Star-Telegram*, a strong parks proponent. Courtesy of the TCU Photo Collection, Mary Couts Burnett Library Special Collections, Texas Christian University, Fort Worth, Texas, 922.

373,000 acres of parkland and expenditures on parks of $462 million between 1963 and 2000.[3]

An enormous side benefit of the Connally legislative triumph for parks was that the Texas legislature put its (or our) money where its mouth was. The legislation tripled the parks budget, appropriating $1.7 million for fifty-eight sites covering 62,000 acres and funding for development of several new sites:[4]

- In 1965, San Jacinto Battleground was transferred to the Texas Parks and Wildlife Department
- In 1966, rising visitor revenues paid off the last of the Palo Duro Canyon revenue bonds
- Martin Dies Jr. State Park was added in 1964
- LBJ State Park and Historic Site was added in 1966
- Fort Leaton State Historic Site was added in 1967
- Fort Richardson State Park and Historic Site was added in 1968
- Dinosaur Valley State Park was added in 1968

More parks and historic sites would be brought online in the years leading up to 1988, according to an excellent 2011 article by John Jefferson in *Texas Parks & Wildlife Magazine*.[5]

There is one event that must be mentioned, although I hesitate to do so; however, it has a direct bearing on Governor John Connally's reputation and popularity: the near-loss of his life during the tragic assassination of President John F. Kennedy in Dallas on November 22, 1963. As Connally recovered and returned to public life, he became one of the most intriguing figures among political leaders in America. That charismatic appeal, coupled with his subject-matter knowledge and immense political skill, would bode well for years to come. After his general election win in 1962—54 percent to 45.6 percent—the governor went on to win races in 1964 and 1966 by 73.8 percent and 72.8 percent, respectively.[6] These margins most assuredly influenced Texas legislators to the point of getting many of his programs passed, including greatly expanding higher education, public education support, teachers' salaries, better libraries, and increased research. He financed these programs by substantially increasing taxes—normally the kiss of death at the hands of the legislature and at the next election. In addition, he promoted and passed a number of reforms of state government, including the parks and wildlife merger in 1963.

But why would John Connally expend his newly found political power by pushing parks system reforms and financing during his first term in 1963?

In 1964, Connally's friend and mentor, President Lyndon Johnson, would shepherd

**ABOVE LEFT**

Texas Parks and Wildlife Commission former chairs Perry Bass (left) and Ygnacio "Nacho" Garza at the Texas Parks & Wildlife Expo, 1994. Courtesy of the Texas Parks and Wildlife Department, Austin, Texas.

**ABOVE**

Texas Parks and Wildlife Commission former Chair Lee Bass (center) at a commission gathering, 2009. Courtesy of the Texas Parks and Wildlife Department, Austin, Texas.

**ABOVE**

From left, Texas Parks and Wildlife Commission former chairs Dan Friedkin, Ralph Duggins, and Dan Allen Hughes at a commission function, 2010. Courtesy of the Texas Parks and Wildlife Department, Austin, Texas.

**RIGHT**

The Honorable John Montford, Texas state senator and chairman of the Senate Finance Committee, which passed the original Sporting Goods Sales Tax, date unknown. Courtesy of the office of the Honorable John Montford.

The Honorable Don Kennard, Texas state senator, at his desk in the Senate chamber, 1962. Courtesy of Senate Media Services, The Texas Senate, Austin, Texas, 62-QY-02.

the federal Land and Water Conservation Fund through Congress. A major part of the act called for funding to be earmarked for state and local communities for (among other things) acquisition and development of recreational projects. But to receive such funding, recipients had to provide an outdoor recreation master plan and state matching funds. The mandated master plan for Texas was prepared by Texas Tech University and utilized to justify Governor Connally's proposal to the legislature in 1967 to pass the $75 million bond issue. When coupled with the federal match, Texas would have the wherewithal to expand the parks system as never before possible, surpassing even the numbers during the Depression years. Now it had more than $100 million to do just that and a governor who wanted to see it through to satisfactory and long-lasting results.

In the twenty-five years after the merger of the agencies, Texas acquired sixty-three parks—forty-seven were obtained before 1963, and many of those were the result of federal action during the period of the Great Depression.[7]

The prospect of these federal funds helped prompt the passage of Texas's matching funds, as was the case in future appropriations by the state. Former Texas Parks and Wildlife Commission Chair Ed Cox Jr. stated it best:

> There was a confluence of events that led to a very substantial acquisition program [during part of the expansion era]. While helpful, I'm not sure the merger [of Game and Fish with the State Parks Board] itself had as much to do with acquisitions as did the availability of large amounts of federal funding. I'm not sure the cigarette tax would have passed had there not been a 50 percent matching fund provision.[8]

But with all good things, there are usually flaws. The bond financing program was no exception. The $1-per-car mandated entrance fee did not generate enough revenue to meet the needs of a rapidly growing Texas or adequately cover debt retirement.[9]

To correct the shortfall and allow park expansion to continue to move forward (and to help draw down the federal matching funds in a timely fashion), the Texas Parks and Wildlife Department turned to Texas State Senator Don Kennard of Fort Worth, a parks and conservation advocate of the first (and lasting) order. With Texas Parks and Wildlife's blessing over the 1968 to 1971 periods, Kennard would develop a financing scheme using state revenue from the sale of cigarettes: a penny-a-pack tax. Though projected to generate substantial and sustainable funding—$16 million annually—for the acquisition of new parks, its passage was the product of dealmaking and compromise, and it came at a cost.

Don Kennard was the product of an urban upbringing who had a healthy love of nature and the outdoors fostered by his father. The elder Kennard loved to hunt, particularly quail. Kennard, in a 1999 Conservation History Association of Texas oral history interview, claimed his dad was a great quail hunter and dog man who loved to get away from the big city and spend time in the open spaces of Texas. He often took young Don along.

From these outings, Kennard discovered a love of nature, particularly canoeing, and he shared with friends—and later, prospective supporters of his conservation work in the legislature—the pure pleasure of getting away from the city. Along the way, he developed a love for Big Bend country and the Rio Grande River.

The Kennard outdoor outings became so popular (along with his historic site and event trips) that people lobbied to get an invitation. I know because in later years (after his time in the legislature), I went on ten or more such trips in the 1980s and 1990s. He always tried to have key legislators and opinion-makers along to share the wonders of nature and foster the connection of historic sites to the need to conserve both. Shades of Stephen Mather!

During his years in the Senate, Kennard seemed to write important conservation and preservation legislation every session, often with the support of Governor Connally, who took office in 1963, the year Kennard went to the Texas Senate.

One particular point of pride for Kennard was his authorship and fight for the Antiquities Code. For this, Kennard, Connally, and their allies had to take on the powerful land commissioner, Jerry Sadler. The fight got so bitter that Sadler choked one of

John Connally (left) with Lieutenant Governor Ben Barnes, date unknown. Courtesy of the Records of Ben F. Barnes, Texas Office of the Lieutenant Governor, Prints and Photographs Collection, Archives and Information Services Division, Texas State Library and Archives Commission, Austin, Texas, 1995/037-017.

Kennard's key supporters, Jake Johnson, on camera. The press loved it, and it sealed the fate of the bill—favorably for Kennard. The House passed it, the Senate concurred, and Connally signed it into law to the lasting satisfaction and pride of Kennard.

Not bad for two urban boys from Fort Worth.

At any point in his career in the legislature, particularly the Senate years (1963 to 1973), Don Kennard could have rested on his conservation laurels. But he had another, more important (as it turned out) major fight for parks and conservation on the horizon.

Throughout the late 1960s and early 1970s, State Senator Don Kennard used the power of chairmanship and interim committee study to make the case for a more substantial and sustainable method of state financing for state parks, wildlife management areas, and historic sites. Anything would have been an improvement. Texas in 1961 was spending less than a nickel per Texan per year on the parks system, and only two parks had been purchased.[10]

Through persistence, homework, and perfect timing, all the legislative rings aligned. With the 1971 Texas legislative session, Kennard perfected not only a penny-a-pack cigarette tax to generate the needed revenue but a fund—Fund 31—in which to deposit and hold the funds, plus a carefully crafted plan detailing how and for what to make distributions: acquisition, planning, and development of state parks and historic sites.

The wagon to which Kennard hitched his park financing plan was a major tax proposal introduced by Lieutenant Governor Ben Barnes. A corporate income tax was not included in the bill. However, the moderate-liberal wing of the Senate (still mostly Democrats), including Kennard, supported a corporate income tax. Barnes needed a liberal cosponsor for the overall bill, so he approached Kennard, who accepted with two conditions: 1) even though he was a cosponsor, he would continue to push for a corporate tax and 2) Barnes had to accept his cigarette tax amendment. Barnes agreed and kept his end of the bargain throughout.

The liberal-moderate coalition thought they had the sixteen necessary votes to pass a corporate income tax. They were wrong—and surprised—when solid-as-Jell-O™ Texas State Senator "Diamond" Jim Bates switched his vote in favor of Barnes. The original bill passed in the Senate, with Don Kennard's parks tax amendment hanging on for dear life.

With Connally's bond money plus the federal matching funds, revenue flowing into Fund 31, and revenue from other assorted accounts, it looked like nothing but smooth sailing for Texas's state parks for the foreseeable future.

But lest you forget, this is Texas, which has never taken to new taxes, and although Barnes's tax package won over the more pro-business stakeholders, it was still going to take $864 million out of Texans' pockets. While most of the state had not heard of Don Kennard, the people of Fort Worth and Tarrant County had and, in 1972, turned him out of office, as he laughingly liked to say, "by popular demand."

Don Kennard could laugh because he understood politics and knew his sponsorship of the tax package was political poison, but he had the courage to act as one of the co-sponsors because he knew from the beginning that his cigarette tax had to be attached to the larger tax package in order to become law.

Considering his body of work, which culminated in the creation of Fund 31 and revenue generated annually by the cigarette tax, Kennard left office (no matter how bitterly at the moment) with deep satisfaction then and for the future, as far as the eye could see.

At its zenith, the cigarette tax generated $16 million annually.[11] In its first four years (1971 to 1975), it generated $53 million, but less than $9 million was appropriated for parkland acquisition.[12]

While I am sure Kennard and other supporters thought they had made the distribution intent clear in floor speeches and bill language—acquisition, planning, and development—there was apparently just enough ambiguity to allow the Texas Parks and Wildlife Department's commissioners and key legislators to flip the use of funds to suit their own purposes and small-vision needs.

Instead of awe-inspiring vistas and areas of wildlife protection for the benefit of nature and Texas citizens and families, Fund 31 monies were used for a new Texas Parks and Wildlife Department headquarters, employee salaries, operations, and never-to-be-overlooked wishes of elected legislators whose future support may very well have hinged on the number of blue-ribbon events that could be photographed and splashed on the front page of the local newspaper. Kennard and others were critical of the method, not the need. Bob Burleson of Belton, a former legislator and sitting Texas Parks and Wildlife Department commissioner who helped draft the bill, was one critic. He appreciated the need for a new headquarters but not in place of—or to the detriment of—acquisition.[13]

The greater irony is that at the beginning of 1975, in spite of the diversions, there was a surplus of $17 million in Fund 31—enough to buy several large-acre (twenty-thousand-acre-plus) park prospects and a like number of wildlife management areas, with enough left over to pay for some real planning.

Why was the money not spent this way? From 1973 to 1983, Texas Parks and Wildlife Department commissioners and staff were, for the most part, at odds with public parks interests.

Big Bend Ranch State Park, 2009. Courtesy of Earl Nottingham, Texas Parks and Wildlife Department, Austin, Texas.

## Leaders for a New Plan for Parks

In most times of park crisis and need for leadership, the Texas parks system inspired leaders who stepped forward and addressed once again the age-old problem of inadequate funding at all levels of park needs: repair, maintenance, operations, local grants, and, most assuredly, new acquisitions. In 1988, after years of failure and denial, Texas Parks and Wildlife Department commissioners voted to purchase a 212,000-acre privately owned ranch, which would become Big Bend Ranch State Park. It would become the largest state park in Texas. It has since been expanded to more than 300,000 acres.

## Conservation con Queso

If this section of parks history reads personal, the reader would be correct. I have known the two principals here for much of my adult life: Bob Armstrong (now deceased) and Andy Sansom, both the epitome of public servants at their best. In matters of the public good and the conservation of natural treasures, their body of work is stellar. Using Big Bend Ranch State Park as a case study will amply demonstrate the personality traits common to both.

All good endeavors usually require patience. In the case of acquiring something as magnificent as Big Bend Ranch State Park, patience became protracted perseverance. Bob Armstrong's love affair with that landscape began on a hunting trip in West Texas in 1970, when he met the owner of the ranch, Robert O. Anderson. Armstrong allowed that if Anderson ever wanted to sell the ranch, it would make a fine state park. The idea apparently struck a chord. Over the next fifteen years, they kept in touch.

Even when Texas leadership and their legislatures were at their frowning worst, Bob Armstrong was at his smiling best. Partly, it was in his DNA, and partly, it was because he had experience as an elected member of the Texas House of Representatives for seven years and Texas land commissioner for eleven years—both institutions that, by the nature of the beast, would try the patience of Job.

Andy Sansom (left) and Bob Armstrong at the ten-year anniversary celebration of Big Bend Ranch State Park, 2009. Photo by George Bristol, author's collection

When the powerful chairman of the Senate's finances, A. M. Akin, told him, "We ain't buying no ranch," Armstrong, a landowner, could understand the elder's fiscal conservatism.[14] With his sunny disposition as a foil, Armstrong probably found the humor in the scene. He would certainly not have held a grudge against the chairman. Who knows, things could change. Besides, there were other life matters that required his attention, and Bob Armstrong was in the middle of a great number of them, particularly those involving fishing, hunting, hiking, Willie and Waylon, flying, family and friends, and almost anything that had to do with conservation and preservation.

In 1988, Andy Sansom—at the urging of Texas Parks and Wildlife Commissioner Ed Cox Jr. and with the blessing of Texas Governor Bill Clements—joined the Texas Parks and Wildlife Department team to scout out new park prospects and find the funding to secure them for the system.

Somewhere in the multitude of financial accounts, Sansom and staff discovered that $25 million of the twenty-year-old "Connally bonds" had been authorized for expenditure but never drawn down.

With the discovery of the Connally bonds, Sansom, who shared Armstrong's dream of purchasing the ranch, arrived on the scene just in time to take the baton. From 1987 to 1988, Armstrong had struggled to find a method of financing through the General Land Office. At one point, Armstrong deputized Lieutenant Governor Bill Hobby to approach the tough—but dealmaking—State Comptroller Bob Bullock. Hobby asked if Bullock could scratch around and find an extra $10 million to finance the purchase.

From left, former Texas Parks and Wildlife Executive Director Carter Smith, Bob Armstrong, Big Bend Supporter James King, and Andy Sansom at the ten-year anniversary celebration of Big Bend Ranch State Park, 2009. Photo by George Bristol, author's collection.

Bullock answered, "No," but he thought he could find $11 million—if Hobby would agree to direct the extra million to a pay raise for the Texas Rangers.

Around the same time, Andy Sansom secretly flew to New Mexico, Connally bond money in hand, to hammer out a deal with Bob Anderson, who, it turned out, was willing to sell below market value. A deal was quickly struck. After eighteen years of patience and perseverance, Bob Armstrong, now a Texas Parks and Wildlife commissioner, made the motion during a commission meeting to buy the Anderson ranch.

Bob Armstrong and Andy Sansom's dream was realized—sort of. It would take more than a decade to develop the ranch into a working and welcoming park.

From 1988 into the 2000s, the miserly Texas state legislature failed to appropriate any funds for developing this magnificent landscape, which has vistas rivalling any in Big Bend National Park. And after 1993, when a fully funded Sporting Goods Sales Tax would have spun off plenty of revenue for appropriation, the legislature not only didn't lift the tax's $32 million appropriation cap, they appropriated less on several occasions.

Sansom and Armstrong weren't happy with the situation, but both had other endeavors and favorite things to keep them smiling. Sansom had his hunting dogs, including his much-beloved Scout, and Armstrong had his own concoction of chili con queso made at El Matt's Restaurant in Austin. Bob Armstrong's chili con queso and a good brace of dogs are just natural smile-makers.

But by 1992 to 1993, much of the parks system's situation had grown dire. Most of the parks were between twenty-five and fifty years old, with neglect at almost every site, even as visitorship increased year in and year out. Even during the war and drought years—up through the "Connally bond" golden years and supplemented by the Kennard cigarette tax—the demand for more and better parks continued to increase and far outstripped appropriations year after year.

What was needed was a better—and more sustainable—method of funding to carry parks forward into a more-prosperous future.

# Chapter 8

# The Sporting Goods Sales Tax: Leadership at Every Level

A s has been proven time and again, Texans (and visitors to Texas) love their parks, and more are visiting every year. With the increase in visitorship, any neglect of the parks system could have economic repercussions. A 2018 to 2019 report from the Outdoor Industry Association concludes that outdoor recreation in Texas contributes $52.6 billion annually to the state economy, supports 411,000 jobs, and produces $3.5 billion in state and local taxes.[1] And a 2019 economic impact study by Ji Youn Jeong and John L. Crompton points out that economic activity from state parks generates an estimated $891 million in sales annually, $688 million in output, $426 million in added value, and $240 million in impact on residents' income, accounting for an estimated 6,801 jobs paying an average salary of $35,320 per year.[2]

Even with matching funds from several sources within the federal government, by 1993, the state parks funding problem was compounded by a decrease in revenue from the cigarette tax enacted in 1971. Even after several increases from the original one-cent-per-pack tax to three cents per pack then five cents per pack in 1979 (with 40 percent allocated to state parks, 40 percent to local parks, and 10 percent to debt retirement), revenue still fell from a high of $19 million per year in 1980 to $12.5 million in 1990—this while visitation increased by 37 percent and many parks fell into disgraceful condition after decades of little maintenance and repairs.[3]

Legislative action was needed and an alternative revenue source identified—a substantial and sustainable source. Two old but successful and popular federal conservation excise taxes were signposts: the Pittman-Robertson Act of 1937, which taxed guns, ammunition, and archery equipment, and the more recent Dingell-Johnson Act of 1950, which taxes fishing tackle, other fishing gear, and fuel and gasoline used by boaters.

Both of these federal "user taxes" have helped fund restoration, planning, and regulation of state hunting and fishing, respectively. If hunting and fishing could be financed by user taxes, why not a state parks program paid for by Texans who use sporting goods equipment?

What was also important was that whatever method was considered had to have the potential to increase in revenue to satisfy an ever-growing population demand. To gain acceptance by the Texas legislature, the funding method would have to be a tax that was not a new tax and a revenue stream that could project a continuing—but modest—annual growth that would flow from the purchasing power of new classes of park visitors: hikers, bikers, climbers, photographers, and birders.

Statistics furnished to the legislature and public over the years proved how right those projections would be. Annual running tabulations by the state comptroller, calculations from the tourism industry, and a series of economic input studies commissioned by the Texas Coalition for Conservation all lent credibility to the case for a tax that was not a new tax but a defined portion (from the sales of sporting goods) of the existing sales tax. Specifically, these items were supported in large measure by the ever-increasing new categories of park participants.

In order to examine and explain the actions and events of the rollercoaster years between 1993 and the present, the reader needs a basic understanding of the legislative dynamics of the Sporting Goods Sales Tax. The rise and fall—and rise again—over those twenty-five-plus years would—and will—determine the future well-being of our state parks system.

If the Sporting Goods Sales Tax adopted in 1993 by the Texas legislature had been a new tax, the legislature probably would have killed it early in the session on opening day. It was a carved-out portion of the existing 6.25 percent general sales tax set aside for the use and benefit of state parks and historic sites. The amount of the Sporting Goods Sales Tax is determined by the Texas comptroller using national market data (and the tax, I might add, has been so carefully structured that, over the years, its validity has rarely been challenged).

Based on projected industry market data, the tax seemed to meet another important criterion as well: its proceeds appeared likely to increase yearly, keeping pace with park visitation and the growing need for adequate repairs and maintenance on a timely and reliable basis.

Speaker of the Texas House of Representatives Pete Laney on the House floor during the legislative session, Austin, Texas, 1997. Courtesy of Bob Daemmrich via Alamy Stock Photo.

Finally, it was a source of revenue that was tied to the health and well-being of the user instead of the destructive habit of cigarettes. Besides, the powerful lieutenant governor, Bob Bullock, wanted the cigarette revenue for cancer research.

Accommodations must be anticipated in any major legislation in order to pass both houses of the legislature. One would think that, given the positives of a sporting goods sales tax, coupled with the declining condition of most parks, and fortified by statewide polls showing solid public support (a number that would only grow in strength in future polls), the bill would be passed without opposition.

That would be wishful thinking. Certain powerful legislative leaders—specifically Lieutenant Governor Bob Bullock, who controlled the Senate, and Speaker Pete Laney, who dominated the House of Representatives—did not appear to have anything against parks personally, but both were opposed to dedicated accounts for specific programs, certainly what the revenue from the Sporting Good Sales Tax would become if enacted as envisioned.

Former Speaker of the Texas House of Representatives Tom Craddick, 2013. Courtesy of the Photography Department, Texas House of Representatives, Austin, Texas.

Edwin Cox Jr., former chairman of the Texas Parks and Wildlife Commission, date unknown. The Edwin L. Cox Jr. Texas Freshwater Fisheries Center in Athens, Texas, is named in his honor for his contributions to natural resource conservation and management in Texas. Courtesy of of Edwin Cox Jr.

Fortunately for Texas and parks, Speaker Laney was fair-minded and sought bipartisan solutions whenever possible. One such move was his appointment of State Representative Tom Craddick, a Republican from Midland, Texas, as chairman of the powerful Ways and Means Committee. This move would have positive consequences as the bill establishing the Sporting Goods Sales Tax moved through the legislature in 1993.

What was crucial from start to finish was the formation of a team, both from inside the ranks of the legislature and from outside, in the form of well-organized groups that could muster facts and put pressure on the members of the House and Senate as they began the process in the 1993 legislative session. It was the parks' great fortune to have both, and both were coordinated from the opening of the session all the way to final passage.

While there were many participants at every level of the process, I will mention a few who were extraordinary in their ability to work together, make deals, then sell the package to House and Senate members while keeping the main thrust of the bill intact.

Because I devoted a portion of the last chapter to Andy Sansom and his role with Bob Armstrong in closing the deal on the Big Bend Ranch State Park, I will pick up the tale here with his role in the Sporting Goods Sales Tax saga.

After a stint in Washington in the early 1970s, when he learned the rhyme and politics of the various conservation movements under the tutelage of Secretary of the Interior Rogers C. B. Morton, Sansom returned to Texas and became executive director of the Texas Nature Conservancy. Due to his successes at the conservancy as a consummate conservation land dealmaker, he soon caught the eye of Ed Cox Jr., chairman of the Texas Parks and Wildlife Commission, who hired him away from the Texas Nature Conservancy in 1987 to head up land and park acquisitions for the Texas Parks and Wildlife Department. Sansom's successes were so outstanding in securing Big Bend Ranch State Park and Devils River State Natural Area that when an opening arose in 1989, Governor Bill Clements and Cox had Sansom appointed the new executive director of the Texas Parks and Wildlife Department. It was a match, if not made in heaven, at least blessed by Mother Nature.

By 1992, when the Texas House Committee on Environmental Affairs reported on the condition of parks, including the fact that cigarette tax revenues were not meeting the parks' financial needs, several recommendations were put forward, including the imperative for a substitute: the Sporting Goods Sales Tax. Andy Sansom was ready to meet the challenge. He would have support at every level of the conservation/parks movement in Texas. From nonprofit organizations to interested industry groups to local park advocates, all stepped up to drive home the benefits of a well-financed and -maintained parks system.

The external support effort was headed by Fred "Corky" Palmer Jr., who had a thriving sporting goods store in Lake Jackson, Texas, and a wide and favorable circle of contacts throughout the industry. As a well-established insider, he was the perfect person to lead the advocacy effort. He and the industry were aided by the fact that most of the sporting goods establishments, whether single stores or national chains, were owned by Texans. They all had a direct stake in the well-being of their industry, Texans, and Texas. Decisions, unlike financial support for legislative initiatives, could be made swiftly, usually with top-dollar results.

That is not true today. The major Texan-owned chain-store giants such as Academy and Oshman's have been bought by out-of-state entities, resulting in varying degrees of participation in park matters.

As for the smaller "mom-and-pop" stores, most have been competed out of business. But in 1993, they were a force to be reckoned with.

When joined with the leadership of local parks groups (members of the Texas Recreation and Parks Society), who worked the Texas legislature from practically every city and town in the state, there was little room for outside opposition.

But no amount of outside support could be effective without a first-class team of legislative insiders.

No legislative endeavor in Texas could have had a better luck of the draw than those leaders who stepped forward to champion, carry, and coauthor the Sporting Goods Sales Tax legislative package that would transfer park financing from the dwindling revenue of the cigarette tax to the blossoming potential of sporting goods sales.

There was Governor Ann Richards, who had enjoyed a love affair with all things natural since she was a young girl and who had often gone hunting and fishing with her father. While she had no real power over the legislative process, she set the tone in public and private speeches and by example—like canoeing on the Rio Grande or hunting with her "good ol' boy" friends.

One such friend was Ygnacio "Nacho" Garza, former mayor of Brownsville and passionate advocate for parks, whose physical stature of six feet, six inches matched his enthusiasm for parks as chairman of the Texas Parks and Wildlife Commission. Throughout his tenure and chairmanship, Garza would be a tower of strength, especially in the cause of parks—state and local—and specifically in the push to enact the Sporting Goods Sales Tax.

Waiting in the House of Representatives was Rene Oliveira of Brownsville, a personal and political ally of Garza. Oliveira was first elected to the House in 1980 and served until 2019, with a short break from 1987 to 1990, when he ran for the Texas Senate—but lost—then regained his House seat four years later.

By 1993, Rene Oliveira was again in a position of power, serving on the Ways and Means Committee and as chair of the Mexican American caucus.

In the 1993 session, he was tasked by the chair of Ways and Means, Tom Craddick, to carry the Sporting Goods Sales Tax legislation. With the support of Speaker Pete Laney,

Fred "Corky" Palmer Jr., coordinator of outside organizations for support of the original 1993 Sporting Goods Sales Tax, date unknown. Courtesy of Fred Palmer Jr.

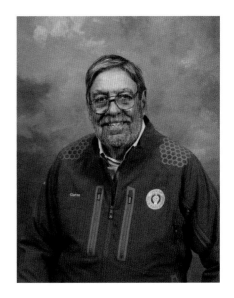

Ygnacio "Nacho" Garza, former chair of the Texas Parks and Wildlife Commission, January 2022. Courtesy of Ygnacio Garza.

Former Chair of the Texas House of Representatives Ways and Means Committee Rene Oliveira, 2017. Courtesy of the Photography Department, Texas House of Representatives, Austin, Texas.

John Montford, former Texas state senator and chairman of the State Senate Finance Committee, which guaranteed passage of the Sporting Goods Sales Tax, ca. 1993. Courtesy of the office of the Honorable John Montford.

Craddick, Garza, the Texas Parks and Wildlife Commission, and a wide range of supporting organizations that included local parks organizations and portions of the sporting goods industry, it passed the House with ease, then was sent to the Senate.

By design, the bill landed in the Senate Finance Committee, chaired by Senator John Montford of Lubbock, a committed friend of parks. Because of Montford's position and power, he was able to obtain the blessing of Lieutenant Governor Bob Bullock, a must in the scheme of legislation timing, floor action, and passage. In typical Montford style, all points in the flow of the Sporting Goods Sales Tax bill were covered. It passed the Senate without objection. With the concurrence of the House and Senate, House Bill 706 became law. It should be noted that Senator John Montford was named one of *Texas Monthly*'s "Top 10 Best Legislators" five times.[4]

A final note. In order to comply with the fiscal policy of the legislature, the bill set the original two-year appropriation at $27 million. This amount was arrived at because it was the estimated revenue to be derived from the cigarette tax that would be generated during each of the next two years (biennium).

### Sporting Goods Sales Tax Totals 1993-2023

| FY | Total SGST Estimates per CPA | Annual % Change | Biennial Totals | Biennial % Change |
|---|---|---|---|---|
| 1993 | 58,251,000 | | | |
| 1994 | 61,113,000 | | | |
| 1995 | 64,166,000 | 5.0% | 125,279,000 | |
| 1996 | 67,297,000 | 4.9% | | |
| 1997 | 70,520,000 | 4.8% | 137,817,000 | 10.0% |
| 1998 | 73,179,000 | 3.8% | | |
| 1999 | 76,075,000 | 4.0% | 149,254,000 | 8.3% |
| 2000 | 80,008,000 | 5.2% | | |
| 2001 | 84,230,000 | 5.3% | 164,238,000 | 10.0% |
| 2002 | 87,119,000 | 3.4% | | |
| 2003 | 90,905,000 | 4.3% | 178,024,000 | 8.4% |
| 2004 | 93,821,000 | 3.2% | | |
| 2005 | 97,125,000 | 3.5% | 190,946,000 | 7.3% |
| 2006 | 104,831,000 | 7.9% | | |
| 2007 | 108,396,000 | 3.4% | 213,227,000 | 11.7% |
| 2008 | 112,512,000 | 3.8% | | |
| 2009 | 116,652,000 | 3.7% | 229,164,000 | 7.5% |
| 2010 | 122,854,000 | 5.3% | | |
| 2011 | 126,888,000 | 3.3% | 249,742,000 | 9.0% |
| 2012 | 122,900,000 | -3.1% | | |
| 2013 | 128,432,000 | 4.5% | 251,332,000 | 0.6% |
| 2014 | 130,600,000 | 1.7% | | |
| 2015 | 135,200,000 | 3.5% | 265,800,000 | 5.8% |
| 2016 | 137,200,000 | 1.5% | | |
| 2017 | 140,600,000 | 2.5% | 277,800,000 | 4.5% |
| 2018 | 165,000,000 | 17.4% | | |
| 2019 | 168,500,000 | 2.1% | 333,500,000 | 20.1% |
| 2020 | 170,200,000 | 1.0% | | |
| 2021 | 216,900,000 | 27.4% | 387,100,000 | 16.1% |
| 2022 | 196,900,000 | -9.2% | | |
| 2023 | 207,900,000 | 5.6% | 404,800,000 | 4.6% |

It is also important to note that the 40/40/10 split between state parks, local parks, and debt retirement would hold true over the next twelve years—at least on paper. There were a number of years when the Sporting Goods Sales Tax appropriation (set and capped in 1995 at $32 million) was less than $32 million.

And therein lies the saga of the failure of the Texas legislature to fix and then stick with a financial solution that was sustainable and substantial enough to meet the needs of a growing user population and a parks system that was established in 1923, rescued in the Depression of the 1930s, enlarged under Governor Connally's reorganization and meaningful bond initiative, then financed during the 1970s and early 1980s by the cigarette tax and the federal government's matching Land and Water Conservation Fund.

While the original bill transferred financing of state and local parks from cigarettes to sporting goods, it did so with the sponsors' and supporters' intent that, in the future, it would follow the projected rise in revenue generated year-to-year by sales of the designated sporting goods supporting it.

What sponsors and supporters didn't contemplate was that the $32 million annual appropriation would be capped permanently. The chart on page 194 shows how enduring that cap would be. It remained for twelve years, although there were some years when the legislature would appropriate less than $32 million. Over the same period of time, parks continued to deteriorate, while the numbers of visitors continued to increase.

A natural train wreck was about to happen. By the turn of the century (2001 to 2002), the most damning fact about the shameful condition of parks was that hundreds of toilets were in need of repair or replacement!

## The Dark Decade

If there were periods over the seventy years of the Texas state parks history that were deemed "golden," then the period from 1995 to 2007 certainly earned the title "the dark decade."

Again, there were exceptions in 2005 and 2007, when it looked like the onerous and artificial $32 million cap on state parks funding from the Sporting Goods Sales Tax might be swept aside, and the tax would support the parks in the manner envisioned by the original supporters and bill sponsors. But that was yet to come.

There was also a single new park exception, which was accomplished without a dime's worth of state legislative financial support. Through the support of local, private, and public contributions, an Eagle Mountain Lake transaction was completed between 2006 to 2007. The state sold four hundred acres of undeveloped state parkland to the Tarrant Regional Water District for the purpose of converting them to a local park.

The funds from the sale ($9.3 million) flowed to the state's general revenue account to be held until a piece of land (of around five thousand acres and less than one and a half hours away from Fort Worth) could be obtained at a future date for a new state park.

For a number of reasons, it would take five years (until 2011) to identify and acquire that piece of land for a state park and another decade to fund development. During the years in between, there was mischief aplenty, wrapped in legislative intrigue and spite, dishonest scheming on the part of the Legislative Budget Board, an oil billionaire secretly purchasing neighboring land and other prospective tracts to block the deal, and a major sports owner and chairman of the Texas Parks and Wildlife Commission stepping in to save the funding day.

Then, to top things off, there was the matter of murder!

Murder? How and why?

The short version is that a scoundrel was flirting with a waitress in The Mule Lip bar in Mingus, Texas, west of Fort Worth. An elderly rancher tried to intervene, but the no-good persisted. The rancher pulled a gun and shot him. In the criminal case, the rancher received a light sentence, but he lost the civil suit and was ordered to pay a substantial settlement, large enough to require him to sell his land.

Fortunately, the Texas Parks and Wildlife Department had funds from the Eagle Mountain sale ready and waiting to purchase the landscape that would become Palo Pinto Mountains State Park.

As Texas moves into the next hundred years, there must be serious thought given on ways and means to move the purchase/development process along in a timelier fashion. Suffice it to say that one new park per decade does not meet the needs of a population that is growing each year, carrying with it ever-increasing numbers of visitors to our state parks.

It was past time for "the dark decade" to come to an end.

# Chapter 9

# Starts and Stops:
# Fickle Legislatures:
# 1994–2016

ven though we would not know it at the time, 2007 would be a major turning point in the fight for full funding with revenue from the Sporting Goods Sales Tax.

Sensing a chance for real change in the 2007 legislative session, I kept copious notes and saved all sorts of materials. I had at the back of my mind that there was a story in the making, but I had no concrete plan.

Through a fortunate set of circumstances, what happened in 2007 in the context of conservation and parkland advocacy caught the attention of Dick Bartlett, a top-flight business leader and conservationist, and Shannon Davies of the Texas A&M University Press conservation/environmental division. They asked if I would write a book about my experiences in building a coalition to move park financing from a dream (prior, a nightmare) to a sustainable annual appropriation.

I agreed if they would allow me to write the state parks legislative story into the larger story of my life experiences. Many of those experiences were signposts leading me to—and preparing me for—my work in conservation. We reached an agreement, and, throughout 2010 to 2011, I wrote *On Politics and Parks*.

During the rollout marketing period for the book and shortly thereafter in 2012, several people whose knowledge I trust allowed that they thought the chapter "Parks in a Changing Texas" was a superb piece depicting the trials and tribulations of working the Texas legislature.

Early morning hunt at Bucksnag Lodge, El Campo, Texas, 2010. From left (standing), Bob Armstrong, Dick Bartlett, George Bristol, Andy Sansom, (kneeling) Joey Park, and guide. Author's collection.

When I began to compile the materials I would need to convey the history of Texas's state parks system in this book, I reread the chapter and came to the same conclusion.

Therefore, with the generous permission of Texas A&M University Press, I have used parts of that chapter to convey my experiences and observations leading up to 2007 and beyond, toward another span of darkness before the bright light of success.[1]

## Parks in a Changing Texas

In 1994, I was appointed to the National Park Foundation board of directors by President Bill Clinton and Secretary of the Interior Bruce Babbitt and, after six years, rotated off with deep regret but fired up with knowledge gained during my time on the board. In the summer of 2000, I sought out my friend Andy Sansom, who was by then serving with great distinction and vision as executive director of the Texas Parks and Wildlife Department. I explained that I wanted to put my national park enthusiasm and experience to use in Texas. After an hour or so of conversation and exchange of ideas, he wrote something on a piece of paper, folded it up, and handed it to me. On it was one word: "Money!"

"George," he said, "the department is underfunded, particularly the parks system, but we also need increased appropriations for fish hatcheries, wildlife areas, and a number of other conservation venues." I told him that while I knew the legislative process, I had not worked on conservation and parkland issues specific to Texas and did not know the legislative or conservation players across the state. However, I thought I could raise enough money from friends and associates to give me enough breathing room to learn while beginning to build an organization diverse and strong enough to succeed. Sansom suggested several people I ought to meet and, in December 2000, introduced me to the constituency groups he had assembled over the years to explain the upcoming 2001 legislative budget and issues situation. That was of immense help to me, as I met people who signed on with the project early and who, to this day, I count as supporters and friends. This was the genesis of what would become the Texas Coalition for Conservation.

I visited with friends and the people Sansom had suggested. Most were receptive, but David Gochman of Academy Outdoor Sports and Morton Meyerson, my National Park Foundation partner and friend, were generously supportive. Gochman agreed to chair the coalition. I could not have begun without them.

It was also apparent early on that we would need a rallying cry—a hook—to focus our efforts and those of elected officials, volunteers, and donors. But first I had to immerse myself in the politics, personalities, and processes of the world of Texas conservation in the twenty-first century. I would never know as much as those with a single mission, but I needed to know enough to communicate with each on some level of intelligence and sophistication.

The year 2001 looked to be a good year to begin, partly because there were no huge issues that required immediate mobilization, even though the state senate situation was in a rare state of flux. After Texas Governor George W. Bush was elected president, his seat was vacated. Lieutenant Governor Rick Perry became governor, vacating *his* seat. The Senate then, for the first time in history, elected a new lieutenant governor from among their own—and the Senate had a Republican majority. In late December 2000, State Senator Bill Ratliff, with unanimous support of Democrats, was elected. As he was a moderate Republican, many breathed a sigh of relief. Ratliff had shown throughout his career that he could work with both sides, especially in his role as chairman of the Senate's Education and Finance committees. He would more than meet that expectation, although it would later cost him dearly when he stood for election in his own right the following year. The conservative Republican special-interest contributors forced him out of the race. While lieutenant governor in 2001, out of commitment and gratitude, Ratliff appointed State Senator Rodney Ellis as chair of the Senate Finance Committee, which bode well for me because we were friends of long standing. The lieutenant governor of Texas wields more real power than the governor, in great part because he or she appoints chairs of the various committees. In turn, the chairs become the lieutenant governor's lieutenants on the floor and in committee—for the most part. The lieutenant governor also controls the agenda and legislative floor action. Thus, bills move only when and if the lieutenant governor allows them to move.

The House was still controlled by the Democrats. Speaker Pete Laney and the chairman of the House Appropriations Committee, Rob Junell, were both friends of mine. The committee chair with jurisdiction over park matters was Edmund Kuempel, an old high school mate and a strong advocate for parks. State Senator Buster Brown and I were

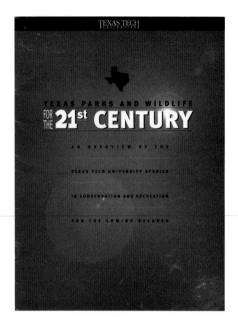

Texas Parks and Wildlife Department 21st Century Texas Tech University study, 2001. Courtesy of the Texas Parks and Wildlife Department, Austin, Texas.

in law school together. At least I had friends with whom I could talk and from whom I could learn.

We were also armed with two excellent reports. The first was from October 28, 2000, by a blue-ribbon committee that had been appointed by Governor Bush. *Taking Care of Texas* addressed private lands, public lands, and water. Each section explored present and future needs in each category. Without going into great detail, the reports proposed the following recommendations to Governor Bush:

- Create a statewide purchase of development rights (PDR) program for retention of private lands to thwart agriculture and habitat fragmentation.
- Reform tax laws to support conservation.
- Develop a comprehensive system to assess outdoor recreation needs.
- Fund the repair, development, and maintenance of existing public properties to meet the needs of a growing and urban population.
- Acquire assets of statewide significance to meet those needs.
- Divest properties that [are] underutilized.
- Ensure adequate quantity and quality of water to protect Texas's land and water ecosystems.
- Include the requirements of fish and wildlife in current water resource management.
- Promote agriculture water uses that also benefit wildlife.
- Protect Texas's springs.

Each of these recommendations was unanimously adopted by men and women who were, for the most part, Republican, with not a radical "tree-hugger" in their midst. Each recommendation was reached based on public testimony, existing studies, and work being completed by what was to be known as "the Texas Tech study"—*Texas Parks and Wildlife for the 21st Century*—published in 2001.

To a degree, the recommendations were complementary. Private lands, new parklands, and water were all tied to meaningful ecosystems. Private landowners were encouraged to open their lands to ecotourism. Water conservation is tied directly to the well-being of fish and wildlife, and, in turn, fishing and hunting are a significant economic engine. The estimated economic benefits of the recommendations totaled more than $36 billion annually in 2000.

The Bush committee left it to the legislature to arrive at methods of financing and amounts to be appropriated. But I would soon learn that reason, common sense, and unanimity carry little or no weight among some elected officials. Both the committee report and the Texas Tech study were more or less buried by those who either cared little for the land and its people or who were simply peeved at someone or the system. I had to obtain bootlegged copies of both reports in order to read the deliberations and recommendations, which were noncontroversial in content, language, and purpose. The documents called for planning and implementing policies and programs that were essential to meeting the needs of a population that would double by 2050. There was little time to waste.

As the 2001 session opened, I went to see my old friends and sought out new ones, particularly people who controlled the purse strings and the legislative process. I went to every appropriations hearing, committee meeting, and legislative session related to conservation or parklands. Some, particularly appropriations meetings, went on into the wee hours. It didn't matter. I was taking notes, learning, and asking questions. I was blessed to have State Representative Myra Crownover from my hometown of Denton explain the process and personalities. She also sat on the Cultural, Recreation, and Tourism Committee and had a passion for parks. On two or three occasions, we went hiking at Ray Roberts Lake State Park near Denton and shared thoughts, which helped me focus on the daunting task of increasing funding for parks.

Sometime during the session, Andy Sansom called on me for advice. He needed an introduction to the chairman of the Senate Finance Committee, Rodney Ellis. There was an opportunity for the Texas Parks and Wildlife Department to benefit (to the tune of $100 million) from a major bond package being considered during the session—if it passed the legislature and a vote of the people. Because Ellis had not served on committees of jurisdiction that affected the parks department in the past, he and Sansom had not had an opportunity to get to know each other well.

Rodney Ellis is a man of tremendous depth and scope. Though most of his pursuits lay in issues important to urban areas—education, jobs, clean air, and the like—he and I went way back and genuinely liked one another. He and Andy Sansom hit it off, too, and there was the bonus that Ellis was a passionate bicyclist who loved to ride through city, state, and national parks. Ellis said that he'd sign on and was good to his word. That became important because Rob Junell, chairman of the House Appropriations Committee, had no love for Andy Sansom, the Texas Parks and Wildlife Department, or parks. It was essential to have the counterbalancing support of the Senate, particularly when the appropriations bills of the House and Senate got to conference.

Conference committees are where proposed bills are agreed on, stripped, modified, or killed. It is essential to have allies who will stand pat or, if necessary, cut the best deal possible. At the right moment (late in the session), Rodney Ellis cut such a deal. It was unexpected—but the right thing to do. In their earlier discussions, Sansom had told Ellis of the rich treasure trove of the Levi Jordan Plantation. Sansom had tried for years to draw attention to its possibilities. With Ellis's blessing, he sought and received $2 million from the state to restore the plantation, which is near Houston and had long been

Katharine Armstrong, former Texas Parks and Wildlife Commission chair, ca. 2001. Courtesy of the Texas Parks and Wildlife Department, Austin, Texas.

rotting away. The artifacts there are some of the richest sources of slave history, art, and lifestyle in Texas. Among items found were old buttons with African carvings on the back (presumably carved on button backs so that slave owners would not see them).

In my naiveté, I took it upon myself to see Rob Junell. For five or ten minutes, he vented loud and clear about his issues with Andy Sansom and the Texas Parks and Wildlife Department. I listened and then told him that I was not there representing Sansom or the department. I was his friend who happened to have a deep commitment to parks for the people, and Texas's parks were in a shameful state of disrepair. I also said that parks were extremely popular and, in most cases when they were contained within a bond issue, tended to guarantee the bond's successful passage. He cooled down and said that he would give it some thought. Perhaps I had some small gift of persuasion. That is all it could have been because I still had much to learn—I knew only enough to be passionate, not knowledgeable. The parks and wildlife part of the bond authorization survived and was included in what was to be known as Proposition 8. Voters passed it by a sizable margin in November 2001.

At the session's end, I thought I had learned a great deal and contributed modestly to the cause. The issue of the bond authorization allowed me to educate myself and others on the need for increased funding for parks and conservation measures, including the important concept of purchase of development rights, which allows farmers and ranchers to retain their lands under favorable tax and payment provisions and forestall further fragmentation of vital habitat in ecosystem holdings.

But in the process and in my inexperience, I didn't pick up on warning signals that Andy Sansom's position as executive director of the Texas Parks and Wildlife Department was in jeopardy. I did know that he was under serious consideration to become the next director of the National Park Service. Unfortunately, that did not happen. In the meantime, while Sansom remained executive director, Katharine Armstrong, the daughter of Tobin and Anne Armstrong of Armstrong Ranch fame, was appointed chair of the Texas Parks and Wildlife Commission.

She called in late June 2001 and asked to see me. We met at her home in San Antonio. We discussed issues and the need for a concerted effort to advocate for passage of Proposition 8. She specifically asked me what I thought her role should be as chair. Because I firmly believe in the concept of noblesse oblige, as demonstrated by the Rockefellers, Mellons, and others who had given their time and treasure to the national parks, I thought she had a golden opportunity to continue that tradition in Texas since she came from one of the landed families. Without in any way abandoning property rights or the crucial and productive conservation efforts of private landowners, she could become a champion for the future enhancement of public lands. I went away pleased that she had been attentive and gracious with her time, and nothing over the summer led me to think differently.

At Andy Sansom's urging, we called a luncheon meeting of all the agencies that would benefit by the passage of Proposition 8. House member Talmadge Heflin, who had shepherded the portion of the appropriations bill dealing with the bond issue, attended. With his assurances that the leadership would support passage, we urged all attending to contact their various constituency groups at the local level.

In August 2001, I set up an election political action committee, began to solicit commitments, and laid out an inexpensive but adequate campaign. At the same time, the Texas Coalition for Conservation continued to grow, holding meetings in Houston, Dallas, and elsewhere. I didn't see much of Sansom in July and August—there was no need for me to see him. I had an organization to build, and I only had to share thoughts on the bond campaign every so often, as it seemed to be falling into place.

My new friend David Gochman again rose to the occasion. Academy Outdoor Sports agreed to a shared advertising campaign as well as shopping bag stuffers and window signs reminding people to vote in November and to vote for Proposition 8. At the end of the campaign, he told me that several hundred thousand pieces had been distributed statewide, and "Vote for Prop 8" ads had run several times in all the communities where Academy had stores. Furthermore, because of his leadership, others in the industry had participated as well.

In August, however, Andy Sansom told me that things had gotten ugly and untenable and that he would be announcing his resignation the next day at the Texas Parks and Wildlife Commission meeting. He had made a deal to resign effective December 31, 2001, however, to allow a smooth transition while remaining available to help on the bond issue as much as he was allowed. I was heartsick. I knew that I was losing a valuable ally and would probably have little to no support from the Texas Parks and Wildlife Department for the foreseeable future.

Regardless of the circumstances, we had to press on. There was the bond issue as well as a Texas Coalition for Conservation-sponsored conference planned for September 14, 2001. "Seeking Common Ground: The Future of Texas Land-Water-Wildlife and Parks" was to be the Texas Coalition for Conservation's first attempt to bring representatives of as many diverse groups as possible into one room to work together on conservation. But it was not to be. September 11, 2001, put all thoughts of proceeding out of mind. Fundraising also came to a halt or slowed down during those dark days when America and the world held its breath.

It seems that while Texas Governor Rick Perry wanted Andy Sansom terminated, he left the details to Katharine Armstrong, the new Texas Parks and Wildlife Commission chair. For whatever reason, she took it on herself to purge all of his friends and vestiges of his time with the agency. Her purge extended beyond the agency to other organizations, including members of the staff and board of the Texas Parks and Wildlife Foundation. At some point, even photos of Sansom, formal and informal, disappeared from the walls

Dr. John Crompton, University Distinguished Professor, Regents Professor, and Presidential Professor for Teaching Excellence, Texas A&M University, College Station, Texas, 2022. Dr. Crompton directed the economic impact studies of Texas state parks in 2005, 2015, and 2019. Courtesy of John Crompton.

Dr. Ji Youn Jeong, Assistant Professor, Department of Tourism, Kyungpook National University, Seoul, South Korea, 2017. Dr. Jeong coauthored the 2005, 2015, and 2019 economic impact study reports. Courtesy of Ji Youn Jeong.

and halls of the Texas Parks and Wildlife Department. This was totally unnecessary. A simple visit between the governor and Sansom would have sealed the deal. Katharine Armstrong's petty and ham-handed action would split the commission and the department's staff. Carol Dinkins, one of the most respected commissioners, resigned in protest. Others grumbled and complained but remained. In February 2002, Bob Cook assumed the position of executive director of the Texas Parks and Wildlife Department.

On November 6, 2001, Proposition 8 passed 62 to 28 percent. After the election, I had a chance to regroup. Shortly before September 11, the Texas Coalition for Conservation had received IRS notification of our nonprofit status. Therefore, we could formally proceed. I concentrated on grant writing and reviving the "Seeking Common Ground" forum. The postponement allowed me time to enhance the program as well as better focus the message and mission on grant requests.

It was becoming clearer that any chance of success in funding parks (or any new conservation venture) had to focus on economic benefits to local communities and the state. It may have been more rewarding to praise the spiritual, physical, and other intrinsic values of our shared natural and cultural treasures, but this would never have had the appeal of the almighty dollar. For me, the epiphany came in a small insert that I had nearly overlooked in a 1998 study by Texas A&M University. Dr. John Crompton, professor in the university's Department of Recreation, Park and Tourism Sciences, and Dr. Ji Youn Jeong, assistant professor in the Department of Tourism at Kyungpook National University in South Korea, had surveyed four or five state parks and come forth with a revelation: parks, if properly maintained and financed, could give economic benefits to local communities, businesses, and merchants far in excess of the amount appropriated to the parks by the state.

Several nights after reading this, I sat at a table with Crompton and State Parks Director Walt Dabney. I told them that I thought a more substantial study was required, and in the next day or so, I went to see Dabney. He was enthusiastic about the possibility of a major park-by-park study. We called Crompton, and the delightful United Kingdom native said that yes, such a study was possible and, in his opinion, long overdue, but that its validity rested on an accurate visitation count. I told Dabney that I thought I could raise the funds to commission a study but that it would be incumbent on his department to verify the counts. I then drove to College Station to meet with Crompton. After spending some time with him, I had a clear understanding of his methods and what it would cost to commission a sample survey to calculate visitors' expenditures and economic impact, not with perfect accuracy, but close enough to make workable assumptions and a valid case. We agreed in principle, subject to funding.

I was adamant about the visitor count because the matter had become an issue with the national parks during my term on the National Park Foundation board. A number had been publicized and then revised downward after a similar study, even though with the adjustment, the number remained huge, more than enough to make the case that national parks continued to be one of the most enduring attractions for both US citizens and foreign visitors. I had every confidence this would be the case in Texas as well. That count was necessary to lend credence to the economic impact survey that the Texas Coalition for Conservation would commission and fund. After some negotiation and discussion of the parks to be selected, we struck a deal. Over the summer and fall of 2002, thirty-seven parks (a good cross-section of existing parks and historical sites) would be surveyed.

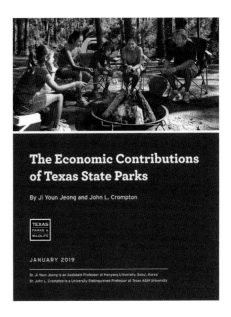

Economic Contributions of Texas State Parks report update, 2019. Courtesy of the Texas Parks and Wildlife Department, Austin, Texas.

With the survey in progress, I turned my intention to the rescheduled "Seeking Common Ground" forum. We wound up with an all-star lineup of speakers, including David Schmidly, who spoke convincingly about the scope of his Texas Tech study (ignored by those apparently uninterested in the collapse of one of Texas's richest assets—its landscape), and John Crompton, who is not only an educator but a motivator and who made a complete case for the benefits derived from well-maintained parks. I came away satisfied that we had established an underlying foundation for our efforts.

The other thing we did right was to mix the forum's characters and content so that the diverse groups could share their missions and experiences with counterparts. A number of participants told me before the meeting that they thought Ducks Unlimited was a hunting club and that they had no idea it was a major rehabilitator of wetlands. Progress ever so small, but progress. In 2002, we would continue to listen and educate ourselves on the priorities and purposes of other groups.

By summer 2002, I had substantially defined the problem. The solution would take time, more organization, refinement of mission, and—eventually—luck or a break, or both. It was becoming apparent that private landowners, water specialists, and hunters and fishermen had well-financed and well-organized advocates—usually on both sides of any position. Parks had little voice and no clout—inside or outside the Texas Parks and Wildlife Department. While my natural inclination was toward parks, I did not think they were the only meaningful aspect of conservation, but I was coming to the conclusion that they were ignored to the point of disrepair and might soon be irrelevant to citizens of Texas as well as to out-of-state visitors. That was confirmed in the Texas Parks and Wildlife Department's 2002 *Land and Water Resources Conservation and Recreation Plan*, which stated:

> The window of opportunity for conservation of natural resources and providing adequate access for outdoor recreation in Texas is closing. The state's population is expanding rapidly, land fragmentation is increasing, and water resources are already stretched in many areas. Failure to ensure adequate water for wildlife now will impose a great cost on the citizens of Texas in the future.

The loss or decline of these resources will have a greater impact on the economy than is readily apparent: it will negatively impact local economic development from the loss of hunting, fishing, and other recreational tourism; it will increase state and federal regulations; it will increase costs to businesses and industries; and it will impact public services, including municipal water supply and treatment. Furthermore, the cost of acquiring land to serve the public's recreational needs will also increase over time.

While I thought the Texas Tech study was an excellent blueprint for the future, its recommendations far exceeded any realistic consideration by a legislature (Democrat or Republican) prone to doing little more than begrudgingly funding the status quo. That certainly applied to parks and even more so to appropriating funds for new land acquisitions crucial to meeting the needs of an ever-increasing urban population. But if the Texas Tech study was too ambitious on the issue of parkland acquisition, the *Land and Water Resources Conservation and Recreation Plan* was the opposite, giving only lip service to acquiring new park assets: a minimum of four new parks of five thousand acres (a valid calculation to meet ecosystem considerations as well as recreational ones), all to be located within an hour and a half driving time from major metropolitan areas—another valid criterion. What was distressing was that this minimalist recommendation was intentionally minimal and had been added begrudgingly. Subsequently, no parks of this magnitude were added to the system, even though strongly supported in public opinion and even though funds were available to add them from Sporting Goods Sales Tax revenues.

Policy advancement on any issue, including setting aside more parklands for recreation, requires commitment not only from the public but also from within appropriate government agencies. In our case, this would not be forthcoming for several years. I knew that the efforts of the Texas Coalition for Conservation and its supporters would have to be mounted without any tangible support from its eventual beneficiary—the Texas Parks and Wildlife Department, which, even into the twenty-first century, was dominated by a "good ol' boy" mentality that weighed heavily on the side of private land and hunting and fishing. With this in mind, we took our show on the road with public forums, testimony, and visits with outdoor columnists.

As 2002 progressed, I became more convinced that the park-by-park analysis might hold the key to our ability to give substance and effective voice to our cause. Because parks are local, they would have relevance to community leaders, elected officials, and local media. They would become more relevant than the distant and amorphous state parks system. They would hit close to home.

In the fall, the Texas Coalition for Conservation held a board retreat to sharpen our mission and focus. Through a facilitator, we arrived at the conclusion that we would give key weight to those areas of concern that called for funding, including parks, water, and purchase of development rights, while at the same time we would attempt to act as an "honest broker" among sympathetic but diverse groups. Parks, water, and development rights each clearly fell within the purview of the Bush study, the Texas Tech study, and the Texas Parks and Wildlife Department study. All needed addressing with ample funding to achieve even modest goals. But the state, like the nation, was in a recession and faced a budget deficit going into the 2003 legislative session—a deficit of $10 billion as it turned out. That threw a damper on any sort of new or increased funding. However, I thought it would be a perfect time to highlight methods of financing used in other states in the areas of parks, purchase of development rights, and water.

Through the Texas office of the Trust for Public Land, the Nature Conservancy, and others, we found measures that had recently been passed in other states that addressed problems with more than platitudes. I also thought it important to invite representatives of states governed mainly by Republicans to a symposium, since Texas's statewide leaders were Republican. Following the 2002 elections, State Representative Tom Craddick became Speaker of the House, and Talmadge Heflin became chairman of the House Appropriations Committee. A wealth of measures had been passed in Republican states by Republican leaders, including Jeb Bush and State Senate Majority Leader Jack Latvia in Florida and former South Carolina legislator Chip Campson. The Florida Forever initiative was a multibillion-dollar program that covered the same needs as Texas's parks—purchase of development rights and water issues, financed by bonds and a documentary stamp tax. South Carolina's Conservation Incentive and Conservation Bank acts were financed by a deed transfer fee. Other methods of financing included state lottery funding, real estate transfer fees, license plates, and dedicated sales taxes. All in all, this was a good mix that should have sparked great interest and thought-provoking dialogue. We even decided to hold the symposium in the capital to facilitate attendance by legislators and staff. Unfortunately, bad weather and bad timing would dampen attendance literally and figuratively.

On Monday, January 27, 2003, it rained. More significantly, the legislative session was just underway, and it is a cardinal rule of legislative advocacy never to push new programs as the session is just beginning. We had a fair crowd, with some legislators and staff (particularly Speaker Craddick), but not all I had anticipated. The symposium speakers did give legitimacy to our contention that parkland and conservation measures were universal in appeal and that citizens were willing to pay for them. The symposium also highlighted the completion of the 2002 to 2003 Texas A&M University economic impact study, and, again, John Crompton's comments drew attention. Most importantly, we demonstrated that the Texas Coalition for Conservation could deliver diverse personalities, philosophies, and causes within a common framework and advance fresh ideas to the benefit of all who cared to listen and learn. The Texas Coalition for Conservation

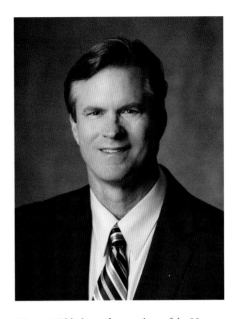

Harvey Hilderbran, former chair of the House Cultural, Recreation & Tourism Committee, 2013. Courtesy of the Photography Department, Texas House of Representatives, Austin, Texas.

was now established as a major player in the conservation arena.

We did catch the attention of the new chair of the Cultural, Recreation and Tourism Committee, Harvey Hilderbran. At some point in February 2003, he and I talked and agreed that there was little chance for enhanced appropriations for anything. However, Hilderbran asked me to give him my best thoughts, with the promise that these might be discussed in interim hearings after the session to amplify the plight of state parks, land fragmentation, and water problems, coupled with methods to finance measures addressing them. Given the budget deficit, that was all we could expect. It was a start.

Then I had a brainstorm. What was lacking in all the reports was a dollar amount for appropriate funding. As I had said many times before (and since), we could pass non-binding and unfunded resolutions of support, even authorizations, but without money, those are like kissing your cousin. So, I wrote to Hilderbran in early March 2003, asking him to file a "shell" bill to fund a billion-dollar bond package for parks, purchase of development rights, and water. Why not? You might as well start high. You can always back off. To bring it back to reality, I suggested that the bill be taken to a public vote in November 2004, with bond funding not to kick in until 2005. After negotiation, we agreed on $500 million.

A "shell" bill is a legislative method of filing before a deadline so that if something unforeseen occurs, there will be a germane bill in play. Any expectations of final passage should never go beyond a faint hope. House Bill 2449 fit that category to a tee. Nonetheless, it was on the table, with specific dollar amounts attached for each potential beneficiary: parks, purchase of development rights, and adequate water conservation programs.

Hilderbran then held a hearing. We expressed our thoughts for the record, and—lo and behold—he passed the bill out of committee, even without a word of support from commissioners or staff, though this was not surprising. That would be it for the session. It was all that could be hoped for, given the circumstances. But unbeknownst to me, favorable notice was taken.

As expected, we didn't have much to show for 2003, although a freshwater fish stamp was authorized to build new fish hatcheries and rehabilitate older ones. Like many of the state's parks, most of Texas's hatcheries were products of the Depression, built with substantial financial help from the Civilian Conservation Corps and Works Progress Administration. (Oh, those ever-intrusive feds!) Additionally, a bill was passed to raise motorboat registration fees and motorboat manufacturers' and dealers' fees, and 85 percent of the increase would go to Fund 9 (hunting and fishing), but 15 percent would flow to Fund 64 (the state parks account). This addition ($2.5 million, as I recall) was welcome and necessary, as many of our state parks are located near lakes and rivers and were in need of boat ramps and other water-related improvements.

The other major accomplishment of the session was the passage of a contingency rider (commonly referred to as the Entrepreneur Rider). Its passage meant that additional funds raised by various fee increases (estimated to be $31.5 million) would flow to Fund 9 and Fund 64 and be spent by the Texas Parks and Wildlife Department during 2004 to 2005. Had it not passed, the department—and parks, in particular—would have been thrown into chaos, though this would come soon enough anyway.

So, 2003 was better than a poke in the eye, except for the local parks grants program, also funded by the Sporting Goods Sales Tax. At the outset, I wondered why the state, given the apparent shortage of funds and the milking of the Sporting Goods Sales Tax for other purposes, would be in the local parks business. Over time, I came to support this local grants program enthusiastically. First, the state was nothing more than a seed-money venture capitalist. At relatively small cost, this program could create significant leverage. Competing communities had to put up dollars or land or both, and successful bidders had to operate their programs with local funds and personnel. Furthermore, by way of the highly respected bidding matrix fashioned by the Texas Parks and Wildlife Department and local communities, taxpayers were guaranteed to get the best projects.

As part of a growing team that was capable of mounting an educational public awareness campaign and advocating effectively, I had now reached a position where I could articulate both message and process with some knowledge and nuance. It was gratifying to hear from folks who not only had received our message but seemed to understand what we were talking about and who wanted to do more the next time. And there would be a next time because important people and institutions were now taking notice.

For all our efforts through 2003, we still lacked a coherent case for substantial increases in funding for parks and the need for a sustainable source of revenue. That was also true for purchase of development rights, but proponents of that crucial legislation were hesitant to place a price tag on the table. When asked about the validity of the $500 million bond package, my standard answer was, "Thank God it never got to a discussion of underlying numbers." The truth lay somewhere between the neglect by the Texas Parks and Wildlife Department to develop a short- and long-term case for funding to adequately finance operations, capital repairs, acquisition, and other essentials, and the fact that many among the commissioners and staff really had no interest in enhancing the status of parks. By reputation, the department was viewed by many as the pleasure ground for those who cared only about "hook and bullet" matters, private lands, and game warden issues. Parks for the use of the greater population were a byproduct of former Governor John Connally's consolidation and enhancement efforts for the 1967 passage of his major parkland acquisition package—$75 million in bonds. No equivalent effort to secure additional parks for people had been forthcoming since that time. Subsequent bond issues, like those in 2001 and 2007, were for repair and renovation.

It was becoming clear that funding needs and a reliable source of revenue had to be joined at the hip and sold together. To do that, we had to make the case that economic benefits far outweighed the appropriated outlay. We had the tools—the first economic impact study of thirty-seven parks, with another forty-two parks commissioned to be surveyed, and the various aforementioned studies (most mandated by the legislature or the Sunset Advisory Commission)—and we had a growing base of supporters.

We were beginning to generate press and community support. I had sent the initial Crompton survey to elected officials and chambers of commerce as well as local media in communities with park sites. In the statehouse, committee chairman Harvey Hilderbran had the heart for the fight but clearly needed additional support. I was about to add another tool—a monthly series of four-color, two-page flyers on the economic and societal benefits of hunting, fishing, water, wildlife appreciation (especially birding), and parks. The pieces were intentionally short and easy to read. With design support from the firm Public Strategies, I crafted every page personally. Great support staff and designers can only take a project so far. By spring and early summer 2004, I knew exactly what I wanted to convey with images and words, and I hoped to provoke thought and make a lasting impression.

We gathered into a master file all pertinent lists: donors, support organizations, media, chambers of commerce, and elected officials, state and local. Each month, from June to October, we sent out a slick position brief. Each month, we got a few more responses and words of appreciation and encouragement. But it was the response that showed up at my office (generously donated by Public Strategies) in June 2004 that was the most amazing and gratifying. There, framed in the doorway, was Ernest Angelo of Midland. Angelo had been a Bush appointee to the Texas Parks and Wildlife Commission but was rotating off after completing his term. By any measure, he fit the "hook and bullet" profile. He would move up or delay a medical procedure so as not to interfere with the opening of dove season. He financially supported the Texas Coalition for Conservation at our annual duck- and goose-hunt outings. He fished all summer in Colorado. He was as conservative as they come. As someone said, he was "the first full-time Republican in Texas." An oilman by profession, he was a public servant at heart, serving as mayor of Midland and on a number of federal and state boards and commissions.

"George," Angelo said, "I've followed your program with interest. I think you're on the right track, and I'd like to help if I can." We visited for a good while, and sometime during the conversation, he allowed that he was about to leave for his summer home in Colorado. I must have asked where because I was scheduled to visit Colorado with my friends Jack and Patsy Martin in July. Angelo said that Beaver Creek, where I was planning to go, wasn't far from his place, and he suggested that I stop by for a day or two of fishing and talking about parks.

Later that summer, I took him up on his offer. After a much-delayed flight, I drove to the Angelo place, arriving around 3:00 a.m. Rather than disturb my hosts, I slept in the car. At dawn, Penny Angelo stuck her head out the door, then hurried away to tell her husband that a strange car was in the driveway. Angelo came out, we had a good laugh about my late-night campout, and I was invited in for a good breakfast. For the rest of the day, we fished in the Taylor River, one of the most beautiful flows in Colorado and full of trout. Then, true to his word (an ongoing trait of Ernest Angelo), we sat down and visited about parks, their positive economic impact, and how they either directly or indirectly pay for themselves—with a substantial return on investment. He asked probing questions—and I had the answers.

By 2004, Texas ranked next to last among states in per capita expenditure on parks, and the case for additional funding could be made from simply the numbers alone. Calculations gathered from the Texas Parks and Wildlife Department, the state's comptroller, and the Texas A&M economic impact report clearly proved the case. User fees and the Sporting Goods Sales Tax paid for all but a small portion of the expense of parks. Sporting Goods Sales Tax revenue had increased and would continue to increase in sufficient amounts to cover even the most ambitious legislative appropriation. Finally, over and above these direct revenues, was the revelation that parks generate significant economic activity and sales within local communities.

What numbers do not enumerate is the spiritual, physical, and family well-being derived from well-maintained and attractive parks, especially for young people. Parks are inexpensive classrooms and fitness centers that provide recreation and renewal.

I asked Angelo why so unlikely a candidate as he would take such an interest. He said that he thought parks made good sense economically and were the last best places where young people and their families could connect or reconnect to natural and cultural treasures. In doing so, he hoped that they would carry a conservation ethic with them throughout their lives.

Our time together was well spent. We mapped out a plan and drafted a letter that I would send to him and that he would share with Speaker Craddick on returning from Colorado. By late August 2004, he called and asked me to send a fuller letter of explanation to Craddick with as many backup materials as I thought appropriate to make our case. He also asked me if I would make an appointment and visit with Craddick. I agreed and scheduled a meeting for right after Labor Day.

I was going to see a representative who had toiled as a Republican in the Democratic-controlled Texas House for thirty-four years. While remaining a partisan Republican, Craddick had honed his legislative skills and abilities to work with members on both sides of the aisle to the degree that he had been appointed to several important committees by Democratic speakers over the years. For years, he was chairman of the all-important Ways and Means Committee. At one time, he had been quite close to Speaker Pete Laney, but they had recently had a falling out, which I believe heightened Craddick's desire to obtain a Republican House. In 2003, his goal of a majority became a reality, and he became the Speaker. Smart, tough, and magnanimous in victory, he honored the tradition afforded him and appointed Democrats to a number of chairs. He also demoted and sometimes belittled Republican members who did not toe his line. Accommodating, yes, but demanding absolute loyalty.

I knew Craddick only by reputation, save for one chance meeting on an airplane. During the flight, he asked where I had been. When I told him I'd been to a national parks meeting, his eyes lit up, and he described at some length how he and his wife, Nadine, loved national and state parks. He recalled with great enthusiasm and joy how much his family looked forward to those outings. I had tucked that fact away. Even so, I didn't know what to expect.

He could not have been more gracious. He could not have been more attentive. My basic pitch was that there simply had to be a lifting of the cap on the Sporting Goods Sales Tax, if not completely, then up to a number adequate to stop the bleeding and start rehabilitating the state parks system. I think we discussed a new cap of $85 million. He kept listening, and I kept talking, pointing out that this increase was not for a new tax but was part of the sales tax revenue flow that had long been diverted to other uses and programs. I said that I thought this increase would pay rich dividends and should be viewed as an investment for the future, particularly in view of the Texas A&M survey, which was being upgraded to seventy-nine parks since we had spoken. Craddick kept listening. Then I raised a serious concern. Lifting the present $32 million annual cap imposed in 1995 by any amount would create the need for additional appropriations, causing a negative fiscal note. A $53 million increase to $85 million in the Sporting Goods Sales Tax might well be a deal-killer.

Craddick smiled and said, "Not if it is accompanied by a 'Dynamic Fiscal Note.'" My face must have conveyed confusion and ignorance. He explained that he, as chairman of the Ways and Means Committee, and John Sharp (at the time the state comptroller) had invented it. The crux of their "invention" was that there would be recognition on the part of the legislature and comptroller that certain expenditures, while creating a temporary negative budget impact, should be viewed as a long-term investment that would generate new and increased revenues.

We both smiled. Clearly, all the work that had been done—and that was being done on the seventy-nine-park survey—would prove that parks are a wise investment. Craddick then told me that there was a problem that had nothing to do with our case or the validity of our calculations. He and the current comptroller, Carole Keeton Strayhorn, did not get along, so much so that the Speaker told me that we would have to seek out members of the legislature who could approach her. I told him that I would work on that and that perhaps I could informally broker the matter, as Strayhorn and I were friends going back to Austin High. He said that would be fine at the right time but that we also needed a member like Jim Keffer, current chairman of Ways and Means, to make a formal request. Keffer would be the most logical member to shepherd the tax part of the measure through the House. All tax matters under Texas law and legislative procedure must originate in the House of Representatives and go through that committee. We ended the meeting on a gratifying note.

Within hours after the meeting, staff members from the Texas Parks and Wildlife Department were nervously calling to find out what was afoot. Because the meeting had been exploratory in nature, I saw no reason to tell anyone. It could have ended on a negative note, so why bother? Too many chefs in the kitchen, particularly at the outset, never complete a meal. They just argue. Much gets burned; nothing gets cooked. At some point, I did brief them, giving my best analysis of what needed to happen to forge a complete package with an attendant but separate lobbying team, media and organization education, distribution of the forthcoming seventy-nine-park study, and a public opinion survey.

In 2001 and 2003, the lobbying efforts of the Texas Coalition for Conservation had been minimal and well within the guidelines of IRS rules. But 2005 was going to be different and more intense. I got a thorough briefing on the law just to be sure of what we and other supporters could do, then went to see David Gochman. Years before, Gochman had set up an organization, the Texas Outdoor Recreation Alliance, which lobbied for the original Sporting Goods Sales Tax legislation and other matters pertaining to the industry. The organization was still in play—on paper. Gochman agreed to renew its activities and help finance the effort through its members and Academy Outdoor Sports. Paige Cooper, who had been the clerk of the Cultural, Recreation and Tourism Committee, and Corky Palmer, a veteran sports product distributor and former Texas Parks and Wildlife Department employee, were chosen to be the lobbying team for the Texas Outdoor Recreation Alliance. I also registered as a lobbyist with the Texas Ethics Commission.

That handled, I went to Brownwood to meet Jim Keffer. I did so through a first-class citizen and park enthusiast, Brad Locker, who was a Texas Outdoor Recreation Alliance member and Republican county chairman of Brown County. Keffer was very receptive to lifting the cap and other aspects of our proposed legislative initiatives to enhance parks. He offered to be the primary cosponsor of what would be Hilderbran's bill. This all made good sense, as Keffer was chair of the Ways and Means Committee that would have to pass the portion of the bill lifting the cap and would have to accept the Dynamic Fiscal Note. We still needed help with Strayhorn because Keffer also had a problem with her.

With Speaker Craddick's assurance that he would talk to the Calendars Committee chair at the right time, the House had come to order, at least in theory. But we had to educate Carole Strayhorn on the validity of our fiscal case, we had to educate the press, and we had to gain the support of Lieutenant Governor David Dewhurst and the Senate.

Nothing was set in concrete, although there was reason to be hopeful that parks were to be given a fair hearing, and the machinery was in motion to substantially increase funding by at least $53 million annually.

From mid-October 2004 until the end of the year, we marshaled our forces and resources. We reached out to every contact and organization that might hold sway with legislators. We supplied informative ammunition. We prepared letters to editors and constructed teams to visit them with supplied informative ammunition. We prepared to issue the upcoming seventy-nine-park survey. We commissioned a public opinion survey that was conducted in early December. We now had a hook, and we could focus on a disciplined, well-run, and adequately funded statewide campaign. For the first time, I felt a real sense of accomplishment, with prospects for success.

But the Texas legislature is set up to kill bills, and it can in its manipulative ways confound seasoned lobbyists, the press, and others not used to being confounded. We weren't even out of 2004, so we had to lead from strength early in 2005 and then apply and continue the pressure. In February 2005, we released the Texas A&M study, which again demonstrated our case that parks—good parks—have direct and indirect economic benefits that will generate a significant return on investment. On February 16, we released the poll data that showed that Texans strongly supported measures to protect natural resources and parks. The support was very strong in every region, political party, and ethnic group. Seven out of ten Texans were willing to pay $12 to $60 per year in additional taxes for new parks as well as land, water management, and natural habitat. To accomplish that, 65 percent of Texans favored lifting the cap on the Sporting Goods Sales Tax, and this included a healthy percentage of those who called themselves "fiscal conservatives."

Two other items of note were apparent. With the poll numbers practically a mirror reflection of earlier polls, Dr. David Hill, founder of Hill Research Consultants, offered an analysis: "The remarkable consistency of these attitudes across time suggests that we are measuring long-term values rather than floating opinions. The values are so well internalized that they are likely to influence public opinion far into the future."

Texans of all persuasions by an equally large percentage did not like the fact that their state legislators could divert park funds from their intended purpose to other programs. That would have been an even greater number if in a poll we could have explained how annual revenue from the Sporting Goods Sales Tax had increased from about $58 million in 1993 to around $100 million in 2006, but that hundreds of millions of dollars had been diverted from park operations and development over a twelve-year period.

The Sporting Goods Sales Tax is a dedicated account to be used by state and local parks for the well-being of Texans. Between park visitor fees and this tax revenue, a great portion of budgeted expenses are generated. According to Comptroller Strayhorn's estimates for fiscal years 2006 through 2007, dedicated sales tax revenue would total $205 million in the biennium, leaving some $141 million after deducting the capped amount of $32 million annually, so why was the legislature hesitant to honor the intent of the 1993 legislation? The overarching reason is the legislature's dislike of truly dedicated accounts. The Sporting Goods Sales Tax account is dedicated in name only—and only for cosmetic purposes. To be binding, a measure to permanently dedicate such revenues would require a constitutional amendment and a vote by the people. Legislators and statewide elected officials knew that such an amendment would pass—park funding measures succeed in the polls—but that would take the matter out of their hands, and that would be unacceptable. Some in the legislature, regardless of party, come to believe that the people's money becomes theirs. To the best of my knowledge, the chairs of the House and Senate committees of jurisdiction introduced bills every session of the remaining years of the twentieth century and early twenty-first century to allow such an amendment to be voted on by the people, but the arguments of State Representative Edmund Kuempel and State Senator Buster Brown fell on deaf ears.

The other reason for the lack of consideration of any increase in the cap—or its outright abolition—was that there had never been a concerted chorus of concern about the plight of parks and the fact that taxpayers and parks had been short-changed for years. At least as far back as the 1970s, when the penny-a-pack cigarette tax dedicated to the acquisition and development of state parks and historic sites was passed, diversions by Texas Parks and Wildlife Department commissioners immediately took place. In a November 1975 article titled "The Strange Case of the Missing Parks," Griffith Smith wrote in *Texas Monthly* of the continuing saga. As noted previously, of the $53 million collected under what was then Fund 31, less than $9 million went to acquisition. What was the Texas Parks and Wildlife Department funding? A new headquarters building, salaries, and projects pushed by influential legislators and commissioners.[2]

Even though to one degree or another we faced these same oppressive forces, House Bill 1292 was introduced by Harvey Hilderbran on February 17, 2005. It raised the cap to $85 million: $58.5 million to state parks, of which $18 million was to be used for acquisition and development; $25.5 million to the local parks grant account; and $2 million for bond debt service. It would not bring the state's parks back to world-class status, but it was a start in the right direction. Furthermore, as the bill moved, we would have an opportunity to amend it if necessary.

Hopes and expectations were high. We had support up and down the line in the House. State Senator John Whitmire of Houston agreed to sponsor and handle the bill in the Senate, and we had the blessing of the Speaker. But we didn't have the Dynamic Fiscal Note, and Harvey Hilderbran, who claimed he was close to Comptroller Strayhorn, would not move. The Ways and Means Committee stood ready, and, by then, a majority of its members had signed on.

Weeks went by with no action in the statehouse. That did not mean inaction on our

Joseph Fitzsimons, 2007 chair of the Texas Parks and Wildlife Commission, 2021. Fitzsimons was relentless in his advocacy for park funding in the 2007 legislative session. Personal collection of Joseph Fitzsimons.

part. Throughout March into April, we met with the editorial boards of major dailies. We sent letters to the editor to all the rest. The response was favorable, with both editorial and column coverage. We had local organizations and individuals visit or call representatives. We hammered home the poll results at every opportunity.

Then the bottom dropped out. By mid to late April 2005, the Speaker and lieutenant governor were in a fight over school financing—and I'm sure other matters. They never seemed to get along. Because of the uncertainty of the cost of school financing, the Speaker pulled down two hundred to three hundred bills with negative fiscal notes. Yes, House Bill 1292 had a negative note, and Strayhorn eventually issued her opinion, saying that while she had confidence that enhanced parks were a good investment, with every prospect of a substantial return on that investment, she had (without telling anyone, to my knowledge) decided not to issue such opinions except for those measures that exceeded more than $100 million in fiscal impact. By May 1, House Bill 1292 was dead. We tried to perfect several legislative substitutes but to no avail.

By session's end, I was ready to throw in the towel—and almost did. But over the summer, Ernie Angelo asked me to hang on and go another round. I said I would think about it but would have to do a great deal of checking, especially with supporters and donors, specifically the large foundations: Houston Endowment, the Brown Foundation, and the Meadows Foundation. I had assured them that our work would be complete by 2005.

During the summer, my interest was again stirred because it was apparent that the parks funding that finally was appropriated in 2005 would not be sufficient to cover rising utility costs, fuel costs, and other expenses. If an additional $4 million was not made available through a process commonly known as "budget reconciliation," many parks would have to be partly closed, staff laid off, and programs curtailed. Some consideration was given, though not wholeheartedly—then Hurricane Rita hit, and any chance of supplemental funding went by the wayside.

But the crisis led to a rallying cry—it seemed perverse that it took such a crisis to motivate protest—and action. All those surveys, polls, letters to the editor, and materials we'd generated suddenly were relevant and useful after all. The Texas A&M survey pointed to the impact on local communities and placed park closings and potential closings in a whole different light. This wasn't just a system-wide failure—it was one that could shut down your local park. That put it right at everyone's doorstep. Before we entered the 2007 legislative session, every major newspaper and most smaller dailies and weeklies ran editorials and columns about the parks crisis, some more than once, and some—like the *Fort Worth Star-Telegram* and *Houston Chronicle*—often.

With this opportunity at hand, another one arose. Texas Parks and Wildlife Commission Chair Joseph Fitzsimons and I had had several conversations about renewing the Texas State Parks Advisory Committee. The committee hadn't done much in the past few years. I told Fitzsimons that it was a good idea as long as the members carried weight and covered the waterfront from conservation to tourism. Fitzsimons is a multigenerational South Texas ranch owner who, by heritage and circumstance, could have stuck to policies regarding private land, water, and property rights, but he was—and is—a generous man who grew into a strong advocate for parks and fully embraced the need for a strong parks council or committee. We recruited several people, then I went to see my friend former State Senator John Montford, who had coauthored the original Sporting Goods Sales Tax legislation in 1993 and had served in the statehouse with distinction. Former Lieutenant Governor Bill Hobby told me that John Montford and Kent Caperton were the best state legislators during his long tenure. Montford went on to serve with great success as the chancellor of Texas Tech University and as president of the Western region of AT&T. Because of his background and his reputation for firm but nonconfrontational leadership, he was the perfect choice to chair the committee. He heard me out and agreed to do so—as long as I would handle the day-to-day lifting. In March 2006, a well-rounded and influential committee met. Our charge was multifold but focused on defining the method of financing that would best fit the needs of Texas's parks within a framework of legislative reality. Of tantamount importance was that the staff spell out those financial requirements on a category-by-category basis. In 2003 and 2005, we had flown by the seat of our pants because we had no true figures from the Texas Parks and Wildlife Department on what was necessary to at least meet requirements adequately.

State Park Advisory Committee Report, 2006. The recommendations established by this report became the foundation for the 2007 legislative effort. Courtesy of the Texas Parks and Wildlife Commission, Austin, Texas.

Over the next several months in formal meetings, subcommittees, and informal discussions, we pulled together a working document that eventually called for substantial increases for operations, major repairs, local parks grants, and acquisition of at least four major new parks near urban centers. We also reaffirmed that the Sporting Goods Sales Tax was the best and most reliable source of revenue. For 2008 to 2009, it was estimated that the tax would generate $110 million annually—more than enough to wholly support our recommendations, particularly if the major repair component ($25 million annually) and the land acquisition component ($15 million annually) were funded through a voter-approved bond issue. However, we also strongly urged that our recommendations be addressed on a pay-as-you-go basis.

This document was not a Cadillac but a good, solid Chevrolet—adequate and meaningful but without frills. We released our findings in late August 2006 to much fanfare

Preserve America Presidential Awards event at the White House, May 12, 2008. Advisory Council on Historic Preservation Chairman John Nau III and First Lady Laura Bush announce awards for the Historic Courthouse Preservation Program in Texas. Courtesy of Tami Heilemann, National Archives at College Park, Still Pictures Collection, National Archives and Records Administration, 7923333.

and good reception from almost all quarters. Our recommendations were presented to Texas Parks and Wildlife commissioners a few days later and were unanimously accepted. From that acceptance came the request that was forwarded to the legislature as the 2008 to 2009 Legislative Appropriation Request. Euphoria reigned, but barely perceptible storm clouds were gathering.

Lieutenant Governor Dewhurst and at least one senator, Steve Ogden, were not happy with the critical press coverage. They thought that somehow it was directed at them. I reviewed all the articles I retained, and very few mentioned either one—or any other legislator—by name. This parks problem was longstanding, going back years when Democrats controlled the statehouse, although Republicans had not done anything to improve the situation since they had gained power. John Montford and Commissioner Ned Holmes were deputized to visit with Dewhurst. I went to see Blaine Brunson, director of budget for the lieutenant governor, and Ogden, who then chaired the Senate Finance Committee. Brunson had been very helpful to me since my first years in Texas conservation work. The crux of my conversation with Brunson was that Dewhurst and Ogden had been caught by surprise, that the Texas Parks and Wildlife Department had never presented a case to them. I told him that all sorts of materials had been sent by the Texas Coalition for Conservation over the years spelling out the crumbling circumstances of our parks, including the studies mandated by various sessions of the legislature or the Sunset Advisory Commission, a legislatively controlled body. Brunson allowed that that was probably true and said that it was unfair for me and others to have gone to so much trouble, only to be ignored by officials and staff who apparently had little time to read, much less study, even basic documents. We then discussed the unhappiness that prevailed. I told him none of our work was meant as a personal affront and that the parks problem went back for decades, particularly the last twelve years after the capping of the Sporting Goods Sales Tax by Democratic leaders. Then I asked, "What would happen if we'd done nothing to highlight the plight of the parks?" "Probably nothing," was Brunson's reply. All in all, it was a pleasant meeting, but he did impart his suspicions of the Texas Parks and Wildlife Department and its habit of changing numbers. I could not comment on that but did say that I would raise hell if it changed the calculations we had recommended. We parted with the understanding that we would stay in touch as the session drew near.

The other sign of a storm was rumors that the Texas Historical Commission was going to make a run at stripping all or some of the historic sites from the Texas Parks and Wildlife Department. Over the years, John Nau, the chairman of the Texas Historical Commission, had coveted some of the sites, even though historic sites had been part of the parks system since the outset, when the San Jacinto monument was built in the 1920s. Like other state parks, they had deteriorated over the years, not due to purposeful neglect on the part of the Texas Parks and Wildlife Department, but because they lacked funding.

The word went out that Nau had the Speaker in his hip pocket. I thought that was a bit crass. John Nau was a big Republican contributor to many legislators, including the Speaker. In my opinion, he was perfectly within his rights to seek support for his point of view. What was vexing, however, was that there seemed to be no clear reasoning behind his desire to take over sites now under the Texas Parks and Wildlife Department. There were no hearings, and there was certainly no thought given to looking at each property to ascertain whether it belonged under a particular state agency, something recommended by the State Parks Advisory Committee. That recommendation was fortified by the recent Texas Historical Commission's Sunset Commission review and the Senate's Government Organization Committee. Both entities would not condone such transfers without adequate review, certainly not unless such a reassignment would mean substantial net savings.

All this aside, it was clear that the battle was to be waged on a political basis, not on a scientific or cost-saving one. It would ultimately nearly wreck the chance to finally lift the cap entirely and provide substantial and sustainable funding for state and local parks— and historic sites. What followed would require an effort unmatched in the history of conservation legislation or politics in Texas.

At this point, I would like to pay tribute to my legislative opponent, John Nau. Although a rough contact sport player during the 2007 session, he immediately turned around and generously supported the Proposition 4 bond ballot measure that was upcoming in November 2007. He would join Peter Holt and Dan Friedkin, future chairs of the Texas Parks and Wildlife Commission, in ensuring the campaign was adequately funded. He lent his private plane to facilitate a "barnstorming" campaign in late October of that year, loaned one of his top lobbyists/public relations experts, Ray Sullivan, to the cause, and personally made fundraising calls as well as calls for political support.

The Texas Outdoor Recreation Alliance would again serve as the lobbying arm, with a budget of $100,000. All supporting organizations were put on notice that they would be called on to mount email campaigns and media efforts. *Texas Monthly* agreed to run a pro bono ad reiterating the plight of parks. A plan was reinstated regarding letters to editors and visits with editorial boards, and this time, we asked local supporters to visit the smaller dailies and send letters. The local parks groups circulated a resolution among cities, towns, and chambers of commerce. More than two hundred local groups would sign on.

Testimony was prepared for the various committee hearings. I had asked Texas A&M University for a new update on the parks survey so we would have reaffirmation from the latest data. Based on seventy-nine state parks, the total annual economic activity was calculated to be an estimated $859 million in sales and $484 million in residents' income, accounting for an estimated thirteen thousand jobs. Not a bad return on an investment of less than one-tenth of 1 percent of the budget, particularly given that Texas was second from last among all states in per capita expenditure on parks. Almost any increase would produce a greater return.

Specific tasks were assigned to John Montford, former State House Member Clyde Alexander, and Texas Parks and Wildlife commissioners, as well as major political donors who supported parks. The chairman, commissioners, and staff of the Texas Parks and Wildlife Department weighed in within the limits of their legal boundaries, providing resource materials and support. By the opening gavel in January 2007, I thought we had done everything possible to bring outside influence to bear on an institution that bordered on indifference and complete inertia with regard to parks and conservation in general.

At the earliest opportunity, State Representative Hilderbran filed House Bill 6—on January 8, 2007—and the governor included it on his list of "emergency items," which meant that it would be on a fast track for legislative action. A companion bill—Senate Bill 252—was filed in the Senate by Craig Estes. Then nothing happened, even though in short course we obtained twenty-five Senate sponsors (out of thirty-one) and more than 120 House sponsors (out of 150). Even with the historic sites brouhaha, the bill should have been moved forward to take advantage of momentum. We had finally

From left, Clyde Alexander, George Bristol, Dan Allen Hughes, and Carter Smith, June 2015. Author's collection.

positioned park enhancement and funding as a major legislative agenda item, but nothing happened.

Not until February 21 was a hearing in the House held. Then, to confuse matters, a substitute bill (House Bill 12) was filed on March 9 but did not pass on the House floor until May 3, very late in the process.

Nothing on the surface seemed to be occurring. Backroom doors were opening and shutting frequently, however. Transparency was ignored. Tempers flared in some quarters. From time to time, we would hear bits and pieces—the number of parks recommended to be transferred to the Historical Commission moved from thirty-four to zero to twenty-one and every number in between. The major problem was that the Speaker would not step in and slam the gavel down for a resolution. In the meantime, the House Appropriations Committee was left waiting to assign numbers to complement the various funding slots of House Bill 12, so they left big-ticket items pending, subject to the bill moving and passing the Senate. It was turning into a dangerously delayed mess. The key players were the Speaker, who kept hands off; John Nau, who coveted what wasn't his but didn't want transparency; and Harvey Hilderbran, who was trapped, not knowing which way to turn and not having a House support team with any firepower. The latter problem was clearly of Hilderbran's own making. Others and I had urged him to assemble such a team to help him through the process. But Hilderbran wanted the credit all to himself. As we would learn, he came within an inch of receiving all the blame for abject failure. But we were not to be counted out yet.

We redoubled our visitation and email campaign efforts, so much so that someone at one friendly office asked me to turn off the "bubble machines." We went back to news

Texas House of Representatives legislative session, Austin, Texas, May 27, 2007. Texas State Representative Sylvester Turner, bottom center, delivers an impassioned speech in favor of the Texas Budget legislation during a night session of the House. Other representatives, left to right, are Susan King, David Swinford, Norma Chavez, Turner, Beverly Woolley, and Sid Miller. Presiding above is Speaker Tom Craddick. On the right in the background is Ron Wilson, assistant parliamentarian. Courtesy of Harry Cabluck, Associated Press.

sources and editorial boards and explained that the entire effort was in jeopardy. The measure was stuck in the House because of the historic sites issue and in the Senate because Lieutenant Governor Dewhurst would not let either Senate Bill 252 or park appropriations move.

Finally, on May 17, 2007, two weeks before the session's end, the lieutenant governor called a meeting of all interested parties—Texas Parks and Wildlife commissioners, three citizen leaders (including me), senators, and staff of the Senate and Texas Parks and Wildlife Department who dealt with budgets and appropriations. The lieutenant governor began by smiling at me and saying, "We've gotten the message." It was time to hammer out a deal. We went through what we had asked for in the various categories and what might realistically pass out of the Senate Finance Committee. There were holes, but the numbers were closing. Then Dewhurst said that he wanted $25 million for the USS *Texas*. This was not a surprise because the State Parks Advisory Committee had given that item back to the legislature. Since it had been given to Texas by the federal government (which was glad to get rid of it), the battleship had been planted in a saltwater marsh that had continuously eroded the great ship's outer hull and innards. Even with two or three major repairs, it had always fallen back into serious disrepair—rotting and rusting because enough funds were never forthcoming to permanently dry-dock the vessel. To do so would cost millions of dollars, so we had concluded that the legislature needed to decide once and for all what to do. The lieutenant governor had decided on the figure of $25 million over the biennium without any supporting analysis. This would be part of a bond package to be announced, he said.

And so, it was time to vote and declare victory for the time being. Despite the flaws, machinations, and hypocrisy, a significant increase in funding in every category save acquisition would be enacted. It was a new beginning, with one more hurdle ahead.

Legislatures usually run true to form. The odds increase if the speaker has significant power, has appointed allies from the opposing party, has majority ownership of his own House, and has a majority status in the Senate. Throw in a governor with little power, and you have a winner. That is, unless in the course of a session, that Speaker alienates the governor, the lieutenant governor, a majority of the Senate, and a new majority of his own House, consisting of mostly Texas Democrats and fifteen or so Republican members who are ready to risk life and limb in revolt.

Rumors began to float that there would be a move to vacate the Speaker's chair, a dethronement of monumental consequence. On Thursday night, May 24, 2007, the explosion erupted. Heated criticism came from Republicans, with Democrats egging them on. Finally, there was a call for a vote to end Craddick's reign. He ruled that the motion was out of order. His handpicked parliamentarian ruled against him. He fired her on the spot and replaced her with strong-willed allies with cast-iron stomachs. The battles and verbal abuse raged back and forth. Craddick held firm, but a new, previously unseen resolve ran through the House—and a coalition of Republicans and Democrats broke the quorum and shut down business two days before adjournment. It now looked like sayonara to House Bill 12.

At the time, many of my friends in the House galleries were in agreement: "Throw the bum out!" But I was horrified and maddened because Tom Craddick held the fate of our bill in his hands.

While all this theater was afoot, House Bill 12 was having its own problems. As mentioned previously, Hilderbran had been urged to recruit wise and strong co-leaders, but, wanting all the credit himself, he had sent as his representative to the House-Senate Conference Committee his clerk, a person of little weight when matched against the senators and their staffs. Todd Kercheval was outclassed to the point of jeopardizing acceptance of the bill by me, others, and the Texas Parks and Wildlife Department. Instead of a straightforward parks funding bill with a resolution about the historical sites jurisdiction thrown in, it became a Christmas tree with every imaginable garish ball attached. It was so bad that Hilderbran called, wondering if he should pull the bill. I tried to calm him down and said I'd poll some of the most affected and get back to him. Sometime late Saturday afternoon, the staff of the Texas Parks and Wildlife Department decided that, on principle, it should be pulled, but there was enough good to make it digestible—barely. I called Hilderbran back, only to discover the House revolt had exploded and the quorum was broken. No business could be conducted. Finally, I reached him and said that while we agreed that we had been poorly represented, there was enough good and necessary that we ought to live with the bad.

Overnight and into early Sunday morning, John Montford, Clyde Alexander, and I, with the help of our team, called and begged our friends in the House to return to establish a quorum. Sometime later that day, that occurred. But we were not home free yet. It seemed the Speaker had a major water bill that Lieutenant Governor Dewhurst wanted as his legacy, and Dewhurst held House Bill 12 in the Senate, awaiting passage of the water bill. But on the vote for this bill in the House, Harvey Hilderbran voted "present, not voting," and it lost by one vote. The word came to me from the Senate that unless the water bill was turned around, we could say goodbye to House Bill 12. I tried to reach Hilderbran. Then I called his clerk, Kercheval, who said, "We are ready to negotiate." I can't recall whether the pregnant silence came before or after my expletive in response, but I told him that there was no time left to negotiate and to tell Hilderbran to switch his vote or face grave consequences—from the press, his colleagues, me, and every constituency group I could reach.

It is impossible for me to make sense of that mentality. All one can do is yell at it loud enough to make it react before it is distracted. The water bill was reconsidered and passed, as was House Bill 12—the last bill in the last hour of the eightieth session of the Texas legislature. After nearly seventy-two hours of a nonstop ride and practically no sleep for many, the session ended.

The good news was that the bill did lift the cap on the Sporting Goods Sales Tax. It did direct a preponderance of new funding to parks in every category for every need save acquisition. Then it wandered off in all sorts of small favors and mischief-making riders.

Somewhere in the give-and-take of conference committee swapping and last-minute additions, some House or Senate committee members were instructed—cowardly and secretively—to write in several draconian measures for no other reason than to make life miserable for personnel at the Texas Parks and Wildlife Department. Among the most vengeful was a directive that would require the department to hire twenty-three auditors each year to pore over every expenditure and income source to the penny for each park in the state system. The purpose was not to find waste or wrongdoing—although those committee members would have been delighted to have had the windfall come their way—it was spitefulness for being put in the harsh spotlight of allowing the state parks to fall to the level of neglect and disrepair that was highlighted by most state newspapers and media leading up to the 2007 legislative session.

The irony is that while no wrongdoing or malfeasance was discovered, several findings prompted the department to make some needed adjustments. In the end, nothing damaged the department. To the contrary, after the pettiness, time consumption, and precious expenditure of funds, what remained was better agency recordkeeping and accountability.

Interestingly enough, two of the principal perpetrators of the call for auditors and other narrow-minded measures were thrown out of office or defeated at the polls in short order.

In addition to the petty political retribution, there was an insert saying that future funding was subject to appropriations, meaning the increase could be honored—or not—by future legislatures.

The Senate sponsor publicly declared victory for the parks, but I wasn't so sure. There were significant increases, particularly when coupled with the new bond package—Proposition 4—that added more funding to capital projects. It did raise the bar and aid a system so starved that crumbs might have seemed like a gourmet meal. This was far more than crumbs, even more than the proverbial half a loaf. Was it worth all my effort and the efforts of so many others? If so, what lessons were learned?

For all my criticism of some in the statehouse and the legislative process, I thoroughly enjoyed the opportunity to start with a nearly blank slate and move parks funding to a position of much higher priority among the many elected officials who care—and there are many who do care on both sides of the aisle. Above all, I was lucky to meet and be befriended by an extraordinarily diverse collection of Texans dedicated to the task of leaving our state better than they found it: Republicans and Democrats, urbanites and rural dwellers, liberals and conservatives, regardless of race and gender, who generously gave time and money. And for all the ups and downs and heartburn, Harvey Hilderbran deserves a special note of appreciation. He came early and stayed late. He was there when others stood aside.

At the end of the 2007 session and again in 2009, we were successful in raising the bar and then keeping it from being lowered. We certainly raised awareness of a problem that demanded attention and action, but problems remained and loomed especially large. The Sporting Goods Sales Tax, for one: to be or not to be? That was truly the question. Why must the entire machinery of funding for Texas parks grind to a halt every other year when, following the comptroller's estimate of revenue from taxes (every year since 1993 has shown an increase), there is a hue and cry that our state and local parks are again being shortchanged by millions of dollars? A better method of funding might have merit. But every time the possibility of switching to a real estate transfer fee, documents fee, or fund from lottery revenues was mentioned, it was shot down by the affected industry's lobbyists. Even when House Bill 12 called for a joint House and Senate study of the Sporting Goods Sales Tax, it went nowhere because at least two methods appeared to raise more revenue than the existing formula. Now, because the Texas legislature is not about to add more to direct parks funding, we are left with the Sporting Goods Sales Tax. In my opinion, it is by far the best source because it is derived from those who most enjoy and use parks and outdoor recreation. That has been the continuing recommendation of two sunset commissions, the State Parks Advisory Committee, and, by implication, the inaction of the House and Senate interim committees.

What is not widely recognized is the underlying thrust of the State Parks Advisory Committee's ten-year recommendation. In its entirety and within the categories of

Fire covering 96 percent of Bastrop State Park, as seen from the entrance to the park, September 5, 2011. Courtesy of Chase Fountain, Communications Division, Texas Parks and Wildlife Department, Austin, Texas.

need, no consideration was given to appropriations exceeding the revenues generated by the Sporting Goods Sales Tax. When the Advisory Committee arrived at the $105 million annual appropriations recommendation, we did so in recognition of basic ongoing needs—not bells and whistles—within the present bounds of Sporting Goods Sales Tax revenues. What we did highlight was that revenue stream had risen and would continue to rise year in and year out.

If legislators and their staffs will become involved and stay involved, if the power and lack of transparency of the Legislative Budget Board (a permanent joint committee of the Texas legislature that develops budget and policy recommendations for legislative appropriations, completes fiscal analyses for proposed legislation, and conducts evaluations and reviews to improve the efficiency and performance of state and local operations) is curtailed, and if the finally determined appropriation for the Texas Parks and Wildlife Department is given over to the agency without hidden agendas or cuts, then our parks can survive in bad times. In better times, they can be enhanced. In the best of times, perhaps, with a substantial and sustainable flow of funds voted on by the people of Texas, they can be allowed to become a parks system of the first order. The ultimate beneficiary will be Texas citizens and out-of-state and foreign tourists. Local businesses and communities will flourish. A sense of state pride will be restored, enhanced, and perpetuated.

So, what happened to the budget and the recommendations of the Legislative Budget Board? It is not a pretty picture.

When the final budget numbers for 2012 to 2013 were finalized in 2011, only $27 million per year was realized from the Sporting Goods Sales Tax, even though the Texas comptroller certified $125 million per year in revenue. That is less than the original cap of $32 million per year established in 1995. Coupled with the questionable recommendations fashioned by Legislative Budget Board staff, there was no room for error or negative circumstance.

The year 2011, however, was not only a financial disaster as far as park appropriations go—it was a disaster, period.

Monstrous fires and lingering drought covering most of the state triggered some of the worst damage to parks ever recorded. The Bastrop State Park fire in September 2011 was the largest state parks fire in history, sweeping through the beautiful and historic stands of Lost Pines, threatening most of the seventy-plus-year-old Civilian Conservation Corps structures (all were saved by the heroic efforts of Texas Parks and Wildlife Department employees supported by private individuals and Texas businesses), destroying sixteen hundred homes, and killing two people. At its end, 96 percent of the park was destroyed.

This story, in varying degrees, was tragically retold in practically every area of the state.

And what of any contribution from the state for the ruin caused by the fire at Bastrop? Not much until a lawsuit was settled for $20 million, including negligence by a commercial company.

For all the trauma and tragedy 2011 visited on parks—and Texas in general—with budget slashing and wildfires, there were, as is often the case, silver linings.

It is impossible to imagine any lining remaining from fires that burned across Texas, ultimately claiming more than four million acres statewide, nearly three thousand homes, and ten deaths. In Central Texas alone, specifically in the Bastrop State Park area, 33,000 acres were blackened and 1.5 million trees destroyed.

In 1951, a group of lumbermen championed a state program to develop better strains of trees for production. They persuaded Texas Governor Allan Shivers to support their

Former Texas Parks and Wildlife Department Executive Director Carter Smith, 2018. Courtesy of the Texas Parks and Wildlife Department, Austin, Texas.

cause. One of the first strains that the newly formed Tree Improvement Program decided to cultivate was the drought-tolerant loblolly pine from Bastrop. This species had evolved to develop a number of traits that protected it from the heat of Texas's summers and fires—at least most fires. The seeds were harvested from the area and sent to East Texas for cultivation and then to the Texas Forest Service's Indian Mound Nursery, where they grew to seedlings.[3]

The Lost Pines ecosystem is a unique forest housed principally in Bastrop State Park. Its uniqueness derives from the fact that in years past, probably during the Little Ice Age around 1850, the contiguous forest stretching from East Texas through the Bastrop area, perhaps as far as Mexico, split. The Central Texas strain developed into a heat-resistant specimen.

Ninety-five percent of those loblolly pines would be consumed by the Labor Day fire. The Lost Pines were lost—but not forever.

Through an act of fate, another near loss was avoided. In 1992, Brookshire Brothers grocers had agreed to store one thousand pounds of pine seed in a company freezer at no charge—enough to plant fourteen million seedlings. After several years of unsuccessful attempts to seek a market for this particular strain and after the nursery went out of business in 2008, the Texas Forest Service decided to take the unused and unsold seeds to a nearby landfill.[4]

The disposal date was set for three weeks after Labor Day 2011. After the fire, the light bulb of surprised remembrance came on.

Today, that one thousand pounds of seed has been more than enough to restock the burned-out hole of thirty-three thousand acres of Lost Pines.

There will be more about this horrific event and the heroic response to save the park—during and after the fire—in the chapter on philanthropy.

After a disastrous 2011, the good news was we had gained statewide attention, with expanding support from all corners and sections. The most encouraging was the public opinion polls (there were five such polls commissioned by the Texas Coalition for Conservation directly—as well as polls commissioned by others) that supported our findings. Clearly, year in and year out, the people of Texas demonstrated—by 70 percent or more—that they loved their parks, were willing to pay for them, and strongly disapproved of the legislature directing Sporting Goods Sales Tax revenue to other programs or to balance the budget.

As discussed previously, the 2007 parks bill passed on the last day of the session. It lifted the cap and allowed 94 percent of Sporting Goods Sales Tax revenue to be directed to parks and 6 percent to historic sites. Everyone celebrated. Awards were passed out.

However, the benefits of the bill were not fully realized due to the language inserted by the Senate in conference requiring all revenue to be subject to legislative appropriation. It was a pig with lipstick, but a pig, nonetheless. But the issue and the reality of the legislative action was now out in the open. It would stay out in the open until the time was right and the signals were favorable.

That would occur in 2015. The Speaker of the House was Joe Straus (a conservationist by nature). The lieutenant governor was Dan Patrick, who had campaigned on an open budget process and truth in appropriation. He signaled he would support a bill that was open and fair and provided full funding of all the revenue generated by the Sporting Goods Sales Tax.

The 2015 legislature took major steps to improve the Sporting Goods Sales Tax situation with two modifications. First, it eliminated the prescribed distribution of funds between accounts to give the legislature discretion on how to direct funds and adapt to changing priorities and needs. Second, it dedicated the full 94 percent of the Sporting Goods Sales Tax to the Texas Parks and Wildlife Department as was originally intended in the 2007 legislation. For the first time, the full 94 percent of the Sporting Goods Sales Tax was appropriated to the Texas Parks and Wildlife Department for the 2016 to 2017 biennium, amounting to more than $261 million.

From left, former Texas Parks and Wildlife Commission chairs Robert Brown, Joseph Fitzsimons, and John Parker, 2003. Courtesy of the Texas Parks and Wildlife Department, Austin, Texas.

It felt like we were finally at a point where it might be possible to permanently lift the "cap" imposed by the appropriations requirement, allowing for substantial increases maintained on a sustainable basis year after year.

If ever a time called for new leadership to step to the forefront in the manner of conservation giants explored in prior pages, then the decade leading up to 2023 was such an occasion.

In late 2007, following the bruising legislative session when some improvements were made—at great cost—finding a replacement for retiring Texas Parks and Wildlife Department Executive Director Bob Cook became an immediate priority.

After a several-month search conducted by Commission Chairman Joseph Fitzsimons, Carter Smith, a Texas outdoorsman by DNA, degree, and disposition, was chosen to lead the Texas Parks and Wildlife Department.

No better choice could have been made. The agency called for it. The leadership of the state demanded it, and the diversity of the constituency groups required it.

Smith would inherit a department of approximately three thousand employees in thirteen divisions, including state parks, wildlife, law enforcement, and coastal and inland fisheries. Through historical circumstance, legislative pressure, favoritism, and outside constituency persuasion, most divisions tended to act and operate as independent entities.

Smith not only had to mend the rifts at the Capitol that had grown and simmered over the past decade or so, but he also had to draw the divisions into a more coherent and unified force for nature and conservation, not to mention administrative sanity.

He was up to the task and seemed to relish the challenge. His good-natured outward appearance was fortified by a first-class mind that seemed to grasp all aspects of each division's strengths and weaknesses. He was able to demonstrate that he understood the situation and was ready to articulate its solution to legislators, community leaders, and competing constituency groups.

In short order, state parks advocates were meeting with various leaders of the wildlife side of the title—the "hook and bullet" crowd. Mutual letters of support for parks funding and fish and game issues were circulated on a regular basis. Joint visits to legislators became more frequent. Legislators became more receptive.

Slowly but surely, old wounds began to heal. Carter Smith began to mold a coherent team that extended from appointed chairs and commissioners to elected leaders to business and media communities and on down to local conservation chapters.

It wasn't that he did it alone, but by his example, he encouraged others to follow his lead.

In the Teddy Roosevelt tradition, Carter Smith not only helped propel parks to become a popular issue again, he also made it possible for those of us in the advocating trenches to show it was the patriotic and right thing to do.

If Teddy Roosevelt had teammates and bench strength at the national level, Carter Smith was fortunate beyond the telling to have a string of Texas Parks and Wildlife Commission chairs second to none. From Joe Fitzsimons to Peter Holt to Dan Friedkin to Dan Allen Hughes to Ralph Duggins to Reed Morian to the present chair, Arch H. "Beaver" Aplin III, the leaders who served during this decade were always on call to help move the causes of the Texas Parks and Wildlife Department forward. This certainly applied to parks, as will be demonstrated in chapter ten in the constitutional amendment effort.

While there were downtimes and disappointments, each year, the legislative session grew better. Staff morale vastly improved, and constituency groups fell in line willingly and enthusiastically.

Thus, Texans and their leaders recognize that quality leadership must be sought out and encouraged. Without visionary leadership, matters of state—in this instance, parks—have and will continue to fall back into failure and disrepair.

By the time all the rings of the forces governing Texas's state parks had aligned, thanks in great part to Carter Smith's efforts to unite, the stage was set for the improbable to become possible.

# Chapter 10

# The Essential Answer: A Constitutional Amendment

L et it be said at the outset of this chapter that many in and out of the halls of the Capitol of Texas had grown skeptical of the chances of passing a constitutional amendment (or anything closely resembling one) to permanently fix the historic underfunding that had stymied Texas's parks for much of their existence.

From 1923, when the Texas legislature gave the State Parks Board life—but no financial support—to passage of the Sporting Goods Sales Tax in 1993, with all its failed remedies to follow, the whisper of a constitutional amendment blew away on the winds of improbability.

Yes, there were bright periods along the way: the Civilian Conservation Corps years (mostly federal money), which dried up with the outbreak of World War II; the surprising flash of legislative generosity when the Texas legislature appropriated $1.5 million in 1945 for the purchase of the far West Texas lands that would become Big Bend National Park; and Governor John Connally's bond and appropriations initiatives that added much to the park landscape. The latter ultimately failed to cover the cost of bonds and operations and had to be supplemented with income from the cigarette tax passed in 1971 and that, after twenty years, provided neither substantial nor sustainable cash flow to satisfy expectations of Texans constantly yearning for the outdoor experience. Add to that the fact that much of the cigarette revenue was siphoned off to non-park projects, and you had another failed attempt at funding stability.

**Texas Parks and Wildlife Department**
**Sporting Goods Sales Tax Totals 1993-2023**

| FY | Total SGST Estimates per CPA | Annual % Change | Biennial Totals | Biennial % Change |
|---|---|---|---|---|
| 1993 | 58,251,000 | | | |
| 1994 | 61,113,000 | | | |
| 1995 | 64,166,000 | 5.0% | 125,279,000 | |
| 1996 | 67,297,000 | 4.9% | | |
| 1997 | 70,520,000 | 4.8% | 137,817,000 | 10.0% |
| 1998 | 73,179,000 | 3.8% | | |
| 1999 | 76,075,000 | 4.0% | 149,254,000 | 8.3% |
| 2000 | 80,008,000 | 5.2% | | |
| 2001 | 84,230,000 | 5.3% | 164,238,000 | 10.0% |
| 2002 | 87,119,000 | 3.4% | | |
| 2003 | 90,905,000 | 4.3% | 178,024,000 | 8.4% |
| 2004 | 93,821,000 | 3.2% | | |
| 2005 | 97,125,000 | 3.5% | 190,946,000 | 7.3% |
| 2006 | 104,831,000 | 7.9% | | |
| 2007 | 108,396,000 | 3.4% | 213,227,000 | 11.7% |
| 2008 | 112,512,000 | 3.8% | | |
| 2009 | 116,652,000 | 3.7% | 229,164,000 | 7.5% |
| 2010 | 122,854,000 | 5.3% | | |
| 2011 | 126,888,000 | 3.3% | 249,742,000 | 9.0% |
| 2012 | 122,900,000 | -3.1% | | |
| 2013 | 128,432,000 | 4.5% | 251,332,000 | 0.6% |
| 2014 | 130,600,000 | 1.7% | | |
| 2015 | 135,200,000 | 3.5% | 265,800,000 | 5.8% |
| 2016 | 137,200,000 | 1.5% | | |
| 2017 | 140,600,000 | 2.5% | 277,800,000 | 4.5% |
| 2018 | 165,000,000 | 17.4% | | |
| 2019 | 168,500,000 | 2.1% | 333,500,000 | 20.1% |
| 2020 | 170,200,000 | 1.0% | | |
| 2021 | 216,900,000 | 27.4% | 387,100,000 | 16.1% |
| 2022 | 196,900,000 | -9.2% | | |
| 2023 | 207,900,000 | 5.6% | 404,800,000 | 4.6% |

Chart of Sporting Goods Sales Tax revenue and distribution from 1993 to 2021. Courtesy of the Texas Parks and Wildlife Department, Austin, Texas.

It fell to the enactment of the Sporting Goods Sales Tax in 1993 to attempt to remedy the seemingly endless search for a funding mechanism that would create a revenue source that would be substantial and reliable enough to meet the needs of a parks system that was again falling into disrepair, allow for enhancement of existing facilities, allow for proper planning, and have some left over for new park acquisitions.

The projections of a Sporting Goods Sales Tax fund held great promise (and would hold true as demonstrated in the chart at left). In every year from 1993 to 2019, revenue from the Sporting Goods Sales Tax increased annually. The problem was that the allowable appropriation was capped in 1995 (just two years after passage) at $32 million, and that amount was split with the local parks grants program and debt retirement. Both programs suffered as park facilities fell further behind in repairs—small and major—and adequate personnel to serve growing numbers of visitors was not forthcoming—indeed, staffing levels were curtailed.

While some right-minded legislators attempted to address the problem, their efforts were thwarted by those in leadership positions who saw no reason to strive for a first-class state parks system and/or had a deep-seated aversion to dedicated funds—funds tied up by law that leave no room for legislators to move, divert, or leave in place to balance the budget. By 2007, the twelfth year of the imposition of the artificial $32 million cap, with no legislative attempts to remove or raise the cap in sight, lack of funding had caused such dire circumstances in the parks that the staff at the Texas Parks and Wildlife Department was forced to seek other sources of revenue.

Several measures helped but did not solve the problem.

As noted in chapter nine, in 2003, the Seventy-Eighth Legislature passed House Bill 2351, requiring 15 percent of boat registration revenue to be transferred to Fund 64, the state parks' account. The logic behind the enactment was (and is) that many of our parks host boating activities. Over the years (2003 to 2017), this change in revenue allocations produced roughly $3 million annually.[1]

Beginning in 2008, the legislature began to use the Sporting Goods Sales Tax for debt service on park-related bonds. In 2013, the legislature allowed the Texas Parks and Wildlife Department to receive funding from the Sporting Goods Sales Tax to cover the cost of employee benefits.[2]

All these actions helped at the edges but did not approach the appropriations levels necessary to obtain Cadillac (or even used-car) status for our parks. They just helped keep the doors open—barely—and in some years, not. There were also two bond issues authorized by the legislature that were approved by substantial margins of the citizens of Texas at the ballot box. Their purpose, as far as parks were concerned, was to fund capital construction and repair projects. Again, much needed and helpful in the short term but much more expensive in the long run than outright appropriations from revenue generated by the Sporting Goods Sales Tax. At the time of passage in each of the two years (2001 and 2007), $84 million and $108 million, respectively, in Sporting Goods Sales Tax revenue was collected, but only $32 million and $20.5 million were appropriated. Basically, margins like these would hold true year in and year out, with revenue available on a pay-as-you-go basis to cover capital construction and repair projects. However, this less-expensive option (general revenue appropriation) was not available; thus, the more costly bond financing was the only alternative, and needs were immediate.

The one bit of good news was that the plight of the parks was now an open secret. Due to the publicity generated by the legislative debate leading up to passage of the 2007 bill and bond issue later that year, there began to be open conversations about the need for a permanent and unassailable solution to the problem: a constitutional amendment! The large number of coauthors who signed on to State Representative Harvey Hilderbran's House Bill 12 in 2007 was encouraging: 120 out of 150 members in the House and twenty-five out of thirty-one members in the Senate.

While legislation was not drafted to address such an amendment, the number of supporting members in each chamber was more than the two-thirds required in both houses to pass a constitutional amendment that would place the issue before Texas voters. If that transpired, there was no question, based on ongoing polling data, that it would pass by an overwhelming margin.

The whisper would become a conversation—now and then. However, the time for an amendment was not at hand. Such an opportunity had to await legislative circumstances, outlast a national recession that created budgetary shortfalls, and endure crippling floods and fires—more stumbling blocks to making good on the promise of a parks system second-to-none, or at least a system that would attract Texas citizens and tourists from other states and abroad.

Unfortunately, there was nothing permanent about the improvements captured in Hilderbran's bill due to the language inserted at the last minute of the 2007 session. Even though the $32 million cap was lifted, it remained in the hands of the legislature to determine amounts to be appropriated. After a two-year increase to $66.5 million and $57 million, respectively, the amounts for the following fiscal years of 2010 and 2011 dropped back to a wholly inadequate $24 million (2012) and $25 million (2013). The numbers for the following biennium were not much better.

As Texas arrived at 2014, not only were our state parks in a woeful state of disrepair and deterioration, but there was also no room for meaningful planning for the future. There was certainly no discussion about additional park acquisitions. Even the purchase of the proposed Palo Pinto Mountains State Park in 2011 was left in limbo, even though it was financed with no state funds.

It was a pitiful state of affairs, so much so that it was beginning to catch the attention of key legislators and influential citizens, including past and present Texas Parks and Wildlife commissioners.

In the fall of 2014, an active program of lobbying, fundraising, and renewed education on the disrepair of our aging parks was organized and put into play. Ninety-one percent of the playgrounds in Texas state parks were thirty years old or older, and 50 percent were in need of replacement. Ninety percent of the restrooms in Texas state parks were thirty years old or older; three hundred required removal or replacement.[3]

On the positive side of the equation was the growing call for constructive and permanent action by the Texas legislature. An updated *Economic Contributions of Texas State Parks* by Dr. John Crompton of Texas A&M University was commissioned by the Texas Coalition for Conservation and was circulated to legislators, news media, local officials, and key leaders.

This 2014 study (validated by the earlier 2005 study and a later one in 2019) showed an estimated $774 million in sales, $568 million in output, $351 million in value added, and $202 million in impacts on residents' income. Healthy numbers in any economy but essential to most of the small towns across Texas hosting state parks.[4]

Polls taken during this time (and the one in 2019 to follow) demonstrated that across the decades, Texans valued their parks, were willing to pay for their parks, did not approve of the diversions of Sporting Goods Sales Tax revenue for purposes unrelated to parks, and would support a constitutional amendment to ensure a permanent stream of revenue generated by the Sporting Goods Sales Tax. By large margins, ranging from 68 to 76 percent, Texans affirmed their commitment to their parks.

As David Hill of Hill Research Associates, which conducted the polling, explains:

Aside from highly visible presidential elections, political operatives and advocates working at state and local levels to persuade voters to choose a particular candidate or back a ballot measure often face serious barriers and impediments to these objectives. Perhaps the greatest of these impediments is the electorate's lack of interest in or passion about some corners of politics and low levels of knowledge about candidates, offices, and policy topics. Researchers encounter these challenges, too. Pollsters ask questions and dutifully record the answers of potential voters, but many come away with the sense that "public opinion," as measured by most polls, is uninformed, fragile, and ephemeral. Political scientist George Bishop, informed by these observations, has argued that most polling today provides a mere "illusion of public opinion" that is not reliable as a guide to most operatives and advocates.

It was in the context of this conundrum that we first began polling Texans' attitudes and opinions about conservation and parks topics in 1999 and continued to poll through 2019, spanning two decades. From the outset, we guarded against simplistic questions such as "Do you support conservation programs?" or "Do you want to support Texas parks?" that would provide little more than socially desirable responses. Several strategies were key to our deeper dive into opinions, transcending the illusionary. First, we always sought to measure the intensity of opinions with questions such as "Do you support this goal strongly or just somewhat?" Second, we forced voters to prioritize their preferences: "Okay, you want conservation programs and parks, but do you place a higher priority on competing programs like schools or traffic management?" Third, we tested the ultimate commitment: expressing a commitment to raising taxes to pay for these programs.

Another important research strategy was to move beyond measuring opinions to gauging deeper human constructs of beliefs and values. Opinions come and go based on the latest news cycle. But beliefs and values run deep and long, resistant to change. The best example of this was a question that asked poll respondents to agree or disagree (using a five-point Likert scale) with this statement: "All of God's creation deserves protection, including our land, water, animal habitat, and other natural areas." In 1999, an astounding 91 percent of voters agreed with that statement. An even more astounding 51 percent agreed STRONGLY with this heavily value-laden statement. It was from that moment on that I knew that the effort of Texas conservationists and parks advocates to find a permanent source of funding was not just another advocacy campaign but was rather what the Blues Brothers, Jake and Elmo, described as their own quest to save an orphanage: "a mission from God." But we didn't stop there. We plumbed the deeper recesses of Texans' hearts and minds, seeking reactions to deep value statements like these:

- "Unless we protect Texas's natural areas, we will lose the very things that make Texas a special place in which to live."
- "If state leaders don't purchase and protect some of Texas's natural areas today, they will be lost forever to development."

As well as the counterpoint value:

- "The free market and not government should decide whether land gets developed or not."

Based on the initial poll, our assessment was that only 17 percent of Texas voters were solidly in the conservationist, pro-parks camp, willing to support anything and pay for it, and only 24 percent were firmly anti-conservationist, disapproving of anything. This left a large majority in the middle who were open to some means of financing conservation and park efforts. The preferred option seemed to be sales taxes on sporting goods and outside recreation. Subsequently, the policy track of the effort moved in that direction.

- Later research in 2004 confirmed the public preference for sales taxes and suggested that two bedrock principles should be embedded in a public finance plan:

  Texas should spend for parks and conservation on a pay-as-you-go basis, not incurring debt by bonding; and,

  Any sales taxes should fall on users—that is for products and services indicating use of parks and outdoor activities.

Polling in subsequent years reflected continuing support for these perspectives. As we moved closer to developing an actual ballot question for voters, we ran into an impediment discussed above—lack of information. A statewide poll in 2019 found that only one in four Texas voters was familiar with the then-applicable Texas sales tax on sporting goods, a tax we wanted to dedicate to parks and conservation. This presented a potential quirk for advocacy. Suggesting that we could spend more for conservation and parks without any increase in taxes threatened to be "too good to be true" in the minds of skeptical voters. So, an important part of the narrative that led to passage in a statewide election was explaining that the money had always been there, but it was just being spent by legislators for other purposes. As this storyline coincided with a skeptical and cynical view of most leaders' trustworthiness, it overcame the too-good-to-be-true narrative.

Two final observations are worth noting about public opinion over this time period. First, there was remarkable stability in opinions across the two decades of research. Second, there was broad consensus on the core issues.

Stability in attitudes about parks, conservation, and funding across the years was especially astonishing because the "Great Recession" occurred smack in the middle of the time period, potentially slacking appetites for conservation spending as opposed to financial relief to taxpayers. But the economic downturn didn't even seem to be a speedbump on the road to eventual passage of the amendment to secure permanent funding.

The breadth of support for parks, conservation, and funding also largely defied the tribal splits that have come to plague the politics of Texas and the nation. Whether it was liberal versus conservative, Republican versus Democrat, native versus newcomer, Anglo versus minority, urban versus rural, Dallas versus Houston versus Austin versus San Antonio, there was broad agreement that parks and conservation are important and that a secure means of financing should be approved. In our fractured state and nation, this was truly amazing and perhaps a phenomenon not to be duplicated on any other public policy issue of our time.

Despite the broad consensus, there were some shades or degrees of difference that portend positively for securing the long-term future of parks and conservation in Texas. The younger generation clearly exhibits a stronger allegiance to conservation and outdoor recreation than their parents and grandparents. Outdoor activities are key to the lifestyles of many Texans under the age of forty-five. Also, the growing Hispanic or Latino population is imperative. Generally, we have found that Hispanics share a more communitarian spirit when it comes to providing public amenities like parks. While the older generation of Hispanic males may be cautious about new funding for parks and conservation programs, Hispanics as a whole are—and will be—users of parks, and support for parks and conservation funding will likely follow for most.[5]

Armed with this positive and updated data, strategy meetings began to be held in several important areas: further education that would be needed to make our case, strategic targeting of elected state officials, and fundraising for a full-blown lobbying effort in and through the upcoming 2015 legislative session. Regarding each strategy, the parks were blessed with growing and effective groups of individuals and organizations that could make the case and contribute or raise the funds to see us through.

But above all else, the right key leaders, once again, stepped forward to give direction at every important and necessary juncture.

In the House, Speaker Joe Straus gave his blessing to the planned legislation. State Representative Ryan Guillen, chair of the Culture, Recreation, and Tourism Committee, introduced House Bill 82. State Representative Lyle Larson also filed a back-up bill, House Bill 158. It turned out to be less than hoped for. In short order, once the legislature went into session, more than a hundred House members signed on as cosponsors

Former Texas Parks and Wildlife Commission Chair Dan Allen Hughes, date unknown. Hughes was an unflinching advocate for state park funding. Courtesy of Dan Allen Hughes.

(enough to pass a constitutional amendment bill if the opportunity arose). It is worth noting here that more than fifty organizations signed on to help secure cosponsors for Guillen's bill. Their presence and pressure were invaluable throughout the process.

On the Senate side, the support of the lieutenant governor, Dan Patrick, was an absolute must. In many respects, the power of the lieutenant governor of Texas is greater than that of all others: governor or speaker. Patrick controlled all committee chair assignments, the flow of the legislative calendar, and whose bills would move forward and whose would die. In the fall of 2014, his position on parks was unknown, if it existed at all.

Into that vacuum stepped Dan Allen Hughes Jr., an oil and gas entrepreneur and chairman of the Texas Parks and Wildlife Commission. As it turned out, he was an absolute devotee of parks for the people of Texas. His passion for the outdoors grew from boyhood experiences when he visited state parks and learned to hunt and fish. Later in life, Hughes was inspired by Bill Osbourne, a member of the Texas Parks and Wildlife Commission. Hughes thought to himself that a seat on the commission at some point in the future would be one of his life's goals. Equally important, Dan Allen Hughes developed a sense of fairness: "parks for all the people" was not just a slogan but a guiding light.

In 2009, Governor Rick Perry named Hughes to the Texas Parks and Wildlife Commission and, in 2014, appointed him chairman. During that first term, Hughes learned of the Sporting Goods Sales Tax and the shabby treatment of parks left in the wake of legislative diversion and denial. Over a five-year course, 2009 to 2014, he became a strong advocate for consistent, full utilization of all revenue generated by the Sporting Goods Sales Tax for parks. His argument was simple: as a successful businessman, he saw no way for proper and permanent planning if appropriations were hit-and-miss from one year to the next.

In the fall of 2014, Chairman Hughes and Lieutenant Governor Patrick met. Patrick wanted to talk about education, highways, and other weighty issues facing the state. Hughes only wanted to talk about parks.

At some point in the conversation, Dan Allen Hughes won out. Patrick agreed to help with the enabling legislation and consistent appropriations.

Patrick would stand by his word.

When the Texas legislature met in January 2015, all was ready on all fronts. The first order of business was to demonstrate the width and breadth of our support, first in the House (where the bill would originate) and then in the Senate. As mentioned previously, in short order, we had 109 House cosponsors, more than enough to guarantee passage of House Bill 82 and nine more than needed to pass the two-thirds requirement for a constitutional amendment, should we ever get to that point.

By mid-March, it appeared that we were set to pass Chairman Guillen's bill with room to spare. Then a change occurred. For reasons never fully explained, word came down that Representative Lyle Larson's House Bill 158 would be the vehicle to support. While still favorable to parks, it was not a fully dedicated funding measure. It got parks funding further down the road than ever imagined, in greater amounts, and with a fond hope based on assurances that funding would be consistent in years to come.

That was signaled with the passage of 2016 to 2017 appropriations. The Texas Parks and Wildlife Department allocation for the biennium was $261.1 million, a significant increase in its own right, but it was also the first time in history that the full 94 percent of Sporting Goods Sales Tax revenue was appropriated to the Texas Parks and Wildlife Department for parks.

With Dan Patrick's unwavering support, Larson's bill and the 100 percent appropriations easily passed the Senate.

There were joy and handshakes all around—again.

Media reports, newspaper columns, and editorial pages praised the legislature in glowing terms. Awards were gratefully bestowed. Even some members of the House and Senate who had little or nothing to do with the success took credit where none was due. Amidst all the backslapping and awards-giving, no one paid attention to the complementing Senate Bill 1366, which had been sponsored and passed by State Senator Lois Kolkhorst and State Representative Larry Gonzales. The bill appeared to be a much-needed correction of the tax code for those who cared to look. Few did. Even the bill's sponsors thought they had fixed the financing problem until an adverse ruling by Comptroller Glenn Hegar proved otherwise.

Bastrop State Park flood, May 25, 2015.
Photo by George Bristol, author's collection.

The reasons for the lack of scrutiny were several-fold, but two were of major significance: for the first time in the history of the Sporting Goods Sales Tax, 100 percent of the revenue for fiscal years 2016 and 2017 ($129 million and $132 million, respectively) was appropriated and allocated fully; and second, the legislative session of 2015 had no more signed off, sine die, than terrible rains and flooding hit Texas, destroying several parks, wildlife management areas, and other facilities. Bastrop State Park, which had not recovered from the fires of 2011, was struck with water so powerful that it knocked out the park dam and a campground downstream. There went much of the funding planned for major repairs in other parks.

Even though it looked like the Texas Parks and Wildlife Department was again snakebit following a success, it did have the 100 percent appropriation to renew and restore facilities and fill personnel slots left vacant for years. The remainder of 2015 and into 2016 seemed to flow smoothly without incident and with much to be thankful for.

In early 2017, I happened to set aside a day to visit the Capitol and check in with a few friends, one being Ryan Guillen, who deserves more credit than he received. His House Bill 82 got the ball rolling, gathering a hundred-plus House sponsors before Lyle Larson moved in to take credit with his own bill.

Ryan Guillen was not a happy man and no longer chairman. A conflict between House Bill 158 and Senate Bill 1366 had been discovered and ruled on by State Comptroller Glenn Hegar. The amounts to be credited to the Texas Parks and Wildlife Department held conflicting language, and the final interpretation was that the Texas Parks and Wildlife Department was limited to amounts appropriated by the legislature. Each succeeding legislature would continue to call the shots, and the roller coaster appropriations process loomed large again. Angry though he was, Guillen had already filed a bill (House Bill 78) to correct the conflict. Surely, this was a simple oversight miswritten in the closing days of the 2015 session. Surely a meeting with Speaker Joe Straus and Lieutenant Governor Dan Patrick would expose the problem and be quickly dispatched.

Meetings were arranged, cases were made, and surprise at the consequences of Senate Bill 1366 and the comptroller's ruling appeared to be genuine. Calls went out for support for House Bill 78, with letters to the editors of all newspapers, great and small. And nothing happened.

Representative Lyle Larson would not even sign on to rescue his own 2015 bill.

After the initial shock over what had occurred, I assured Guillen that I thought the fix was a simple one and that his bill would correct the conflict. I made several calls, specifically to Dan Allen Hughes. We agreed to set appointments with the speaker and lieutenant governor. Surely, with quick action in the House on Guillen's bill and acceptance by the Senate, that would be that.

We met with the Speaker and his staff first. Our message was twofold: Senate Bill 1366 could open the floodgate of diversion of Sporting Goods Sales Tax revenue, leaving parks funding to the whims of future legislatures; and second, it would re-create the inability to properly plan long-term. With assurances made that both issues would be addressed, we went to the lieutenant governor's office. He immediately gave his word that, even though state revenue was tight, he would do everything he could to get park funding as close to 100 percent as possible, and he would investigate the best way to fix the problem caused by the negative interpretation of the conflict. By the end of the meeting, we felt good about the prospects: full or near-full appropriations and a legislative fix to the conflict. We paid our respects to Representative Guillen and thanked him for introducing House Bill 78. He asked us to round up cosponsors, specifically State Representative Lyle Larson, to request that he coauthor House Bill 78.

Larson immediately agreed to see us.

He listened attentively.

He agreed it was most unfortunate.

He took a copy of Guillen's bill.

He never lifted a finger to help.

His inaction remains puzzling.

At the conclusion of the session, Texas's parks wound up with no correction of the conflict, but, true to his word (and that of Speaker Straus), Lieutenant Governor Patrick delivered on his promise: 90 percent of Sporting Goods Sales Tax revenue ($139 million) for fiscal year 2018 and 87 percent ($138 million) for fiscal year 2019.

Not 100 percent, but a huge sum when compared to the 40 percent allocation averages in years past. Based on the appropriations of the most recent years, there was a hint in the trend line that the Texas legislature had come to the realization that substantial appropriations went hand in hand with sustainable revenue.

But without a cure of the conflict caused by the two bills, the fate of future appropriations faced the possibility of future meddling. Given the history of parks funding throughout the decades, there was legitimate, lingering fear that that could happen, perhaps sooner rather than later.

The problem remained. Even though a high percentage of the dollars available were appropriated, there was the same old nagging possibility that highly adequate could plunge to severely inadequate in the next and future legislative sessions. The roller coaster ride would start anew, and necessary funding and planning would fly off the tracks—again.

Then, with faint praise for leadership and legislators, the parks and conservation advocates disappeared into the fog of historic doubts.

The results of the 2017 legislative session were bittersweet. After much joy-making and award-presenting following the apparent success of House Bill 158 (in 2015), coupled with full funding of the Sporting Goods Sales Tax revenue for parks and historic sites in 2016 to 2017, the permanent sustainability provision was undermined by the passage of the conflicting Senate Bill 1366. This last-minute bill inadvertently negated all the good that was to have flowed from the intent of House Bill 158.

There was a momentary period of gratitude and relief. But when all was said and done, there remained the problem of lack of permanency that precluded planning for long-needed repairs and capital improvements. The proof lay in the ever-increasing amount of deferred maintenance—$800 million!—and increasing annually.

At some point over the remainder of 2017 and into 2018, the whisper of a constitutional amendment began anew.

Who heard it first? Who knows!

It may have been Joe Fitzsimons, former chairman of the Texas Parks and Wildlife Commission, rancher, and advocate for private property rights and parks for people, who was driving or flying to his ranch house in South Texas. Maybe he slapped the steering wheel or dashboard and exclaimed, "Enough is enough!" and determined to do something about it. He would eventually form the Texas Coalition for State Parks to support a lobbying effort. Or maybe it was the very savvy president of the Texas Wildlife Association, David Yeates, talking to his friend State Representative John Cyrier about the disappointing failure to fix the parks funding problem as they drove to a fall football game at Texas A&M University. Representative Cyrier told me that he was shocked to find the permanent fix articulated in 2015 had been torpedoed and left ignored and unresolved in 2017. It turned out a number of his colleagues felt the same disappointment.

Or it could have been State Senator Lois Kolkhorst, who, with six state parks and eight historic sites in her district (the most of any senatorial district in Texas), stayed keenly attuned to all things parks. Her attention, coupled with a passion to get Texans—particularly children—into the outdoors, ensured that she would be interested in any suggestion that would address a permanent solution: perhaps a constitutional amendment?

Or maybe Ralph Duggins, newly appointed chairman of the Texas Parks and Wildlife Commission, while casting a line for trout, began to think about the pride his grandfather had in the contributions he was able to make to Missouri as chairman of that state's Conservation Commission—none more so than its conservation funding program that had raised more than a billion dollars for parks and other natural venues.

Former Texas Parks and Wildlife Commission Chair Ralph Duggins, date unknown. Duggins played a major role in passing the Proposition 5 constitutional amendment in 2019. Courtesy of the Texas Parks and Wildlife Department, Austin, Texas.

At that moment, Duggins knew that it was time to extend his grandfather's gift to him to the citizens of Texas, particularly its children. And the only way to make it lasting was to cloak it in the protective cover of a constitutional amendment! It was time for a full-fledged conversation on plans and levels of support. The support was there.

The whisper was starting to become a well-orchestrated chorus.

What is known—and important—is that those leaders were absolutely essential to any chance of success. Joe Fitzsimons, with initial and substantial financial support from his own checkbook and that of Dan Allen Hughes, got the organizational ball rolling over the spring and summer of 2018. He hired Logan Spence, former chief of staff to the lieutenant governor, to head the lobbying effort during the upcoming session. He fortified the lobbying team with John Montford, who not only had sponsored the original Sporting Goods Sales Tax in the Senate but had signed on as chairman of the revitalized State Parks Advisory Committee, which, among its supporting roles, called for a constitutional amendment in 2014. I recommended Jenifer Sarver as our media consultant. She had worked on the 2015 effort and could articulate the issues without having to learn the ropes.

During the same time frame, State Representative John Cyrier had let it be known that he wanted to play a major role in perfecting legislation that would once and for all address the state parks funding issue—a constitutional amendment.

Simultaneously, State Senator Lois Kolkhorst was drawing up similar bill language for her sponsorship in the Senate. Senate Bill 26 and Senate Joint Resolution 24 would become the vehicles adopted to move the bill through both houses of the Texas legislature.

Senate Bill 26's low number granted by Lieutenant Governor Patrick practically guaranteed passage by the Senate, as it would be part of his "must-pass" legislative priorities.

Texas Representative John Cyrier promoting Proposition 5, October 2019. Cyrier authored the House legislation creating Proposition 5. Courtesy of the office of the Honorable John Cyrier.

By early September 2018, everything seemed to be heading in the right and, just as importantly, the same direction. There were differences to be negotiated but nothing that would derail the effort, partly because Cyrier and Kolkhorst held power and respect among their colleagues in the House and Senate and partly because they were dedicated to making it work this time.

It was time to introduce the latest plan to a broader audience of potential—and necessary—supporters. From my early days of planning strategy and educating those audiences about the position of conservation as it relates to state parks, I determined that public parks needed to be a partner with private landowners and advocates. All too often, they were at loggerheads for no valid reason; that was just the way it was.

It was Texas's own version of conservation "Hatfield and McCoy." Fortunately, we were able to break down those barriers to the point that by an organizational luncheon in the fall of 2018, there was legitimate comradeship based on common ground. By the time the Texas legislature opened in January 2019, we were at fifty or so supporting groups, and that would grow to seventy-four by session's end.

> This constitutional amendment dedicates the revenue received from the existing state sales and use taxes that are imposed on sporting goods to the Texas Parks and Wildlife Department and the Texas Historical Commission to protect Texas's natural areas, water quality, and history by acquiring, managing, and improving state and local parks and historic sites while not increasing the rate of the state sales and use taxes.

Proposition 5 Ballot Language

The ballot language of a constitutional amendment is most important. It must be a clear and easy statement of the fact(s) of the issue to be presented to the voters. It also must touch on the motivating factors that polling data or common sense dictate. For example, "no new taxes" was a hot-button issue and an absolute must. Its absence could have cast a shadow over the rest of the amendment. Placing it at the end of the sentence gave it the added emphasis—the last thought before a vote was cast.

Bill language was finalized. Hearings were held in the House and Senate committees of jurisdiction. The proponents were out in force and recruited several articulate advocates such as Ed Whitacre, former chairman of the boards of AT&T and General Motors. His message was spot on: parks were not only good for the spiritual, mental, and physical well-being of Texans but also for their pocketbooks, particularly for the citizens in hosting communities. But in order to ensure a continuing flow of park benefits, they must be sustained on a reliable basis—year in and year out.

While all of this was in play, the sponsors—Cyrier and Kolkhorst, with a host of supporters—fanned out over the Capitol to nail down at least twenty-one senators and one hundred House members.

By the time they had finished, thirty-one senators and 150 House members supported the park legislation. How did that happen? Teamwork, true bipartisanship, and a great deal of educational advocating over almost twenty years. A lone House member would eventually withdraw his support, but no matter.

Cyrier called on me to approach State Representative Chris Turner, chairman of the Democratic Caucus. I did. Turner delivered every member of the caucus, and Cyrier asked him to coauthor the House bill. This camaraderie prevailed in both chambers throughout the session. It is a role model of legislative civility, decency, and positive results.

Why, for all this effort, was the two-thirds support in both houses necessary? It is the law in the Texas Constitution governing the rules of the legislature that such margins are required to move a constitutional amendment from legislation to a ballot measure to be voted on by a simple majority on a date determined by the legislature.

In a sense, the easy part of the constitutional amendment effort had been accomplished. Chairman Cyrier and Senator Kolkhorst had the full blessing and support of the lieutenant governor and Speaker Dennis Bonnen, a full-blown media program, active and productive support from the seventy-four recruited organizations and others, and unabated personal visits by present and past Texas Parks and Wildlife commissioners led by Chairman Ralph Duggins. The call for a constitutional amendment had reached a full-throated choir. Yes, all the legislative rings had aligned, and Senate Joint Resolution 24 and Senate Bill 26 were the law of the land. But now we had to present the proposition to the people, who would be called on to cast their ballots for Constitutional Amendment 5 (Proposition 5) on November 5, 2019.

To give the entire team a roadmap to a successful outcome, I had quietly commissioned and raised the funds for a statewide poll by Hill Research Associates, which had conducted four earlier polls in 1999, 2005, 2009, and 2014. On July 16, representatives from every sector of the sponsoring and support team met in Chairman Cyrier's business office to hear the results.

The numbers were impressive, but there were a few cautionary notes. All elections at the beginning—and often throughout the process—involve mystery and doubt. That is especially true for off-year special elections, principally because turnout is traditionally low. Low turnout allows a well-organized or riled-up minority to become, in effect, a majority. But this was unlikely due to the continuing popularity of parks among all groups of Texans.

According to David Hill of Hill Research Associates,

Texans' sentiments on the issues (parks, Sporting Goods Sales Tax, etc.) covered by this poll has remained remarkably stable over the past decade, suggesting that these opinions are more than ephemeral or transient views; rather, we see attitudes that are closer to bedrock beliefs and values that persist for a generation or more. That trendline certainly held through the election of 2019.[6]

Attention was turned to the "mother's milk of politics"—money. Texas is a huge state, with twenty Designated Market Areas (television) that are widely diverse in race and philosophy. To put an election budget together for a special election with a guaranteed low turnout is at best a challenge. First, because Proposition 5 was not a "hot-button" social issue and had seemingly no opposition, there was little motive to contribute and little in the coffers. There was even a negative in the fact that the poll results were so good: many who supported parks might have shrugged their financial shoulders with an attitude of "why bother—it's in the bag."

During August 2019, a working budget and fundraising plan were cobbled together. It was clear that few thought that there was reason to be concerned and, thus, contributed in lesser amounts—far less than needed.

Fortunately, the news media in September began to pick up the story and strongly endorse the measure—all except the *Dallas Morning News*. Once again, the *Fort Worth Star-Telegram* led the way!

To coordinate the moving parts of the campaign, Rob Johnson, a superb campaign strategist, was hired.

The supporting organizations began to report back firm and enthusiastic commitments. Parks friends groups began to campaign. By the end of August, all was in place—except a commitment of contributions sufficient to finance a satisfactory campaign. At that moment, Ralph Duggins's conservation DNA kicked into high gear. He marshaled an eloquent plea that all of us had come this far, and it was time to ensure success—with a margin as large as possible—by backing the campaign to the fullest degree possible. The "possible" came directly from Ralph Duggins's efforts and from others inspired by the generosity the Duggins group demonstrated. By early September 2019, there was adequate money in the bank and a plan in place.

**ABOVE, LEFT AND RIGHT**
Exterior and interior of an educational brochure used during
the election effort to pass Proposition 5 by 88 percent of the vote,
September–October 2019. Courtesy of Ernest Cook and the
Texas Conservation Alliance, Dallas, Texas.

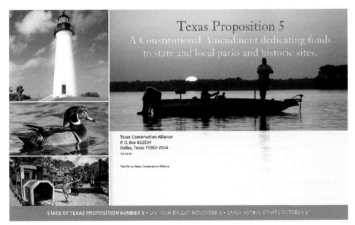

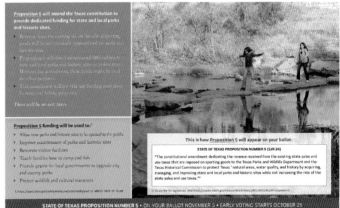

**ABOVE, LEFT AND RIGHT**
The two sides of a postcard used during the Proposition 5
election effort, September–October 2019. Courtesy of
Ernest Cook and the Texas Conservation Alliance,
Dallas, Texas.

Unannounced and unknown by most involved in the formal political action committee, Ernest Cook had been at work throughout the spring and summer selling his ideas for a nonprofit-financed election education campaign. Cook knew much about Texas politics and formulations, having worked the "ballot measure vineyards" for years under Trust for Public Land conservation initiatives. After careful research and legal blessing, he set a goal of raising $500,000 and reaching nine hundred thousand households through a two-piece mail campaign.

Ernest Cook recognized another opportunity: an education program that would provide voters with objective information about the proposal, leaving them to make up their own minds on whether to vote "Yes" or "No." Why would an education program be effective? Surveys show that there are two main reasons given by voters for opposing spending measures for parks and conservation: 1) they do not understand how the money will be used, and 2) they do not want new taxes. In the case of the Sporting Goods Sales Tax amendment, no new taxes would be imposed. And the funding would be used to improve and care for state and local parks in communities throughout Texas, with widespread public benefits. A voter education program that focused on these points was likely to be effective in overcoming any doubts about supporting the measure on election day.

A major advantage to an education program is that it can be paid for with grants from private foundations. Federal law prohibits these institutions from earmarking grants for lobbying purposes—and campaigns that aim to persuade voters to vote one way or the other on a ballot measure are considered a type of lobbying. But communications to voters that provide strictly objective information about a ballot measure are a permissible project for a private foundation to fund. Here are the key differences between a ballot measure lobbying campaign and an education program:

| LOBBYING CAMPAIGN | EDUCATION CAMPAIGN |
| --- | --- |
| Urges a "yes" or "no" vote | Does not take a position on the measure |
| Offers opinions | Communicates only factual information |
| Conveys messages, soundbites | Provides substantial information that allows a voter to evaluate the merits of a proposal |
| Targets swing voters or urges base to turn out | Aims to educate the electorate generally |
| Funded by non-deductible campaign contributions | May be funded by private foundations as well as by deductible charitable contributions |

The task was to select an organization that was clearly associated with the values represented by the Sporting Goods Sales Tax amendment, was recognized for its educational work, and was willing to undertake the task. Indicators pointed to the Texas Conservation Alliance, a nearly fifty-year-old wildlife conservation organization with a track record of protecting rivers, forests, and other wildlife habitats.

Cook explained to the Texas Conservation Alliance his goal of raising and spending $500,000 for the program over the following six months. He assured Janice Bezanson, the organization's executive director, that he would carry much of the load for fundraising and designing and implementing the education program.

The next step was fundraising. There was a window of only a few months for the necessary funds to be raised. With an election in early November 2019 and widespread early voting, voter communications would have to go out in mid-October. That meant final decisions about spending the money would have to be made by August, and funding commitments would be needed by July at the latest. Ultimately, several Texas foundations committed a total of $505,000 to the education campaign.

When the fundraising effort reached its conclusion, Cook commented, "This is the easiest money I've ever raised."

Cook elected to use direct mail as the sole means of carrying out the education program. Although modern ballot measure campaigns use a variety of strategies to communicate with voters, direct mail was particularly well-suited to this education program for several reasons:

- This would surely be a low-turnout election. History shows that turnout in odd-year November elections in Texas ranges from 5 to 12 percent of registered voters. Communication strategies reaching a mass audience—like TV or newspaper advertising—would therefore be largely wasted.

- In contrast, by analysis of voting records, direct mail can be targeted fairly precisely to households with at least one voter likely to participate in the November election. On Cook's advice, the Texas Conservation Alliance engaged a direct mail expert with broad experience in ballot measures for parks and conservation. He determined that the universe of households including at least one likely voter consisted of approximately one million mailing addresses. If the education program could reach virtually all of these households, regardless of political affiliation and residence (urban or rural), it would clearly demonstrate that it met the test of communicating broadly with the electorate rather than targeting a particular demographic.

- Direct mail can present sufficient information to fully inform voters and allow them to reach their own conclusions.

- Direct mail allows the communication to be fully controlled and vetted by legal counsel to ensure it does not represent a lobbying communication. In this case, every word of text, design of the mailers, and even choice of photos were carefully reviewed by an independent legal expert.
- Educational mail from a public charity such as the Texas Conservation Alliance can be delivered very inexpensively, costing only twelve to thirteen cents for each piece.

Following templates from previous direct mail efforts on which he had worked, Ernest Cook designed and wrote—with helpful advice from Janice Bezanson—the text for a trifold brochure and an oversized postcard. Each went through more than half a dozen revisions based on reviews and recommendations of counsel, the Texas Parks and Wildlife Department, and other advisers. With just over $500,000 in hand, the education program ultimately sent two pieces of mail to each of 952,000 households in every corner of the state.

On November 5, 2019, Texans had a chance to have their say. The results of the Proposition 5 constitutional amendment vote? Eighty-eight percent approved; 12 percent disapproved.

Hereafter, unless both houses vote by a two-thirds majority, the legislature will be unable to reduce full funding for parks and historic sites and, even then, by only 50 percent. That would be a hardship, but only temporarily. They'd have to vote again in two years. In my judgment, based on the voters' positive vote, the size of the victory, and the self-constraints written into the law by the members themselves, the Texas legislature will not meddle much with our parks and historic sites—at least for a while.

With the huge infusion of Sporting Goods Sales Tax funds (plus additional unanticipated windfalls) for fiscal years 2022 and 2023 assured, some of those dreams delayed and plans deferred are ready to jump off the architects' and engineers' desks at the Texas Parks and Wildlife Department.

That infusion of funds—coupled with the likely prospect that the Texas legislature will leave the Sporting Goods Sales Tax revenue alone—gives hope for continuity, with a constant, but non-confrontational, reminder that Texans did, indeed, direct the legislature to do what they should have been doing all along. Because of that overwhelming support, legislators would meddle with the parks at their own peril.

What these dreams deferred will be and what they will address will take time to sort through, but changes will take place over several years—not decades—just in time to kick off a new age of Texas state parks development in the next centennial—2023 to 2123.

State Representative John Cyrier (left) and State Senator Lois Kolkhorst (right) with Texas Governor Greg Abbott at the signing of Senate Bill 26 and Senate Joint Resolution 24, June 24, 2019. The legislation, coauthored by Representative Cyrier and Senator Kolkhorst, placed Proposition 5 on the ballot to stop the diversion of funds from state parks and historical sites. Courtesy of the office of the Honorable John Cyrier.

# Chapter 11

# Private Park Philanthropy: An Essential Partner

B ecause national and state parks are creatures of legislative action and governmental guidance, there is a tendency to overlook the need for—and legitimacy of—private philanthropy as an integral part of park creation and continuing support.

Nothing could be further from the truth.

From the outset, our parks have benefited from the time and treasure of those who have been touched by the handiwork of the Creator.

Much of park gifting has centered on national parks, but state and local parks require and have received similar interest and dedication. In the early 1900s, Texas individuals and organizations stepped forward to contribute money or lands and historic sites for the benefit of Texas citizens. That spirit of gifting has carried forward to this day.

I turn the clock back to Thomas Jefferson and his purchase of the Virginia Natural Bridge for twenty shillings from King George III on July 5, 1774—two years before the Declaration of Independence—that became one of the seeds for public parks supplemented by private philanthropy in America.[1]

Although Jefferson did not envision his purchase as a prelude to a national or state park, he did deem it "the most sublime of nature's wonders" and allowed only a two-room cabin to be built as a retreat for himself and many visiting luminaries, including John Marshall, James Monroe, and Sam Houston.[2] He allowed no other development on the property. Later, private owners caused all manner of tourist attractions to be built nearby, but not on the site itself.

**RIGHT**

*Texas*, the musical, at Palo Duro Canyon State Park, ca. 1970. Courtesy of Curatorial Services, Texas Parks and Wildlife Department, Austin, Texas, 2010.5.4.

**RIGHT**

Civilian Conservation Corps structure at the Fort Worth Nature Center & Refuge, 2016. Photo by George Bristol, author's collection.

**RIGHT**

Natural Bridge State Park, Virginia, date unknown. After more than 240 years and an increase in nearby development, Natural Bridge finally became a state park in 2016. Courtesy of the Virginia Department of Conservation and Recreation, Richmond, Virginia.

Fortunately, in 2013, when 1,500 acres that included the bridge were about to be put up for sale, the Virginia Conservation Legacy Fund, with a $9.1 million loan from the Virginia Clean Water Revolving Loan Fund, purchased the property. In short order, on September 24, 2016, Natural Bridge State Park opened under the supervision of the Virginia Department of Conservation and Recreation, in affiliation with the National Park Service. Until the loan is paid in full, it is the only state park in Virginia located on private land.[3]

Even though some of the surrounding areas were developed, the cradling 1,500 acres remain more or less intact to this day. Part of the reason is the strong influence of Jefferson's inaction in not developing more than the rustic retreat. While his twenty-shilling purchase was an act of private philanthropy, his persuasive conservation was another form of philanthropy. He would write that he "viewed it as a public trust and would under no consideration permit the bridge to be injured, defaced, or masked from public view."[4]

Sign directing visitors to Natural Bridge State Park, Virginia, date unknown. Courtesy of Andriy Blokhin via Adobe Stock.

But what was most significant was that this set the precedent for private giving for public benefit—not quite a park at the beginning of Jefferson's action, but an illuminating idea that would circulate around the growing nation, particularly as the population moved west into the awesome landscapes that inspired gigantic gifts of private lands and dollars in the decades to come.

From the creation of Yellowstone National Park—our first national park—in 1872 forward, many of our parks have been held in private hands until created by Congress, purchased to protect until accepted by congressional action, and added to and supplemented by private donations in all manner of ways where government funding fell short.

Even before the founding of the National Park Service, Mr. and Mrs. William Kent donated the land and forest in 1907 that is now Muir Woods National Monument.[5] In 1916, George Dorr and a group of like-minded citizens in Maine donated the lands that became Acadia National Park.[6]

As we discovered in an earlier chapter, Stephen T. Mather, first director of the National Park Service (1916), was a man of action, courage, and wealth. More often than not, he would use his wealth to punctuate and support his actions. In 1915, he put up his own money and that of wealthy friends to buy the Tioga Road in Yosemite National Park. The next year, he bought land in Glacier National Park, then deeded it to the National Park Service as the site for a headquarters for the park. He also persuaded Horace Albright and Robert Sterling Yard to come work with him through the crucial first year

of the National Park Service by paying for their salaries out of his own pocket. By example, he demonstrated the many ways one could support parks by private contributions. And he encouraged private giving even as he battled with Congress for adequate funding for a growing parks system.

Over the years, there have been many other contributors to parks and park projects, but a special place must always be reserved for the Rockefellers—John D. Rockefeller Jr. and Laurance Rockefeller. Father and son would stretch their park generosity from the 1920s into the twenty-first century. Their direct contributions and influence on others to follow suit cannot be measured in dollars alone. But the breadth of their democratic donations are there for all to see in every section of the country and many states: Grand Teton National Park, Acadia National Park, Great Smoky Mountains National Park, Blue Ridge Parkway, Virgin Islands National Park, Yosemite National Park, and Glacier National Park.

Most of those gifts were to acquire and preserve lands until congressional action could expand the land holdings within or bordering parks. More millions went for museums such as the Mesa Verde National Park Museum. In 1992, Laurance and Mary Rockefeller gave their historic Vermont estate, valued at $21.4 million with a $7.5

million endowment, to establish the Marsh-Billings-Rockefeller National Historical Park.[7] Even in death, Laurance Rockefeller continued giving to our parks, deeding the family estate abutting Grand Teton National Park to the National Park Service.

After the Rockefellers, another family tradition contributed generously to the enhancement of our natural and historic heritage. On the historic front, $10.5 million of Richard King Mellon Foundation funds were donated to purchase Civil War battlefield lands: Antietam, Fredericksburg, Gettysburg, and Petersburg. Particular emphasis was placed on seacoasts and Great Lakes shorelines that led to several national seashores and lakeshore sites.[8]

While it does not appear that the Mellons played any significant role in the creation of Padre Island National Seashore in Texas, they made several land purchases over the

Grand Teton National Park, 1982. Photo by George Bristol, author's collection.

years in the state. One made through their Conservation Fund, Christmas Mountains, did not come close to meeting the state's criteria for a state park or wildlife management area and was nearly sold to the highest bidder.[9] It was finally donated to the Texas State University system and is administered by Sul Ross University.[10]

I bring this failure of purpose to the reader's attention to point out the delicate relationship between private donors and public administrators. In the case of lands for public benefit, there must be a clear understanding of end results. Certainly, one such standard must prevent the selling of a freely contributed gift to the highest bidder after it has been held for a prescribed number of years. In 1996, the Mellons, through the Richard King Mellon Foundation, bought the Chinati Mountains tract (thirty-nine thousand acres) and turned around and gave it to the Texas Parks and Wildlife Department for park or wildlife management.[11] Today, it is one of the premiere natural areas in the state's system.

Unfortunately, there have been several instances where offers of significant landscapes have been lost because the donor, rightly or wrongly, thought Texas Parks and Wildlife Department rules and regulations for acceptance were too stringent, added too much additional cost to the gift, or were just plain stupid.

Conversely, the department has turned down (and had every right to do so) properties that had too many self-serving stipulations, unenforceable demands, or even potential illegalities.

However, for the most part, details for donation and acceptance are worked out in advance, with resulting benefit for all parties—most assuredly, the people of Texas.

Over the decades of the twentieth century and into the twenty-first, private donations from individuals, families, foundations, and corporations have saved, preserved, enhanced, or created park holdings to the benefit of touring Americans and foreign visitors.

This phenomenon of private gifts for the public good reached its apex in 2016, when more than $500 million was raised by the National Park Foundation in the leadup to the centennial of the National Park Service.

In the tradition of the Rockefellers and other private donors and in the spirit of the centennial, Roxanne Quimby, cofounder of Burt's Bees, and her foundation began purchasing land in Maine in 2001 with the goal of amassing significant acreage for a new national park. She announced her plans in 2011 but was met with opposition from state and federal politicians. Not to be deterred, she reset her goals (for the time being) and set out to create a national monument that only required a proclamation by the president under the Antiquities Act. On the eve of the centennial, she donated the land (valued at $60 million), plus $20 million as an endowment, and a commitment for $20 million more in future support. President Barack Obama proclaimed the eighty-seven thousand acres as the Katahdin Woods and Waters National Monument.[12]

Clara Driscoll, a generous early contributor to many historic sites, 1903. Courtesy of the Adina Emilia De Zavala Papers, Dolph Briscoe Center for American History, University of Texas at Austin, Austin, Texas, di_00930_02.

Many park gifts, no matter how generous, often take patience to gain park status, but they are all the sweeter when completed. Thank God for the Rockefellers and Quimbys of the nation and gift givers at all levels of giving.

I am quite certain Clara Driscoll of Texas never heard of Roxanne Quimby—a matter of birth dates—and Roxanne probably never heard of Clara. But I am certain they would have joined forces to enhance the common good had they met.

The many contributions to state parks by women are covered in depth in chapter two, but Clara Driscoll's generous private gifts helped set the stage for the long line of philanthropists who would make a difference for Texas state parks and historic sites in the decades to come. Clara Driscoll was a Texas citizen—a true original—of wealth and privilege, the heiress of a ranching, oil, and business fortune. Later in life, she would have to take over the entire estate and run its affairs, which, by all accounts, she did most successfully. But it was her encounter with the magnificent restoration and preservation of historic buildings in Paris and other cities of France while she studied abroad that drove what became a lifelong passion for historic preservation.[13]

Upon returning to Texas in 1899, she became acquainted with the tragic deterioration of the Alamo and its surrounding grounds through Adina Emilia De Zavala, a leader in the Daughters of the Republic of Texas. To purchase the Alamo site and surrounding grounds, $75,000 was needed. The Daughters of the Republic of Texas did not have the money. Clara did. Through a series of cash payments and notes, the owners had a sale, and Clara had what was to become Texas's single most-popular tourist attraction—the Alamo—which she deeded to the Daughters of the Republic of Texas.[14]

While Clara, Adina, and the women of the De Zavala chapter of the Daughters of the Republic of Texas were busy saving the Alamo, which included persuading the Texas legislature to appropriate funds to repay Clara while conveying the entire Alamo site to the Daughters of the Republic of Texas, other chapters and organizations were at work.[15]

In 1907, the Daughters of the Republic of Texas pressured the Texas legislature to buy more than three hundred acres of the San Jacinto battlefield (and, while they were at it, appropriate funds for future improvements).[16] Following close behind were other efforts by the Daughters of the Republic of Texas, Daughters of the American Revolution, Texas Federation of Women's Clubs, and the Texas Garden Clubs to secure, preserve, and protect a number of Texas Revolution (1836) sites, including Washington-on-the-Brazos, where the Texas Declaration of Independence was signed.[17] (On a personal note, in 1986—Texas's 150th anniversary—as chair of the Texas Conservation Foundation, I was able to persuade Phillips Petroleum and Diamond-Shamrock to donate two hundred-plus acres of unused land to enlarge the state's San Jacinto Battlefield holdings.)

These several sites were deemed by proclamation and documentation to be among the first state parks of Texas.

But their status was always tenuous because there was no state parks system to legitimize their standing. No matter. The women of Texas, through their donations of money, time, and political savvy (not to mention power, with the prospect of the right to vote for women growing year after year, culminating in 1920), were demonstrating that private contributions for the common good had merit and support. In this case, their gifts helped preserve historic sites for public viewing, which, in turn, would foster citizen pride in statehood history.

Mother Neff's gift by her will in 1921 of six acres of private land is covered in an earlier chapter as well. However, that act of conveyance had far-reaching consequences that need to be explored.

Dedication ceremony for Mother Neff State Park, 1938. Courtesy of the Pat Neff Archive, Texas Collection, Baylor University, Waco, Texas.

It did not hurt the cause of parks that shortly after Mother Neff's death, then-Governor Pat Neff expanded the Neffs' gift to the state by some 250 acres and deemed it Texas's first state park. By example, the gifts of the Neffs gave legitimacy to the practice of contributing private lands for public benefit for parks and conservation. This not only satisfied the philanthropic spirit of generous Texans, but it would also play a key role in the task of fulfilling the dictates of a skeptical Texas legislature that directed only donated and maintained lands could be accepted by the newly formed State Parks Board. Surely, by holding up the generous example of the Neffs, it made David Colp's and other members' task of soliciting private donations easier.

It has been pointed out that a great number of legislators did not want Neff to succeed and were not going to accept whatever number of qualifying properties Colp presented to the 1925 session of the Texas legislature.

Nonetheless, in 1924, with great media attention and ballyhoo, Governor Neff, Colp, members of the board, highway commissioners, and other state celebrities, after much organizing, sailed forth across Texas to drum up support and donations of lands. The crowds were large and receptive, media attention was statewide, and land donations were forthcoming.

Their stop in Meridian is perhaps the best example of their success. Ten thousand citizens of Central Texas poured out to hear the governor and others extol the benefits of a state park in their area, not to mention a state park adjacent to a new state highway.

At the end of the forays, they not only had stirred up enthusiastic support and media attention, but they also had twenty-three sites in hand, which were proudly presented to the legislature for approval at the 1925 session. They were promptly rejected. They

**ABOVE**
Robert O. Anderson and his wife, Barbara Anderson, Aspen, Colorado, July 11, 1965. Courtesy of Margaret Durrance, Durrance Collection, Aspen Historical Society, Aspen, Colorado, 2018.002.1130.

**RIGHT**
Early morning at Big Bend Ranch State Park, December 29, 2014. Courtesy of Sam Rosenzweig, author's grandson.

would be turned over to the State Parks Board in 1927—once Pat Neff was out of office. But in doing this, the Texas legislature would establish another pattern that held true for many periods during the first hundred years: no appropriation for operations or maintenance and certainly not a dime for acquisition of new parklands.

Some gifts come to parks and conservation venues through reduction of price. There is no greater example of this than Robert O. Anderson's generous offer in 1988 to sell his three hundred thousand - acre ranch bordering Big Bend National Park to the state for $8.8 million below its market value. Today, that ranch is Big Bend Ranch State Park, the largest park in the Texas state parks system.

Other contributions come in-kind through the gifting of time or materials. None is more dramatic than the response to the devastating fire at Bastrop State Park and surrounding area in 2011. With a series of phone calls and emails, the heavy equipment industry rushed road graders and bulldozers to the park. Because of this instantaneous generosity, much was saved, including the historic Civilian Conservation Corps cabins and structures. At the other end of the giving scale, the local friends group raised more than $151,000, with donations ranging from small denominations to $25,000. Due to the size of the devastation, every gift counted—large, small, and in-kind.

I want to devote another moment to the pine seed story related earlier. Although not an act of philanthropy in the true sense of the word, it was a gift of enormous consequence.

The heartbreak of the 2011 Bastrop fire affected many victims with death, injury, loss of homes, loss of wildlife, and a 33,421-acre hole in the Lost Pines of Bastrop and Fayette counties, much of which was in Bastrop State Park.

Bastrop State Park fire, September 6, 2011. Courtesy of Chase Fountain, Communications Division, Texas Parks and Wildlife Department, Austin, Texas.

Given the nature of the pines, they might never have been replaced. That is until Tom Byram, a Texas Forest Service geneticist, called the Texas Parks and Wildlife Department with a miracle that was three weeks shy of never happening. Byram and the Forest Service were in possession of one thousand pounds of pine seeds—Lost Pine seeds!

Enough seeds to grow millions of trees were sitting in a freezer at the Brookshire Brothers's facilities in Lufkin, Texas. Because they had been there a good while with no potential buyer or other offer, Byram had decided to haul the seeds to the local landfill. The drop-dead date was to have been in September 2011. The fire occurred on September 4, 2011.

The seeds, the park, and the forest had a new lease on life.

**ABOVE**
Civilian Conservation Corps cabin
at Bastrop State Park, 2008. Photo by
George Bristol, author's collection.

**RIGHT**
Brookshire Brothers, Carthage, Texas,
July 22, 2017. Courtesy of Michael Barera
via Wikimedia Commons.

Those seeds were shipped to state and private nurseries (including the Lady Bird Johnson Wildflower Center) to grow into 450,000 seedlings—enough to reforest the burned-out area, including Bastrop State Park.

A reviving forest—with the help of donated seeds, Bastrop State Park, August 2021. Courtesy of G. Lamar via Wikimedia Commons.

Philanthropy? Maybe not. But a gift? By every meaning of the word!

From 2007 through 2017, positive changes began to occur on both the legislative and private giving fronts (the legislative actions for 2007 through 2015 and 2019 have been covered in earlier chapters). During that period, private contributions were encouraged by timing and necessity—fire, flood, budget constraints, and legislative directives.

Another extraordinary event in Texas park and conservation philanthropy occurred in December 2010. The Texas Parks and Wildlife Commission voted to acquire an additional eighteen thousand acres of West Texas land bordering the Devils River—regarded as the most pristine waterway in the state.[18] Though a stellar action in and of itself, it was the motivation behind the action that raised it to the level of the extraordinary. With no natural disaster, imminent sale to a shady buyer, toxic waste destroyer, or any other dire potential consequence, a group of patriotic Texas citizens came together to raise $10 million for no more apparent reason than a mutual love of nature at its awe-inspiring best.

"This land is a treasure for all generations to come," said Texas Parks and Wildlife

DOLANS FALLS, DEVIL'S RIVER, NEAR DEL RIO, TEXAS

OA4310

Old postcard of Dolan Falls at Devils River near Del Rio, date unknown. Courtesy of the Texas Parks and Wildlife Department, Austin, Texas.

Department Commissioner Dan Allen Hughes Jr., one of the contributors. Cash contributions were coupled with the generosity of the owner of the Devils River Ranch, Rod Sanders of Dallas, who dropped his selling price by nearly $3 million in order to make all the pieces of financing come together. The private part of the equation was rounded out with $2.7 million in state acquisition funds and $1.3 million from the federal Land and Water Conservation Fund.

By action of the commissioners, the Texas Parks and Wildlife Department now controlled some thirty-seven thousand acres (nineteen thousand acres were previously acquired in 1988), protecting what would become a state natural area under its jurisdiction.[19]

The origin of Palo Pinto Mountains State Park, one of the most recent examples of private philanthropy, was prompted in 2006 with the Texas General Land Office's announcement to sell four hundred acres of underutilized land adjacent to Eagle Mountain Lake near Fort Worth. The prospect of selling that natural gem to a developer of any sort did not sit well with many in Tarrant County and beyond. In almost simultaneous actions, the Tarrant Regional Water District (which eventually became the owner of record of the land, developing it into a fine local park—Eagle Mountain Park), the Trust for Public Land, and Texas Parks and Wildlife Commission Chairman Joseph Fitzsimons raised their concerned voices and vowed to take action. The *Fort Worth Star-Telegram* (as always on parkland issues) joined the cause.

Within a short time, a committee of Fort Worth and Tarrant County individuals and institutions raised the $9.3 million necessary to buy the Eagle Mountain acreage from the state. Governor Rick Perry proclaimed the effort a great success and vowed that the funds would be used to purchase a property befitting a major state park within an hour-and-a-half drive from Fort Worth. Fitzsimons, who had worked tirelessly to make this monumental transaction a reality, further confirmed that the funds raised would be used exclusively for the purchase of suitable lands to meet the criteria of a park located the recommended distance from Fort Worth and sized at five thousand acres.

It was the perfect demonstration of public/private cooperation, a coordinated partnership joining state and local entities to set the stage for a new state park. By the time the newest park was finally negotiated, purchased, and planned, it would be the first

in twenty years—in a state whose population would explode to twenty-seven million citizens and visitation to state parks would approach ten million annually. In 2021, the Texas legislature finally funded the first phases of development of the new park in the following manner: state appropriations, $12.5 million; highway department, $9 million; and private-partner funding, $8.5 million, for a total of $30 million.[20]

To encourage private-sector giving, a very generous supporter and former Texas Parks and Wildlife commissioner, Kelsey Warren, activated a $3 million challenge grant to develop the first phase of the Palo Pinto Mountains State Park project.[21]

This is not the complete story of the public/private partnership that will comprise the Palo Pinto Mountains State Park saga. Only the future will witness its completion. Then the story will start again with another park or, to the point, several parks—one hopes at least ten in the next few years.

No treatment of conservation philanthropy in Texas would be complete without rec-

Palo Pinto Mountains State Park, the latest park to be added to the Texas state parks system, 2019. The park is in the opening stages of its development. Courtesy of Jonathan Vail, Jonathan Vail Photography.

**ABOVE**

From left, Palo Pinto Mountains State Park ranger, former Texas Parks and Wildlife Foundation Executive Director Anne Brown, current Texas Parks and Wildlife Foundation Executive Director Susan Houston, and Texas Parks and Wildlife Department State Parks Division Director Rodney Franklin, August 3, 2020. Courtesy of Jonathan Vail, Jonathan Vail Photography.

**RIGHT**

Renderings of the new Palo Pinto Mountains State Park, date unknown. Courtesy of the Texas Parks and Wildlife Department, Austin, Texas.

Government Canyon State Natural Area, 2018. Courtesy of Chase Fountain, Texas Parks and Wildlife Department, Austin, Texas.

ognizing the contributions of San Antonio ranchers and business leaders Tim and Karen Hixon. Nearly every project of note over the past several decades seems to have had their stamp of approval as well as their financial backing. So apparent were these continuous acts of participation and generosity that both, in their own time, were asked to serve on the Texas Parks and Wildlife Commission. Both would do so with distinction.

Their most outstanding achievement, however, was the leadership they provided for the private-sector side of a monumental multifaceted effort to expand and enhance an environmental gem: Government Canyon, which acquired its name from the military supply route that ran through the canyon in the 1850s.

What began as a modest undertaking—a small acreage that protected the health and

Powderhorn Ranch Wildlife Management Area (future State Park) at sunrise, 2017. Courtesy of Jonathan Vail, Jonathan Vail Photography.

sustainability of the Edwards Aquifer near San Antonio—became a major venture encompassing twelve thousand acres close to a major urban center. In 1991, the Hixons formed a powerful coalition with the City of San Antonio, Bexar County, San Antonio Water District, Edwards Aquifer Authority, Trust for Public Land, and Texas Parks and Wildlife Department with the goal of purchasing the property and protecting it from development.

The Government Canyon State Natural Area opened in 2005 under the auspices of the Texas Parks and Wildlife Department. But neither a park nor a natural area simply opens its doors and runs itself. Here is where great staffing comes into play. Deirdre Hisler stepped in to manage Government Canyon as its first superintendent. No park or natural area could hope for a better leader. Deirdre rose to the occasion at every turn. She was a force of nature with a gentle touch—who could morph into a hammer on the rare occasions one was needed.

Together, the Hixons, Deirdre, and the coalition members would fashion a natural area and center second to none. It is the model all such projects across the country should emulate—and many have.

Serving twice as chairman of the Texas Parks and Wildlife Commission, Dan Friedkin is another example of the private citizen who is somehow called—and answers.

Dan Friedkin could have been successful in a hundred different pursuits (in many instances, that has been the case). He could have chaired any number of government agencies. He could simply have gone about the business of accumulating wealth.

But he has a deep sense of sharing and an equal love of nature and the outdoors. He chose to conserve and preserve Texas's most treasured landscapes and historic sites. Thus, he pursued a seat on the Texas Parks and Wildlife Commission. It was a timely fit.

During his tenure, he championed the acquisition of the 17,351-acre Powderhorn Ranch on Matagorda Bay. The land was donated to the Texas Parks and Wildlife Department, first as a wildlife management area and, hopefully soon, as a state park. Because of this accomplishment and other acts of personal generosity toward the people of Texas, it has been announced that T. Dan Friedkin will be inducted into the Texas Conservation Hall of Fame in 2023—our state parks' centennial year. Another timely fit!

Once again, the Texas state parks system had attracted the right person at the right time. It now becomes the charge of future elected officials and private citizens to seek out those drawn to the cause of nature's conservation for the benefit of *all* Texans.

From Thomas Jefferson to Palo Pinto Mountains State Park, the history of private giving has not only demonstrated the generosity of contributors but the essential necessity of such support during times of opportunity, including natural disasters or government denial, inaction, or mischief.

Whatever the situation, our parks—and conservation in general—have benefitted greatly from the gifts of institutions and citizens who understand that nature is a pillar essential to the well-being of our democracy and our citizens' shared sense of pride. It must be recalled year after year that these are gifts to ourselves.

# Chapter 12
# A Brighter Future

One hundred years.

Ten decades.

All part of the ongoing history of the eighty-nine Texas state parks that exist today.

Four devastating wars.

The women's right to vote.

A Great Depression.

A magnificent response: Franklin Delano Roosevelt and the Civilian Conservation Corps.

Two crippling droughts bracketed by floods, fires, hurricanes, and a pandemic.

The Civil Rights Act of 1964 and Voting Rights Act of 1965.

The golden years of progress (1963 to 1990).

The lean years of denial (1993 to 2017).

The gradual acceptance (often grudgingly) of the policy of public land for the people, which climaxed in a constitutional amendment overwhelmingly approved by Texans in 2019.

ventually, enough seeds of progress took root—deep and strong—in time to celebrate a fully and permanently funded Texas state parks system in 2023.

And to thoroughly make the point that they love their state parks, the people of Texas rushed to parks—and kept coming—when they (and other outdoor venues) reopened in 2020 during the pandemic.

If our state parks can continue to attract, even while they are in various stages of disrepair, think how much more they will mean to our citizens when they are repaired to excellence or brought onstream as new additions, undergirded by visionary long-range planning!

There is much to consider and celebrate as we peer at the fast-fading first hundred years and into the unknown future. In doing do, we will recognize much from the past. May we have the wisdom to enlarge on the good and reject the bad going forward.

But wherever we take our parks in the twenty-first century and the next hundred years, all dreams and aspirations must be grounded in a solid and lasting financial foundation derived from both public and private sources.

Walter Bristol, Mother Neff State Park, August 2020. Photo by George Bristol, author's collection.

# A Solid Financial Foundation for Parks

*Dear Mr. Bristol,*

*After careful review of budget and appropriations memos and conversations, I hope the following information will help provide a better understanding and clearer picture of the Texas Parks and Wildlife Department's Sporting Goods Sales Tax appropriations in the 2021 legislative session for the 2022 to 2023 biennium.*

*The total Sporting Goods Sales Tax cash allocation estimates per the comptroller's office for both the Texas Parks and Wildlife Department (93 percent) and Texas Historical Commission (7 percent) are $196.9 million for fiscal year 2022 and $207.9 million for fiscal year 2023, totaling $404.8 million for the 2022 to 2023 biennium.*

*To break that down further, the total statutory dedication of Sporting Goods Sales Tax cash allocations per the comptroller's office for the Texas Parks and Wildlife Department are $183.12 million for fiscal year 2022 and $193.35 million for fiscal year 2023, totaling $376.46 million for the 2022 to 2023 biennium. The Texas Parks and Wildlife Department received 100 percent of its 93 percent share of available Sporting Goods Sales Tax allocations. Rider 14 (c) in Senate Bill 1 (87R), the General Appropriations Act, provides the informational listing for Sporting Goods Sales Tax allocations for the following purposes (please note that the amounts below do not include unexpended balances or fringe amounts):*

- *State Parks Salary, Operating, and Equipment (Strategies B.1.1., B.1.2., and B.1.3.):*
  - *Fiscal Year 2022: $99,451,129*
  - *Fiscal Year 2023: $101,725,616*
  - *Total: $201,176,745*
- *State Parks Capital Construction and Repairs (Strategy D.1.1.):*
  - *Fiscal Year 2022: $22,569,166*

- *Fiscal Year 2023: $30,237,834*
- *Total: $52,807,000*
- *Local Parks Salary, Operating, and Grants (Strategies B.2.1. and B.2.2.):*
- *Fiscal Year 2022: $18,963,569*
- *Fiscal Year 2023: $18,959,113*
- *Total: $37,922,682*
- *Land Acquisition (Strategy D.1.2.)*
- *Fiscal Year 2022: $3,500,000*
- *Fiscal Year 2023: $3,500,000*
- *Total: $7,000,000*

*As a result of the increase in interest in the outdoors and subsequent purchase of sporting goods during the COVID-19 pandemic, the revised estimate of Sporting Goods Sales Tax revenue for fiscal year 2021 per the Comptroller's Biennial Revenue Estimate in January 2021 also reflected an additional $41.85 million for the Texas Parks and Wildlife Department.*

*Sincerely,*

*Allison Winney*

This November 15, 2021, exchange between Allison Winney, intergovernmental affairs specialist with the Texas Parks and Wildlife Department, and the author has been highlighted for an important reason.

Compared to the dire straits experienced in the mid-2000s, as revealed in the following Texas Parks and Wildlife Department summary update of the budget shortfall in fiscal year 2006, it is a complete reversal of the financial picture of Texas state parks.

*March 30, 2006*
*TEXAS STATE PARKS SUMMARY UPDATE*
*Fiscal Year 2006 Budget Shortfall—A Historical Perspective*

*The Texas state parks system's budget has been in continuous decline for many years in relation to the costs to operate the system. The cost of maintaining the parks system has grown due to the cumulative effects of unfunded personnel costs, additional areas to manage, and operating cost increases. These costs are compounded by the added costs of an aging infrastructure of buildings and support facilities. Thirty-one of the parks [in existence today] were built by the Civilian Conservation Corps in the 1930s, and many others include historic buildings that are more than a hundred years old. All of these factors have caused operational needs to far exceed authorized funding levels.*

*Staffing levels are critically low in most parks and are due to worsen as the state parks budget is reassessed and redistributed in order to meet the authorized funding level for fiscal year 2006. The only way that the State Parks Division has been able to pay for the increased* cost of operations such as fuel, utilities, and supplies is through reductions in the number of staff, thus using salaries in order to pay the bills.

The cumulative effects of the costs have resulted in a state parks operating deficit of more than $6 million. This figure does NOT take into consideration the cost of equipment replacement and facility maintenance. Replacement of vehicles and equipment such as tractors, mowers, and other power equipment needed to properly maintain park sites has not occurred in a timely manner for many years. As an example, the state parks system has a vehicle fleet of 935 vehicles, of which more than two-thirds are more than eight years old. More than half of the fleet vehicles have accumulated more than 100,000 miles, yet the parks system received authorization for the purchase of only two vehicles in the 2004 to 2005 biennium. Unserviceable large mowers and tractors are routinely used for parts to fix other broken-down equipment, diverting staff resources from other duties.

Many facilities are in poor condition. Bathrooms in some parks are in such bad condition that they are difficult to keep clean and should be entirely replaced. Failure to provide quality services will eventually result in visitor dissatisfaction and loss of revenue on which parks depend for operational funding.

Texas Parks and Wildlife has requested additional funding for the state parks system during past legislative sessions but has not been successful in these requests. Park funding has remained essentially static over the past five years.

A small increase in funding has come in 2006 due to the comptroller's certification of increased revenue generated by state parks above original revenue projections. These funds are not adequate to fully restore services at parks, however. In order to properly care for the resources entrusted to the parks system and provide the customer service desired, funding will need to be substantially increased above this amount.

The following memorandum from then Texas Parks and Wildlife Department Executive Director Bob Cook to Texas Parks and Wildlife employees on December 2, 2005, emphasizes the depths to which state parks had fallen:

To: All TPWD Employees
From: Robert L. Cook, Executive Director, Texas Parks and Wildlife Department
Re: Staff Reductions

Regretfully, earlier this week, thirty-nine (39) employees in the State Parks Division were notified that their positions are being eliminated as part of a reduction in force. These employees were placed on paid emergency leave and will remain on the Texas Parks and Wildlife's payroll until the effective date, January 31, 2006. In addition, to minimize the number of people who are losing their jobs, forty-four (44) vacant positions are also being eliminated.

*The Department has sought, and will continue to seek, additional funding for state parks and other department programs, but this action was necessary in the face of reduced operating funds and increased expenses over the past several years. We have high expectations that additional department funding will be secured so that future reductions may be avoided.*

*This issue will be discussed in more detail at a Town Meeting at Austin headquarters on Monday, December 5 at 10 a.m. in the Commission Hearing Room. Audio from that session will be available on WILDnet for field employees to access.*

*Thank you for your continued dedication to performing our mission.*

As a side note, Bob Cook was a good and competent leader who got caught up in the whirlwind of legislative animosities and budget shortfalls. When coupled with declining morale across the agency and mixed leadership and support at the top, the Texas Parks and Wildlife Department was in a crisis of confidence.

It would take the appointment of Joseph Fitzsimons as chair of the Texas Parks and Wildlife Commission to draw commissioners into the fray. There was great talent (and political clout) waiting to be tapped. Walt Dabney, director of Texas State Parks, was a talented and articulate spokesperson for parks whom the chairman encouraged to continue making the case for parks. Fitzsimons and I also renewed and enlarged the Texas State Parks Advisory Committee, composed of political and professional leaders from across the state, with John T. Montford as its chair. Both groups, working in tandem throughout the 2007 legislative session, set the wheels in motion for future consideration of a permanent solution to Texas state parks' financial well-being—the constitutional amendment.

In their entirety, these exchanges encompass the full journey of our parks—from one of the direst financial times to the fulfillment of the long-elusive goal of a financing method that meets all the needs of Texas parks in the twenty-first century and beyond. And it transpired without raising an existing tax or creating a new one.

By the votes of the Texas legislature and the people of Texas, the full appropriation of the Sporting Goods Sales Tax was honored for fiscal years 2022 and 2023. While that was not the first time that 100 percent of the Sporting Goods Sales Tax appropriation was granted (in fact, it would be the eighth year in a row that 100 percent or near that amount was allocated), it was the first time the people of Texas had a direct say in ensuring that would be the case, and it was accomplished with little argument or skullduggery among members of the legislature. For the most part, the goodwill engendered throughout the 2019 session held. We can only hope it will continue unabated into the future. Whether it does or not will, in large measure, determine the fate of Texas's state parks in the second century of their existence.

The unanticipated $41.85 million that helped fill the Texas Parks and Wildlife Department's coffers in 2021 and an additional $68.1 million for specific purposes (also

From left, Evelyn, Mark, and Jennifer C. Bristol, the author's daughter-in-law, Mother Neff State Park, August 2020. Photo by George Bristol, author's collection.

unanticipated) that was added to fiscal years 2022 and 2023 were significant for a couple of reasons.

First, they demonstrate how popular—indeed necessary—state parks and the outdoors are to Texas's citizens and how, as Texans rushed in unprecedented numbers to the state's natural and historical treasures, they bought Sporting Goods Sales Tax products in record amounts in the face of the pandemic. Second, upon certification—and without argument—those funds were appropriated by the legislature rather than being diverted or tucked away for future use.

Though small in amount ($7 million), the allocation designated for land acquisition as a Sporting Goods Sales Tax appropriation is also significant. Supporters hope that this will become a permanent designation by future legislatures that will recognize that these purposeful, targeted designations, as well as increased funding for new park acquisitions, are important tools in parkland expansion and enhancement.

While the aforementioned numbers are absolutely essential in the present and immediate future, they are also positive signals that a viable Texas state parks system will meet the needs of a diversified and expanding population—close to thirty million in 2023.

To continue to make the future attractive and attracting, we of the present must make certain that our positive vote of 88 percent in 2019 continues to be honored, particularly since polls conducted over two decades have demonstrated unwavering support for our parks year after year.

Therefore, we can conclude this look into the past with thoughts of improvement for the future. By necessity, any improvement must begin with consistent and adequate financing. That has now happened. It appears that stability will be the order of the day for the foreseeable future.

## Thoughts for the Future

Before turning the page on the centennial of our state parks in 2023, we must recognize that some of the future is behind us and must be addressed. It should also be noted that the suggestions to follow are the author's alone, written to raise issues and keep them in the forefront of our thoughts. What follows is a call for someone across the stretches of the Lone Star State to come forward with better ideas.

The author and reader must also recognize that plans and financing can—and will—change. There will be recessions or depressions that will impact appropriations. There will be fires, floods, hurricanes, and pandemics that will alter priorities. And surely, there will be petty grievances and greed that will attempt to divert funding away from well-laid plans to projects without plan or merit. We can only work to see that such possibilities are forestalled at the outset.

But for now, let's plan for a positive future.

Over recent decades, Texas has let $800 million in deferred maintenance accumulate. Hardly a park has escaped the wear and tear of time and use.

If we adopted a policy of addressing that backlog over ten years, we could make all worn parks new and put a great many Texas citizens to work in the process. The challenge will be to appropriate enough each year to rapidly shrink the backlog.

We seem to be headed in that direction. One only has to look at Allison Winney's analysis for fiscal years 2022 and 2023 to see that the State Parks Capital Construction and Repairs allocation of $52.8 million is almost as large as the entire parks budget during the 2003 to 2006 period.

Simultaneously, I believe that Texas should identify at least ten new state park sites to be purchased and developed by 2033. There is no benefit in buying land (except on a

A long line of cars waiting for entry into Enchanted Rock State Natural Area, March 17, 2018. The popular park turns away more than forty thousand visitors each year. Courtesy of Earl Nottingham, Texas Parks and Wildlife Department, Austin, Texas.

short-term basis) and holding it in perpetuity without purpose. Buy and develop as soon as possible—new parks are needed now! Then let's set plans in motion to purchase ten additional parks in each of the remaining decades to follow as Texas moves toward its second state parks centennial in 2123.

With Texas parks approaching ten million visitors annually, overcrowding, delays, and early closures are the unfortunate order of the day in many parks. With deferred maintenance addressed on a regular schedule to refresh existing parks and ten new parks opened to complement the old, the shortage of space and delays could be relieved, and more than $1 billion annually in sales could be generated in park communities! This, in turn, should signal greater collections from the Sporting Goods Sales Tax, generating more funding for parks and more revenue from park receipts.

There is no way all the aspirations for the future of our Texas parks can be explored in one book, especially when it is a given that legislative action (or inaction), climate change, unexpected damage, and unrecognized opportunities might change plans.

I have chosen several items that need readdressing since they will continue to be important factors in the future, just as they were in the first hundred years: economic impact, race, and conservation vs. preservation.

## Tools of the Trade: Economic Impact Studies, Polls, and Private Support

Over the course of the decades that spanned 2000 to 2019, three studies (*The Economic Contribution of Texas State Parks*—one original in 2005 and two updates in 2014 and 2019) were conducted by Dr. Ji Youn Jeong and Dr. John L. Crompton of Texas A&M University. All were commissioned by the Texas Coalition for Conservation. All were invaluable in making the case to legislators and local leaders that, among a number of other benefits of state parks, the millions of dollars generated by park visitors each year had a positive economic impact on the state as a whole and particularly on the counties in which the parks resided.

As an example, Bastrop State Park, according to summaries of the park's impact, generated $893,269 in labor income, $1,679,242 in added value, $3,061,673 in output, 35.6 jobs, and $88,791 in sales tax for the county in 2014. By 2019, the park generated $2,291,122 in labor income, $4,001,585 in added value, $7,778,667 in output, 65.8 jobs, and $114,099 in sales tax for the county.[1]

It must be pointed out that greater appropriations from the state—when designated to be spent in such categories as park repairs, maintenance, and personnel—create local jobs.

As the 2019 *Economic Contributions of Texas State Parks* study update demonstrates, parks are a job maker: "[In 2019,] economic activity generated an estimated $891 million in sales, $688 million in output, $42.6 million in added value, and $240 million in residents' income and accounted for an estimated 6,801 jobs paying an average salary of $35,320 per year."[2]

In fact, greater appropriations, in my opinion, lead to side benefits that are often overlooked, if acknowledged at all.

Even though Dr. David Hill has written an excellent explanation of the reach of polling (and its drawbacks) in chapter ten, I want to suggest that it is necessary to continue to place the issues—including funding—of parks among the top five or so topics that routinely capture and hold the attention of private citizens and elected officials.

In order to accomplish this objective, there must be a regular commissioning of new polls to bring parks to the forefront of the conversation—and, more importantly, to the forefront for some three hundred or more specific souls: statewide elected officials, state senators, and state House members, as well as capital news reporters and other news and media outlets. This small population group pays attention to polls, even with all the criticism about pollsters—as long as those polls remain credible over time.

But even legitimate polls, like other forms of persuasion—i.e., economic impact analyses—need to be updated on a regular basis. The clients need fresh data, and the recipients—especially elected officials—need to be reassured with regularity. For the most part, these officials are creatures of suspicion who must be braced on a regular basis.

It is also a truth that elected bodies such as the Texas legislature frequently turn over their leadership and membership. Thus, the situation often occurs that each session includes members who have never experienced any of the pieces that make up the state parks legislative puzzle. They must be educated—and swiftly, at that. The time between election day in November and the start of the next session is only a matter of two months. This is where leadership at the top—governor, speaker, lieutenant governor, and bill sponsors—as well as private citizens must play key roles.

If most of these elected leaders announce their support (or opposition), they can carry many of those freshmen members along. The example of State Representative John Cyrier is a case in point. During the 2019 constitutional amendment push, he received the support of the newly elected speaker, Dennis Bonnen, then went out on the floor, into hallways and offices, and signed every House member as a cosponsor. The same results occurred in the Senate through the tireless efforts of State Senator Lois Kolkhorst.

The latest polling in early summer 2019 set the stage. Polls not only showed the depth and strength of support for a constitutional amendment, they also demonstrated that that depth was so telling that even the most spineless of legislators could take comfort in the fact that support for parks would not draw the ire of any constituent group.

Finally, it is necessary, even in noncontroversial times, for major issues to have a support group(s) to keep benefits and backing of state parks squarely before elected officials and local leaders. Local leaders, especially, can be of enormous benefit should a situation arise that requires local jawboning.

All of these separate tools in the ongoing arena of state parks history contribute to the renewal that must constantly occur, lest something damaging be slipped into the legislative process—unnoticed, unstoppable, or unnecessary.

## A Final Look at Private Philanthropy

Even though more-than-adequate space has been devoted to private philanthropy—as well as to the benefits of economic impact studies and polling—it merits a final emphasis as we look, in closing, to the future.

As we have seen at the national and state levels, many parks and historic sites would not exist today were it not for the generous concern of private citizens who held or purchased landscapes for future public benefit. Others deeded over their holdings to help create a new park or protect an existing one.

In Texas, that spirit of generosity has again been rekindled. In the first decade of the centennial, five properties are waiting in the queue to be developed into full state park status: Albert & Bessie Kronkosky State Natural Area, Chinati Mountains State Natural Area, Davis Hill State Park, Palo Pinto Mountains State Park, and Powderhorn Ranch Wildlife Management Area and State Park. All have been brought to life by gifts of land or cash—or both—with the hope that all would be converted in whole or in part as new additions to the Texas parks system. This is a good way to begin the hundred-year march toward one hundred new parks created by public funds and private contributions.

The Texas Parks and Wildlife Department has been fortunate to have the support of its nonprofit partner, the Texas Parks and Wildlife Foundation, over the past thirty years. With strong and engaged directors and complementing professional staff, the organization has raised some $220 million for Texas parks as of 2019.

And with a 2019 legislative directive calling for a public/private match, the foundation has all but completed the private-sector portion of $9 million to fund Texas's newest state park—Palo Pinto Mountains State Park.

Perhaps the celebration of the state parks centennial in 2023 will spark additional gifts from those who wish to utilize some of their treasure to preserve "beauty spots to be held in sacred trust by the State for the public good, now and forever."[3]

**ABOVE**
Albert & Bessie Kronkosky State Natural Area, 2012. Courtesy of Chase Fountain, Texas Parks and Wildlife Department, Austin, Texas.

**RIGHT**
Chinati Mountains State Natural Area, 2010. Courtesy of Earl Nottingham, Texas Parks and Wildlife Department, Austin, Texas.

Powderhorn Ranch Wildlife Management Area,
2017. Courtesy of Jonathan Vail, Jonathan
Vail Photography.

Fishing for black drum, Goose Island State Park, July 11, 2021. Courtesy of Chase Fountain, Texas Parks and Wildlife Department, Austin, Texas.

**ABOVE**
Learning about nature, Lake Casa Blanca International
State Park, 2016. Courtesy of Chase Fountain, Texas
Parks and Wildlife Department, Austin, Texas.

# On the Matter of Race

While the Civil Rights Act of 1964 and Voting Rights Act of 1965 opened many doors, including those of state parks, they opened as a matter of law, not necessarily of the heart. That is not to say that all White Texans were rude or threatening as they gathered around campfires and canoe dockings. For the most part, the vast majority of those who take to park trails, picnic tables, and waterways are not concerned with who's in the next campground or cabin—White, Black, or Brown. They are there to get away from the "isms" and divisions that hammer at their daily lives. They want a beer, a soda, a grilled hamburger, a light-free look at the heavens, perhaps an end-of-campfire ghost story or bragging rights about that day's catch or birding count. Above all else, they want to be with themselves and their family and friends, at peace and renewed. But herein lies the rub.

> You've got to be taught
> To hate and fear,
> You've got to be taught
> From year to year,
> It's got to be drummed
> In your dear little ear
> You've got to be carefully taught.
>
> Rodgers & Hammerstein
> "You've Got to Be Carefully Taught"
> *South Pacific*
> 1949

This poem-turned-song by one of America's greatest musical show teams embodies the observations of Dr. KangJae "Jerry" Lee and Charles Jordan that are spelled out in chapter five. Unless one has parents and grandparents—or at least another devoted adult—to counter those who adhere to racist sentiments, the results of the song will become the reality at home, school, playground, and state park.

Unfortunately, Dr. Lee makes the case that there has been so much hate, fear, and ignorance hammered into those "dear little ears" over the generations that there are almost no park traditions on which to draw that might allow goodwill to take root. And that is the continuing problem. Norman Rockwell-like images of four-to-a-family settings make us feel good about ourselves, our country, or our state, but where does the chance for welcoming interaction with others of a different skin color come into play?

Day of birding, Sheldon Lake State Park and Environmental Learning Center, date unknown. Courtesy of Earl Nottingham, Texas Parks and Wildlife Department, Austin, Texas.

The solution must be open to all citizens, but not all citizens will avail themselves of the opportunity. Even though Texas is closing in on ten million park visitors annually, that leaves twenty million Texans who do not visit our parks, either rarely or ever.

Yet we know, to a certain degree, that all demographic groups, according to the polls, support the park ethic, and they proved that in 2019, when 88 percent of voters cast their ballots in favor of parks. The results are not a sign that those favorable voters have gone—or will go—to their state parks, but it does give some indication that they are not forever lost to the wonders of the outdoors and the benefits accrued while there. Thus, it must be up to those of us who have enjoyed the opportunities of solace and renewal afforded by waterfalls and calls of the wild to find ways—inside and outside our parks—to reach those who might be open to the wonders available to all, including those of different skin colors.

We must also be mobilized to reach out and within to recruit leaders who can take the time, in turn, to recruit potential conservation champions of different colors and outlooks.

Whatever the plan and programs devised to take new messages to this population, they must be shared and shaped outside the parks—as well as within. And they must target all generations. It will not be just the young who must be persuaded but those parents and grandparents who have little or no knowledge of what great good lies in the great outdoors. It will not be easy, and it might well fail. But it must be attempted—again and again.

As an example, Stephen Mather gathered the leading newspaper, magazine, and business owners of his time for an outing of several days camping in Yosemite to persuade them to use their organizations' influence to sway the people and then, in turn, the United States Congress of the need for national parks and a national park service to govern them. While he was at it, he and some of his friends bought the Tioga Road in Yosemite and deeded it to the park.

The point here is that it doesn't take hundreds of recruits to effect change. But it does take time. Even with forceful and effective leadership focused on the task of making the Sporting Goods Sales Tax revenue permanent, it took nearly twenty years to accomplish.

Discrimination's roots are much deeper. But with a few good leaders in and out of the Texas Parks and Wildlife Department, change can come. Even with that effort, prejudice will remain, but with perseverance, our hope is that it will be countermanded by our better angels.

Taking a family selfie, Martin Dies Jr. State Park. 2015. Courtesy of Chase Fountain, Texas Parks and Wildlife Department, Austin, Texas

Plaque created in recognition of the wrong of segregation, which held until 1964 amid passage of the Civil Rights Act, Bastrop State Park, 2022. Courtesy of the Texas Parks and Wildlife Department, Austin, Texas.

Camping fun, Bastrop State Park, 2015.
Courtesy of Jonathan Vail, Jonathan Vail
Photography.

# Conservation vs. Preservation

Which purpose it is to conserve the scenery and the natural and historic objects and the wildlife within and to provide for the enjoyment of the same in such a manner and by such means as will leave them unimpaired for the enjoyment of future generations.

National Park Service Act of 1916, known as the "Organic Act"

Lacking national and state parks, conservation in America—and Texas—might never have blossomed into one of our most cherished concepts, and any meaningful preservation policy would have fared no better—if, indeed, it had fared at all.

"Without the national parks, the history of conservation becomes predictable and, therefore, ordinary."[4] Alfred Runte's thoughts could apply to many of Texas's state parks as well. It must be remembered, however, that the early position of Neff, Colp, and others in their camp was, at best, a nod toward conservation (proper use of nature) and a wink at preservation (protection of nature from any use).[5] For most of the early history of state parks in Texas, conservation in its primitive form won out, to no one's surprise. Expanding highways and exploding automobile travel could only lead to a collision.

It was not that Neff, Colp, and others did not recognize and appreciate magnificent natural beauty and its contribution to tourist attractions; it was simply that industry and commerce served the public good more. That is how early arguments for Texas parks evolved: tourism, public good, conservation, then preservation. To a great degree, this debate was at the center of Governor—and citizen—Pat Neff's sales pitch. It does not appear that this pitch was a recognized, hard-and-fast plan. It is safe to say that Neff knew that something was amiss and needed to be addressed—but only as a means to keep tourists coming and automobiles rambling over the state's highways.

But the more he studied the issue, the more he began to realize there was a connection between conservation, preservation, and the public's well-being. Apparently, he read and took to heart the work of Governor Al Smith of New York and Horace Albright, director of the National Park Service, who both saw the benefit of parks in broader ecological terms. Governor Smith would write: "The influence of these parks on the national sanity in days like these [referring to the Depression] may not be exactly measurable, but it is far-reaching and enormously beneficial."[6]

One only has to look at the public's reaction in Texas to the news that state (and national) parks were reopening after the lockdown of the 2020 pandemic to prove this statement true: record numbers of visitors spending record amounts of money on sporting goods equipment, gasoline, motels, and cafés as they hiked, biked, swam, and fished

Swimming in the lake, Cleburne State Park, July 21, 2009. Courtesy of the Texas Parks and Wildlife Department, Austin, Texas.

with abandon.

Slowly but surely, preservation began to enter Neff's papers and speeches. Parks could serve the public good beyond their traditional recreational value—as outdoor natural museums and classrooms. This would dictate that the natural wonders of wildlife, wildflowers, and waterways be preserved in a manner that would pay homage to the dual mission of the National Park Service Act of 1916.

> It is my conviction that the beauty spots that we have today are not ours to enjoy and then destroy, but they are a God-given heritage, to be preserved, just as the Great Architect of the Universe left them.[7]

> Texas Governor Pat M. Neff
> Parks Speech
> 1924

To fulfill God's handiwork, Neff (as covered in chapter three) asked the Texas legislature to appropriate $50,000. The legislature would have none of it—not a dime. Not a tithe. By their inaction, the legislature set up the real possibility that some, or all, of the parks that Governor Neff, Chairman Colp, and members of the first State Parks Board had secured were in danger of reverting back to the donors. Then in 1927 came the surprise legislative gifting of the twenty-three state parks to the State Parks Board once Governor Neff was safely out of office and in Washington, DC, on assignment by appointment of President Calvin Coolidge.

But in what already was—and would continue to be—a predictable trend, there was no supporting appropriation attached.

Even into the early 1930s, Texas "had no state park worthy of the name."[8] Though hardly perceived, even by Neff or his park advocates, two philosophies began to creep into speeches and plans. Neff, in his 1924 parks speech and thereafter, began to speak about the "beauty spots" and the need to preserve them as products of God's doing.

That conservation vs. preservation conflict continues to this day. Even as we take positive steps to open more park spaces to the public as well as repair present ones, we must be mindful of the need to maintain, as best we can, the careful balance between conservation and preservation. Both are essential parts of an equation that is so necessary to continue the citizenry's honoring of the dual mission of the national and state parks concept. Unlike some who favor one philosophy over the other, I find it necessary for both to exist side by side in harmony.

The tension between the two is the very essence of our public parks concept: an admiring visitor, drawn for a weekend away by ancient urges to be one with nature as well as with family or friends, knows instinctively that what they wish to experience must be

preserved. Otherwise, these treasured landscapes may become no more appealing than what the visitor left behind. Conversely, there must be accommodations, numerous and attractive enough to satisfy that visitor's needs.

Campsites, trails, parking lots, roads, and other amenities are necessary to meet visitors' needs and also to serve as visible parameters to "stay on the trails" so that these natural venues are there both for us and for generations yet to come.

We won't hit the mark every time, nor will all the destroyers be banished from these landscapes. But we can be instructed and guided by park policy and employees dedicated to the proposition that men, women, and nature can live in harmony, at least in those areas we have chosen to protect. And we can do so by our own example of civility and citizenship.

Family camping, Bastrop State Park, date unknown. Courtesy of Earl Nottingham, Texas Parks and Wildlife Department, Austin, Texas.

# Epilogue
## Looking to the Past to Secure the Future: A Final Observation

So, why parks?

All the principals discussed in this book began their own journeys to enlightenment sometime early in life by coming upon wildlife, wildflowers, and waterfalls. Those initial encounters would be the first signs pointing down the nature trail—a road they might sometimes leave but never forsake.

At some point, they reached a stage in life when personal satisfaction was not enough. They wanted others to have an opportunity to share in the natural blessings of the country that was becoming America—and our state, Texas. There was much to share. At the same moment, they also reached a position of influence sufficient to have their voices heard—and heeded.

If we wish to have those sorts of unselfish leaders always at the ready, we must have those "breathing spots of beauty" available in their ageless natural state, accessible to all citizens. For somewhere in the mix of humanity that visits year in and year out, there will be a boy or girl who will honor, renew, and expand the gift.

As I have stated many times in speeches and in writings, the imperative for conserving and preserving the last best places is to let our people be of the earth—to be renewed and moved in a wholesome setting. From that connection—or reconnection—comes deeper and more lasting civility and patriotism. Having a shared sense of place and a shared stake in that place gives people pride of ownership and fosters responsible citizenship. There is a human need to connect with land, water, and wildlife. It does not matter what station in life one inhabits—rich or poor. If the well-off require getaways to recreate and renew, it stands to reason that the rest of us need places to recreate and renew as well.

We must use the next century not only to preserve the Great Architect of the Universe's handiwork—but to preserve more of it. The gift must be ever-expanding in order to ensure that there will be gift enough for all, regardless of skin color or position.

To that point, this quote from Stephen Mather is a fitting close: "What God-given opportunity has come our way to preserve wonders like these before us. We must never forget or abandon our gift."[1]

# Appendix A
# Texas State Parks

## Abilene State Park
Tuscola, Texas

Courtesy of Earl Nottingham, Texas Parks
and Wildlife Department, Austin, Texas.

## Atlanta State Park
Atlanta, Texas

Courtesy of Earl Nottingham, Texas Parks
and Wildlife Department, Austin, Texas.

**Balmorhea State Park**
Toyahvale, Texas

Courtesy of Earl Nottingham, Texas Parks and Wildlife Department, Austin, Texas.

**Barton Warnock Visitor Center**
Terlingua, Texas

Courtesy of Earl Nottingham, Texas Parks and Wildlife Department, Austin, Texas.

### Bastrop State Park
Bastrop, Texas

Courtesy of Chase Fountain, Texas Parks and Wildlife Department, Austin, Texas.

### Bentsen-Rio Grande Valley State Park
Mission, Texas

Courtesy of Chase Fountain, Texas Parks and Wildlife Department, Austin, Texas.

**Big Bend Ranch State Park**
Presidio, Texas

Courtesy of Chase Fountain, Texas Parks and Wildlife Department, Austin, Texas.

**Big Spring State Park**
Big Spring, Texas

Courtesy of Chase Fountain, Texas Parks and Wildlife Department, Austin, Texas.

## Blanco State Park
### Blanco, Texas

Courtesy of the Texas Parks and
Wildlife Department, Austin, Texas.

## Bonham State Park
### Bonham, Texas

Courtesy of Chase Fountain, Texas Parks
and Wildlife Department, Austin, Texas.

**Brazos Bend State Park**
Needville, Texas

Courtesy of Chase Fountain, Texas Parks and Wildlife Department, Austin, Texas.

**Buescher State Park**
Smithville, Texas

Courtesy of Chase Fountain, Texas Parks and Wildlife Department, Austin, Texas.

## Caddo Lake State Park
Karnack, Texas

Courtesy of the Texas Parks and
Wildlife Department, Austin, Texas.

## Caprock Canyons State Park
Quitaque, Texas

Courtesy of Chase Fountain, Texas Parks and
Wildlife Department, Austin, Texas.

### Cedar Hill State Park
Cedar Hill, Texas

Courtesy of Chase Fountain, Texas Parks and Wildlife Department, Austin, Texas.

### Choke Canyon State Park— Calliham Unit
Calliham, Texas

Courtesy of Chase Fountain, Texas Parks and Wildlife Department, Austin, Texas.

## Choke Canyon State Park—
## South Shore Unit
Calliham, Texas

Courtesy of Chase Fountain, Texas Parks
and Wildlife Department, Austin, Texas.

## Cleburne State Park
Cleburne, Texas

Courtesy of Bryan Frazier, Texas Parks
and Wildlife Department, Austin, Texas.

### Colorado Bend State Park
#### Bend, Texas

Courtesy of the Texas Parks and Wildlife Department, Austin, Texas.

### Cooper Lake State Park—Doctors Creek Unit
#### Cooper, Texas

Courtesy of Earl Nottingham, Texas Parks and Wildlife Department, Austin, Texas.

## Cooper Lake State Park— South Sulphur Unit
Sulphur Springs, Texas

Courtesy of Earl Nottingham, Texas Parks and Wildlife Department, Austin, Texas.

## Copper Breaks State Park
Quanah, Texas

Courtesy of Chase Fountain, Texas Parks and Wildlife Department, Austin, Texas.

## Daingerfield State Park
Daingerfield, Texas

Courtesy of Earl Nottingham, Texas Parks and Wildlife Department, Austin, Texas.

## Davis Mountains State Park
Fort Davis, Texas

Courtesy of Chase Fountain, Texas Parks and Wildlife Department, Austin, Texas.

## Devils River State Natural Area
### Del Rio, Texas

Courtesy of Jonathan Vail, Jonathan Vail Photography.

## Devil's Sinkhole State Natural Area (Rocksprings Visitor Center)
### Rocksprings, Texas

Courtesy of Chase Fountain, Texas Parks and Wildlife Department, Austin, Texas.

## Dinosaur Valley State Park
Glen Rose, Texas

Courtesy of the Texas Parks and Wildlife Department, Austin, Texas.

## Eisenhower State Park
Denison, Texas

Courtesy of Chase Fountain, Texas Parks and Wildlife Department, Austin, Texas.

### Enchanted Rock State Natural Area
Fredericksburg, Texas

Courtesy of the Texas Parks and
Wildlife Department, Austin, Texas.

### Estero Llano Grande State Park
Weslaco, Texas

Courtesy of Chase Fountain, Texas Parks
and Wildlife Department, Austin, Texas.

### Fairfield Lake State Park
Fairfield, Texas

Courtesy of the Texas Parks and Wildlife Department, Austin, Texas.

### Falcon State Park
Falcon Heights, Texas

Courtesy of the Texas Parks and Wildlife Department, Austin, Texas.

### Fort Boggy State Park
Centerville, Texas

Courtesy of Chase Fountain, Texas Parks and Wildlife Department, Austin, Texas.

### Fort Leaton State Historic Site
Presidio, Texas

Courtesy of Chase Fountain, Texas Parks and Wildlife Department, Austin, Texas.

### Fort Parker State Park
Mexia, Texas

Courtesy of Susan Metcalf Loomis, Texas Parks and Wildlife Department, Austin, Texas.

### Fort Richardson State Park & Historic Site / Lost Creek Reservoir State Trailway
Jacksboro, Texas

Courtesy of the Texas Parks and Wildlife Department, Austin, Texas.

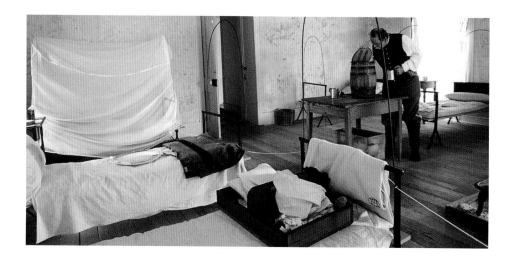

**Franklin Mountains State Park**
El Paso, Texas

Courtesy of Chase Fountain, Texas Parks and Wildlife Department, Austin, Texas.

**Galveston Island State Park**
Galveston, Texas

Courtesy of Chase Fountain, Texas Parks and Wildlife Department, Austin, Texas.

## Garner State Park
Concan, Texas

Courtesy of Chase Fountain, Texas Parks
and Wildlife Department, Austin, Texas.

## Goliad State Park & Historic Site
Goliad, Texas

Courtesy of Chase Fountain, Texas Parks
and Wildlife Department, Austin, Texas.

**Goose Island State Park**
Rockport, Texas

Courtesy of Chase Fountain, Texas Parks and Wildlife Department, Austin, Texas.

**Government Canyon State Natural Area**
San Antonio, Texas

Courtesy of Earl Nottingham, Texas Parks and Wildlife Department, Austin, Texas.

### Guadalupe River State Park
Spring Branch, Texas

Courtesy of Chase Fountain, Texas Parks and Wildlife Department, Austin, Texas.

### Hill Country State Natural Area
Bandera, Texas

Courtesy of Earl Nottingham, Texas Parks and Wildlife Department, Austin, Texas.

**Honey Creek State Natural Area**
Spring Branch, Texas

Courtesy of the Texas Parks and
Wildlife Department, Austin, Texas.

**Hueco Tanks State Park
& Historic Site**
El Paso, Texas

Courtesy of Chase Fountain, Texas Parks
and Wildlife Department, Austin, Texas.

### Huntsville State Park
Huntsville, Texas

Courtesy of the Texas Parks and Wildlife Department, Austin, Texas.

### Indian Lodge
Fort Davis, Texas

Courtesy of Chase Fountain, Texas Parks and Wildlife Department, Austin, Texas.

**Inks Lake State Park**
Burnet, Texas

Courtesy of Chase Fountain, Texas Parks and Wildlife Department, Austin, Texas.

**Kickapoo Cavern State Park**
Brackettville, Texas

Courtesy of the Texas Parks and Wildlife Department, Austin, Texas.

## Lake Arrowhead State Park
Wichita Falls, Texas

Courtesy of Chase Fountain, Texas Parks and
Wildlife Department, Austin, Texas.

## Lake Bob Sandlin State Park
Pittsburg, Texas

Courtesy of the Texas Parks and Wildlife
Department, Austin, Texas.

### Lake Brownwood State Park
Lake Brownwood, Texas

Courtesy of Earl Nottingham, Texas Parks and Wildlife Department, Austin, Texas.

### Lake Casa Blanca International State Park
Laredo, Texas

Courtesy of Chase Fountain, Texas Parks and Wildlife Department, Austin, Texas.

### Lake Colorado City State Park
Colorado City, Texas

Courtesy of the Texas Parks and Wildlife
Department, Austin, Texas.

### Lake Corpus Christi State Park
Mathis, Texas

Courtesy of Chase Fountain, Texas Parks
and Wildlife Department, Austin, Texas.

## Lake Livingston State Park
Livingston, Texas

Courtesy of Chase Fountain, Texas Parks and Wildlife Department, Austin, Texas.

## Lake Mineral Wells State Park
Mineral Wells, Texas

Courtesy of Earl Nottingham, Texas Parks and Wildlife Department, Austin, Texas.

## Lake Somerville State Park—Birch Creek Unit

Somerville, Texas

Courtesy of Earl Nottingham, Texas Parks and Wildlife Department, Austin, Texas.

## Lake Somerville State Park—Nails Creek Unit

Ledbetter, Texas

Courtesy of the Texas Parks and Wildlife Department, Austin, Texas.

## Lake Tawakoni State Park
Wills Point, Texas

Courtesy of the Texas Parks and Wildlife Department, Austin, Texas.

## Lake Whitney State Park
Whitney, Texas

Courtesy of Earl Nottingham, Texas Parks and Wildlife Department, Austin, Texas.

## Lockhart State Park
### Lockhart, Texas

Courtesy of Chase Fountain, Texas Parks and Wildlife Department, Austin, Texas.

## Longhorn Cavern State Park
### Burnet, Texas

Courtesy of Chase Fountain, Texas Parks and Wildlife Department, Austin, Texas.

## Lost Maples State Natural Area
Vanderpool, Texas

Courtesy of Leroy Williams, Texas Parks and Wildlife Department, Austin, Texas.

## Lyndon B. Johnson State Park & Historic Site
Stonewall, Texas

Courtesy of Chase Fountain, Texas Parks and Wildlife Department, Austin, Texas.

## Martin Creek Lake State Park
Tatum, Texas

Courtesy of Earl Nottingham, Texas Parks and Wildlife Department, Austin, Texas.

## Martin Dies Jr. State Park
Jasper, Texas

Courtesy of Chase Fountain, Texas Parks and Wildlife Department, Austin, Texas.

## McKinney Falls State Park
Austin, Texas

Courtesy of Chase Fountain, Texas Parks and Wildlife Department, Austin, Texas.

## Meridian State Park
Meridian, Texas

Courtesy of Earl Nottingham, Texas Parks and Wildlife Department, Austin, Texas.

### Mission Rosario State Historic Site
Goliad, Texas

Courtesy of Larry D. Moore via
Wikimedia Commons.

### Mission Tejas State Park
Grapeland, Texas

Courtesy of Chase Fountain, Texas Parks
and Wildlife Department, Austin, Texas.

### Monahans Sandhills State Park
Monahans, Texas

Courtesy of the Texas Parks and Wildlife Department, Austin, Texas.

### Mother Neff State Park
Moody, Texas

Courtesy of Earl Nottingham, Texas Parks and Wildlife Department, Austin, Texas.

## Mustang Island State Park
Corpus Christi, Texas

Courtesy of the Texas Parks and Wildlife
Department, Austin, Texas.

## Old Tunnel State Park
Fredericksburg, Texas

Courtesy of Chase Fountain, Texas Parks
and Wildlife Department, Austin, Texas.

**Palmetto State Park**
Gonzales, Texas

Courtesy of Earl Nottingham, Texas Parks and Wildlife Department, Austin, Texas.

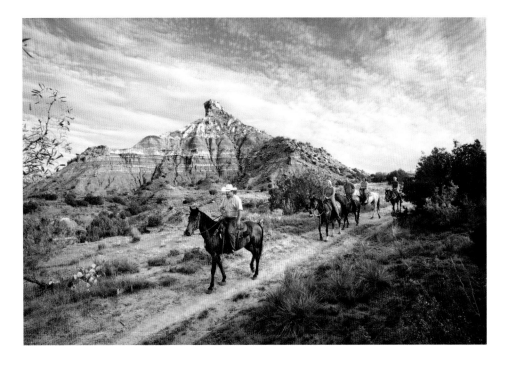

**Palo Duro Canyon State Park**
Canyon, Texas

Courtesy of Tomas L. Pantin, Texas Parks and Wildlife Department, Austin, Texas.

## Pedernales Falls State Park
Johnson City, Texas

Courtesy of the Texas Parks and Wildlife
Department, Austin, Texas.

## Possum Kingdom State Park
Caddo, Texas

Courtesy of the Texas Parks and Wildlife
Department, Austin, Texas.

## Purtis Creek State Park
Eustace, Texas

Courtesy of Earl Nottingham, Texas Parks and Wildlife Department, Austin, Texas.

## Ray Roberts Lake State Park— Isle du Bois Unit
Pilot Point, Texas

Courtesy of Earl Nottingham, Texas Parks and Wildlife Department, Austin, Texas.

### Ray Roberts Lake State Park— Johnson Branch Unit
Valley View, Texas

Courtesy of the Texas Parks and Wildlife Department, Austin, Texas.

### Resaca de la Palma State Park
Brownsville, Texas

Courtesy of Chase Fountain, Texas Parks and Wildlife Department, Austin, Texas.

### San Angelo State Park
San Angelo, Texas

Courtesy of the Texas Parks and Wildlife Department, Austin, Texas.

### Sea Rim State Park
Sabine Pass, Texas

Courtesy of Chase Fountain, Texas Parks and Wildlife Department, Austin, Texas.

### Seminole Canyon State Park & Historic Site
Comstock, Texas

Courtesy of Chase Fountain, Texas Parks and Wildlife Department, Austin, Texas.

### Sheldon Lake State Park & Environmental Learning Center
Houston, Texas

Courtesy of Bryan Frazier, Texas Parks and Wildlife Department, Austin, Texas.

## South Llano River State Park
Junction, Texas

Courtesy of Chase Fountain, Texas Parks and Wildlife Department, Austin, Texas.

## Stephen F. Austin State Park
San Felipe, Texas

Courtesy of the Texas Parks and Wildlife Department, Austin, Texas.

## Tyler State Park
### Tyler, Texas

Courtesy of Chase Fountain, Texas Parks and Wildlife Department, Austin, Texas.

## Village Creek State Park
### Lumberton, Texas

Courtesy of the Texas Parks and Wildlife Department, Austin, Texas.

## Wyler Aerial Tramway
El Paso, Texas

Courtesy of Wikimedia Commons.

## Zaragoza Birthplace State Historic Site
Goliad, Texas

Courtesy of Rob McCorkle, Texas Parks and Wildlife Department, Austin, Texas.

# Appendix B

# The Original Twenty-Three State Parks

---

## AUTHOR'S NOTE

*This list of the original twenty-three state parks (with accompanying information) is used with the generous permission of author James Wright Steely, whose excellent book* Parks for Texas: Enduring Landscapes of the New Deal *thoroughly recounts the rise of Texas state parks during and leading up to the 1930s.*

The following is a list of the parks in the First Official State Parks "System" of 1927, with brief descriptions provided by Marian Rather Powell, chair, Parks and Playgrounds Committee, Texas Federation of Women's Clubs, in a March 19, 1927, article in the *Dallas News.*\* These parks, accepted by the Fortieth Legislature, appeared in Senate Concurrent Resolution 13 and then in the *Dallas News* roughly in the order they were donated. In Senate Concurrent Resolution 13, the parks were listed by donated name, sometimes different from the name of the host community; in Marian Powell's article, they were listed by community name first, often leaving off the name given them by the donor. For clarity, the parks are listed here in alphabetical order by community, with original names in parentheses if not included in Powell's information. Powell's notes in her article appear to be the only details in one place describing the camping park "system" of 1927. Neither the original deeds nor any comprehensive descriptions survive in David E. Colp's files or in records at the Texas State Archives or Texas Parks and Wildlife Department. While few of these parks served the public for some time under local management, and still fewer received elaborate facilities in the 1930s, most claimed the "state park" title only briefly, and Powell's notes represent their only known descriptions.

- Alto Frio (Mayhew State Park): twenty-five acres on the Frio River

- Beeville State Park: 128 acres; ninety-five miles from San Antonio and sixty miles from Corpus Christi on the main highway

- Big Spring State Park: two hundred acres on the Big Spring Mountain, 3,150 feet above sea level

- Brownsville (Barreda State Park): seventy-five acres, with great variety of timber

- Campbellton (Mary Campbell State Park): thirty acres, fronts the Atascosa River

- Canadian (Young State Park): ten acres, containing the only running water and shade in that section

- Crosbyton State Park: fifty acres on the Brazos River

- Crowell (Fergeson [sic] Brothers State Park): thirty-five acres

- Fort Worth (John Henry Kirby State Park): one hundred acres on Sycamore Creek

- Frio River State Park: fifty acres between Pearsall and Dilley, halfway between San Antonio and Laredo on the Meridian Highway

- Hillsboro (Jefferson Davis State Park): thirty-five acres, the former site of the Old Settlers' Association

- Kerrville (Schreiner State Park): forty-four acres on the Guadalupe River

- Laredo (Mackin State Park): 118 acres on the Meridian Highway

- Llano (Robinson State Park): sixty-nine acres

- Lovelady (Abram and Lucy Womack Memorial State Park): thirty acres

- Marshall State Park: 120 acres; a key to the Caddo Lake

- Palestine (Howard Gardner Memorial State Park): twenty-five acres

- San Angelo (Johnson Memorial State Park): fifty acres fronting the Concho River; a wonderful pecan grove

- Smithville (Buescher State Park): one hundred acres; small dam across the creek

- Sterling City (Foster State Park): 532 acres on one fork of the Concho River

- Three Rivers (Tips State Park): thirty acres on the Nueces [actually Frio] River

- Van Horn (Thomas State Park): eighty acres; waterfalls and canyon

- Wayside State Park: 120 acres, about thirty miles from Amarillo on the edge of Palo Duro Canyon; rugged and very beautiful

*From "State Accepts 24 New Parks / Mrs. Ben Powell, Austin, Presses Resolution in Legislature," *Dallas News*, March 19, 1927, and *House Journal* (1927), 1543–44.

# The Legislation That Started It All: 1923 Parks Bill

# HOUSE JOURNAL.

### THIRTY-EIGHTH LEGISLATURE, SECOND CALLED SESSION

## PROCEEDINGS.

### FIRST DAY.

Hall of the House of Representatives,
Austin, Texas,
Monday, April 16, 1923.

In obedience to the proclamation of his excellency, Pat M. Neff, Governor of Texas, convening the Thirty-eighth Legislature to meet in special session at Austin, the seat of government, this, the 16th day of April, A. D. 1923, the members of the House of Representatives assembled in the Representative Hall and at 9 o'clock a. m., the House was called to order by Hon. R. E. Seagler, Speaker.

Speaker Seagler then directed the Clerk to call the roll.

The roll was called and the following members were present:

Abney.
Amsler.
Arnold.
Atkinson.
Avis.
Baker of Milam.
Baker of Orange.
Baldwin.
Barker.
Barrett.
Beasley.
Bell.
Bird.
Bonham.
Burmeister.
Cable.
Carpenter
of Matagorda.
Carter of Hays.
Chitwood.
Coffee.
Covey.
Cowen.
Culp.
Davenport.
Davis.
DeBerry.
Driggers.
Duffey.
Dunlap.
Dunn.
Durham.
Edwards.
Faubion.
Fields.
Finlay.
Fugler.
Gipson.
Green.
Greer.
Hardin of Erath.
Harris.
Henderson
of Marion.
Henderson
of McLennan.
Houston.
Howeth.
Hughes.
Irwin.
Jacks.
Jennings.
Johnson.
Kemble.
Lackey.
Laird.
Lane.
LeMaster.
LeStourgeon.
Lewis.
Loftin.
Looney.
McBride.
McDaniel.
McDonald.
McFarlane.
McKean.
McNatt.
Martin.
Mathes.
Maxwell.
Melson.
Merritt.
Montgomery.
Moore.
Morgan
of Liberty.
Morgan
of Robertson.
Pate.
Patman.
Patterson.
Perdue.
Pinkston.
Potter.
Quaid.
Quinn.
Rice.
Robinson.
Rogers.
Rountree.
Rowland.
Russell of Trinity.
Sackett.
Sanford.
Satterwhite.
Shearer.
Simpson.
Smith.
Sparkman.
Stell.
Stewart of Jasper.
Stewart of Reeves.
Storey.
Stroder.
Sweet.
Teer.
Thompson.
Thrasher.
Turner.
Vaughan.
Wells.
Westbrook.
Wessels.
Wilmans.
Wilson.
Winfree.
Young.

Absent.

Bobbitt.
Brady.
Bryant.
Dodd.
Hardin
of Kaufman.
Lusk.
Shires.
Stevens.
Stewart
of Edwards.
Stiernberg.
Strickland.
Williamson.

Absent—Excused.

Blount.
Carpenter
of Dallas.
Carson.
Carter of Coke.
Collins.
Crawford.
Dielmann.
Dinkle.
Downs.
Frnka.
Harrington.
Hendricks.
Hull.
Jones.
Lamb.
Merriman.
Miller.
Pool.
Pope.
Price.
Purl.
Russell
of Callahan.
Wallace.

read severally, the following enrolled bills and resolutions:

S. C. R. No. 17, Relating to the treatment of convicts in the penitentiary.

S. J. R. No. 2, Relating to the Prison Commission.

S. B. No. 73, "An Act relative to State parks; creating a State Parks Board to investigate prospective park sites in the State and report to the Legislature with recommendations; authorizing the board to solicit and accept donations of land for State park purposes; making an appropriation for expenses of the board; providing that localities may pay expenses of the board in visiting such locality to investigate and inspect land for park purposes, and declaring an emergency."

H. B. No. 109, "An Act levying and providing for the payment of a State occupation tax on refining, compounding, manufacturing, blending or preparing gasoline or gasoline substitutes from petroleum or natural gas measured by intrastate sales, and levying a State occupation tax on intrastate selling of gasoline or gasoline substitutes brought into the State from outside the State based on the first intrastate sale thereof after the same is brought into the State; requiring reports to be made, and records to be kept, and permitting inspections thereof by proper public officials, and prescribing penalties for failure to comply with the act in order to facilitate collection of such occupation taxes; providing for interest on delinquent taxes and penalties; making disposition of the taxes after collected; providing for suits for taxes, penalties and interest and compensation of officers bringing same; defining gasoline; declaring the legislative intent as to parts of the act being held invalid; repealing the present gasoline occupation tax law; defining 'person' as used in this act, and declaring an emergency."

H. B. No. 186, "An Act to amend Section 3 and 20 of House bill No. 13 passed at the Regular Session of the Thirty-eighth Legislature and approved by the Governor on February 28, 1923, and being 'An Act providing for the licensing, bonding and regulating of private employment agents; limiting the fee charged by such agents; providing for the cancellation of such license; prescribing the duties of the Commissioner of Labor Statistics for the State of Texas with reference to the enforcement of this act; providing for recoveries on said bond; fixing penalties for the violation of this act; creating a special fund for the enforcement of this act and appropriating same for said purposes; repealing certain laws and all laws or parts of laws in conflict herewith and declaring an emergency,' and to further amend said House bill No. 13 by adding after Section 20 thereof a new section to be known as Section 20a; the purpose of these amendments is to permit the issuance of licenses to residents of this State to engage in the business of employment agents; to remove discrimination against alien residents of this State who desire to engage in said business; to require certain statements to be made in application for license and to fix the amount and form of bond required to be given by those who are licensed to engage in the business; and to define certain offenses and prescribe penalties therefor; and to provide for restraining by injunction of any person or persons pursuing the business of employment agents or conducting an employment office without first having obtained a license therefor, and declaring an emergency."

H. B. No. 5, "An Act making appropriation to pay salaries of judges and the support of the Judicial Department of the State government for the two years beginning September 1, 1923, and ending August 31, 1925."

H. B. No. 25, "An Act amending Section 1 and 2 of Chapter 78, General Laws, Second Called Session, Thirty-sixth Legislature, as amended by Chapter 61 of the General Laws, First Called Session, Thirty-seventh Legislature; making it unlawful for any person, directly or indirectly, to possess or receive for the purpose of sale, or to manufacture, sell, barter, exchange, transport, export, deliver, take orders for, solicit or furnish spirituous, vinous or malt liquors or medicated bitters capable of producing intoxication, or any other intoxicant whatever, or to possess, receive, manufacture or knowingly sell, barter, exchange, transport, export, deliver, take orders for, solicit or furnish any equipment, still, mash, material, supplies, device or other thing for manufacturing, selling, bartering, exchanging, transporting, exporting, delivery, taking orders for, soliciting or furnishing any such liquors, intoxicants or beverages, and making it unlawful for any person, directly or indirectly, to possess or receive for the purpose of sale,

Appendix D

# 2019 Polls and Public Support

# Texas Parks 2019 voter opinion survey

June 23-27, 2019

## Background

- Methodology
  - Sample of 608 likely voters for November 2019
  - Interviews conducted June 23-27, 2019
    - 360 were conducted on cell phones
    - 120 were conducted on landlines
    - 128 were conducted using an online panel
  - Margin of error of ±4.0% for 608 cases
  - Results weighted to match past odd-year electorate profile
  - Typical interview took about 8-17 minutes
- Contributors
  - Dr. David B. Hill, Director, Hill Research Consultants
  - Dr. Stephen N. White, Assistant Director

2

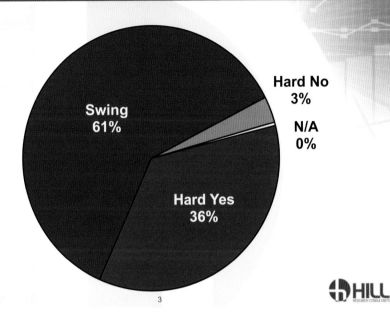

# Sporting goods tax ballot segmentation

Swing
61%

Hard No
3%

N/A
0%

Hard Yes
36%

3

HILL
RESEARCH CONSULTANTS

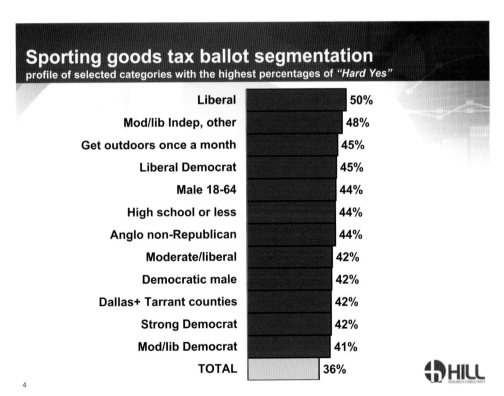

# Sporting goods tax ballot segmentation
profile of selected categories with the highest percentages of *"Hard Yes"*

| | |
|---|---|
| Liberal | 50% |
| Mod/lib Indep, other | 48% |
| Get outdoors once a month | 45% |
| Liberal Democrat | 45% |
| Male 18-64 | 44% |
| High school or less | 44% |
| Anglo non-Republican | 44% |
| Moderate/liberal | 42% |
| Democratic male | 42% |
| Dallas+ Tarrant counties | 42% |
| Strong Democrat | 42% |
| Mod/lib Democrat | 41% |
| TOTAL | 36% |

HILL
RESEARCH CONSULTANTS

4

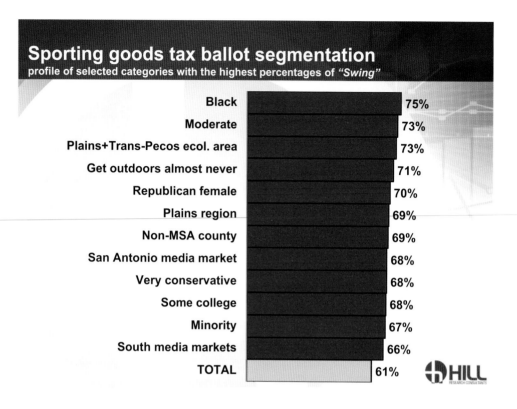

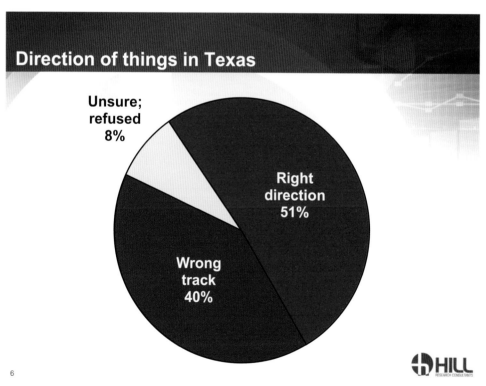

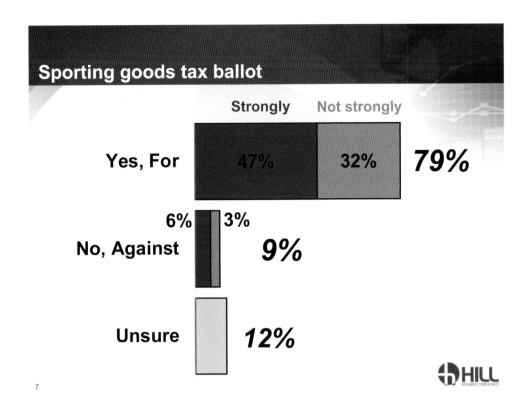

# Sporting goods tax ballot

| | Strongly | Not strongly | |
|---|---|---|---|
| Yes, For | 47% | 32% | **79%** |
| No, Against | 6% | 3% | **9%** |
| Unsure | | | **12%** |

7

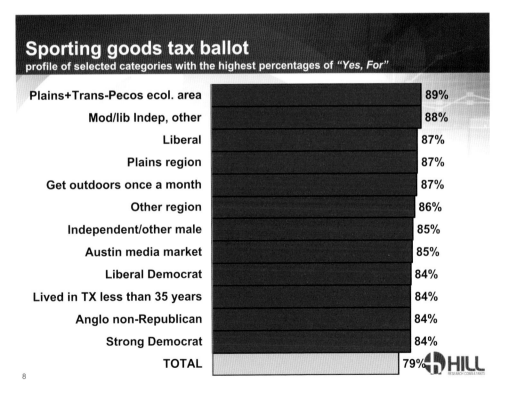

# Sporting goods tax ballot
**profile of selected categories with the highest percentages of *"Yes, For"***

| | |
|---|---|
| Plains+Trans-Pecos ecol. area | 89% |
| Mod/lib Indep, other | 88% |
| Liberal | 87% |
| Plains region | 87% |
| Get outdoors once a month | 87% |
| Other region | 86% |
| Independent/other male | 85% |
| Austin media market | 85% |
| Liberal Democrat | 84% |
| Lived in TX less than 35 years | 84% |
| Anglo non-Republican | 84% |
| Strong Democrat | 84% |
| TOTAL | 79% |

8

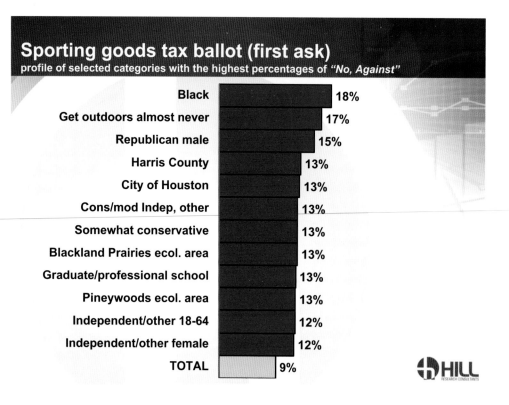

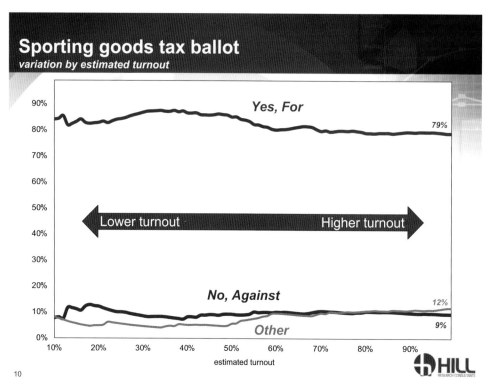

## Parts or details of the proposition:
### Strength of support

| | Support (all) | Support strongly | Support somewhat | Oppose |
|---|---|---|---|---|
| Ultimate purpose is to protect Texas' natural areas, water quality, & history by acquiring, managing, & improving state & local parks & historic sites | 90% | 62% | 28% | 8% |
| Requires no new taxes or fees; rather, it simply dedicates the existing sales tax collected on the sale of sporting goods to our parks & historic sites | 88% | 59% | 29% | 9% |
| Will dedicate all revenue from the existing sales tax on sporting goods, so that those dollars can be used only by the Texas Parks & Wildlife Department & the Texas Historical Commission | 84% | 56% | 28% | 14% |
| Will dedicate all revenue from the existing sales tax on sporting goods, so that those dollars can be used only [by the Texas Parks & Wildlife Department & the Texas Historical Commission/for Texas parks & historic sites] | 86% | 53% | 32% | 12% |
| Will dedicate all revenue from the existing sales tax on sporting goods, so that those dollars can be used only for Texas parks & historic sites | 87% | 51% | 37% | 10% |
| Changes state practices for spending existing sales tax dollars from purchases of sporting goods & recreational products, such as those used for hunting, fishing, wildlife watching, & camping | 79% | 44% | 35% | 15% |
| Was placed on the ballot after approval by solid majorities of each party & both houses in the Texas Legislature | 76% | 35% | 41% | 13% |
| Adds a few words to Section 7, Article 8 of the Texas Constitution | 60% | 21% | 39% | 15% |

11

## Best 3 combination of strongest parts or details of the proposition – swing voters only

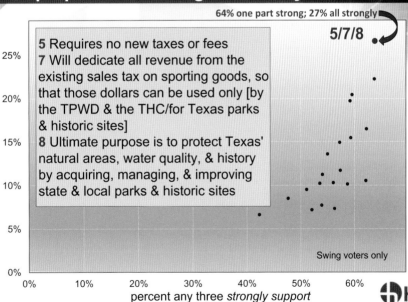

# Familiarity with the Texas sporting goods sales tax

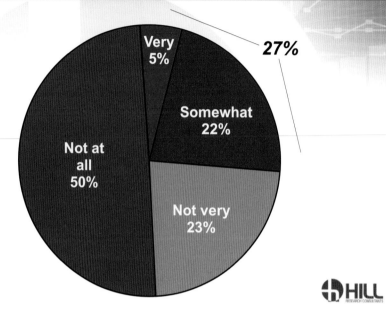

**Very** 5%

**27%**

**Somewhat** 22%

**Not at all** 50%

**Not very** 23%

HILL

13

# Acquiring, maintaining & operating state & local parks with revenue from the existing sales tax on sporting goods purchases

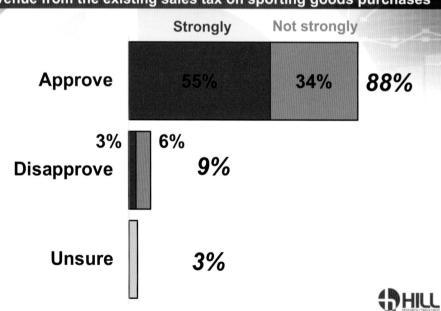

Strongly    Not strongly

**Approve**    55%    34%    **88%**

3%    6%

**Disapprove**    *9%*

**Unsure**    *3%*

HILL

14

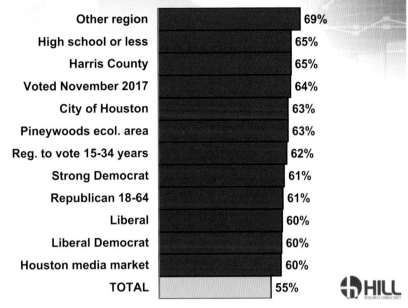

## Acquiring, maintaining & operating state & local parks with revenue from the existing sales tax on sporting goods purchases
profile of selected categories with the highest percentages of *"Approve Strongly"*

| Category | Percentage |
|---|---|
| Other region | 69% |
| High school or less | 65% |
| Harris County | 65% |
| Voted November 2017 | 64% |
| City of Houston | 63% |
| Pineywoods ecol. area | 63% |
| Reg. to vote 15-34 years | 62% |
| Strong Democrat | 61% |
| Republican 18-64 | 61% |
| Liberal | 60% |
| Liberal Democrat | 60% |
| Houston media market | 60% |
| TOTAL | 55% |

15

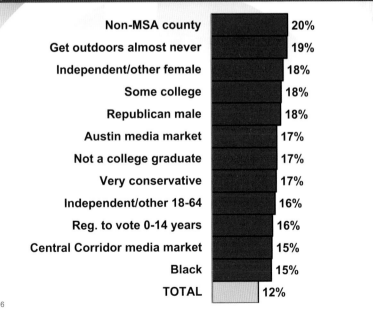

## Acquiring, maintaining & operating state & local parks with revenue from the existing sales tax on sporting goods purchases
profile of selected categories with the highest percentages of *"Do Not Approve"*

| Category | Percentage |
|---|---|
| Non-MSA county | 20% |
| Get outdoors almost never | 19% |
| Independent/other female | 18% |
| Some college | 18% |
| Republican male | 18% |
| Austin media market | 17% |
| Not a college graduate | 17% |
| Very conservative | 17% |
| Independent/other 18-64 | 16% |
| Reg. to vote 0-14 years | 16% |
| Central Corridor media market | 15% |
| Black | 15% |
| TOTAL | 12% |

16

## Agreement with opinions that other Texans have expressed about issues related to Texas land, parks, natural habitat and other natural areas

| | Agree (all) | Agree strongly | Agree somewhat | Dis-agree |
|---|---|---|---|---|
| In an increasingly urban state, public parks are an important way for families to enjoy the great outdoors together without spending a lot of money | 98% | 77% | 20% | 2% |
| With the rapid growth of Texas, up to 1000 newcomers a day, we must protect Texas' last remaining natural areas today so that they won't be lost forever to development | 94% | 76% | 18% | 5% |
| A system of well-maintained & easily accessible state parks is essential to healthy living & the active lifestyle that Texans need | 96% | 72% | 24% | 4% |
| A system of well-maintained & easily accessible [state/local] parks is essential to healthy living & the active lifestyle that Texans need | 94% | 71% | 23% | 4% |
| A system of well-maintained & easily accessible local parks is essential to healthy living & the active lifestyle that Texans need | 93% | 70% | 23% | 4% |
| Unless we protect Texas' natural areas & historic sites, we will lose the very things that make Texas a special place in which to live | 91% | 69% | 22% | 8% |
| Texas' land, water & wildlife are part of God's creation & this proposal helps fulfill our moral responsibility to care for & protect them | 89% | 64% | 24% | 9% |
| Improving & maintaining Texas state parks & historic sites will produce proven economic benefits, including millions in new spending by tourists & visitors, while boosting employment in the Texas tourism industry | 90% | 54% | 36% | 7% |

HILL
RESEARCH CONSULTANTS

17

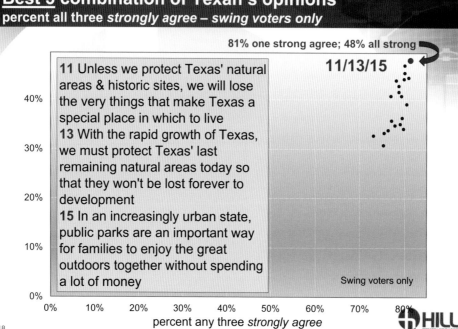

## Best 3 combination of Texan's opinions
### percent all three *strongly agree – swing voters only*

81% one strong agree; 48% all strong

11/13/15

11 Unless we protect Texas' natural areas & historic sites, we will lose the very things that make Texas a special place in which to live
13 With the rapid growth of Texas, we must protect Texas' last remaining natural areas today so that they won't be lost forever to development
15 In an increasingly urban state, public parks are an important way for families to enjoy the great outdoors together without spending a lot of money

Swing voters only

percent any three *strongly agree*

HILL
RESEARCH CONSULTANTS

18

## Arguments being made _for_ the proposed amendment to the Texas sporting goods sales tax

| | Convincing (all) | Very convincing | Somewhat convincing | Not convincing |
|---|---|---|---|---|
| Will ensure these funds can only be spent on public parks & historic sites, & not for any other purposes | 89% | 59% | 30% | 10% |
| Will conserve Texas natural areas & create new parks & trails, giving more kids access to outdoor activities that will improve their overall physical health & well-being | 90% | 59% | 31% | 10% |
| Ensures there will be funding to protect Texas water quality, natural areas, beaches & wildlife, so that our children & grandchildren & future generations can enjoy them the same way we do | 92% | 54% | 38% | 8% |
| Will once-and-for-all ensure that sporting goods sales taxes are spent exactly as promised for parks & historic sites, backed by strict financial accountability, transparency and budgetary disclosures | 86% | 48% | 38% | 13% |
| Will create more parks, natural areas & places for recreation close to home to improve our quality of life | 85% | 42% | 43% | 14% |

HILL RESEARCH CONSULTANTS

19

## Best 3 combination of strong arguments made for the Amendment – swing voters only

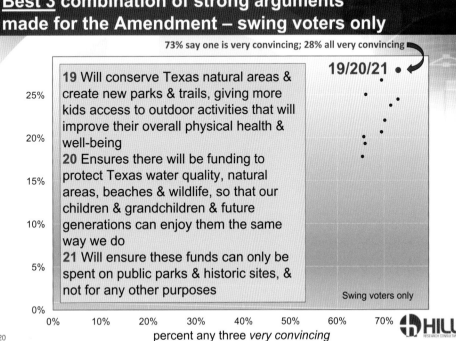

73% say one is very convincing; 28% all very convincing

19/20/21

**19** Will conserve Texas natural areas & create new parks & trails, giving more kids access to outdoor activities that will improve their overall physical health & well-being

**20** Ensures there will be funding to protect Texas water quality, natural areas, beaches & wildlife, so that our children & grandchildren & future generations can enjoy them the same way we do

**21** Will ensure these funds can only be spent on public parks & historic sites, & not for any other purposes

Swing voters only

percent any three _very convincing_

HILL RESEARCH CONSULTANTS

20

## Arguments being made _against_ the proposed amendment to the Texas sporting goods sales tax

|  | Convincing (all) | Very convincing | Somewhat convincing | Not convincing |
|---|---|---|---|---|
| Would permanently change the Texas Constitution by setting aside special funding for the environment, while the Constitution should only deal with the most fundamental issues in our democracy | 48% | 18% | 30% | 50% |
| Will take millions in funding away from more critical needs like public education, affordable healthcare, & transportation; while parks & natural areas are nice, we must prioritize & fund other more important needs first | 54% | 16% | 37% | 45% |
| State government already spends too much & this Amendment gives government bureaucrats more taxpayer dollars to waste on projects that will not benefit the average Texan | 40% | 16% | 25% | 58% |
| Is backed by radical liberal environmental groups that want to spend taxpayer dollars to protect insignificant species of fish & insects, which will cost the state jobs | 33% | 12% | 20% | 65% |

HILL
RESEARCH CONSULTANTS

21

## Best 3 combination of strong arguments against the Amendment – swing voters only

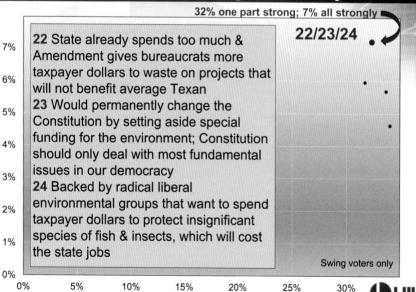

32% one part strong; 7% all strongly

22/23/24

**22** State already spends too much & Amendment gives bureaucrats more taxpayer dollars to waste on projects that will not benefit average Texan

**23** Would permanently change the Constitution by setting aside special funding for the environment; Constitution should only deal with most fundamental issues in our democracy

**24** Backed by radical liberal environmental groups that want to spend taxpayer dollars to protect insignificant species of fish & insects, which will cost the state jobs

Swing voters only

percent any three _very convincing_

HILL
RESEARCH CONSULTANTS

22

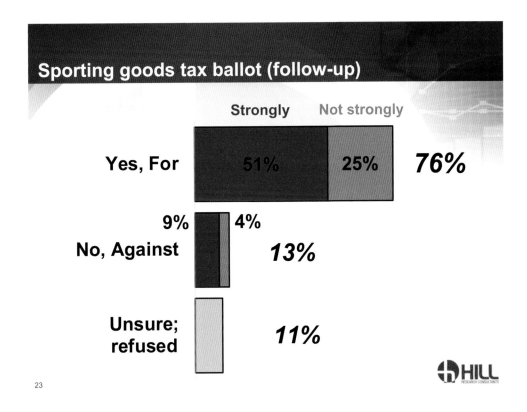

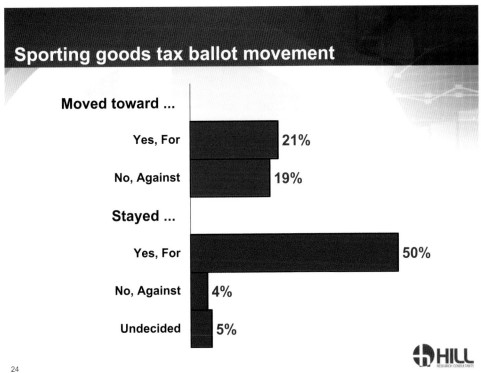

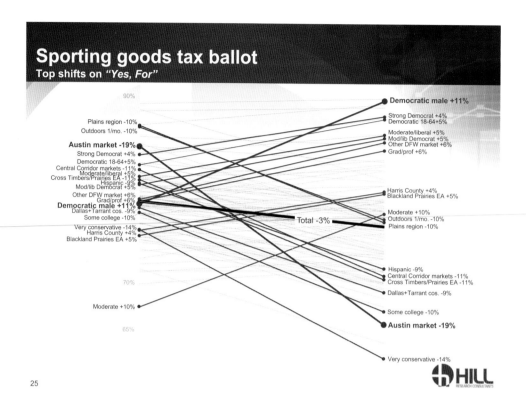

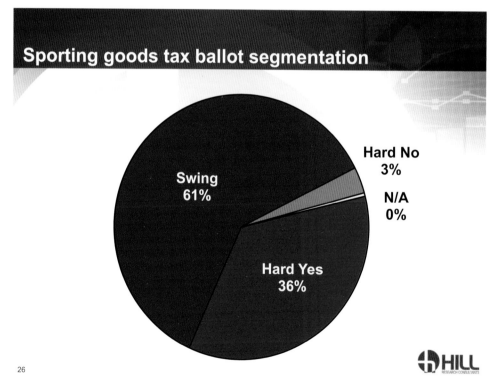

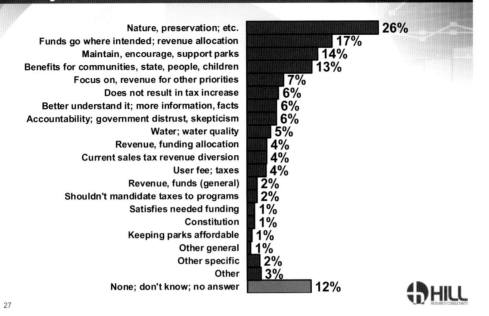

## One or two most important issues in deciding how you should vote on this Amendment

| Issue | % |
|---|---|
| Nature, preservation; etc. | 26% |
| Funds go where intended; revenue allocation | 17% |
| Maintain, encourage, support parks | 14% |
| Benefits for communities, state, people, children | 13% |
| Focus on, revenue for other priorities | 7% |
| Does not result in tax increase | 6% |
| Better understand it; more information, facts | 6% |
| Accountability; government distrust, skepticism | 6% |
| Water; water quality | 5% |
| Revenue, funding allocation | 4% |
| Current sales tax revenue diversion | 4% |
| User fee; taxes | 4% |
| Revenue, funds (general) | 2% |
| Shouldn't mandidate taxes to programs | 2% |
| Satisfies needed funding | 1% |
| Constitution | 1% |
| Keeping parks affordable | 1% |
| Other general | 1% |
| Other specific | 2% |
| Other | 3% |
| None; don't know; no answer | 12% |

27

## Top issues, by selected categories of voters

| | DFW mm | Gulf mm | Cen Corr | Men | Women | Under 55 | 55-69 | 70+ | D | R |
|---|---|---|---|---|---|---|---|---|---|---|
| | % | % | % | % | % | % | % | % | % | % |
| Nature; Historic Preservation Environ/wildlife | 17 ⬌ | 32 | 30 | 21 ⬌ | 30 | 33 ⬌ | 22 | 23 | 30 | 23 |
| Funds go where allocated | 20 | 15 | 14 | 19 | 15 | 12 | 19 | 18 | 17 | 19 |
| Maintain, support parks | 20 | 14 | 9 | 15 | 13 | 14 | 11 | 16 | 16 | 12 |
| Benefits for state, people, children | 10 | 16 | 14 | 9 | 16 | 13 | 13 | 12 | 19 | 9 |

28

# Appendix E
## Proposition 5 Campaign

Proposition 5
Campaign Report
Prepared by: Sarver Strategies

Texas Coalition for State Parks

## Executive Summary

Sarver Strategies was pleased to lead communications efforts in support of the Proposition 5 campaign. We managed a six-week campaign that leveraged a surround-sound strategy that included earned media, social media, a website, grassroots engagement and paid media. Our strategy relied heavily on the active engagement of the 75-member coalition we helped build and sustain during the Legislative Session. We developed core messaging for the campaign and executed a strategy that pushed those messages consistently and creatively across all available channels. This was truly a team effort with all partners and vendors working collaboratively to get out the vote. Partners in this campaign included Ashley Schlosser and Mary Green with Live Out Loud Media, Butch Ewing with Bruce & Eddy Design, Glenda Beasley with Marketing Mileage and Jennifer Swanson, Matt Portillo and Karen Creasey on the Sarver Strategies team. The resounding 88% victory on November 5, is indicative of this team's hard work, and the active engagement of all Coalition partners and supporters. We are pleased to have been a part of such an historic campaign. The following two pages include topline highlights from the campaign, followed by a more detailed breakdown of specific earned and social media highlights.

## Earned Media Highlights

Our earned media efforts were designed to both educate the media and Texas voters about the Constitutional Amendment campaign, and the importance of voting yes on Prop. 5 to support Texas' parks and historic sites. Our efforts yielded statewide coverage with more than 300 individual stories in every media market in the state. We drafted 13 press releases, five media alerts, 10 opinion editorials and numerous pitches. We supported Environment Texas' seven-city media tour. We made hundreds of phone calls to reporters to ensure coverage of Prop. 5. Highlights included editorials by Sen. Kolkhorst, Rep. Cyrier, Joseph Fitzsimons, Ed Whitacre and Regent Kevin Eltife, among others. Coalition members David Yeates, Janice Bezanson, John Shepperd and George Bristol were among many interviewed throughout the campaign. Every major newspaper (with one major exception) endorsed Proposition 5. Detailed earned media highlights are on page 4-8 of this report, with links to individual media hits linked on pages 9-21.

## Social Media Highlights

We had an active and engaged social media presence on Facebook, Twitter and Instagram. We developed 30 individual memes throughout the campaign, sent 173 tweets, made 88 posts on Instagram and 109 posts on Facebook. We cultivated an extremely engaged Facebook following, with more than 2,400 members. We made 10,245,854 impressions and had an average daily each of 202,443 from August 1 through November 15. Our Twitter handle garnered 97,887 total impressions with a total reach of 142,2019. On Instagram we garnered 557,708 impressions, reaching 177,700 users and securing 221 followers. Throughout the campaign our followers regularly interacted with our content – and with one another, becoming an important voice on behalf of the campaign. (Detailed social media highlights on page 22-36.)

**Texas Coalition**
*for* **State Parks**

## Website

Our website, www.SupportTexasParks.org, was created to be the hub of the campaign, with key information about the amendment, the campaign, the election and our coalition. It was regularly updated with social media and earned media content. In addition, it housed all resources for the media and for interested stakeholders, making it a one-stop-shop for all things related to Prop. 5. Throughout the campaign we had 23,059 visitors to the website with 25,127 visits and more than 30,000 page views.

## Grassroots Engagement

Our Coalition partners were instrumental in keeping their audiences informed and engaged. We helped them do so by creating easily leveraged content, including sample newsletter copy, an FAQ document, a one-pager, posters, social media content and talking points, among other assets. We kept everyone engaged through a regular newsletter (with more than 420 recipients). We sent 19 e-mails to our audience, alerting them about important media hits, milestones in the campaign and sharing content for them to distribute. In addition to our Coalition members and cultivated audience, we also engaged with Texas Legislators, creating a set of social media memes specifically unbranded so lawmakers could make them their own. We regularly produced requested content, including social media memes, letters, newsletter copy and other materials as needed by Coalition members and partner organizations.

## Paid Media

While paid media was overseen by Johnson Strategies, we collaborated on strategy and content, including crafting all digital ads and drafting a radio script for an ad featuring Nolan Ryan. The broadcast media (radio and TV) campaign reached more than 5,655,243 impressions against the target of ages 55+. Adding the additional reach of ages 18+, we estimate more than 11 million impressions were delivered.

Nearly 3,000 30-second TV and radio ads ran from October 21-November 5, 2019, primarily in Houston and Dallas, including in-game spots during the World Series on both radio and TV. Coverage in Austin and San Antonio ran on the Ken Milam outdoor radio show. Statewide coverage ran on the Houston Texans game broadcast on 25 radio stations, and on the Texas Fishing and Outdoor Show broadcast on 30 radio stations.

Nolan Ryan's 30-second radio ad was added to all radio stations in the last two weeks of the flight, which was excellent timing for the heightened interest in the World Series. His voice played in-game for Game 5 and 6 on the Dallas radio stations carrying the event (the Houston radio station carrying the game was sold out at time of placement). TV ads ran pre-game in Houston during the World Series Game 5 and in-game in Dallas for the final Game 7.
TV and radio station selection was based on top-ranking stations, cable broadcast zones and programming to deliver the top 10 zip codes of persons most likely to vote for Prop. 5. In addition, outdoor, political show programming and market timing opportunities such as the purchase of sports and sports talk programming were implemented to resonate with potential supportive voters.

**Texas Coalition**
**for State Parks**

## EARNED MEDIA OVERVIEW

In support of Proposition 5 in the Texas Constitutional Amendment Election of 2019, Sarver Strategies designed and implemented a public relations and marketing campaign to educate media and Texas voters on the importance of passing Proposition 5 to support our state parks and historic sites. We drafted content, pitched the media, responded to incoming inquiries and supported partner outreach efforts. In addition to serving as campaign spokespersons directly, we worked to source spokespeople to publicly speak about the proposition and coordinated their interviews with Texas print, radio and television outlets. A selection of key interviews secured throughout the campaign included:

- Representative John Cyrier with Spectrum News and the Texas Tribune
- Joseph Fitzsimons with the Houston Chronicle and the Texas Tribune
- George Bristol with the Courthouse News Service
- Senator Lois Kolkhorst with the Texas Tribune
- Environment Texas and other parks advocates on tour interviews with:
  - Spectrum News (Austin & San Antonio)
  - KVUE-TV
  - KEYE-TV
  - KXAN-TV
  - KUT-FM
  - Austin Chronicle
  - Telemundo/KTDO-TV (El Paso)
  - ABC KVIA-TV (El Paso)
  - KWES-TV Channel 9 (Midland)
  - WOAI-TV / Channel 4 (San Antonio)
  - KABB-TV (San Antonio)
  - KSAT-TV (San Antonio)
  - San Antonio Express News (San Antonio)
  - Rivard Report
- Janice Bezanson with KCEN-TV/Channel 6/Central Texas News
- Beaver Aplin (founder of Buc-ees) interview on the Mark Davis show
- David Yeates with News 4 and Fox 29 in San Antonio
- John Shepperd with KSKY radio and The Word (DFW area)

The following is a list of the press materials (op-eds, letters to the editors, press releases, media alerts) we utilized to drive the media portion of this campaign. A comprehensive compilation of all media hits acquired can be viewed in the full media coverage section of our campaign report.

**Texas Coalition for State Parks**

## PRESS RELEASES:

- Release – Six Week Countdown to Election Day (launch release)
- Media Alert – Voter Registration Deadline
- Media Alert – Early Voting
- Media Alert – Final Week of Early Voting
- Media Alert – November 5th Voting Day for Texans
- Media Alert – Prop 5 Passes Texas Election
- State parks supporters to launch 7 city, 13 park tour to promote Prop 5 (Austin event)
- State parks supporters to launch 7 city, 13 park tour to promote Prop 5 (Houston event)
- State parks supporters to launch 7 city, 13 park tour to promote Prop 5 (Dallas/FW area event)
- State parks supporters to launch 7 city, 13 park tour to promote Prop 5 (San Angelo event)
- State parks supporters to launch 7 city, 13 park tour to promote Prop 5 (Midland event)
- State parks supporters to launch 7 city, 13 park tour to promote Prop 5 (El Paso event)
- State parks supporters to launch 7 city, 13 park tour to promote Prop 5 (San Antonio event)

## REGIONAL RELEASES ON ECONOMIC IMPACT DRAFTED & DISTRIBUTED:

- East Texas Area Economy
- Lufkin Area Economy
- Texarkana Area Economy
- Galveston Area Economy
- El Paso Area Economy
- Del Rio Area Economy
- Corpus Christi Area Economy
- Brazos Valley Region Economy
- Beaumont Area Economy
- Bastrop Area Economy
- Amarillo Area Economy
- Abilene Area Economy

## OPINION EDITORIALS AND LETTERS TO THE EDITOR

- Sen. Kolkhorst & Rep. Cyrier op-ed written and placed in the Dallas Morning News: Vote in November to fund our state parks for future generations of Texans *Also ran in*: Odessa American

- Joseph Fitzsimons op-ed written and placed in the Austin American-Statesman: OPINION: PROP. 5 WILL KEEP TEXAS PARKS OPEN FOR EVERYONE

- Ed Whitacre (former chairman and CEO of GM and AT&T) op-ed written and placed in the San Antonio Express-News Opinion: State parks are good for business; *Also ran in*: Laredo Morning Times: Opinion: State parks are good for business

**Texas Coalition for State Parks**

## Social Media Analytics

### TWITTER: @SUPPORTTXPARKS

POTENTIAL AUDIENCE REACH

**97,887**
TOTAL IMPRESSIONS

**142,108**
TOTAL REACH

FOLLOWERS

**166%**
INCREASE

**88**
FOLLOWERS

Followers as of Aug. 1    Followers as of Nov. 15

### ACTIVITY TIMELINE – IMPRESSIONS OVER TIME

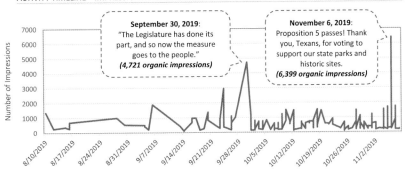

**September 30, 2019:**
"The Legislature has done its part, and so now the measure goes to the people."
*(4,721 organic impressions)*

**November 6, 2019:**
Proposition 5 passes! Thank you, Texans, for voting to support our state parks and historic sites.
*(6,399 organic impressions)*

Number of Impressions — 7000, 6000, 5000, 4000, 3000, 2000, 1000, 0

8/10/2019, 8/17/2019, 8/24/2019, 8/31/2019, 9/7/2019, 9/14/2019, 9/21/2019, 9/28/2019, 10/5/2019, 10/12/2019, 10/19/2019, 10/26/2019, 11/2/2019

### TWITTER: @SUPPORTTXPARKS

TWITTER ACTIVITY OVERVIEW

**214**
TOTAL MENTIONS OF @SUPPORTTXPARKS TWEETS
(Including 173 @SupportTXParks generated tweets and 41 unique user mentions)

**539**
TOTAL PROFILE VISITS

**1,553**
ENGAGEMENTS

**1.6%**
ENGAGEMENT RATE

**Texas Coalition** **for State Parks**

*(8 likes / 3 retweets / 15 engagements / **1,754 impressions**)*

## INSTAGRAM SNAPSHOT: @SUPPORTTEXASPARKS

supporttexasparks

**88 posts**   **221 followers**   **73 following**

**Support Texas Parks**
Vote FOR #Prop5onNov5
www.supporttexasparks.org
starlocalmedia.com/rowlettlakeshoretimes/news/voters-show-support-for-state-p...

## 88 POSTS | 557,708 IMPRESSIONS | 177,700 USERS REACHED | 221 FOLLOWERS

**November 6, 2019:**
Proposition 5 passes!
Thank you, Texans, for
voting to support our
state parks and historic
sites.
.
#SupportTexasParks
#TXLege #VoteTexas
*80 Likes*

**Texas Coalition for State Parks**

## FACEBOOK SNAPSHOT: @SUPPORTTEXASPARKS

AUDIENCE AMPLIFICATION

LIFETIME TOTAL LIKES

# 10,245,854

TOTAL IMPRESSIONS
(Aug. 1 to Nov. 15)

# 202,443

AVERAGE DAILY REACH
(Aug. 1 to Nov. 15)

## 102.1%

INCREASE

## 2,456

LIKES
(PREVIOUSLY
219)

Likes as of Aug. 1        Likes as of Nov. 15

FACEBOOK PAGE POST REACH OVER TIME (UNIQUE VISITORS, Aug. 1 to Nov. 15)

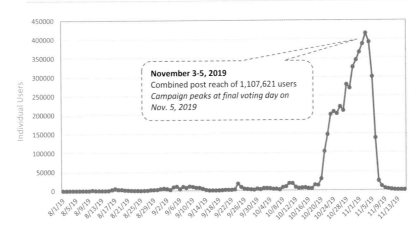

**November 3-5, 2019**
Combined post reach of 1,107,621 users
*Campaign peaks at final voting day on
Nov. 5, 2019*

## FACEBOOK SNAPSHOT: @SUPPORTTEXASPARKS

TOTAL CLICKS ON PAGE POSTS DEMONSTRATING ENGAGEMENT (Aug. 1 to Nov. 15)

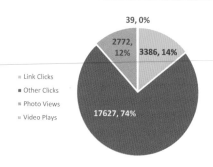

39, 0%

2772, 12%

3386, 14%

17627, 74%

■ Link Clicks
■ Other Clicks
■ Photo Views
■ Video Plays

# 23,824

UNIQUE CLICKS
BY FACEBOOK USERS

TOP 5 MOST ENGAGING POSTS (rated by highest engagement via total comments, likes, shares)

11/5/19          (Post type: Photo)

 **Texas Coalition for State Parks**

Proposition 5 passes! Thank you, Texans, for voting to support our state parks and historic sites. #SupportTexasParks #TXLege #VoteTexas

*171,753 Total Reach (ORGANIC!) / 15,161 Reactions, Comments & Shares / 6,971 Post Clicks*

Texas Coalition
for State Parks

8/16/19          (Post type: Link, Photo)

Texas Coalition for State Parks

Love Texas parks and historical sites? Vote YES on Prop. 5 on Nov. 5 to
ensure consistent funding for these important Texas treasures. Learn more
at our brand new website: www.SupportTexasParks.org.
#SupportTexasParks #Prop5onNov5

*46,349 Total Reach (31,819 Organic – 15,277 Paid) / 1,858 Reactions, Comments & Shares*
*1,451 Post Clicks*

9/6/19  (Post type: Photos)

Texas Coalition for State Parks

This afternoon, Governor Greg Abbott held a ceremonial signing of the
legislation that paved the way for Prop. 5 to be on the ballot this November.
He was joined by bill authors, Rep. John Cyrier and Sen. Lois Kolkhorst,
who championed this legislation and expertly shepherded it through the
Legislative Process gaining near-unanimous support. Now it's time for
Texas to do it's job and vote YES on #Prop5onNov5 to #SupportTexasParks

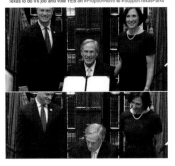

*45,687 Total Reach (15,121 Organic – 30,566 Paid) / 1,383 Reactions, Comments & Shares*
*2,657 Post Clicks*

10/18/19         (Post type: Link, Photo)

 **Texas Coalition for State Parks**

#PSA! The first day of early voting is Monday, October 21, 2019. This is the actual language you will see on the ballot. Just remember: vote YES on Prop. 5! Learn more at https://www.supporttexasparks.org/election/ #SupportTexasParks #Prop5onNov5 #txlege

*34,279 Total Reach (26,719 Organic – 8,844 Paid) / 2,707 Reactions, Comments & Shares*
*1,338 Post Clicks*

10/10/19         (Post type: Link, Photo)

 **Texas Coalition for State Parks**

"This November voters will decide if they want to dedicate the Sporting Goods Sales Tax to solely fund state parks and historical sites...Prop. 5 would automatically send that money to the" Texas Parks and Wildlife department and the Texas Historical Commission. Thank you to KAMR Local 4 News for sharing. Vote YES for #Prop5onNov5. #SupportTexasParks #txlege

www.supporttexasparks.org

*25,858 Total Reach (ORGANIC!) / 1,285 Reactions, Comments & Shares / 2,327 Post Clicks*

**Texas Coalition**
**for State Parks**

## VIDEO ANALYTICS SNAPSHOT

| Video | | Views ⌄ | Finishes | Likes | Comments | Impressions | Downloads | Unique Impressions | Unique Viewers | Avg. % Watched |
|---|---|---|---|---|---|---|---|---|---|---|
| | Vote YES on Prop...<br>Uploaded 2 months ago | 1,638 | 476 | 0 | 1 | 46,830 | 0 | 17,357 | 1,504 | 72 |
| | Vote YES on Prop...<br>Uploaded 2 months ago | 1,182 | 442 | 0 | 0 | 3,661 | 2 | 2,283 | 1,127 | 24 |
| | Vote YES on Prop...<br>Uploaded 2 months ago | 75 | 36 | 1 | 0 | 1,581 | 1 | 486 | 70 | 21 |
| | Vote YES on Prop...<br>Uploaded 2 months ago | 33 | 10 | 0 | 0 | 1,424 | 8 | 423 | 32 | 11 |
| | Prop 5 Texas Parks<br>Uploaded a month ago | 23 | 13 | 0 | 0 | 742 | 0 | 224 | 17 | 27 |

| 5 | 2,951 | 54,238 | 977 | 4,920 |
|---|---|---|---|---|
| VIDEOS POSTED | TOTAL VIEWS | TOTAL IMPRESSIONS | TOTAL FINISHES | TOTAL UNIQUE VIEWERS |

# Notes

**Chapter 1 – Genesis: The National Parks**

1. "John Muir," BrainyQuote (Xplore), accessed March 21, 2020, https://www.brainyquote.com/search_results?q=john%2Bmuir.

2. Walter L. Buenger, "Progressive Era," *Handbook of Texas* (Texas State Historical Association, May 1, 1995), https://www.tshaonline.org/handbook/entries/progressive-era.

3. Frederick Jackson Turner, *The Frontier in American History* (New York: Henry Holt and Company, 1920), 1, https://www.gutenberg.org/files/22994/22994-h/22994-h.htm.

4. "Featured Letter: A Difficult Trip to Natural Bridge," Jefferson Quotes & Family Letters | Monticello (Thomas Jefferson Foundation, July 2009), https://www.monticello.org/research-education/for-scholars/papers-of-thomas-jefferson/featured-letters/a-difficult-trip-to-natural-bridge/.

5. Henry David Thoreau, *The Maine Woods*, vol. 3 (Boston and New York: Houghton Mifflin and Company, 1864), https://www.gutenberg.org/files/42500/42500-h/42500-h.htm.

6. Dayton Duncan and Ken Burns, *The National Parks: America's Best Idea: An Illustrated History* (New York: Alfred A. Knopf, 2009), 11.

7. Frederick Law Olmsted, *Yosemite and the Mariposa Grove: A Preliminary Report, 1865* (Yosemite National Park: Yosemite Association, 2009), 8–9.

8. Olmsted, *Yosemite and the Mariposa Grove*, 9.

9. Olmsted, *Yosemite and the Mariposa Grove*, 11.

10. Olmsted, *Yosemite and the Mariposa Grove*, 12, 18.

11. "Visitation Numbers," National Park Service (US Department of the Interior), accessed March 21, 2020, https://www.nps.gov/aboutus/visitation-numbers.htm#:~:text=Out%20of%20the%20423%20parks,these%20visitor%20statistics%20were%20collected.

12. "Stats Report Viewer," National Park Service (US Department of the Interior), accessed March 21, 2020, https://irma.nps.gov/STATS/SSRSReports/Park%20Specific%20Reports/Annual%20Park%20Recreation%20Visitation%20(1904%20-%20Last%20Calendar%20Year)?Park=YOSE.

13. Duncan and Burns, *The National Parks*, 163.

14. Olmsted, *Yosemite and the Mariposa Grove*, 27.

15. "John Muir," BrainyQuote.

16. "Monuments Protected Under the Antiquities Act," National Parks Conservation Association, June 8, 2021, https://www.npca.org/resources/2658-monuments-protected-under-the-antiquities-act.

17. Gerald A. Diettert, *Grinnell's Glacier: George Bird Grinnell and Glacier National Park* (Missoula: Mountain Press Pub. Co., 1992), 99.

18. "Quick History of the National Park Service," National Park Service (US Department of the Interior), accessed March 18, 2020, https://www.nps.gov/articles/quick-nps-history.htm#:~:text=On%20August%2025%2C%201916%2C%20President,those%20yet%20to%20be%20established.

19. "Visitation Numbers," National Park Service.

**Chapter 2 – Texas Women in the State Parks Movement**

1. "History and Mission," General Federation of Women's Clubs, June 4, 2021, https://www.gfwc.org/about/history-and-mission/.

2. Mrs. Grady Rash, "Daughters of the Republic of Texas," *Handbook of Texas* (Texas State Historical Association, 1952), https://www.tshaonline.org/handbook/entries/daughters-of-the-republic-of-texas.

3. Elizabeth Hayes Turner, "Ballinger, Betty Eve (1854–1936)," *Handbook of Texas* (Texas State Historical Association, 1976), https://www.tshaonline.org/handbook/entries/ballinger-betty-eve.

4. "History," Daughters of the Republic of Texas, accessed March 7, 2022, https://www.drtinfo.org/about-drt/history.

5. "San Jacinto Battleground State Historical Park," Texas State Historical Association, accessed 2020, https://www.tshaonline.org/handbook/entries/san-jacinto-battleground-state-historical-park.

6. Gina Manlove, "San Jacinto Celebrates Joining the Texas Historical Commission," San Jacinto Museum of History, September 13, 2019, https://www.sanjacinto-museum.org/About_Us/News_and_Events/News/San_Jacinto_and_THC_Partnership/.

7. Megan Seaholm, "Texas Federation of Women's Clubs," *Handbook of Texas* (Texas State Historical Association, February 1, 1996), https://www.tshaonline.org/handbook/entries/texas-federation-of-womens-clubs.

8. "Texas Federation of Colored Women's Clubs," Texas Woman's University Libraries Woman's Collection - Texas Association of Women's Clubs (Texas Woman's University, 1997), https://twu.edu/library/womans-collection/collections/civic-organizations/tawc/.

9. "Timeline of Voting & Elections in Texas," The League of Women Voters of Texas, accessed March 5, 2022, https://lwvtexas.org/content.aspx?page_id=22&club_id=979482&module_id=485202.

10. "Palestine to Houston Highway Campaign by Post Party," *Houston Post*, June 20, 1915, vol. 30, no. 78 edition, sec. Auto, 44, https://www.newspapers.com/image/96211202/.

11. Martha Deeringer, *Flower of the Wilderness: Mother Neff and the State Parks of Texas* (Bradenton: BookLocker.com, Inc., 2014).

12. Thomas E. Turner, "Neff, Pat Morris (1871–1952)," *Handbook of Texas* (Texas State Historical Association, 1976), https://www.tshaonline.org/handbook/entries/neff-pat-morris.

13. James Wright Steely, *Parks for Texas: Enduring Landscapes of the New Deal* (Austin: University of Texas Press, 1999).

14. Martha Deeringer, *Flower of the Wilderness.*

15. "Women Urged to Vote for Amendment," *McKinney Daily Courier-Gazette*, July 2, 1923, 5, https://www.newspapers.com/image/63470429.

16. June M. Steele, *Phebe Warner: Community Building in the Texas Panhandle, 1898-1935: A Thesis in History*, Thesis, Texas Tech University, 2000, https://ttu-ir.tdl.org/handle/2346/17310?locale-attribute=en.

17. Austin E. Burges, "Transformation of 'Cave Springs,' Sabine Bottoms: Narrative of What One Woman Can Do Who Has a Well-Defined Plan and Follows It," *Galveston Daily News*, April 24, 1921, 15, https://www.newspapers.com/image/22134667/?terms=.

18. Mrs. W. C. Martin, "State Park System Is Needed to Further Move of Acquainting Texans with State," *Fort Worth Star-Telegram*, July 13, 1924, vol. XLIV, no. 164 edition, sec. Society and Clubs, 29, https://www.newspapers.com/image/634503444/?terms=.

19. "Mrs. J. F. Welder Succumbs at 94," *Victoria Advocate*, September 10, 1958, 113th Year, no. 126 edition, 1, 3.

20. Allison Baughman, "Marian 'Mamie' Rather Powell," East Texas History, July 2019, https://easttexashistory.org/items/show/22.

21. D. E. Colp Letter to Mrs. Ben H. Powell, January 26, 1927.

22. "Neal, Margie Elizabeth (1875–1971)," *Handbook of Texas* (Texas State Historical Association, 1976), https://www.tshaonline.org/handbook/entries/neal-margie-elizabeth.

23. Mrs. Ben Powell, "Texas Federation of Women's Clubs Report, Division of Parks and Playgrounds, 1925-1927" (Texas Federation of Women's Club, n.d.).

24. Mrs. Ben Powell Letter to D. E. Colp, February 19, 1927.

25. Mrs. Ben Powell Letter to D. E. Colp, n.d.

26. Mrs. Ben Powell Letter to Mrs. R. D. Rather, March 9, 1917.

27. D. E. Colp Letter to Mrs. E. A. Bellis, March 17, 1927.

28. "State Accepts 24 New Parks: Mrs. Ben Powell, Austin, Presses Resolution in Legislature," *Dallas Morning News*, March 19, 1927, vol. XLIL, no. 170 edition, 2, https://archives.dallasnews.com/uncategorized/IO_7b85e554-05c6-4182-9263-7e34028c3d20/.

29. D. E. Colp and the State Parks Association Letter to Miss Julia D. Owens, May 7, 1927.

30. "Lady Bird Johnson," Lady Bird Johnson, accessed September 2020, http://www.ladybirdjohnson.org/about.

31. Danna McDonald, *Sale of Enchanted Rock*, Thesis, Texas Parks and Wildlife Archeology Library, 1978.

32. Jane Dunn Sibley and Jim Comer, *Jane's Window: My Spirited Life in West Texas and Austin* (College Station: Texas A&M University Press, 2013).

33. State Task Force on Texas Nature Tourism, "Nature Tourism in the Lone Star State: Economic Opportunities in Nature" (Austin: Texas Parks and Wildlife Department and the Texas Department of Commerce, 1994).

34. Dan Parker, "Birding Trail's First Site Opens Friday in Rockport," *Corpus Christi Caller-Times*, September 7, 1995, vol. 113, no. 250 edition, sec. B, 13, https://www.newspapers.com/image/759077503.

35. Jennifer L. Bristol, personal interview with Madge Lindsay, February 2020.

36. Gillian Swanson, "Mid-Valley City Shows Interest in Birding Center," *The Monitor*, September 25, 1997, sec. Valley & State, 27, https://www.newspapers.com/image/330671560.

37. Cheryl Smith, "World Birding Center Will Nest in Mission: Surprise Decision Comes after Legislature Intervenes," *The Monitor*, April 30, 1999, 1, https://www.newspapers.com/image/331041047/?terms=.

38. Jennifer L. Bristol, personal interview with Carter Smith, December 2021.

## Chapter 3 – Genesis: The State Parks

1. Rebecca Conard, "The National Conference on State Parks: Reflections on Organizational Genealogy," *The George Wright Forum* 14, no. 4 (1997): 28–43, http://www.georgewright.org/144conard.pdf.

2. Jeffrey Fritz Crunk, "Breathing Spots for the People: Pat M. Neff, David E. Colp, and the Emerging Idea of State Parks in Texas, 1900–1925," Thesis, Baylor University, 1994, 23, 87.

3. Dorothy Blodgett, Terrell Blodgett, and David L. Scott, *The Land, the Law, and the Lord: The Life of Pat Neff: Governor of Texas, 1921-1925, President of Baylor University, 1932–1947* (Austin: Home Place Publishers, 2007), 4.

4. Jorjanna Price, "1920 Census Data Hints at Today's Texas," Texas Association of Counties, 2020, https://www.county.org/County-Magazine-Main/September-October-2020/1920-census-data-hints-at-todays-Texas.

5. "To Love the Beautiful: The Story of Texas State Parks," Texas State Library and Archives Commission, November 7, 2016, https://www.tsl.texas.gov/exhibits/parks/index.html.

6. "To Love the Beautiful."

7. Pat Morris Neff, *The Battles of Peace* (Fort Worth: Pioneer Publishing Company: The Bunker Press, 1925), 128, https://www.google.com/books/edition/The_Battles_of_Peace/ojsVAAAAYAAJ?hl=en.

8. James Wright Steely, *Parks for Texas: Enduring Landscapes of the New Deal* (Austin: University of Texas Press, 1999), 4.

9. H. Allen Anderson, "Palo Duro Canyon State Scenic Park," *Handbook of Texas* (Texas State Historical Association, 1976), https://www.tshaonline.org/handbook/entries/palo-duro-canyon-state-scenic-park.

10. "Lasting Legacies," American Forests, April 3, 2012, https://www.americanforests.org/blog/lasting-legacies/.

11. John Muir, "Studies in the Sierra," *Overland Monthly* 12–14 (1874), https://vault.sierraclub.org/john_muir_exhibit/writings/studies_in_the_sierra/.

12. Robert S. Maxwell, "Jones, William Goodrich (1860–1950)," *Handbook of Texas* (Texas State Historical Association, February 1, 1995), https://www.tshaonline.org/handbook/entries/jones-william-goodrich.

13. Maxwell, "Jones, William Goodrich."

14. Crunk, "Breathing Spots for the People," 80.

15. Crunk, "Breathing Spots for the People," 64.

16. Crunk, "Breathing Spots for the People," 65.

17. Crunk, "Breathing Spots for the People," 72.

18. Crunk, "Breathing Spots for the People," 73.

19. Crunk, "Breathing Spots for the People," 62.

20. Crunk, "Breathing Spots for the People," 63.

21. Crunk, "Breathing Spots for the People," 76.

22. Crunk, "Breathing Spots for the People," 82.

23. Crunk, "Breathing Spots for the People," 85.

24. Crunk, "Breathing Spots for the People," 86.

25. Crunk, "Breathing Spots for the People," 86.

26. Crunk, "Breathing Spots for the People," 87.

27. "About Lead Belly," About Lead Belly (The Lead Belly Foundation), accessed May 21, 2020, https://www.leadbelly.org/leadbelly.html.

28. Roger Catlin, "The Incomparable Legacy of Lead Belly," *Smithsonian Magazine*, February 23, 2015, https://www.smithsonianmag.com/smithsonian-institution/incomparable-legacy-of-lead-belly-180954390/.

29. Crunk, "Breathing Spots for the People," 111.

30. Steely, *Parks for Texas*, 8.

31. Ben H. Procter, "Great Depression," *Handbook of Texas* (Texas State Historical Association, October 1, 1995), https://www.tshaonline.org/handbook/entries/great-depression.

32. Procter, "Great Depression."

33. Procter, "Great Depression."

34. Phebe Kerrick Warner, "Depression Boosts State Parks," *Texas Federation News*, April 1933, 9.

35. Arthur M. Schlesinger Jr., *The Coming of the New Deal* (Boston: Houghton Mifflin, 1958), 335.

36. Steely, *Parks for Texas*, 14.

37. Steely, *Parks for Texas*, 34–35.

38. Steely, *Parks for Texas*, 53.

39. Steely, *Parks for Texas*, 53.

40. Procter, "Great Depression."

41. "Winston Churchill Quotes," BrainyQuote (Xplore), accessed March 26, 2022, https://www.brainyquote.com/authors/winston-churchill-quotes.

**Chapter 4 – A New Deal for Texas State Parks**

1. The National Park Service worked with a number of counties and municipal entities since not all parks in Texas were overseen by the Texas State Parks Board.

2. Sections of this chapter are based on Cynthia Brandimarte, *Texas State Parks and the CCC: The Legacy of the Civilian Conservation Corps* (College Station: Texas A & M University Press, 2013) and Cynthia A. Brandimarte, "Built Sturdy, Left Fragile: State Parks after the New Deal," in *A Century of Design in the Parks: Preserving the Built Environment in National and State Parks* (Santa Fe: National Center for Preservation Technology and Training | National Park Service, 2016), 154–165.

3. Ben H. Procter, "Great Depression," *Handbook of Texas* (Texas State Historical Association, October 1, 1995), https://www.tshaonline.org/handbook/entries/great-depression.

4. The array of New Deal programs constituted Roosevelt's response after he entered the White House in March 1933. His administration quickly created federal agencies to monitor and regulate industry, employ men and women in mammoth projects like the Boulder Dam (later Hoover), and provide others with work in community organizations funded by Washington. The Works Progress Administration alone put eight million unemployed Americans to work on projects that ran the gamut from building roads and dams for hydroelectric power in the Tennessee Valley to writing state guidebooks and recording oral histories of former slaves.

5. Kenneth Holland and Frank Ernest Hill, *Youth in the CCC* (Washington: American Council on Education, 1942), 8.

6. "Congressional Record: Proceedings and Debates of the First Session of the Seventy-Third Congress (March 4, 1933-April 3, 1933)," 77 Congressional Record: Proceedings and Debates of the First Session of the Seventy-Third Congress (March 4, 1933–April 3, 1933) § (1933), 650, govinfo.gov/app/details/GPO-CRECB-1933-pt1-v77/.

7. At first, this was accomplished by the Office of Employment in the Department of Labor, but there was a desire to place this employment function at the state level. In the interim, Secretary of Labor Frances Perkins had to set up some thirty offices around the country. These Reemployment Service offices were in operation for a brief time.

8. Valentina Kachanovskaya, "New Deal: Distribution and Impact of Funds in the States" (dissertation, University of Arizona, 2016), 39.

9. The Civilian Conservation Corps was established by an act of Congress, approved on June 28, 1937 (50 Stat. 31), as amended, to succeed the Emergency Conservation Work Act established by Executive Order 6101 on April 5, 1933, under an act of March 31, 1933 (48 Stat. 22), as amended. The Civilian Conservation Corps became part of the Federal Security Agency by Reorganization Plan I, effective July 1, 1939, in accordance with the Reorganization Act of 1939 (53 Stat. 561).

10. James Steely demonstrates in *Parks for Texas: Enduring Landscapes of the New Deal* (Austin: University of Texas Press, 1999), Appendix C (234–235), the relationship between state parks and Texas's congressional delegations. He also notes that local economies received a good portion of the $2,300-per-month federal operating costs. Factoring in inflation, that 1935 amount is equivalent to roughly $50,000 per month in 2022.

11. Steely, *Parks for Texas*, Appendix B, 231–233.

12. Westbrook remained a presence until the end of January 1934, when he moved to Washington, DC, to become assistant director of the Federal Emergency Relief Administration, which sponsored the nationwide Civil Works Administration program under presidential adviser Harry Hopkins. The Civil Works Administration completed some park projects over the winter of 1933 to help desperate folks through a tough winter. Westbrook selected some of those park projects. See Steely, *Parks for Texas*, 58, 67.

13. Conrad Louis Wirth, *Parks, Politics, and the People* (Norman: University of Oklahoma Press, 1980), Chapter 5.

14. The "SP" indicated "State Park," but there were other prefixes: for example, "CP" meant "County Park"; "MA," "Municipal Area"; "SCS," "Soil Conservation"; "PE," "Private Erosion" project; etc. Likewise, each Civilian Conservation Corps company, initially consisting of two hundred men, was identified by a number that included an "8," designating Texas.

15. During the Second New Deal, District III became Region VII.

16. Michelle Williams, interview with James W. Steely at Bastrop State Park, *Terra Incognita*, Historic Sites and Structures Program, Texas Parks and Wildlife Department, September 8, 2008.

17. Wirth, *Parks, Politics, and the People*, Chapter 5.

18. Steely, *Parks for Texas*, 65. See also Joseph M. Speakman, "Into the Woods: The First Year of the Civilian Conservation Corps," *Prologue Magazine*, 2006, https://www.archives.gov/publications/prologue/2006/fall/ccc.html.

19. Steely, *Parks for Texas*, 65, 73.

20. Ralph Edward Newlan et al., "Bastrop State Park, National Historic Landmark Nomination Form," Bastrop State Park, National Historic Landmark Nomination Form § (1997), https://npgallery.nps.gov/GetAsset/d14f407f-937d-446a-8cf1-2256cd8e6cce. As of 1997, Bastrop was among only six state or interstate parks designated as a National Historic Landmark.

21. For information on Olin Boese, see Martha Doty Freeman, "Abilene State Park: A History of the Development of a Cultural Landscape, 1875–2003," Historic Sites and Structures Program, Texas Parks and Wildlife Department, August 2003.

22. David Carlton, personal interview with Russell Cashion at Bastrop State Park, March 30, 2003.

23. Dale Martin, personal interview with W. R. Patrick at Bastrop State Park, March 31, 2003.

24. Cindy Brown, personal interview with Julian Cavazos at Bastrop State Park, September 16, 2005.

25. John C. Paige, *The Civilian Conservation Corps and the National Park Service: 1933-1942: An Administrative History* (Washington: National Park Service, US Department of the Interior, 1985), 15. Native Americans could comprise up to 10 percent of the total—5 percent in the territories of Alaska (outside the continental US), Puerto Rico, the Virgin Islands, and Hawaii. See Office of the Director, *The Civilian Conservation Corps: What It Is and What It Does* (Washington: Federal Security Agency, Civilian Conservation Corps, 1941), 5.

26. Dennis Cordes, personal interview with Gardner Hill at Bastrop State Park, March 30, 2003.

27. Scarlett Wirt and Mark Thurman, personal interview with Thomas Earl Jordan at Bastrop State Park, March 30, 2003. Jordan's transcript is used here because of its range and descriptiveness; other interviews recount similar experiences. While enrolled in the Civilian Conservation Corps, Jordan worked at Tyler and Possum Kingdom State Parks. His 2007 obituary does not mention his contribution to Texas state parks.

28. Wirt and Thurman, interview with Thomas Earl Jordan.

29. Dan K. Utley and James W. Steely, *Guided with a Steady Hand: The Cultural Landscape of a Rural Texas Park* (Waco: Baylor University Press, 1998), 72. These classes were available to the enrollees during the spring of 1935.

30. Diane E. Williams, "Historic Resources Study: Brief Narrative and Report, Blanco State Park, Blanco County, Texas," Historic Sites and Structures Program, Texas Parks and Wildlife Department, 2008, 16.

31. Wirt and Thurman, interview with Thomas Earl Jordan.

32. Wirt and Thurman, interview with Thomas Earl Jordan.

33. Luther C. Wandell, "A Negro in the CCC," *Crisis* 42 (August 1935): 244–254.

34. Erin Blakemore, "The New Deal Program That Sent Women to Summer Camp," History.com (A&E Television Networks, July 7, 2020), https://www.history.com/news/

new-deal-women-summer-corps; "Camp Tera to Continue: Mrs. Roosevelt Still Hopes Girls May Get Facilities Like CCC," *New York Times*, October 24, 1933, 16, https://www.nytimes.com/1933/10/24/archives/camp-tera-to-continue-mrs-roosevelt-still-hopes-girls-may-get.html?searchResultPosition=12.

35. Janelle Taylor and Tom Johnson, personal interview with Louise Sellers in Dallas, Texas, October 26, 2004.

36. Kenneth Heger, "Dangers in the Civilian Conservation Corps: Accident Reports, 1933-1942," *Prologue Magazine*, 2011, https://www.archives.gov/publications/prologue/2011/winter/ccc-accidents.html.

37. For example, James Laswell, *Shovels and Guns: The CCC in Action* (New York: International Pamphlet 45, 1935).

38. *Sparks*, January 1940, 10–12.

39. "State Parks Board Minutes" (Austin: State of Texas, June 13, 1934), 60.

40. Steely, *Parks for Texas*, 97. Although the State Parks Board and the Civilian Conservation Corps played a small role in support of the celebration, the Centennial Commission did undertake initiatives at several Civilian Conservation Corps parks, notably Fort Parker, Goliad, and Mission Tejas.

41. Both the Works Progress Administration and the National Youth Administration employed women. Their work was typically gendered, including work in sewing rooms and school lunch programs, and their numbers were usually smaller than those of men hired. White women tended to benefit from more opportunities. Some women were hired as teachers, and some were assigned to Civilian Conservation Corps camps.

42. Steely, *Parks for Texas*, 104–105.

43. Utley and Steely, *Guided with a Steady Hand*, 128.

44. Big Bend National Park remained staffed with a Civilian Conservation Corps company through March 1942.

45. Joan Pearsall, Harold Toy, and Fred McNeil, "History of Texas Parks Board, Updated Narrative Consolidation" (Austin: Departmental History Project Research Files, Texas Parks and Wildlife Department Administrative Records and Other Materials, Archives and Information Services Division, Texas State Library and Archives Commission, June 24, 1974), 19.

46. Paige, *The Civilian Conservation Corps*, 34.

47. Thomas R. Cox, *The Park Builders: A History of State Parks in the Pacific Northwest* (Seattle: University of Washington Press, 1988), 107.

48. Cox, *The Park Builders*, 86.

49. Conrad L. Wirth, "Civilian Conservation Corps Program of the United States Department of the Interior (March 1933 to June 30, 1943)" (Report to Harold L. Ickes, Secretary of the Interior, 1944), 31, https://digitalcommons.unomaha.edu/slceslgen/57/.

## Chapter 5 – War, Peace, Drought, and a War Within

1. "Texas Parks Civilian Conservation Corps Drawings Database," Texas State Library and Archives Commission, accessed June 21, 2020, https://www.tsl.texas.gov/apps/arc/CCCDrawings/.

2. John R. Jameson, *The Story of Big Bend National Park* (Austin: University of Texas Press, 1996), 3.

3. Jameson, *The Story of Big Bend National Park*, 3.

4. Jameson, *The Story of Big Bend National Park*, 3.

5. Jameson, *The Story of Big Bend National Park*, 8.

6. "Texas's Gift to the Nation: The Establishment of Big Bend National Park," National Park Service (US Department of the Interior, August 3, 2020), https://www.nps.gov/bibe/learn/historyculture/tgttn.htm.

7. James Wright Steely, *Parks for Texas: Enduring Landscapes of the New Deal* (Austin: University of Texas Press, 1999), 7.

8. Steely, *Parks for Texas*, 8.

9. Steely, *Parks for Texas*, 8.

10. Steely, *Parks for Texas*, 146.

11. Alice J. Rhoades, "Quinn, Frank David (1894–1971)," *Handbook of Texas* (Texas State Historical Association, June 1, 1995), https://www.tshaonline.org/handbook/entries/quinn-frank-david.

12. Rhoades, "Quinn, Frank David (1894–1971)."

13. Steely, *Parks for Texas*, 148.

14. Jameson, *The Story of Big Bend National Park*, 44, 48.

15. Robert A. Calvert, "Texas Post World War II," *Handbook of Texas* (Texas State Historical Association, February 1, 1996), https://www.tshaonline.org/handbook/entries/texas-post-world-war-ii.

16. Calvert, "Texas Post World War II."

17. Farzad Mashhood, "How Dry Is It? Conditions Are Bad but Pale in Comparison to 1950s Drought," *Austin American-Statesman*, August 4, 2011, vol. 141, no. 10 edition, A1, A6, https://www.newspapers.com/image/434895240, A1.

18. Mashhood, "How Dry Is It?," A6.

19. "To Love the Beautiful: The Story of Texas State Parks: 'So Would Hell,'" Texas State Parks in the 1950s (Texas State Library and Archives Commission, November 16, 2016), https://www.tsl.texas.gov/exhibits/parks/1950s/page1.html.

20. Leah Scarpelli, "Why Don't More African-Americans Visit State Parks?," *Texas Standard*, June 7, 2016, https://www.texasstandard.org/stories/why-dont-more-african-americans-visit-state-parks/.

21. Charles Jordan, "Urban Greenscapes: Conservation and Parks in America," *Texas Coalition for Conservation*, lecture presented at the Symposium on Conservation and Park Funding, February 2003.

22. Christopher Long, "Ku Klux Klan," *Handbook of Texas* (Texas State Historical Association, 1952), https://www.tshaonline.org/handbook/entries/ku-klux-klan.

23. Cynthia A. Brandimarte, "Built Sturdy, Left Fragile: State Parks after the New Deal," in *A Century of Design in the Parks: Preserving the Built Environment in National and State Parks* (Santa Fe: National Center for Preservation Technology and Training | National Park Service, 2016), 160.

24. Vicki Betts, "For the Citizens of East Texas: The Desegregation of Tyler State Park," *Chronicles of Smith County, Texas* 51 (2021): 2–9.

25. Betts, "For the Citizens of East Texas."

26. Betts, "For the Citizens of East Texas."

27. Betts, "For the Citizens of East Texas."

## Chapter 6 – President and Mrs. Lyndon B. Johnson: Forces for Nature

1. Sam Houston Johnson, *My Brother Lyndon*, ed. Enrique Hank Lopez (New York: Cowles Book Co., 1969), 179.

2. Deborah Lynn Self, "The National Youth Administration in Texas, 1935–1939," Thesis, Texas Tech University, 1974, 47.

3. Kenneth E. Hendrickson Jr., "National Youth Administration," *Handbook of Texas* (Texas State Historical Association, May 1, 1995), https://www.tshaonline.org/handbook/entries/national-youth-administration.

4. Marjorie Arp, "N.Y.A. Program, Not a Movement, Johnson Says," *The Daily Texan*, October 4, 1935, vol. 37, no. 15 edition, 1, 6, https://repositories.lib.utexas.edu/handle/2152/97530.

5. Arp, "N.Y.A. Program," 6.

6. Self, "The National Youth Administration in Texas," 4.

7. "National Youth Administration Projects in Texas," The Living New Deal, accessed March 22, 2021, https://livingnewdeal.org/?s=NYA%2BTexas.

8. Sara Dant, "LBJ, Wilderness, and the Land and Water Conservation Fund," *Forest History Today*, 2014, 16–21, 21.

9. George Bristol, personal interview with Former Texas State Senator Joe Christie, April 2021.

10. Camille Wheeler, "Enchanted Rock: Rock of Ages," *Texas Co-Op Power*, May 2010, 26–27.

11. Anne Thompson, "She Was Green before Green Was Cool," NBCNews.com (NBCUniversal News Group, July 12, 2007), https://www.nbcnews.com/id/wbna19732051.

## Chapter 7 – The Golden Years: 1963–1980

1. George Bristol, personal interview with Andrew Sansom, March 4, 2022.

2. John Jefferson, "The Golden Age of Park Acquisitions," *Texas Parks & Wildlife Magazine*, August 2011, https://tpwmagazine.com/archive/2011/aug/ed_1_stateparks/.

3. James Wright Steely, *Parks for Texas: Enduring Landscapes of the New Deal* (Austin: University of Texas Press, 1999), 193.

4. Steely, *Parks for Texas*, 193.

5. Jefferson, "The Golden Age of Park Acquisitions."

6. "Elections of Texas Governors, 1845–2010," Texas Almanac, accessed August 16, 2021, https://www.texasalmanac.com/articles/elections-of-texas-governors-1845-2010.

7. Jefferson, "The Golden Age of Park Acquisitions."

8. Jefferson, "The Golden Age of Park Acquisitions."

9. Jefferson, "The Golden Age of Park Acquisitions."

10. Griffin Smith Jr., "The Strange Case of the Missing Parks," *Texas Monthly*, November 1975, 89–144.

11. Jefferson, "The Golden Age of Park Acquisitions."

12. Smith, "The Strange Case of the Missing Parks," 90.

13. Smith, "The Strange Case of the Missing Parks," 90.

14. Dave McNeely, "Armstrong's Dip," *Fort Worth Weekly*, August 13, 2014, https://www.fwweekly.com/2014/08/13/armstrongs-dip/.

## Chapter 8 – The Sporting Goods Sales Tax: Leadership at Every Level

1. Kelly Pohl and Megan Lawson, "State Funding Programs for Outdoor Recreation: Texas Sporting Goods Sales Tax" (Outdoor Industry Association, 2018).

2. Ji Youn Jeong and John L. Crompton, "The Economic Contributions of Texas State Parks" (Austin: Texas Coalition for Conservation, 2019), 2.

3. Pohl and Lawson, "State Funding Programs for Outdoor Recreation."

4. "The Best and Worst Legislators, 1973-2021," *Texas Monthly*, February 7, 2022, https://www.texasmonthly.com/the-best-and-worst-legislators-1973-2021/.

## Chapter 9 – Starts and Stops: Fickle Legislatures: 1994–2016

1. George Lambert Bristol, *On Politics and Parks* (College Station: Texas A&M University Press, 2013).

2. Griffin Smith Jr., "The Strange Case of the Missing Parks," *Texas Monthly*, November 1975, 90.

3. Dave Harmon, "Seeds to Reforest Lost Pines Were Almost Lost to Landfill," *Austin American-Statesman*, September 1, 2012, https://www.statesman.com/story/news/local/2012/09/01/seeds-to-reforest-lost-pines-were-almost-lost-to-landfill/9902010007/.

4. Harmon, "Seeds to Reforest Lost Pines Were Almost Lost to Landfill."

## Chapter 10 – The Essential Answer: A Constitutional Amendment

1. Gene McCarty, Email to George Bristol. *Sporting Goods Sales Tax*, December 10, 2020.

2. McCarty, Email to George Bristol.

3. Dan Allen Hughes, "Editorial: Preserve Our Parks; Preserve Our Way of Life," March 1, 2015.

4. Ji Youn Jeong and John L. Crompton, "The Economic Contributions of Texas State Parks" (Austin: Texas Coalition for Conservation, 2014), 4.

5. David B. Hill, "Voter Opinion Surveys" (Hill Research Consultants, 2019).

6. Hill, "Voter Opinion Surveys."

## Chapter 11 – Private Park Philanthropy: An Essential Partner

1. John Murray, "Thomas Jefferson's Land Grant for Natural Bridge and 157 Acres in Botetourt County," Jefferson Quotes & Family Letters | Monticello (Thomas Jefferson Foundation, July 5, 1774), https://tjrs.monticello.org/letter/1975.

2. Carrie Hunter Willis and Etta Belle Walker, *Legends of the Skyline Drive and the Great Valley of Virginia* (Richmond: The Dietz Press, 1940), 81–84, https://www.gutenberg.org/files/33018/33018-h/33018-h.htm#Page_81.

3. Rachel Lucas, "Natural Bridge Officially Becomes a State Park, Affiliated with National Park Service," WSLS 10 News, September 24, 2016, https://www.wsls.com/news/2016/09/24/natural-bridge-officially-becomes-a-state-park-affiliated-with-national-park-service/.

4. Susan Stein, "Natural Bridge (Engraving)," Monticello (Thomas Jefferson Foundation), accessed March 7, 2022, https://www.monticello.org/site/research-and-collections/natural-bridge-engraving.

5. "The Kent Family and Conservation," National Park Service (US Department of the Interior, October 28, 2021), https://www.nps.gov/articles/the-kent-family-and-conservation.htm.

6. "George B Dorr," National Park Service (US Department of the Interior, February 24, 2022), https://www.nps.gov/people/george-b-dorr.htm.

7. Barry Mackintosh, "Philanthropy and the National Parks in the 20th Century," National Park Service (US Department of the Interior, July 6, 2018), https://www.nps.gov/articles/philanthropy-and-the-national-parks.htm#:~:text=Philanthropy%20is%20more%20than%20a,special%20interest%20in%20their%20welfare.

8. Mackintosh, "Philanthropy and the National Parks in the 20th Century."

9. Wayne Bell, "Behind the Story of the Christmas Mountains," Houston Public Media, June 16, 2008, https://www.houstonpublicmedia.org/articles/news/2008/06/16/10771/behind-the-story-of-the-christmas-mountains/.

10. "History of Christmas Mountains," Texas State University System, August 24, 2018, https://www.tsus.edu/about-tsus/research/History.html.

11. "Chinati Mountains State Natural Area," Texas Parks and Wildlife Department, March 16, 2022, https://tpwd.texas.gov/state-parks/chinati-mountains.

12. Melanie Garunay, "President Obama Designates National Monument in Maine's North Woods," National Archives and Records Administration, August 24, 2016, https://obamawhitehouse.archives.gov/blog/2016/08/24/president-obama-designates-national-monument-maines-north-woods.

13. "Driscoll, Clara (1881–1945)," Encyclopedia.com, accessed November 22, 2021, https://www.encyclopedia.com/women/encyclopedias-almanacs-transcripts-and-maps/driscoll-clara-1881-1945.

14. "Driscoll, Clara (1881–1945)."

15. "Driscoll, Clara (1881–1945)."

16. Sally Anne S. Gutting, "Honoring Texas Heroes: The San Jacinto Monument and Its Cornerstone," Houston History, 2007, 20–28, https://houstonhistorymagazine.org/wp-content/uploads/2011/11/V4-N2-Gutting-Honoring-Texas-Heroes.pdf, 21.

17. Mrs. Grady Rash, "Daughters of the Republic of Texas," Handbook of Texas (Texas State Historical Association, 1952), https://www.tshaonline.org/handbook/entries/daughters-of-the-republic-of-texas.

18. "TPW Commission Approves Devils River Land Acquisition," Texas Parks and Wildlife Department, December 20, 2010, https://tpwd.texas.gov/newsmedia/releases/?req=20101220b.

19. "Devils River State Natural Area," Texas Parks and Wildlife Department, September 5, 2017, https://tpwd.texas.gov/state-parks/devils-river/park_history.

20. Joe Nick Patoski, "'All It Took Was 25 Years': Legislature Ponied Up Cash for Underfunded Texas Parks," Texas Observer, June 11, 2019, https://www.texasobserver.org/all-it-took-was-25-years-legislature-ponies-up-cash-for-underfunded-texas-parks/.

21. Lydia Saldaña, "Bringing a Park to Life," Texas Parks & Wildlife Magazine, December 2020, https://tpwmagazine.com/archive/2020/dec/ed_2_palopinto/index.phtml.

**Chapter 12 – A Brighter Future**

1. Ji Youn Jeong and John L. Crompton, "The Economic Contributions of Texas State Parks" (Austin: Texas Coalition for Conservation, 2014 and 2019), 68, 65.

2. Jeong and Crompton, "The Economic Contributions of Texas State Parks" (2019), 2.

3. Pat Morris Neff, The Battles of Peace (Fort Worth: Pioneer Publishing Company: The Bunker Press, 1925), 135.

4. Alfred Runte, National Parks: The American Experience, 1st ed. (Lincoln: University of Nebraska Press, 1979), Preface, https://www.nps.gov/parkhistory/online_books/runte1/index.htm.

5. "Conservation vs Preservation and the National Park Service," National Park Service (US Department of the Interior), accessed January 23, 2022, https://www.nps.gov/teachers/classrooms/conservation-preservation-and-the-national-park-service.htm#:~:text=Conservation%20is%20generally%20associated%20with,protection%20of%20nature%20from%20use.

6. Jeffrey Fritz Crunk, "Breathing Spots for the People: Pat M. Neff, David E. Colp, and the Emerging Idea of State Parks in Texas, 1900–1925," Thesis, Baylor University, 1994, 133.

7. Crunk, "Breathing Spots for the People," 129.

8. Dora A. Padgett, ed., "What about Pennsylvania?," Planning and Civic Comment: January - March 1940 6, no. 1 (1940): 29–30, https://ia902609.us.archive.org/24/items/planningcivilcom05washrich/planningcivilcom05washrich.pdf.

**Epilogue – Looking to the Past to Secure the Future: A Final Observation**

1. Horace M. Albright and Marian Albright Schenck, Creating the National Park Service: The Missing Years (Norman: University of Oklahoma Press, 1999), 101.

# Bibliography

About Lead Belly. The Lead Belly Foundation. Accessed May 21, 2020. https://www.leadbelly.org/leadbelly.html.

Albright, Horace M., and Marian Albright Schenck. *Creating the National Park Service: The Missing Years*. Norman: University of Oklahoma Press, 1999.

Alter, Jonathan. *The Defining Moment: FDR's Hundred Days and the Triumph of Hope*. New York: Simon & Schuster, 2007.

Anderson, H. Allen. "Palo Duro Canyon State Scenic Park." *Handbook of Texas*. Texas State Historical Association, 1976. https://www.tshaonline.org/handbook/entries/palo-duro-canyon-state-scenic-park.

Anderson, H. Allen. "Warner, Phebe Kerrick (1866–1935)." *Handbook of Texas*. Texas State Historical Association, 1952. https://www.tshaonline.org/handbook/entries/warner-phebe-kerrick.

Arp, Marjorie. "N.Y.A. Program, Not a Movement, Johnson Says." *The Daily Texan*, October 4, 1935, Volume 37, No. 15 edition. https://repositories.lib.utexas.edu/handle/2152/97530.

Associated Press. "Senator Margie Neal Slated for High Post." *Fort Worth Record-Telegram*, January 8, 1929, Volume XXXIII, Number 69 edition. https://www.newspapers.com/image/636065418/?terms=.

Barnes, Michael. "Jane Sibley, 95, Saved the Austin Symphony." *Austin American-Statesman*, May 22, 2019. https://www.statesman.com/news/20190522/jane-sibley-who-saved-austin-symphony-has-died.

Baughman, Allison. "Marian 'Mamie' Rather Powell." East Texas History, July 2019. https://easttexashistory.org/items/show/22.

Bell, Wayne. "Behind the Story of the Christmas Mountains." Houston Public Media, June 16, 2008. https://www.houstonpublicmedia.org/articles/news/2008/06/16/10771/behind-the-story-of-the-christmas-mountains/.

"The Best and Worst Legislators, 1973–2021." *Texas Monthly*, February 7, 2022. https://www.texasmonthly.com/the-best-and-worst-legislators-1973-2021/.

Betts, Vicki. "For the Citizens of East Texas: The Desegregation of Tyler State Park." *Chronicles of Smith County, Texas* 51 (2021): 2–9.

Blakemore, Erin. "The New Deal Program That Sent Women to Summer Camp." History.com. A&E Television Networks, July 7, 2020. https://www.history.com/news/new-deal-women-summer-corps.

Blodgett, Dorothy, Terrell Blodgett, and David L. Scott. *The Land, the Law, and the Lord: The Life of Pat Neff: Governor of Texas, 1921-1925, President of Baylor University, 1932-1947*. Austin: Home Place Publishers, 2007.

Brandimarte, Cynthia A. "Built Sturdy, Left Fragile: State Parks after the New Deal." In *A Century of Design in the Parks: Preserving the Built Environment in National and State Parks*, 154–65. Santa Fe: National Center for Preservation Technology and Training | National Park Service, 2016.

Brandimarte, Cynthia. *Texas State Parks and the CCC: The Legacy of the Civilian Conservation Corps*. College Station: Texas A&M University Press, 2013.

Brands, H. W. *Traitor to His Class: The Privileged Life and Radical Presidency of Franklin Delano Roosevelt*. New York: Doubleday, 2008.

Bristol, George Lambert. *On Politics and Parks*. College Station: Texas A&M University Press, 2013.

Bristol, George. Personal Interview with Andrew Sansom. March 4, 2022.

Bristol, George. Personal Interview with Former Texas State Senator Joe Christie. April 2021.

Bristol, Jennifer L. Personal Interview with Carter Smith. December 2021.

Bristol, Jennifer L. Personal Interview with Madge Lindsay. February 2020.

Brown, Cindy. Personal Interview with Julian Cavazos at Bastrop State Park. September 16, 2005.

Buenger, Walter L. "Progressive Era." *Handbook of Texas*. Texas State Historical Association, May 1, 1995. https://www.tshaonline.org/handbook/entries/progressive-era.

Burges, Austin E. "Transformation of 'Cave Springs,' Sabine Bottoms: Narrative of What One Woman Can Do Who Has a Well-Defined Plan and Follows It." *Galveston Daily News*, April 24, 1921. https://www.newspapers.com/image/22134667/?terms=.

Butler, Ovid, ed. *Youth Rebuilds: Stories from the C.C.C.* Washington: The American Forestry Association, 1934.

"Caddo Lake Park to Be Suggested." *Fort Worth Star-Telegram*, August 19, 1928, Volume XLVIII, Number 201 edition. https://www.newspapers.com/image/634559126/?terms=.

Calvert, Robert A. "Texas Post World War II." *Handbook of Texas*. Texas State Historical Association, February 1, 1996. https://www.tshaonline.org/handbook/entries/texas-post-world-war-ii.

"Camp Tera to Continue: Mrs. Roosevelt Still Hopes Girls May Get Facilities Like CCC." *New York Times*, October 24, 1933. https://www.nytimes.com/1933/10/24/archives/camp-tera-to-continue-mrs-roosevelt-still-hopes-girls-may-get.html?searchResultPosition=12.

Carlton, David. Personal Interview with Russell Cashion at Bastrop State Park. March 30, 2003.

Carr, Ethan. *Wilderness by Design: Landscape Architecture and the National Park Service*. Lincoln: University of Nebraska Press, 1998.

"Catholic Order Honors Victorian." *Victoria Advocate*, April 5, 1957, 111th Year, No. 332 edition. https://www.newspapers.com/image/440862934/?terms=.

Catlin, Roger. "The Incomparable Legacy of Lead Belly." *Smithsonian Magazine*, February 23, 2015. https://www.smithsonianmag.com/smithsonian-institution/incomparable-legacy-of-lead-belly-180954390/.

"Chinati Mountains State Natural Area." Texas Parks and Wildlife Department, March 16, 2022. https://tpwd.texas.gov/state-parks/chinati-mountains.

Cole, Olen, Jr. *The African-American Experience in the Civilian Conservation Corps*. Gainesville: University Press of Florida, 1999.

Colp, D. E. Letter to Mrs. Ben H. Powell, January 26, 1927.

Colp, D. E. Letter to Mrs. E. A. Bellis, March 17, 1927.

Colp, D. E., and the State Parks Association. Letter to Miss Julia D. Owens, May 7, 1927.

Conard, Rebecca. "The National Conference on State Parks: Reflections on Organizational Genealogy." *The George Wright Forum* 14, no. 4 (1997): 28–43. http://www.georgewright.org/144conard.pdf.

Connally, John B., Jr. "State of the State." *Legislative Reference Library of Texas*. Address presented at the Regular Session of the Fifty-Eighth Legislature of the State of Texas, January 16, 1963. https://lrl.texas.gov/legeLeaders/governors/displayDocs.cfm?govdoctypeID=6&governorID=37.

Connor, Seymour V. "Briscoe, Mary Jane Harris (1819–1903)." *Handbook of Texas*. Texas State Historical Association, 1952. https://www.tshaonline.org/handbook/entries/briscoe-mary-jane-harris.

"Conservation vs Preservation and the National Park Service." National Park Service. US Department of the Interior. Accessed January 23, 2022. https://www.nps.gov/teachers/classrooms/conservation-preservation-and-the-national-park-service.htm#:~:text=Conservation%20is%20generally%20associated%20with,protection%20of%20nature%20from%20use.

Cordes, Dennis. Personal Interview with Gardner Hill at Bastrop State Park. March 30, 2003.

Cox, Thomas R. *The Park Builders: A History of State Parks in the Pacific Northwest*. Seattle: University of Washington Press, 1988.

Crunk, Jeffrey Fritz. "Breathing Spots for the People: Pat M. Neff, David E. Colp, and the Emerging Idea of State Parks in Texas, 1900–1925." Thesis, Baylor University, 1994.

Dant, Sara. "LBJ, Wilderness, and the Land and Water Conservation Fund." *Forest History Today*, 2014.

Deeringer, Martha. *Flower of the Wilderness: Mother Neff and the State Parks of Texas*. Bradenton: BookLocker.com, Inc., 2014.

"Devils River State Natural Area." Texas Parks and Wildlife Department, September 5, 2017. https://tpwd.texas.gov/state-parks/devils-river/park_history.

Diettert, Gerald A. *Grinnell's Glacier: George Bird Grinnell and Glacier National Park*. Missoula: Mountain Press Pub. Co., 1992.

"Driscoll, Clara (1881–1945)." Encyclopedia.com. Accessed November 22, 2021. https://www.encyclopedia.com/women/encyclopedias-almanacs-transcripts-and-maps/driscoll-clara-1881-1945.

Duncan, Dayton, and Ken Burns. *The National Parks: America's Best Idea: An Illustrated History*. New York: Alfred A. Knopf, 2009.

Egan, Timothy. *The Worst Hard Time: The Untold Story of Those Who Survived the Great American Dust Bowl*. New York and Boston: Houghton Mifflin Co., 2006.

"Elections of Texas Governors, 1845–2010." Texas Almanac. Accessed August 16, 2021. https://www.texasalmanac.com/articles/elections-of-texas-governors-1845-2010.

"Enchanted Rock State Natural Area." Enchanted Rock State Natural Area History. Texas Parks & Wildlife Department, September 11, 2018. https://tpwd.texas.gov/state-parks/enchanted-rock/park_history.

Engbeck, Joseph H., Jr. *By the People, for the People: The Work of the Civilian Conservation Corps in California State Parks, 1933–1941*. Sacramento: California State Parks, 2002.

"Featured Letter: A Difficult Trip to Natural Bridge." Jefferson Quotes & Family Letters | Monticello. Thomas Jefferson Foundation, July 2009. https://www.monticello.org/research-education/for-scholars/papers-of-thomas-jefferson/featured-letters/a-difficult-trip-to-natural-bridge/.

Freeman, Martha Doty. "Abilene State Park: A History of the Development of a Cultural Landscape, 1875–2003." Historic Sites and Structures Program, Texas Parks and Wildlife Department, August 2003.

Ganzel, Bill. "Farming in the 1930s." Wessels Living History Farm, 2003. https://livinghistoryfarm.org/farminginthe30s/intro/.

Garunay, Melanie. "President Obama Designates National Monument in Maine's North Woods." National Archives and Records Administration, August 24, 2016. https://obamawhitehouse.archives.gov/blog/2016/08/24/president-obama-designates-national-monument-maines-north-woods.

Garwood, W. St. John. "Powell, Benjamin Harrison (1881–1960)." *Handbook of Texas*. Texas State Historical Association, 1976. https://www.tshaonline.org/handbook/entries/powell-benjamin-harrison.

"George B Dorr." National Park Service. US Department of the Interior, February 24, 2022. https://www.nps.gov/people/george-b-dorr.htm.

Good, Albert H. *Park and Recreation Structures: Administration and Basic Service Facilities; Recreational and Cultural Facilities; Overnight and Organized Camp Facilities*. National Park Service. Washington: National Park Service, 1938. http://npshistory.com/publications/park_recreation_structures/index.htm.

Good, Albert H. *Patterns from the Golden Age of Rustic Design: Park and Recreation Structures from the 1930s*. Lanham: Roberts Rinehart Publishers, 2003.

Gutting, Sally Anne S. "Honoring Texas Heroes: The San Jacinto Monument and Its Cornerstone." *Houston History* 4, no. 2, 2007. https://houstonhistorymagazine.org/wp-content/uploads/2011/11/V4-N2-Gutting-Honoring-Texas-Heroes.pdf.

Harmon, Dave. "Seeds to Reforest Lost Pines Were Almost Lost to Landfill." *Austin American-Statesman*, September 1, 2012. https://www.statesman.com/story/news/local/2012/09/01/seeds-to-reforest-lost-pines-were-almost-lost-to-landfill/9902010007/.

Heger, Kenneth. "Dangers in the Civilian Conservation Corps: Accident Reports, 1933–1942." *Prologue Magazine* 43, no. 4, 2011. https://www.archives.gov/publications/prologue/2011/winter/ccc-accidents.html.

Hendrickson, Kenneth E., Jr. "National Youth Administration." *Handbook of Texas*. Texas State Historical Association, May 1, 1995. https://www.tshaonline.org/handbook/entries/national-youth-administration.

Hendrickson, Kenneth E., Jr. "Replenishing the Soil and the Soul of Texas: The CCC In the Lone Star State as an Example of State-Federal Work Relief During the Great Depression." *Faculty Papers, Midwestern State University*, 2, 1 (1974): 37–48.

Hendrickson, Kenneth E., Jr. "The Civilian Conservation Corps in the Southwestern States." Essay. In *The Depression in the Southwest*, edited by Donald W. Whisenhunt. Port Washington: Kennikat Press, 1980.

Hill, David B. Report. *Voter Opinion Surveys*. Hill Research Consultants, 2019.

Himmel, Richard L. "Jones, Mary Smith (1819–1907)." *Handbook of Texas*. Texas State Historical Association, February 1, 1995. https://www.tshaonline.org/handbook/entries/jones-mary-smith.

"History and Mission." General Federation of Women's Clubs, June 4, 2021. https://www.gfwc.org/about/history-and-mission/.

"History of Christmas Mountains." Texas State University System, August 24, 2018. https://www.tsus.edu/about-tsus/research/History.html.

"History." Daughters of the Republic of Texas. Accessed March 7, 2022. https://www.drtinfo.org/about-drt/history.

Holland, Kenneth, and Frank Ernest Hill. *Youth in the CCC*. Washington: American Council on Education, 1942.

Hughes, Dan Allen. "Editorial: Preserve Our Parks; Preserve Our Way of Life," March 1, 2015.

Jameson, John R. *The Story of Big Bend National Park*. Austin: University of Texas Press, 1996.

Jefferson, John. "The Golden Age of Park Acquisitions." *Texas Parks & Wildlife Magazine*, August 2011. https://tpwmagazine.com/archive/2011/aug/ed_1_stateparks/.

Jeong, Ji Youn, and John L. Crompton. Report. *The Economic Contributions of Texas State Parks*. Austin: Texas Coalition for Conservation, 2014.

Jeong, Ji Youn, and John L. Crompton. Report. *The Economic Contributions of Texas State Parks*. Austin: Texas Coalition for Conservation, 2019.

"John Muir." BrainyQuote. Xplore. Accessed March 21, 2020. https://www.brainyquote.com/search_results?q=-john%2Bmuir.

Johnson, Charles W. "The Army and the Civilian Conservation Corps, 1933–1942." *Prologue: The Journal of the National Archives*, 1972.

Johnson, Charles W. "The Civilian Conservation Corps: The Role of the Army." Dissertation, University of Michigan, 1968.

Johnson, Lyndon B. "Remarks at the University of Michigan." The American Presidency Project, May 22, 1964. https://www.presidency.ucsb.edu/documents/remarks-the-university-michigan.

Johnson, Sam Houston. *My Brother Lyndon*. Edited by Enrique Hank Lopez. New York: Cowles Book Co., 1969.

Jones, Nancy Baker. "Perry, Hally Ballinger Bryan (1868–1955)." *Handbook of Texas*. Texas State Historical Association, 1976. https://www.tshaonline.org/handbook/entries/perry-hally-ballinger-bryan.

Jordan, Charles. "Urban Greenscapes: Conservation and Parks in America." *Texas Coalition for Conservation*. Lecture presented at the Symposium on Conservation and Park Funding, February 2003.

Kachanovskaya, Valentina. "New Deal: Distribution and Impact of Funds in the States." Dissertation, University of Arizona, 2016.

"The Kent Family and Conservation." National Park Service. US Department of the Interior, October 28, 2021. https://www.nps.gov/articles/the-kent-family-and-conservation.htm.

Lady Bird Johnson. Accessed September 2020. http://www.ladybirdjohnson.org/about.

"Lasting Legacies." American Forests, April 3, 2012. https://www.americanforests.org/blog/lasting-legacies/.

Laswell, James. *Shovels and Guns: The CCC in Action*. New York: International Pamphlet 45, 1935.

Long, Christopher. "Ku Klux Klan." *Handbook of Texas*. Texas State Historical Association, 1952. https://www.tshaonline.org/handbook/entries/ku-klux-klan.

Lucas, Rachel. "Natural Bridge Officially Becomes a State Park, Affiliated with National Park Service." WSLS 10 News, September 24, 2016. https://www.wsls.com/news/2016/09/24/natural-bridge-officially-becomes-a-state-park-affiliated-with-national-park-service/.

Mackintosh, Barry. "Philanthropy and the National Parks in the 20th Century." National Park Service. US Department of the Interior, July 6, 2018. https://www.nps.gov/articles/philanthropy-and-the-national-parks.htm#:~:text=Philanthropy%20is%20more%20than%20a,special%20interest%20in%20their%20welfare.

Manlove, Gina. "San Jacinto Celebrates Joining the Texas Historical Commission." San Jacinto Museum of History, September 13, 2019. https://www.sanjacinto-museum.org/About_Us/News_and_Events/News/San_Jacinto_and_THC_Partnership/.

Martin, Dale. Personal Interview with W. R. Patrick at Bastrop State Park. March 31, 2003.

Martin, Mrs. W. C. "State Park System Is Needed to Further Move of Acquainting Texans With State." *Fort Worth Star-Telegram*, July 13, 1924, Volume XLIV, Number 164 edition, sec. Society and Clubs. https://www.newspapers.com/image/634503444/?terms=.

Mashhood, Farzad. "How Dry Is It? Conditions Are Bad but Pale in Comparison to 1950s Drought." *Austin American-Statesman*, August 4, 2011, Vol. 141, No. 10 edition. https://www.newspapers.com/image/434895240.

Maxwell, Robert S. "Jones, William Goodrich (1860–1950)." *Handbook of Texas*. Texas State Historical Association, February 1, 1995. https://www.tshaonline.org/handbook/entries/jones-william-goodrich.

McCarty, Gene. Letter to George Bristol. *Sporting Goods Sales Tax*, December 10, 2020.

McClelland, Linda Flint. *Building the National Parks: Historic Landscape Design and Construction*. Baltimore: Johns Hopkins University Press, 1998.

McClelland, Linda Flint. *Presenting Nature: The Historic Landscape Design of the National Park Service, 1916–1942*. Washington: National Park Service, 1993.

McDonald, Danna. "Sale of Enchanted Rock." Thesis, Texas Parks and Wildlife Archeology Library, 1978.

McNeely, Dave. "Armstrong's Dip." *Fort Worth Weekly*, August 13, 2014. https://www.fwweekly.com/2014/08/13/armstrongs-dip/.

"Monuments Protected Under the Antiquities Act." National Parks Conservation Association, June 8, 2021. https://www.npca.org/resources/2658-monuments-protected-under-the-antiquities-act.

"Mrs. J. F. Welder Succumbs at 94." *Victoria Advocate*, September 10, 1958, 113th Year, No. 126 edition. https://www.newspapers.com/image/440452259.

Muir, John. "Studies in the Sierra." *Overland Monthly* 12–14 (1874). https://vault.sierraclub.org/john_muir_exhibit/writings/studies_in_the_sierra/.

Murray, John. "Thomas Jefferson's Land Grant for Natural Bridge and 157 Acres in Botetourt County." Jefferson Quotes & Family Letters | Monticello. Thomas Jefferson Foundation, July 5, 1774. https://tjrs.monticello.org/letter/1975.

"National Youth Administration Projects in Texas." The Living New Deal. Accessed March 22, 2021. https://livingnewdeal.org/?s=NYA%2BTexas.

"Neal, Margie Elizabeth (1875–1971)." *Handbook of Texas*. Texas State Historical Association, 1976. https://www.tshaonline.org/handbook/entries/neal-margie-elizabeth.

Neff, Pat Morris. *The Battles of Peace*. Google Books. Fort Worth: Pioneer Publishing Company: The Bunker Press, 1925. https://www.google.com/books/edition/The_Battles_of_Peace/ojsVAAAAYAAJ?hl=en.

Newlan, Ralph Edward, James W. Steely, Susan Begley, and Ethan Carr, Bastrop State Park, National Historic Landmark Nomination Form § (1997). https://npgallery.nps.gov/GetAsset/d14f407f-937d-446a-8cf1-2256cd8e6cce.

Office of the Director. *The Civilian Conservation Corps: What It Is and What It Does*. Washington: Federal Security Agency, Civilian Conservation Corps, 1941.

Olmsted, Frederick Law. *Yosemite and the Mariposa Grove: A Preliminary Report, 1865*. Yosemite National Park: Yosemite Association, 2009.

"Oral History Collection." Austin: Texas Parks and Wildlife Department, n.d.

Padgett, Dora A., ed. "What about Pennsylvania?" *Planning and Civic Comment: January - March 1940* 6, no. 1 (1940): 29–30. https://ia902609.us.archive.org/24/items/planningcivilcom05washrich/planningcivilcom05washrich.pdf.

Paige, John C. *The Civilian Conservation Corps and the National Park Service: 1933–1942: An Administrative History*. Washington: National Park Service, US Department of the Interior, 1985.

"Palestine to Houston Highway Campaign by Post Party." *Houston Post*, June 20, 1915, Vol. 30, No. 78 edition, sec. Auto. https://www.newspapers.com/image/96211202/.

Parker, Dan. "Birding Trail's First Site Opens Friday in Rockport." *Corpus Christi Caller-Times*, September 7, 1995, Vol. 113, No. 250 edition, sec. B. https://www.newspapers.com/image/759077503.

Patenaude, Lionel V. "The New Deal and Texas." Dissertation, University of Texas at Austin, 1953.

Patoski, Joe Nick. "'All It Took Was 25 Years': Legislature Ponied Up Cash for Underfunded Texas Parks." *Texas Observer*, June 11, 2019. https://www.texasobserver.org/all-it-took-was-25-years-legislature-ponies-up-cash-for-underfunded-texas-parks/.

Pearsall, Joan, Harold Toy, and Fred McNeil. Report. *History of Texas Parks Board (Updated Narrative Consolidation)*. June 24, 1974. Austin: Departmental History Project Research Files, Texas Parks and Wildlife Department Administrative Records and Other Materials, Archives and Information Services Division, Texas State Library and Archives Commission, 1974.

Pohl, Kelly, and Megan Lawson. Report. *State Funding Programs for Outdoor Recreation: Texas Sporting Goods Sales Tax*. Outdoor Industry Association, 2018.

Powell, Marian. "Marian Powell Papers: Legislative History of the Law That First Created the State Parks Board," March 4, 1957.

Powell, Mrs. Ben. Letter to D. E. Colp, February 19, 1927.

Powell, Mrs. Ben. Letter to D. E. Colp, n.d.

Powell, Mrs. Ben. Letter to Mrs. R. D. Rather, March 9, 1917.

Powell, Mrs. Ben. Report. *Texas Federation of Women's Clubs Report, Division of Parks and Playgrounds, 1925–1927*. Texas Federation of Women's Club, n.d.

Price, Jorjanna. "1920 Census Data Hints at Today's Texas." Texas Association of Counties, 2020. https://www.county.org/County-Magazine-Main/September-October-2020/1920-census-data-hints-at-todays-Texas.

Procter, Ben H. "Great Depression." *Handbook of Texas*. Texas State Historical Association, October 1, 1995. https://www.tshaonline.org/handbook/entries/great-depression.

"Quick History of the National Park Service." National Park Service. US Department of the Interior. Accessed March 18, 2020. https://www.nps.gov/articles/quick-nps-history.htm#:~:text=On%20August%2025%2C%201916%2C%20President,those%20yet%20to%20be%20established.

Rash, Mrs. Grady. "Daughters of the Republic of Texas." *Handbook of Texas*. Texas State Historical Association, 1952. https://www.tshaonline.org/handbook/entries/daughters-of-the-republic-of-texas.

Rhoades, Alice J. "Quinn, Frank David (1894–1971)." *Handbook of Texas*. Texas State Historical Association, June 1, 1995. https://www.tshaonline.org/handbook/entries/quinn-frank-david.

Runte, Alfred. *National Parks: The American Experience. National Park Service*. 1st ed. Lincoln: University of Nebraska Press, 1979. https://www.nps.gov/parkhistory/online_books/runte1/index.htm.

Saldana, Lydia. "Bringing a Park to Life." *Texas Parks & Wildlife Magazine*, December 2020. https://tpwmagazine.com/archive/2020/dec/ed_2_palopinto/index.phtml.

Salmond, John. *The Civilian Conservation Corps, 1933–1942: A New Deal Case Study*. Durham: Duke University Press, 1967.

"San Jacinto Battleground State Historic Site." Texas Historical Commission, March 19, 1970. https://www.thc.texas.gov/historic-sites/san-jacinto-battleground-state-historic-site.

"San Jacinto Battleground State Historical Park." Texas State Historical Association. Accessed 2020. https://www.tshaonline.org/handbook/entries/san-jacinto-battleground-state-historical-park.

Scarpelli, Leah. "Why Don't More African-Americans Visit State Parks?" *Texas Standard*, June 7, 2016. https://www.texas-standard.org/stories/why-dont-more-african-americans-visit-state-parks/.

Schlesinger, Arthur M., Jr. *The Coming of the New Deal*. Boston: Houghton Mifflin, 1958.

Seaholm, Megan. "Texas Federation of Women's Clubs." *Handbook of Texas*. Texas State Historical Association, February 1, 1996. https://www.tshaonline.org/handbook/entries/texas-federation-of-womens-clubs.

Self, Deborah Lynn. "The National Youth Administration in Texas, 1935–1939." Thesis, Texas Tech University, 1974.

"Seminole Canyon State Park & Historic Site." Seminole Canyon State Park & Historic Site History. Texas Parks & Wildlife Department, July 8, 2019. https://tpwd.texas.gov/state-parks/seminole-canyon/park_history.

Sibley, Jane Dunn, and Jim Comer. *Jane's Window: My Spirited Life in West Texas and Austin*. College Station: Texas A&M University Press, 2013.

Smith, Griffin, Jr. "The Strange Case of the Missing Parks." *Texas Monthly*, November 1975.

Smith, Cheryl. "World Birding Center Will Nest in Mission: Surprise Decision Comes after Legislature Intervenes." *The Monitor*, April 30, 1999. https://www.newspapers.com/image/331041047/?terms=.

*Sparks*, January 1940.

Speakman, Joseph M. "Into the Woods: The First Year of the Civilian Conservation Corps." *Prologue Magazine* 38, no. 3, 2006. https://www.archives.gov/publications/prologue/2006/fall/ccc.html.

Spooner, F. Ed. *Mrs. W. C. Martin Posing in 1905 Cadillac Model E Automobile. Detroit Public Library Digital Collections.* Accessed June 3, 2021. https://digitalcollections.detroitpubliclibrary.org/islandora/object/islandora%3A229677.

Staff Correspondent. "Senators Rise in Turn to Praise Miss Neal." *Fort Worth Star-Telegram*, March 5, 1934, Volume LIV, Number 33 edition. https://www.newspapers.com/image/635915952/?terms=.

"State Accepts 24 New Parks: Mrs. Ben Powell, Austin, Presses Resolution in Legislature." *Dallas Morning News*, March 19, 1927, Vol. XLIL, No. 170 edition. https://archives.dallasnews.com/uncategorized/IO_7b85e554-05c6-4182-9263-7e34028c3d20/.

*State Parks Board Minutes*. Report. Austin, Texas: State of Texas, 1934.

State Task Force on Texas Nature Tourism. Report. *Nature Tourism in the Lone Star State: Economic Opportunities in Nature.* Austin: Texas Parks and Wildlife Department and the Texas Department of Commerce, 1994.

"Stats Report Viewer." National Park Service. US Department of the Interior. Accessed March 21, 2020. https://irma.nps.gov/STATS/SSRSReports/Park%20Specific%20Reports/Annual%20Park%20Recreation%20Visitation%20(1904%20-%20Last%20Calendar%20Year)?Park=YOSE.

Steele, June M. Thesis. *Phebe Warner: Community Building in the Texas Panhandle, 1898-1935: A Thesis in History.* Thesis, Texas Tech University, 2000. https://ttu-ir.tdl.org/handle/2346/17310?locale-attribute=en.

Steely, James Wright. *Parks for Texas: Enduring Landscapes of the New Deal*. Austin: University of Texas Press, 1999.

Stein, Susan. "Natural Bridge (Engraving)." Monticello. Thomas Jefferson Foundation. Accessed March 7, 2022. https://www.monticello.org/site/research-and-collections/natural-bridge-engraving.

Sterner, Richard. *The Negro's Share: a Study of Income, Consumption, Housing and Public Assistance.* New York: Harper & Brothers Publishers, 1943.

"Surviving the Dust Bowl." PBS. Public Broadcasting Service, January 29, 2019. https://www.pbs.org/wgbh/americanexperience/films/dustbowl/.

Swanson, Gillian. "Mid-Valley City Shows Interest in Birding Center." *The Monitor*, September 25, 1997, sec. Valley & State. https://www.newspapers.com/image/330671560.

Taylor, Janelle, and Tom Johnson. Personal Interview with Louise Sellers in Dallas, Texas. October 26, 2004.

Texas Thirty-Eighth Legislature, General Laws, First, Second, and Third Called Sessions § (1923).

"Texas Federation of Colored Women's Clubs." Texas Woman's University Libraries Woman's Collection - Texas Association of Women's Clubs. Texas Woman's University, 1997. https://twu.edu/library/womans-collection/collections/civic-organizations/tawc/.

"Texas' Gift to the Nation: The Establishment of Big Bend National Park." National Park Service. US Department of the Interior, August 3, 2020. https://www.nps.gov/bibe/learn/historyculture/tgttn.htm.

"Texas Parks and Wildlife Department: Civilian Conservation Corps." Texas Parks and Wildlife Department. Accessed June 1, 2021. https://tpwd.texas.gov/spdest/programs/ccc/.

"Texas Parks Civilian Conservation Corps Drawings Database." Texas State Library and Archives Commission. Accessed June 21, 2020. https://www.tsl.texas.gov/apps/arc/CCCDrawings/.

Thompson, Anne. "She Was Green before Green Was Cool." NBCNews.com. NBCUniversal News Group, July 12, 2007. https://www.nbcnews.com/id/wbna19732051.

Thoreau, Henry David. *The Maine Woods. The Project Gutenberg EBook* 3. Vol. 3. 20 vols. The Writings of Henry David Thoreau. Boston and New York: Houghton Mifflin and Company, 1864. https://www.gutenberg.org/files/42500/42500-h/42500-h.htm.

"Timeline of Voting & Elections in Texas." The League of Women Voters of Texas. Accessed March 5, 2022. https://lwvtexas.org/content.aspx?page_id=22&club_id=979482&module_id=485202.

"To Love the Beautiful: The Story of Texas State Parks." Texas State Library and Archives Commission, November 7, 2016. https://www.tsl.texas.gov/exhibits/parks/index.html.

"To Love the Beautiful: The Story of Texas State Parks: 'So Would Hell.'" Texas State Parks in the 1950s. Texas State Library and Archives Commission, November 16, 2016. https://www.tsl.texas.gov/exhibits/parks/1950s/page1.html.

Tompkins, Shannon. "Hurricane Harvey Recovery a Slow, Costly Process for State's Parks, Other Areas." *Houston Chronicle*, December 7, 2017. https://www.chron.com/sports/outdoors/article/Hurricane-Harvey-recovery-a-slow-costly-process-12361071.php.

Toney, Sharon Morris. "The Texas State Parks System: An Administrative History, 1923–1984." Dissertation, Texas Tech University, 1995.

"TPW Commission Approves Devils River Land Acquisition." Texas Parks and Wildlife Department, December 20, 2010. https://tpwd.texas.gov/newsmedia/releases/?req=20101220b.

Turner, Elizabeth Hayes. "Ballinger, Betty Eve (1854–1936)." *Handbook of Texas*. Texas State Historical Association, 1976. https://www.tshaonline.org/handbook/entries/ballinger-betty-eve.

Turner, Frederick Jackson. *The Frontier in American History. The Project Gutenberg EBook*. New York: Henry Holt and Company, 1920. https://www.gutenberg.org/files/22994/22994-h/22994-h.htm.

Turner, Thomas E. "Neff, Pat Morris (1871–1952)." *Handbook of Texas*. Texas State Historical Association, 1976. https://www.tshaonline.org/handbook/entries/neff-pat-morris.

US Government Printing Office, 77 Congressional Record: Proceedings and Debates of the First Session of the Seventy-Third Congress (March 4, 1933–April 3, 1933) §. Part 1 (1933). govinfo.gov/app/details/GPO-CRECB-1933-pt1-v77/.

Utley, Dan K., and James W. Steely. *Guided with a Steady Hand: The Cultural Landscape of a Rural Texas Park*. Waco: Baylor University Press, 1998.

"Visitation Numbers." National Park Service. US Department of the Interior. Accessed March 21, 2020. https://www.nps.gov/aboutus/visitation-numbers.htm#:~:text=Out%20of%20the%20423%20parks,these%20visitor%20statistics%20were%20collected.

Wandell, Luther C. "A Negro in the CCC." *Crisis* 42 (August 1935): 244–54.

Warner, Phebe Kerrick. "Depression Boosts State Parks." *Texas Federation News*, April 1933.

Wheeler, Camille. "Enchanted Rock: Rock of Ages." *Texas Co-Op Power* 67, no. 11, May 2010.

Williams, Diane E. Report. *Historic Resources Study: Brief Narrative and Report, Blanco State Park, Blanco County, Texas*. Historic Sites and Structures Program, Texas Parks and Wildlife Department, 2008.

Williams, Michelle. Interview with James W. Steely at Bastrop State Park. *Terra Incognita*. Historic Sites and Structures Program, Texas Parks and Wildlife Department, September 8, 2008.

Willis, Carrie Hunter, and Etta Belle Walker. *Legends of the Skyline Drive and the Great Valley of Virginia. The Project Gutenberg EBook*. Richmond: The Dietz Press, 1940. https://www.gutenberg.org/files/33018/33018-h/33018-h.htm#Page_81.

"Winston Churchill Quotes." BrainyQuote. Xplore. Accessed March 26, 2022. https://www.brainyquote.com/authors/winston-churchill-quotes.

Wirt, Scarlett, and Mark Thurman. Personal Interview with Thomas Earl Jordan at Bastrop State Park. March 30, 2003.

Wirth, Conrad L. Report. *Civilian Conservation Corps Program of the United States Department of the Interior (March 1933 to June 30, 1943)*. Report to Harold L. Ickes, Secretary of the Interior, 1944. https://digitalcommons.unomaha.edu/slceslgen/57/.

Wirth, Conrad Louis. *Parks, Politics, and the People*. Norman: University of Oklahoma Press, 1980.

"Women Lawmakers Equal to Any Man." *Austin American-Statesman*, February 17, 1929, Volume 15, Number 192 edition. https://www.newspapers.com/image/384243152/?terms=.

"Women Urged to Vote for Amendment." *McKinney Daily Courier-Gazette*, July 2, 1923. https://www.newspapers.com/image/63470429.

"Women's Clubs: Women and Volunteer Power, 1868-1926 and Beyond." National Women's History Museum, March 17, 2014. https://www.womenshistory.org/articles/womens-clubs.

Worster, Donald. *Dust Bowl: The Southern Plains in the 1930s*. New York: Oxford University Press, 1979.

# Index

Italicized page locators refer to images.

Parks outside of Texas are identified by state when possible.

Parks within Texas are identified with the nearest city when possible.

Swanson, Gillian: on World Birding Center location, 45

Sweetwater, Texas: Civilian Conservation Corps (CCC) camp in, 116

Swinford, David, *222*

Taft, William Howard: Glacier National Park created by, 15

*Taking Care of Texas* report (2000), 200–201

Tarrant Regional Water District, 195, 266

Tassin, Sidney, *36*

*Texas*, USS, 140, *141–42*, 143, 222. *See also* Battleship *Texas* Historic Site

Texas Association of Women's Clubs, 24

Texas Coalition for Conservation: Ernest Angelo and, 210–11; flyers produced by, 210; growth of, 203; legislative symposium (2003) of, 207–8; mission and focus sharpening by, 206–7; nonprofit status of, 204; origins of, 198–99; "Seeking Common Ground" forum of, 203, 205; Sporting Goods Sales Tax reform and, 190, 213, 217–18; surveying commissioned by, 204–5, 228, 234, 281

Texas Coalition for State Parks, 242; Proposition 5 (2019) campaign literature from, *369–81*

Texas Conservation Alliance, 249, 250; flier from, *247*

Texas Department of Forestry: creation of, 65

Texas Federation of Colored Women's Clubs, 24–25; Fort Worth chapter, *24*

Texas Federation of Literary Clubs, 24

Texas Federation of Women's Clubs, 24–25, 1926 conference of, 33; Good Roads Movement and, 27, 30; Katie Owens Welder and, 31; preservation activities of, 29–30, 32–35, 260, 346–47; Seguin Shakespeare Club chapter of, *24*; State Parks Board and, 33, 70

Texas Forest Service: Indian Mound Nursery of, 228; loblolly pines and, 228, 263

Texas Game, Fish and Oyster Commission, 58, 120

Texas Garden Clubs, 29, 260; State Parks Board and, 70

Texas Good Roads Association, 66

Texas Highway Department, 165; Big Bend National Park and, 151; created, 58

Texas Historical Commission, 41; San Jacinto Battleground State Historical Site transferred to, 23; Sporting Goods Sales Tax and, 244, 274; Texas Parks and Wildlife Department's historic sites rumored to be transferred to, 219, 221

*Texas Monthly*, 215, 220; on John Montford, 194

Texas Nature Conservancy, 192. *See also* Nature Conservancy

Texas Outdoor Recreation Alliance, 213, 220

Texas Parks and Wildlife Commission: Beatrice Pickens and, 36; Big Bend Ranch State Park and, 187, 188; chairs of, 178, *181*, *229*, 230; Dan Allen Hughes as chair of, 238; Dan Friedkin as chair of, 271; Devils River State Natural Area and, 265; Ed Cox Jr. as chair of, 182, 187, 192; Ernest Angelo and, 210; Hixons and 269; Joseph Fitzsimons as chair of, 216, 242, 266; Katharine Armstrong as chair of, 202, 203–4; Kelsey Warren and, 267; State Parks Board as progenitor of, 36; Texas state parks funding and, 182, 194, 196, 218, 220, 222, 245, 276; Ygnacio Garza as chair of, 193. *See also* State Parks Board

Texas Parks and Wildlife Department: donations to, 258; Enchanted Rock and, 38–40; establishment of, 178–79; "good ol' boy" mentality in, 206; Government Canyon State Natural Area and, 270; racial equality policy of, 160; women leaders of, 36. *See also* State Parks Board

*Texas Parks and Wildlife for the 21st Century* report (2001), 200–201

Texas Parks and Wildlife Foundation, 203, 283

Texas Rehabilitation and Relief Commission, 83, 85–86, 89, 90, 96

Texas Relief Commission, 82, 165. *See also* Texas Rehabilitation and Relief Commission

Texas Revolution: preservation of historic sites from, 20–21, 23, 260

Texas state parks, *297–343*; bill creating (1923), 350–51; Civilian Conservation Corps

(CCC) and, 36, 77–78, 83, 88, 89–121, 124–33; conservation in, 293; drought (1950s) and, 153, 155; economic impact of, 204, 214, 234, 281–82; funding of, 35–36, 104, 106; historical continuity in, 130–31; original listed (1927), 346–47; public support for, 169, 228, 234, 246, 290; racial equity in, 160, 289–90; recommendations for, 278–79, 81; segregation in, 155–60 289–90; women and establishment of, 19–42, 117–18. *See also specific parks*

Texas State Parks Advisory Committee, 219, 222; on Proposition 5 (2019), 243; renewal of, 216–17, 277; on Texas state parks funding, 225–26, 243

Texas State Parks Association, 31

Texas State Parks Board. *See* State Parks Board

Texas Veterans Association, 21

Texas Woman's University: Little Chapel in the Woods at, 166

Thomas State Park, 347

Thoreau, Henry David, 5; pictured, *5*; Walden Pond of, *6*

Timaja Reed Plateau, *143*

Tips State Park, 347

Townsend, Everett E., 146

*T.R. Register, et al v. J.D. Sandefer, Jr., et al.* (1950), 158

Transcendentalism, 2, 5

Tree Improvement Program, 227–28

Trust for Public Land, 207, 248, 266, 270

Tugwell, Rexford, *93*

Tunnel, Curtis, 40

Turner, Chris, 245

Turner, Sylvester, *222*

Tyler State Park (Tyler, Texas), *342*: architectural inspiration of, 100; bathhouse at, *101*; Civilian Conservation Corps (CCC) and, 125; segregation at, 157–60, *158*

Tyler State Park for Blacks (Tyler, Texas), 159–60

## About the Author

After successful careers in politics, then business, George Bristol turned to a complementary endeavor that would utilize his skills and reflect a lifelong love of nature and parks: advocate for parks and people. In 1994, he received a presidential appointment to the National Parks Foundation, launching his new journey. He established the Texas Coalition for Conservation in 2001 and began an eighteen-year effort that culminated in the people of Texas overwhelmingly voting to direct all revenue generated from the Sporting Goods Sales Tax to state parks—as originally intended.

For his advocacy, Bristol has been awarded honors at every level of the conservation spectrum, including the prestigious National Cornelius Amory Pugsley Medal. Bristol is a father of three and grandfather of four. He and his wife, Gretchen Denny, live in Fort Worth.